THE MUSIC OF HINDOSTAN

Rabindranath Tagore.

from a drawing by W. Rothenstein

THE MUSIC OF HINDOSTAN

A.H. FOX STRANGWAYS

MANOHAR
2026

First published 1914
Reprinted 2021, 2023, 2026

ISBN 978-93-90035-72-4

Published by
Ajay Kumar Jain *for*
Manohar Publishers & Distributors
4753/23 Ansari Road, Daryaganj
New Delhi 110 002

Printed at
Replika Press Pvt. Ltd.

PREFACE

HINDOSTAN is, technically, the Indus and Ganges basins; and it is with the music of that part of India that this book primarily deals. It contains reference also to the system of the Carnatic, though that has been more fully treated of in C. R. Day's *Music of Southern India and the Deccan.*

The study of Indian music is of interest to all who care for song, and of special interest to those who have studied the early stages of song in mediaeval Europe or ancient Greece. For here is the living language of which in those we have only dead examples. It is hardly possible in the case of modern European Folk-song to study melody pure and simple, for we have no large body of such song of which we can certainly say that it was not influenced at all by the current conception of harmony. But here is melody absolutely untouched by harmony, which has developed through many centuries tendencies which have the force of laws; and the examination of these enables us to some extent to separate the respective contributions of melody and harmony to the final effect in our own music. Those to whom this aspect of the subject appeals are recommended after glancing at Chapters I and II to look at Chapters VI, VII, VIII, and XII.

Others may be more interested in that technical side of the art which tabulates the facts of song, and their taste has been consulted in Chapters IV and V; others, again, to whom the main charm of the music lies in the memories of India which it revives, may find more of what they would care to read in the Introduction and the first three chapters.

In the hope of being useful to those who may wish to make further investigation into the subject a large number of technical terms has been admitted into the text. These have almost always been translated where they occur, and they appear also in the Index. It would, however, take more than one volume to do justice to all the details, and they have not as a rule been elaborated except to illustrate some principle.

Two branches of the music have been left untouched—the instruments and the notation. About the latter there is very little to say except that it is a Tonic Sol-fa notation of which the various local scripts and special signs are easily mastered. The typical instruments have been admirably described and illustrated by Day; the more interesting part, the technique, can, of course, be communicated only orally, with the instrument in hand. But India is now, instrumentally, at the same stage as mediaeval Europe, with a great variety of means of supporting the voice but absolutely no sense of orchestration; and though a close study of its instruments would probably reveal more than one ancestor of those which our orchestra employs, it would hardly throw much light on any principle of art, and has therefore been omitted. Exception has, however, been made in favour of the drum, the treatment of which is possibly unique.

The India Society have done this book the honour of purchasing copies for distribution to their members for the year 1913. If Indian readers should open it and should be surprised to find the facts given differently from the way to which they are accustomed, they are asked to remember that as there is no one system which is applicable to the whole country, so the circumstance that one set of facts is quoted rather than another need not vitiate the argument; and it is hoped that they will look with a lenient eye upon many solecisms in spelling which are due to sheer ignorance.

The author offers his sincere thanks to many who have helped him in all sorts of ways to gather materials for this book. It would be impossible to make a complete list of them, and he hesitates to give an imperfect list. He hopes that the dozens of English men and women who offered so much hospitality and so many facilities in the winters of 1904 and 1910, the ruling princes and their court officials who arranged opportunities, the private gentlemen who organized concerts and who were ready to discuss their music technically or generally, the numerous musicians who answered with patience and courtesy many questions or who played and sang for many hours, down to his various 'bearers' who knew what he was going to wear before he knew what he was going to do, who caught his trains before he had decided by which one to go, who produced food and transport under the most unlikely and a smiling face under all circumstances, will believe that he has not forgotten their kindness; and that some of his benefactors may even find in these pages enough to make them think it was not wholly wasted.

It would be sanguine to hope that the book could be free from errors both of fact and of proportion. To sift discrepant statements and to get the main features into the proper perspective would have demanded a longer sojourn than twelve months. If it is comparatively free from minor blemishes this is due to the kindness of several who have read the proofs—to Dr. Coomaraswamy for Chapters I and II, also for several illustrations; to Mr. Abdy Williams for Chapter VIII; to Mr. Walter Ford and Mr. E. D. Rendall for some musical illustrations and suggestions; to Dr. A. A. Macdonell, Dr. L. D. Barnett, Mr. F. W. Thomas, Dr. Felber of Vienna, and Dr. Simon of Munich for Chapter X; and to the readers of the Clarendon Press for their very careful supervision of the whole. Grateful acknowledgement is also made to Mr. William Rothenstein for the loan of the copyright of his portrait of Rabindranath Tagore (see p. 92). It was decided to include this portrait before the poet's name was known to Europe; and now, although the need of making it known no longer exists, the portrait is still retained as the frontispiece. The appearance there of one who, more than any other, may be said to personify Indian music in its broadest sense, may serve to remind us of what is surely the truth, that music does not reside in those designs and devices which can be imprisoned in symbols and committed to paper, but that it comes and goes only upon the lips or the fingers of men who are able to feel it or to create it.

TABLE OF CONTENTS

INTRODUCTION

The understanding of music as affected by national characteristics, 1, 2; by an antiquated system, 3; by the absence of harmony, 4, 5; by difference of content, 6, 7. Causes of the particular form taken by Indian music due to the conservatism of India, 7; to its size, 8; to its climate, 9, 10. A concert, 11–13. The future of Indian music, 14–16.

CHAPTER I

A MUSICAL DIARY

Conditions under which these songs were collected and caution with which they should be received, 17, 18. Chanties and labour songs, 19–21. Occupation songs, 20–7. Nagpur, Central Provinces, 29–31. West coast, 32–8. Travancore, 39–45. Maratha bards, 46, 47. Conclusions, 48, 49.

CHAPTER II

A MUSICAL DIARY (*continued*)

Garhwālīs, 50–6. Gurkhas, 57, 58. Panjābis, Cuttack dance, 59. Bhavnagar, 60, 61. Lullabies, 62–7. Children's songs, 68. Conclusions, 69–72.

CHAPTER III

LEGEND, HISTORY, AND THE PRESENT DAY

Absence of the historical sense, 73, 74. Legend, 75–82. History, 83–5. The present day, 86–90. Subbanna and Seshanna of Mysore, 86. Ramachandra of Trivandrum, 88, 89. Sourendro Banerji of Calcutta, 88. Chandra Prabhu of Bhavnagar, 90. Rabindranath Tagore, 92–9.

CHAPTER IV

THE SCALE

The facts of folk-song and folk-instruments, 100–4. List of Sanskrit authorities, 105. Technical terms, 106–8. The *grāmas*, 109–12. Bharata, 113. Date of his system, 114. His twenty-two *śrutis*, 115–18. South India, 119, 120. Transilient scales, 122–6. The *śruti* in practical music, 127–9; and in European music, 130–3.

CHAPTER V

MODE

Scale and mode, 134–6. Indian conception of mode, 137–9. The Greek parallel, 140–3. Mode in actual practice, 144, 145. Appoggiatura, 146, 147. Absolute pitch, 148. *Grāma* and *Rāg*, 149. Ancient and modern mode, 150.

CHAPTER VI

RĀGA

The table of *Rāgs*, 151, 152. Appropriate times and seasons, 153. Sources of *Rāga*, 154, 155. *Tessitura*, 156. A *Rāg* is not a tune, 157; but it conforms to law, 158, 159. Conjunct motion, 160–2. Harmony and harmonization, 163, 164. Instances of *Rāg*, 165–9. Re-entrant *Rāgs*, 170. The drone, 171–3. Comparison with European melody, 174–6; and with the ecclesiastical modes, 177, 178. Imitation, 179. The intervals chosen in melody have no basis in harmony, 180.

CHAPTER VII

GRACE

Grace is inherent in the note, not an appendage to it, 181, 182. Two main kinds of grace, 183. Comparison with Scotch graces, 184, 185; and Hungarian, 186. Grace in the Sanskrit theory, 187. The Mohammedan *Tappa*, 188, 189. Grace may be traced to Sanskrit pronunciation, 190.

CHAPTER VIII

TĀLA

Stress and quantity, 191, 192. Sanskrit metres, 193–200. The transition from poetical to musical metre, 201–3. Metre in music, 204–8. The Carnatic system of Time, 209–14. The Hindostani system, 215, 216. Comparison with the European system, 217–24.

CHAPTER IX

DRUMMING

Indian and European drumming, 225, 226. Drums, 227. Drum-words, 228, 229; drum-phrases, 230; and drum-variants, 231, 232. Instances, 233–40. Augmentation and diminution, 241; and 'convergence' and 'cumulation', 242. The drum used ornamentally not structurally, 243–5.

CHAPTER X

THE SĀMAN CHANT

The *Ṛgveda* accent, 246–8. The *Sāmaveda*, 249–52. Its 'form', 253, 254; its rhythm, 255, 256; its scale, 257–9; its original nucleus, 260. Consonance, 261, 262. The *Gāndhāra grāma*, 263. The *Sāman* scale as transilient, 264. The musical hand, 264, 265. The early Greek scale, 266. Instances of *Sāman* chant, 266–73. Notation, 273. Some technical terms, 274–6. A vocal scale, 276–9.

CHAPTER XI

FORM

Aṃśa and drone take the place of our dominant and tonic as the basis of form, 280, 281. The *Kīrthaṇam*, 282–5. Other forms, 286. The *Khyāl*, 287–99. Subsidiary forms, 299, 300. Specimens of *Rāgs*, 301–16. The cycle of *Rāgs*, 317–19.

CHAPTER XII

MELODY

Melody is homogeneous, 320–2. Conjunct and disjunct motion, 322–8. Climax, 328–30. *Tessitura*, 330–4. Rhythm, cross-metre, 334–6. Analysis of a European, 337, and of an Indian melody, 338. Their characteristics contrasted, 338–42.

	PAGE
APPENDIX I	343
APPENDIX II	345
BIBLIOGRAPHY	346
GLOSSARY AND INDEX	353

LIST OF ILLUSTRATIONS

Rabindranath Tagore. From a drawing by W. Rothenstein — *Frontispiece*

PLATE 1. Music party. Detail from a picture (seventeenth century) in the collection of G. N. Tagore . *To face* p. 14

PLATE 2. Māria Gonds. Circular dance
Gonds and Kanwars. Slow dance, with anklets
Malyas dancing
Malayan women dancing . . . . . . *To face* p. 30

PLATE 3. Kashmīri bīn-player
Nāgasaram-players, Tanjore . . . . . *To face* p. 46

PLATE 4. Rāgi-grinding
Pāṇans
Schoolmistress, Tanjore . . . . . . *To face* p. 63

PLATE 5. Musicians. Detail from an eighteenth-century Rajput cartoon in the collection of A. K. Coomaraswamy . . . . *To face* p. 73

PLATE 6. Detail from a picture of the Surrender of Kandahar in the collection of Sītarām Lal of Benares. Seventeenth century . . . . *To face* p. 77

PLATE 7. Mughal drawing, seventeenth century, of a bīn-player, from an original in the collection of G. N. Tagore . . . . *To face* p. 78

PLATE 8. Dancing girl, South India . . . . . . *To face* p. 80

PLATE 9. Portrait of Numa Khan Katawant, a musician of the court of Jahāngīr, from a picture in the collection of A. K. Coomaraswamy . . . . *To face* p. 83

PLATE 10. Seshanna, vīṇā-player, Mysore
Aiknāth Vishnu Paṇḍit, vīṇā-player, Poona . *To face* p. 86

PLATE 11. Ranganna, drummer, Mysore . . . . . *To face* p. 225

PLATE 12. Bhai Santu, drummer, Amritsar . . . . . *To face* p. 227

PLATE 13. Group of instruments. From the collection in the Museum, Bangalore . . . . . . *To face* p. 228

PLATE 14. Sāmagaḥ, Madras
Sāmagaḥ, Bangalore . . . . *To face* p. 264

TABLE 1. Hindostani Rāgs . . . . *To face* p. 151

TABLE 2. Folk-song variants . . . . *To face* p. 154

Absolutely there is progress, but relatively there is none. Things are better, perhaps; but man is not positively better: he is only different. His virtues and vices undergo change, but on the balance of the account there is no profit. A thousand things move on, and nine hundred and ninety-eight go back: that is progress. And in that there is not much to be proud of, but plenty to take comfort in.

AMIEL.

INTRODUCTION

People who have lived in India have often asked, with various inflexions of voice, 'Do you like'—or, 'Do you really like Indian music?' The more one thinks what the answer to this should be, the more it seems to resolve itself into another—'Do you really understand it?'—to which there can, of course, be no final answer. Indeed, it would be difficult with regard to our own music to reply satisfactorily to the question, or to do more than put down a few of the points that need to be understood.

History crystallized at any given moment into convention, or summed up popularly as association, plays a large part in all that we hear. When we are listening to music and think we are 'understanding' it, we are often making no great intellectual effort at all; our mind is really working in well-worn grooves and exercising little judgment. We listen to a sonata of Beethoven or Brahms which is new to us, as a boy reads a new specimen of his well-known and accredited brand of Weyman or Kipling and finds much what he expected. But when we are confronted with a new composer, and these conventions seem for the moment to be disregarded, when an addition to the orchestra, a new treatment of the voice, an unfamiliar harmony, unconventional counterpoint, or a recast of structure distract our attention from the main issue, there is a great deal to understand and we are apt to flounder. We do not 'like' the music because we do not altogether 'understand' it. It is sometimes thought that understanding is not necessary to liking: that music is like a peach—a thing to be enjoyed, not understood. Without denying that the senses can convey to us things of which the mind can give no account, it may be asked whether there is not a point of view from which even a peach requires to be understood. Do we not like it more, that is, understand more by it, amongst the associations of a sunny garden, or with a pleasant companion, and could a man like it—understand it—at all if only peaches stood between him and starvation, or if he were under sentence of death? A piece of scenery is truly enjoyed only in proportion as a man knows what he is looking for and realizes what he has found. It is a synthesis, but it is analysable, even if we do not consciously analyse. It is the same with music.

Another difficulty in hearing music consists not in the departure from the old-established methods so much as in the substitution of new and strange conventions and associations. Cosmopolitan as the music of Europe is, we still feel the distinction of nationality. In a song by a foreign composer, whether the words are translations from his language or are originals in our own, we are conscious of passages in the music itself which to us, do not seem, to be quite the natural expression of the sentiment of the song. A German hardly seems to get at the conciseness nor a Frenchman at the dignity of what we feel. And it is a true instinct which leads singers to employ the language of the foreign composer rather than a translation, even when it is by Paul England at his best, or than the original English, even when the words are by Scott or Burns. Again, it is difficult for us to seize the point of thought of a Moussorgsky or a Ravel, not merely because they are new, but because they select and develop special aspects of our common heritage of European music. We might summarize such distinctions by saying that music which is to move the listener must be for a German solid and profound, for a Frenchman pungent and antithetical, for a Russian poignant and elemental, while we ourselves find our account best perhaps in humour verging on irony. At the same time the modifications of the general trend of European musical thought, as it is taken up into this or that national mind are slight, and the differences of idiom hardly more than dialectical; we are still travelling in the mother country, but, for the moment, in an unfamiliar part of it. But when we look beyond the 'intense cultivation' of Western democracies, away from the spirit of competition, the method of science, and the claims of 'efficiency', to the calm of the East, where a man's life is his own or at most his family's concern, rather than the State's, where there is time to live it, where truth is found neither in analysis nor compromise, and spiritual food is not contained in tabloids, we do not know what to make of music which is dilatory without being sentimental and utters passion without vehemence.

Another kind of music which has for us an unfamiliar convention is the polyphony of the Middle Ages. Here it is not the place but the time that is unfamiliar; we have suddenly thought away four centuries of our civilization. We step aside from the battle of the styles to contemplate achieved beauty. We wonder where now there are such workmen as those who built these melodies, what their secret was, and what the life of which these were the expression. They move us like forlorn hopes and lost joys, like the places we knew when we were children, like the land to which Blake hurried home from Santa Cruz. They appeal by their freshness and strangeness, but still more by an intimate familiarity. As an Englishman who happened to see for the first time the slope of a Sussex down would feel, apart from its intrinsic beauty, that it was the most English thing that he ever saw, so from these, apart from their intrinsic beauty of tone, the man of religion gets best at that truth which is beyond all limit and condition. Here the different convention helps rather than hinders him; just as his deepest intimations of those thoughts which are beyond words are conveyed to him more easily in Elizabethan language and in Hebrew phraseology than in any other form. It is this strange familiarity, which we are conscious of in Indian melody, that makes us sure that "though our language is different and our habits are dissimilar, at the bottom our hearts are one".

But more imagination is needed to place ourselves at the point of view from which we may enjoy the method of early folk-song, that is, of melody conceived apart from harmony; and it is very difficult for those who have thought all melody with an underlying harmony, tacit or explicit, to accept it without harmony, except after long practice. Consequently they are seldom asked so to accept it; except for specialists, no folk-song is published without accompaniment. The problem is a difficult one, for if a harmonized folk-song, like a restored cathedral, is a persistent lie, yet a folk-song without harmony seems, at any rate for most of us, to fall to pieces, like a picture without perspective. There is another connexion between harmony and melody more intimate still, whereby harmony is no longer a mere adornment to melody which can be added or not, at will, but a vital factor influencing the actual structure of the melody itself. We may harmonize, if we please, 'Green Sleeves' or 'Walsingham' or the 'Agincourt Song' without doing them much harm; but if harmony, as we understand it, had been in the air these tunes could never have come to birth. A tune is just a musical sentence, paragraph, or chapter. And a sentence consists of important and unimportant words, and is not a string of dictionary words. In the same way a tune consists of important and unimportant notes, and depends for its convincingness upon a judicious management of these. But the principles upon which this 'importance' depends are different for melody and for harmony.

The most obvious thing about harmony is that certain combinations are more euphonious than others; the more euphonious are dwelt upon, and the less euphonious skimmed lightly over. The essence of harmony lies in 'substantive' and 'passing' notes, and its progress consists in a training of the ear by which more and more 'passing' notes become 'substantive'. The very various 'chords' that arise in this process give a distinct colour, i. e. importance, to the note to which for the moment they are applied.

On the other hand, the most obvious thing about melody, a succession of single notes, is that the tune 'lies' high or low, that it has, as we say, a high *tessitura* or the reverse. This implies a level on which as a whole the song rests, and in comparison with which its salient passages are high or low. 'Laws' of melody spring into existence as the distance between these two levels, and the manner of passing from one to the other, come to be established and, later, stereotyped—as, for instance, in the 'Final' and 'Reciting' notes of Ecclesiastical music. In the process the intervening notes, and others beyond these two salient points, acquire varying 'importance' subsidiary to that of the two principal notes; and the whole of unharmonized song is laid out with reference to this variety of importance.

But since harmony gives importance, at will, to this or that note of the tune, the 'harmonic' tune will in its turn tend to travel along the most telling points of the harmony and to reinforce its crises; and the significance of such music will be the result of the conflict between melodic idiosyncrasy and harmonic necessity. The compromise between these two impulses will lead to closeness of structure and make for unity, because each checks the tendency in the other to free improvisation. 'Melodic' tune, on the other hand, contains its law in itself, and it has merely to display that law, not to conflict with some other. Provided the 'laws' of melody are not transgressed, one particular structure seems no more desirable than another; and this leads easily to a variety and elaboration of detail, which blunts the sharp outline of *tune* and throws the weight rather upon definition of *mood*. The beauty of harmonic music is that of tilth and culture; of melodic music, that of the briony and the gossamer.

In Europe the conventions of folk-song do not land us in any great difficulties. There is nothing in them which a good artist who is content to eschew conceits and lay aside all preciosity cannot as a matter of fact sing. There are few unsingable intervals because, with the exception of a few people, like the Greeks and Hungarians, the scales in use are the common property of the whole continent. There are few melodic ornaments or eccentric rhythms; they do not thrive when voices are much used in concert. But beyond Europe, at any rate in India, with which we are now concerned, it is very different. An enormous amount of convention, the growth of centuries, stands between us and the reproduction and therefore the appreciation of their melodies, for we understand little of any music we can take no part in. And yet no true musician would turn his back on it if he were convinced that the conventions were interesting in themselves; still less if he felt that there was real art behind the conventions.

Music in India, as elsewhere, is of varying excellence; and it is as rare perhaps to hear the best there as it is in Europe. If we look away, however, from the less worthy kind, which is apt to deal in cheap contrast and to indulge in personal display, to the noblest which is to be found there, our chief difficulty is to feel the religious element in it which an Indian feels. To hold any intelligible language about the emotional content of music is difficult; it is still more difficult when the content is that subject which 'every sensible man keeps to himself'. The range and depth of religious feeling varies in different countries, in one land it rides close, in another it sits loosely, to ethics, and the manifestations of it look different as they proceed from the intellectual or animal extremes of our nature —from the Vedantists or the Tantriks, from the Fourth Gospel or the Song of Solomon. Without questioning the spirituality of the religion of Europe or India, we may call the former practical and the latter contemplative; though it is difficult to say even as much as that without seeming to assert that the converse is never true, which would be absurd. But Europe, certainly England, thinks poorly of a religion that does not result in a good life: while India fixes its attention on the quality of the religion, the amount of realization and of vision it contains, and leaves the good life to follow as a natural consequence. India is still living the age of Faith. It is no accident, therefore, that the nearest analogue we can find to its music is that which culminated in the work of the Cinquecentists. Why it is that the Gregorian Tones portray a self-surrendering faith we can no more explain than we can say why it is that we agree with Heine's description of *Ein' feste Burg* as the Marseillaise of the Reformation, or that we recognize an undemonstrative pietism in Charles Wesley's tunes and an undeniable suitability for their purpose in the hymns of the Salvation Army; but we easily feel that none of these can be divorced from their age or occasion. And though we may be unable to point to definite characteristics in Indian music which are due to its impregnation with a most spiritual form of religion, yet its extraordinary correspondence in detail both of time and tune with the music of Ecclesiastical Europe justifies the view that a peculiar outlook on the world, such for instance as the specifically religious outlook, does bring as a result a peculiar form of music. The best Indian feels towards his music, as perhaps the best of us do towards ours, like the Devout Lover:

> Wheresoe'er my fancy would begin
> Still her perfection lets religion in.
> I touch her, like my beads, with devout care,
> And come unto my courtship as my prayer.

Of this song, given me by S. M. Maitra, the tune is one commonly sung by boatmen in Bengal; the Bengali words are by Indu Bhuśan Ray, the translation by Maitra. The mad woman wandering about hugging a bundle of rags she has collected, with village urchins snatching at them, is a common sight; what is not common is the poet's use of such an image to portray the soul's close communion with God.

Thou art my tiny bundle of old torn rags, my dearest lord; and I am thine own little mad woman holding thee always on my heart.

When I am tired I lay myself down under the tree by the river-side, and sleep in peace, resting my head on thy bosom.

In the streets men point the finger of scorn at me; they laugh at me, they throw dust on me.

Some try to pluck thee from my heart, some tell me to cast thee away. Ah! but how could thy mad woman live without thee, my love!

Pressing thee to my breast I go on my way, and neither fear nor falter; this mad mind of mine cannot be touched by any troubled thoughts.

Long, long years have come and gone, but thou art still the one sweet thing that never grows old. With what talisman holdest thou this mad, mad soul of mine, my love!

My translator said "Men weep when they hear this song".

BHATIAL (BOATMAN'S SONG) (Bengali Words)

Ex. 1.

There is, it is said, no statement which will apply to the whole of India except the geographical one that it is east of Suez. But three statements can be made about it which no one will be disposed to deny—that it is old and large and hot. India has had time to forget more melody than Europe has had time to learn. The elements of tone and rhythm have been combined and recombined, and have left the theory a tangled mass of forgotten systems and the practice an ineradicable instinct. The veneration for the past because of its remoteness, the mental attitude which looks away from the categories of time and space and turns its attention upon the essence of the thing itself, the faith which links the present closely with the time when the gods walked the earth and still points to the visible imprints of their feet—all these have united to personify every element of their music, and piously to

[1] The reason for this way of writing grace-notes is explained in Chapter VII.

preserve names and attributes which have long lost their meaning; so that much of the theory is clear only to those who can read myth. Nor on the practical side has extemporization, as it is there understood, been learned in a day, nor even in the lifetime of any individual; it is, just as much as their fluent public speaking, an inherited instinct of the race. This is, of course, bound up with another peculiarity, the disinclination to spoil a good memory by reliance on the written word or note. The writer heard two girl violinists at Tanjore play by heart in unison for five minutes, and they never once betrayed by a wrong note or by false intonation the fact that they were two and not one. But it is age-long practice rather than memory which has placed at the command of the best singers that inexhaustible wealth of variation with which they make a melody their own, that gift of improvisation which takes on an epic quality, as all crafts do that are handed down from father to son. To walk on the Old Trunk Road is, it has been said, to step into a chapter of Genesis; and in the same way we catch, in these immemorial cadences, the very spirit of the rhapsodists of Homer. Their music is old, but with an age like the eternal youth of Greece, not with a second childhood like the stereotyped formulas of the Troubadours.

The size of a country is to be reckoned not in square miles but by its travelling facilities or their absence. The Norwegian valleys of Helgedal and Lejra Elv are ten miles distant at their nearest point; but as far apart practically, and as different linguistically, as Devon and York. Indian dialects have been variously computed at 141 and 183; it is probably within the mark to say that India comprises 50 peoples, each ranging from thousands to millions, who are mutually unintelligible. If it cannot at present be shown that music and language follow geographically the same lines, it is patent that in each the means of expression is based upon the same general principles of phonetic decay, antithesis, exegesis, and so on, and that both deepen in secluded communities and broaden upon the stream of a universal currency. And the hundreds of names of Indian *Rāgs*, and many more if we count all the variants which, coming from different parts of the country, are included under the same name, are there to show that 'mood' behaves in all respects like dialect. This isolation of the village or the tribe has been repeated in the isolation of the court. The method of Gwalior has been firmly marked off from that of Lucknow or Indore, and these from the methods of Mysore and Tanjore and Trivandrum. Such places formed centres in which local usages were summed up and tabulated; and music that was born in secluded valleys and in trackless deserts was there nursed by royal patronage. If it is too soon to say that the patronage is withdrawn, there are signs that it is rapidly diminishing; and, as for the seclusion upon which this reflective music has so largely thriven, there can be little pride in his profession left to a singer when gramophone records of his best songs can be bought in any large town. In spite of all this it is difficult to believe that Music will lose heart and depart from the earth, least of all from so poetical a race. *Alter erit tum Tiphys, et altera quae vehat Argo Delectos heroas.*

Lastly there is the climate, the effect of which is twofold. Since life is lived under the simplest conditions and much in the open air, day being turned into night and night into day, all times of the twenty-four hours are available, to somebody, for making music. And the character of the music is felt, far more than in Europe where the conditions are more formal, to depend closely upon the hour and season of its performance. It is difficult to gauge the strength of this feeling, since those who believe that the beauty of the music depends on its being heard at the appropriate time are about equal in number to those who do not. The belief is strongest where the music is purest, where it is performed for its own sake rather than for display, and, like every other musical belief, is very old. Another result of the climatic conditions is seen in the simplicity of the instruments. The *Vina,* the most elaborate and the oldest, has not a tithe of the complication of the piano; for the tension of the strings being low, the framework can be simple, and the fingers being on the string, all mechanism is dispensed with. Nor are the gradations between the best and the worst specimens so subtle as in the violin; for the tone is not exposed so much to criticism on plucked as on bowed strings. Neither, of course, is there any comparison in the cost; ten pounds will buy a good instrument for the player's purpose, and the many tens more that may be spent on it are lavished, though not wasted, upon its ornamentation. Meanwhile, for simpler requirements, nature provides the bamboo, out of which an hour's work will fashion a serviceable flute, and man provides the water-pot (*chatti*) over which a skin may be stretched to furnish a quite sufficient drum.[1] It is not the great heat that matters—the difference between midsummer and midwinter is no greater than in Europe—but the all-pervading damp of the rains after the searching heat of June. This swells the wood and softens the glue and so breaks down the tone of elaborately constructed instruments such as we employ.

We have spoken of some difficulties of understanding music which are due to an unfamiliar convention of time or place, or to the absence of a convention to which we are accustomed, or to the presence of a content which appeals less forcibly to us; we have also considered the effect on the particular music which is under discussion, of the conservatism, the broad expanse, and the climate of India. One more cause of the particular form which this music has taken is to be found in the language of the country; for speech is logically, if not also historically, prior to song. Sanskrit, with an infusion of Persian in the north, and in the south incorporating relics of still older tongues, is the basis of all Indian languages. Its pure resonant vowels and clear-cut consonants present the least possible obstacles to good vocalization. The fact that quantity counts for more than accent in its pronunciation has made metre rather than rhythm the decisive element of musical time. The combination of resonant vowels and a metrical language has led to the development of vocal rather than instrumental music. And since the voice employs equable force of tone rather than violent dynamic changes, its deficiency in this respect has been made good on the drum.

That is perhaps as far as the printed page can go in presenting to the eye what can only be apprehended by the ear. To suggest the effect of that which even musical notation only faintly shows, we may borrow a device from the poets. When Homer wanted his reader to feel that Helen's beauty was worth all the ten years' agony of Troy, he made him listen to the old men on the walls talking about her ways as she had moved amongst them in their youth. In that spirit we may read the diary of Pierre Loti in the fifth chapter of his *L'Inde*; and those who have never heard what he speaks of may divine what he means, while those who have heard it may take pleasure in his accuracy of observation and truth of feeling.

[1] *Mṛdānga*, the general word for drum, means 'clay-body'.

"About four o'clock in the afternoon, when the midday heat has passed, the musicians of the Maharajah's orchestra, who have been placed at my disposal for a few hours, enter with noiseless steps, bow ceremoniously, and take their seats on the carpet which has been spread for them in the verandah.

"In the clear-cut profile and dainty features you recognize at once the artist. Gold tinselled turbans are on their heads, and diamonds in their ears. A fold of silk, touched here and there with gold leaf and disposed in the classic style, is thrown over the shoulder and leaves free one side of the body and an arm covered with bangles. From their light drapery steals a faint scent of rose-water.

"They have brought large instruments with brass strings; giant mandolins and overgrown guitars with the scroll of the finger-board ending in the head of some monster. These guitars differ considerably from one another and are intended to produce very different effects; but they have all of them large sound-boards, and occasionally, at the ends of the finger-board, hollow globes looking like fruit on a branch. They are painted, gilded, inlaid with ivory; they are old, well seasoned, and valuable. The mere sight of these queer shapes awakes in me a feeling of mystery—the mystery of India. The musicians smile as they show me them. This one is to be caressed by the finger, that to be stroked by the bow, a third to be plucked with a mother of pearl plectrum, and there is one which is to be played actually by rolling along the strings a little oval piece of ebony. Refinements, these, such as our Western musicians have never known. Then there are drums tuned to different notes and child singers sumptuously dressed. A programme specially printed for me is put into my hand containing the melodious polysyllables of the performers' names.

"By five o'clock they are all there, a score of them, seated on the carpet in the growing twilight while the punkah swings languidly overhead. And now the monster at the end of each guitar has reared its head and the concert is going to begin. What devastating sounds will issue, doubtless, from instruments of such a build, and what a din from the drums! I wait, nerving myself for much noise. Behind the players is an archway standing out against a white porch through which a group of the Maharajah's soldiers are seen standing in the rays of the setting sun, their turbans glowing in the red light to a deeper red, while the musicians form a dim cluster in deep shadow. The sight of their serious faces, and the fixed look with which they regard each other rather than any actual sound, tells you that the concert has begun.

"A note is held on *pianissimo,* almost too high for the ear to distinguish, like the opening phrase of *Lohengrin,* and then through several and various developments passes into a rhythmic movement without any increase in the body of sound. Astonishing it is, this almost silent music issuing from such powerful strings! It is like the buzzing of a fly imprisoned in your hand, or the rustle of a moth's wing against a window-pane, or the death struggle of a dragon-fly. One of the players holds in his mouth a little steel implement, and by the vibration of his cheeks produces the sound of a whispering fountain. Another, on one of the largest of the guitars, coaxed by the hand as if the player were afraid of it, keeps up on the same notes a prolonged Tuwhoo! like the blurred note of an owl, whilst a third instrument, muted, gives the sound of the surf on a distant beach. Then there are taps on the edge of the drumhead with the finger tips which your ear can hardly detect. Suddenly jerks and jolts, utterly unexpected, introduce a mad fit of two seconds duration; the strings vibrate at their full length, and these same drums, struck differently, utter deep, dull sounds like the lumbering stampede of elephants over hollow ground, or the rumbling of a subterranean torrent in some boiling chasm. Then in a moment all grows quiet again, and relapses at last into the whisper with which it began.

"Seated cross-legged on the ground a young Brahman with wonderful eyes holds between his knees an object whose lack of finish contrasts strangely with the refinement of the rest. It is a rough earthenware jar containing pebbles, and its large opening fits closely to the convex of his bared chest. The volume of tone increases or diminishes according as he leaves the jar open or closes it by pressing it to his body. His extraordinarily agile fingers draw from it sounds now twittering, now booming, or again, when the pebbles rattle inside, hard and dry like pattering hail.

"When the melody of one of these guitars makes itself felt above this clamorous silence, it is with a sort of wail by which the sound is dragged from one note to the next, an intense and passionate moan of rising grief, and the sobbing melody instead of being drowned is reinforced by the tumult of the unearthly drumming.

All this brings the listener into closer touch with the poignancy of human suffering than the supremest moments of Western music ever do. . . . The melodies do not, however, speak to us of sorrows so remote or so unintelligible as those of a Mongol or a Chinaman. If not at home in them, we seem at least to understand them. They depict the pain of a highly wrought nature which, though it has travelled down the centuries by another path, is yet not radically different from our own. And the gipsies, though through the medium of a less civilized music, have made us to some extent familiar with these forlorn and feverish accents.

"The human voice had, I found, been kept for the end. One after another tiny fragile-looking boys in rich attire, with eyes almond-shaped and over-large, executed bravura passages with bewildering rapidity. The voices they once had were now broken —already dying, as it were. A man in a gold turban conducted them, to the sound of a truly awe-inspiring prelude, by holding them with his eyes, his head lowered like that of a snake fascinating a bird; and you knew that he was mesmerizing them and could, if he pleased, force to breaking point the delicate structure of their frail organs. The words they articulated to their minor cadences were a prayer to appease an angered goddess.

"Last of all came the turn of the *primo uomo,* a handsome man in the prime of life. He sings and acts for me the laments of a young girl deserted by her lover. Seated like the rest on the ground he is at first buried in thought; his brow puckers; his eye darkens. Then his voice breaks out with the incisive wail of an Eastern bagpipe. In his extreme high notes you are still aware, by its harshness, that the voice is a man's; but in the heart-broken tones I hear—and it is a revelation to me—the very song of anguish; and his play of feature and the tense motions of his tapering fingers accentuate the agony of his despair.

"These players and singers are the servants of the Maharajah. They are to be heard every day within the guarded stillness of his palace walls, while menials pass to and fro with a cat's footfall, or stand with hands joined in supplication. How far other than ours must be the thoughts of this Monarch's heart; how different his outlook upon the sorrow of life, and of love, and of death! But music like this, uncommon in character and distinguished in performance, reveals to me one little corner of his soul better than did our short and formal interview, spoiled by its tiresome punctilio and by the constraint of a language not my own."

Not all Indian music is at this level; and one who determines to hear the real thing must be content to pass hours of boredom and traverse tracts of philistinism, ignorance, and want of skill before he has his reward—as, indeed, may be the case nearer home. But when it comes there is no mistaking it. No doubt there is often that added charm which we get, for instance, in reading poetry in a foreign language, in which the unfamiliar words contain a poetry of their own apart from the poetic use of them; the very *naïveté* of the melody and the old-worldliness and other-worldliness of the setting in which it is heard often compel our feeling for beauty even in very humble specimens of the art. We lose, perhaps, by not understanding the words, but less than we might expect. All their burden is the simplest desires and the simplest fears—the unwearied iteration of *Miserere Domine*, and the unwearying tale of human love.

Causes have been here assigned for this music being what it is; and it would seem that the music will not change until the causes change. Of these the language and the climate are two constant factors. It is shown in Chapter VIII that language, especially verse, has had a determining effect upon the rhythm of the music; and the climate, besides affecting the question of instruments, diminishes the enterprise which is necessary for concerted music. So far, then, it may be predicted that the music will remain metrical rather than rhythmical, vocal rather than instrumental, and individual rather than concerted. The other two factors were the conservatism and the large area of the country. This large area has already been somewhat contracted, and is likely to be still more contracted in the future, by easier and cheaper means of communication; the effect of this, musically, should be to reduce the variety of *Rāg* and *Tāl*, and to make the 'dialects' conform to some common standard. The conservatism will, no doubt, die hard. It seems to many as if all hope for music lay in recovering the traditions and the knowledge which made it so fine in the past. They believe that art can only prosper under munificent patronage, and that when that is removed art must die. In that they may be right; but when they go on to say, or to imply, that the *materia technica* of the art, its precise formularies as they existed in those

PLATE 1

Music Party. Detail from a picture (seventeenth century) in the collection of G. N. Tagore

days, must be sought out and quickened into life, as the only means of awakening an interest which has fallen asleep, they are on more debatable ground. Music cannot stand still. Its whole essence consists in finding short cuts to old roûtes. In the process it does many things that are afterwards seen to be regrettable; they die off, that is all, and the art lives on. The whole of our musical history is full of instances of this. We can appreciate the pope's prohibition of the sharp leading note or Mendelssohn's annoyance at the methods of Berlioz by considering the sort of reception we gave to Wagner's 'substantive' sevenths and chromatic harmony, now become commonplaces, and are giving to French whole-tones and to German pure dissonance. Life is too short to spend wholly in living in the past, and human needs are too imperative to be satisfied by proxy. It is inevitable that the multiple means of expression which Indian music has at its command will be reduced in number, that the fine edges of them will be worn down, and that the real needs will be expressed more simply. For, after all, a man sings because it is a splendid thing to do, and because he cannot help it; and when that is really the case he is not going to be fettered by obsolescent rules.

The process of simplification has already begun. The Carnatic system frankly ignores the niceties (examined in Chapter IV) of intonation. In northern India a number of songs are described as 'in a mixed *Rāg*' or 'not in a *Rāg*' and yet are accepted and enjoyed. The preponderance of common time (*Ādi, Tīntāl*) and of $\frac{3}{4}$ (*Rūpak*) over all the other kinds put together can hardly have been as great in the days when the system of thirty-five *Tāls* was invented. The 'new style' of drumming ignores the 'drum-words' and tends to simplify the elaboration of cross-rhythm.

It is all very sad; but there can be only one remedy—to accept the conditions and to make music first in spite of them, and afterwards on the strength of them. Music which is not built upon the immediate instincts and needs of the people is no music at all; they must make the formal details of their music just as they make their language—by actually singing and speaking. It is as far from the truth to say that 'modes' and 'times' must remain in their primitive condition as to say that poetry of the twentieth century must be in Chaucer's English, or a Bengali love-song in Vedic Sanskrit.

But there are other conditions which need not be accepted. If the rulers of native states realized what a death-blow they were dealing at their own art by supporting or even allowing a brass band, if the clerk in a government office understood the indignity he was putting on a song by buying the gramophone which grinds it out to him after his day's labour, if the Mohammedan 'star' singer knew that the harmonium with which he accompanies himself was ruining his chief asset, his musical ear, and if the girl who learns the pianoforte could see that all the progress she made was as sure a step towards her own denationalization as if she crossed the black water and never returned—they would pause before they laid such sacrilegious hands on Saraswatī. Excuses may be made for such practices, but there is one objection fatal to them all; the instruments are borrowed. We do not hear much about Roman music because it was so easy for them to get Greek slaves; and the importation of the gavotte and the minuet killed the English morris-dancers. To dismiss from India these foreign instruments would not be to check the natural, but to prune away an unnatural growth.

CHAPTER I

A MUSICAL DIARY

THE following pages give an account of musical experiences during a tour through India extending over half a dozen months of 1910–11. The route, determined by other than musical reasons, lay through the Central Provinces, Madras, Bangalore, Mysore, Trichur (exhibition), Travancore, Tanjore, Calcutta, Allahabad (exhibition), Dehra Dun, Lahore, Jhelum, Bhavnagar, Poona. It is hoped that the reader will excuse the use of the first personal pronoun to distinguish a traveller's actual experience from information otherwise obtained.

It must be understood that though many of these melodies were in queer scales, no attempt has been made, beyond an occasional superscript ♯, ♭, or ♮,[1] where the effect was characteristic, to represent niceties of intonation. Where such signs are not appended it does not necessarily mean that the songs were in the normal scale; perhaps the singers were finding their voice and the initial vagaries were not worth recording, or the tune only came once or twice—though generally it came a great many times—or perhaps I was not attending. It would have been good to have been able to note the exact pitch in each case; but the absence of the proper means made this, except in a few instances, impossible. A phonograph cannot be carried on the person or unlimbered and brought into action in half a minute, like a camera; there are also conditions, such as distance of the sound, or movement of the producer (e. g. in dancing) with attendant dust, which preclude its employment altogether. Secondly, as it is impossible for the European reader to reproduce the local colour which is imparted by curiosities of grace-note or of intonation, it is unnecessary to trouble him with them at this stage. And, lastly in attacking

[1] They mean in each case an alteration of less than a semitone, and they are in force, like ordinary accidentals, only till the end of the bar.

a new subject, as for Europeans, in spite of Captain Day's excellent book, this must be called, it is better to treat intonation by itself (see Chapter IV). It is but little, in any case, of language, whether spoken or chanted, that symbols can recreate for us; and when, as here, the choice lies between symbols which falsify but are understood and symbols which tell the truth but are not readily intelligible, there is no doubt which must be adopted to convey a first general impression.

The very simple melodies here recorded may seem to some too trivial to have been worth while. But if art is 'doing common things in an uncommon way', it seems clear that we must be familiar with the common things before we can appreciate the uncommon way of doing them. It is just for lack of this, of familiarity with such simple things as nursery rhymes and games, that we often fail to understand the poetry of a foreign country. It does not, however, occur to us that the same is true of music, because European music, which is all that most of us know, is cosmopolitan, and to understand a foreign composer it is seldom necessary to study the Folk-song of his country. He is using a familiar language, but doing unfamiliar things with it. But as soon as we leave Europe the language of music is not familiar to us, and our first object must be to learn it. We have to be humble, and begin with a 'simple exercise' book.

One caution with regard to these tunes. It would be a mistake to play them on a keyed instrument: they should be played on the violin, or sung, or whistled, or merely thought. Not only because there is then a hope of their being rendered in natural intonation and of getting the sharp edges of the tones rounded by some sort of *portamento*, but also because the temperament of a keyed instrument, in Europe the piano, in India the harmonium, has a unique power of making an unharmonized melody sound invincibly commonplace.

In all the melodies the tonic is C unless otherwise stated. It may be asked what decided in each case which note was the tonic. At the time of hearing the song there was seldom any doubt about it, and the doubtful cases are those for which no special note of the tonic was made at the time. What exactly decided the point at the time is a little difficult to particularize: it was something almost personal—just as when we read a book written by a man whom we actually know we get a better idea of his meaning than others would who do not know him. Tonality depends upon such things as the particular turn of phrase, the repetitions, the accompanying words, and these may, of course, be reproduced on paper. But it is, further, suggested in the extent to which particular notes are made essential or accidental, the exact amount of strength given to a leading note or to an appoggiatura, the emphasis in the accompanying percussion, minute retardations and anticipations, grace-notes at particular places, even the mere expression of face and hand—and most of these defy notation. The sum total of all these guides us, without our quite knowing how, to the general plan of the music, and thereby to its tonic. For a tonic is a tendency rather than a fact. All we could say of our own music is that in proportion as it exists for its own sake, and not for the sake of some other thing—words, or situation, or programme—it has a tendency to centre round some one note. Harmony can mark this note with exceptional precision; and we are apt therefore in looking for the tonic in an unharmonized melody to supply those harmonies mentally, and so to bring what we hope to find. In the Arab tunes, Nos. 52–4, for instance, it is impossible to say without having heard a good deal of Arabian music what they would regard as the tonic.

Except in street cries and sailors' chanties—the former in order to make the voice carry and to secure prompt recognition, the latter to ensure precision of movement—we hardly know in Europe that melodic impulse which finds vent in the occupation songs [1] of the East. The contrast of the two worlds is epitomized for us even before we actually land at Bombay. The A.B. seaman jolts out in a gruff practical voice his

Líghts are bríght and áll 's wéll!

and the Lascar follows with a smooth, dreamy

Ex. 2.

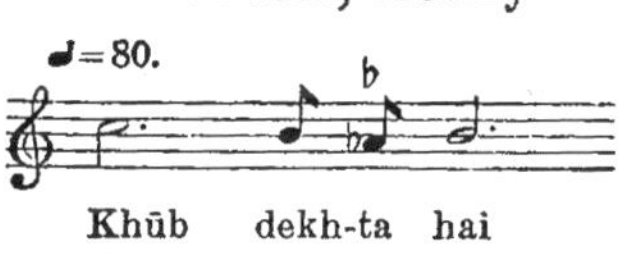

(Good watch is kept)

It is an allegory. On the one hand, the essentials in the fewest possible words, with stress and energy, in matter of fact tones; on

[1] See Karl Bücher, *Arbeit und Rhythmus*, Teubner, Leipzig, 1909.

the other, pitch substituted for stress, a generalization for a statement of fact, and through it all a suggestion that Time has no meaning as opposed to Eternity, with the implication that we *are* in Eternity all the time, though we are apt to forget it.

Neither street cries nor chanties are common in India in the sense in which we understand them. The typical mode of selling wares is not to take them to the customer, but to let him come to them, sit down, and open an interminable bargain. A small amount of coolie labour requires concerted action it is true, and that sometimes necessitates rhythmical motion: but the typical method of work is individual—innumerable baskets, buckets, bamboo poles, contribute their quota, but severally; many shoulders lift the dhooly (palanquin) or many heads the grand piano, but the feet break step; many hundreds of hands man the ropes of the god's car, but the effort, at the instigation of voice or even whip of perambulating priests, is spasmodic.

At any rate, I heard very few songs intended as rhythmical accompaniment to effort, and seem only to have recorded one. Six men were on a roof lifting a block of building stone. The foreman sang the solo.

Ex. 3.

The pull was on the last note of the chorus.

A common use of song is to give words of command to domesticated animals. At a well at Poona the water was drawn by a skin let down by two ropes. When the skin reached the water one rope was slacked and the mouth of the skin opened. The cattle marched slowly down an incline, pulling on the ropes, and, as soon as the contents of the skin had been emptied into the trough which carried the water out over a neighbouring field, backed again up the incline a little slower still. When the well-man started them down he sang

Ex. 4.

[1] The spelling is phonetic.

[2] When the superscript accidental is in brackets it means that the note was sung sometimes one way, sometimes the other.

and when, after a minute's interval he backed them up again, he sang

Ex. 5.

This process went on to my knowledge for three hours, and probably many more.

In the neighbourhood of Madras the wells are worked by the *picotta*. A bamboo pole is balanced crosswise on another; at one end is a weight, at the other a bucket. A man stands at the junction of the poles and throws his weight against the full bucket. Here there is no rhythmic motion to emphasize, and there are no animals to direct; it is merely a question of half a dozen hours and hundreds of bucketfuls. I was unable in a short stay to find a man actually working and singing; so one was persuaded to come to me and sing, a very different thing. This was his melody. The C was slightly sharp; the intervals C–B and B–A seemed to be about equal.

Ex. 6.

Get up on the picotta, Pillaiyar[1] made of cow dung, Pillaiyar made of mud.
I offer rice, cocoanut, cake, wheat, grain.
(counts buckets) . . 9, 10, 11 . .
Have I come here, O maiden, only to sleep?
The fields all wet are ready to receive seedlings.
Get bullocks ready to plough,
Reddish brown, with white horns,
The central bullock black, with white horns.
Harness four together,
Drive them over the wet fields;
After the ground is prepared
The seedlings will grow on the bank of the lake.
(counts) . . 27, 28 . .
The river is dammed,
There are vegetables in the gardens
And mangoes on the trees;

[1] Pillaiyar = Ganesh, the belly god.

I mix these with wheat and curd.
I have a long distance to go,
But I am happy with you here my dear.
Where is your husband?
 (counts) . . 63, 64 . .
He is not to be found here.
He married me and went on board ship.
If I am a chaste woman,
The ship will return with my husband.
 (counts) . . 101, 102 . .
My beloved had sore eyes,
He was jealous and avaricious,
 (counts) . . 116, 117, &c., &c.

Melodies like these are appropriate to particular occupations, and new words are fitted to them from time to time. For the traditional occupations a new tune is seldom invented. The tune for each occupation has a special name. In Behār, every mill-song is a *jātsār*, every cowherd's song a *chāchar*, and so on.[1]

But one comes across tunes in the making from beggars, fakirs, reciters. Some boy acrobats at Bombay gradually formed their petitions into

Ex. 7.

On tour with an Indian civilian we inspected a village school. After the boys had gone through their gymnastics, the 'monkey-leap', the 'crocodile crawl', and the like, we received the pungent and in my case vicarious tribute of marigold wreaths, and the school-master recited a Sanskrit poem of his own composition in honour of the presiding dignitary. Beginning with a mere rise and fall of the voice it settled gradually into a set melody.

Tonic G.?

Ex. 8.

Fakirs at the annual fair at Allahabad, the junction of the two rivers, evolved:

[1] See an article by G. A. Grierson in the *J. R. A. S.*, vol. xviii, p. 210.

Ex. 9.

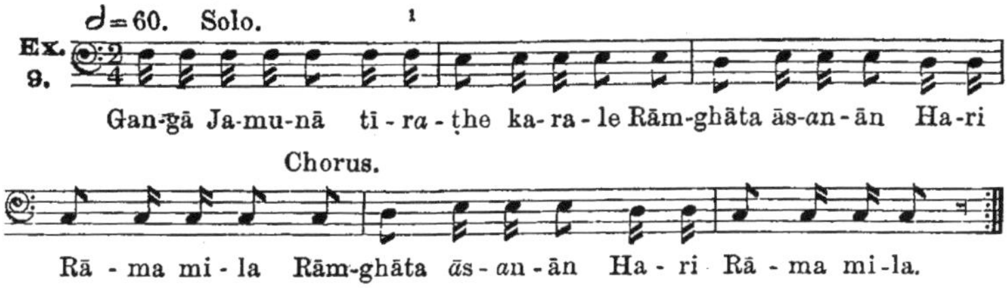

To the Ganges and Jumna pilgrimage make; at the Rāmghat bathing the name of the god Rāma you have got (i.e. if you bathe you will get).

A beggar woman one hundred yards off had a variant of this:

Ex. 10.

A little further on some boy beggars sang:

Ex. 11.

This turned out however to be, apparently, a rendering of a song which was being sung at the time by a celebrated singer at the exhibition, of which two versions were:

Ex. 12.

(1)

(2)

and further developments:

(3)

(4)

so that it does not do to be too sure that every beggar is a composer also.

[1] The italicized *a*'s are inorganic; they are freely inserted for vocalization.

Half a mile away two beggar girls were singing words of which I only made out *Sārīnā*, at the beginning and end:

Ex. 13.

Two coolies at Mussouri, driving ponies up the hill with loads, answered each other with

Ex. 14.

Ex. 15.

There is a slight resemblance in these, as regards melodic figure, to a tune sung by some boys coming home from their work across the Maidān at Calcutta—though that was rather a song from *lack* of occupation:

Ex. 16.

At Bangalore men and women were pulling a roller over a new made road. The voices were rough; the solo enthusiastic but of poor tone, and the chorus consequently took some time to settle down to the tune. Several of the men punctuated the first of the songs with boos and poohs to represent the drum at the places marked *; they were started by the man who scraped the mud off the roller. (Alternate four and six-bar sections.)

Ex. 17.

Ex. 18.

Ex. 19.

The words of No. 19 were:

Draupadī, wife of the Pāndava king, disguised herself as a beggar to get paddy seed for her race to plant in the wilderness. She was afraid of her enemies and cousins, the Kauravas. If she was caught her race would have to spend another twelve years in the wilderness. If gods fare so, what shall we poor mortals do?

The next day, after much searching and delay, I found a woman who was famous for her songs at *rāgī*-grinding. She sat with a friend on the ground before a large mortar, and each stirred with her pestle sometimes in time with the song, sometimes not.[1]

Ex. 20.

(Tamil.) Think of Rāma. Do not waste time. It is short. Always sing of Rāma.

[1] See illustration, p. 62.

Ex. 21.

About Krishna. He used to plague the girls. They complained to his mother. His mother told him to be better behaved.

Ex. 22.

Sin not; or you will go to hell (*Naraka*).

Ex. 23.

(Sanskrit.) Rāma is the only true God whom every one thinks of.

Ex. 24.

(Canarese.) We have several avatārs. This is a world of pain, there is no happiness here. Therefore do meritorious deeds.

Ex. 25.

A Rajah's son sees a beauty in the street and offers her a lakh of rupees.

Ex. 26.

About a wicked Brahman who married a Pariah girl.

With the last dozen songs or so we have begun to cross the rather shadowy line which divides Occupation Songs from ordinary Folk-song.

It was not till I had been some months in India that I found the opportunity I had been waiting for of *overhearing* a folk-melody. I awoke at Madras, about 5.30 a.m., to the sound of singing; it was next door, and seemed to come from a woman about her household duties. In the dim light I scribbled down the following:

Ex. 27.

Most of the phrases were repeated many times, as many as ten; a few only once or twice. The variations were introduced piecemeal; both sections were seldom varied at the same time, though they are shown so here for brevity. The flattening of the D appeared to take place only when there was no mordent, and not always then. I don't know how long she had been going on; what is given took about half an hour to sing.

This humble melody, improvised without shyness on the one hand or any idea of showing off on the other, may serve as an introduction to the tribal songs which follow. It shows the way in which they were varied and expanded, or would have been if there had been time; and the bare themes which are set down in the following pages must be imagined as having been so treated. The rapid succession of variations made it often difficult to note the tune at all, especially as regards that very elusive point, rhythm. The earlier melodies may, like eldest sons, be to some extent experiments; but nothing has been given that I did not satisfy myself was substantially correct. The question of quarter-tones will be dealt with later; any conclusions that may be drawn from these examples as to the general structure of folk-melody will not be vitiated by assuming them all to have been as they are written, and as in fact many of them appeared to be sung, in the (untempered) tones and semitones of the European just scale.

From Nāgpur, where my tour began, I went to Wārsa, a few hours distant by train, where a party of *Mārĭă Gōnds* were to march in from Moholi, a couple of dozen miles away. Owing to some misunderstanding they failed to appear that day at all, and arrived only at nine the next morning at the station, our train, the only one in the day, being due at ten.[1] We found there a crowd of twenty-two under Rainu Patel of Chingli (east of Moholi), a man of fifty, with a striking face full of humour and character, the flat nose and thick lips of the Gond, and a thick-set figure on bow legs. He marshalled his pupils and divided them for singing into two parties of ten and twelve. These songs, being the first of the kind I had heard, could not be noted with any accuracy. The words of three of them were:

1. The bird is crying. Why is the bird crying? It is crying with grief for its mate. Nowhere can she find her mate. The friend is in grief for the friend. She does not find the friend here. In this country he is not found. She must go to the lower country and seek him. If she will go far then she will find him.

2. Quickly, sister, make the *pej* (gruel).

For twenty or thirty years you have not asked me to make the *pej*: why do you ask me now? Where are you going?

I am taking the black bullock to the *bazar*.

If you go I will go too.

No, you must not go. If you go they will say 'See, the brother and sister go together'. It is like a man and wife going together, and that will be a scandal. No, you must not come.

3. The clouds look like rain. There are big drops falling. Rain has fallen in the upper country; the *nalas* are full. Everywhere there is rain. *Dhīmār* (boatman), bring quickly your boat.

What pay will you give me?

I will give you the bracelet on my arm.

I am not married; what use is a bracelet to me?

I have no money in my hand. I will go with (i.e. marry) you. Launch your boat.

They next arranged themselves in a close packed circle for

[1] I mention this not to reproach them or the Malguzar (village headman) who organized the meeting and no doubt did his best, but to show by a typical instance the sort of difficulties, over and above the mistakes one made oneself, which have rendered these records necessarily imperfect.

dancing, with Rainu sometimes in the middle, sometimes prowling round outside and exhorting individuals. In the second dance they linked hands behind each others backs; in the third they broke from their circular into a serpentine movement, and looked like a section of a giant centipede crawling about. Most of the dancing consisted, here as elsewhere, merely in revolving slowly 'widdershins' with a shuffling gait, bending their bodies towards the centre and clapping their hands in rhythm. The interesting point in the dancing was the treatment of the blank beat (*khāli*). Thus, putting R for right foot, L for left, F for forwards, and B for backwards, the ordinary rhythms were danced thus:

Three time 1 2 (3), 1 2 (3),
RF LF RB, LF RF LB

Four time 1 2 (3) 4, 1 2 (3) 4,
RF LF RB LF, RF LF RB LF

Five time
1 2 (3) 4 (5), 1 2 (3) 4 (5),
RF LF RB LF RB, LF RF LB RF LB

And similarly with
Six time 1 (2) 3 (4) 5 6 (our $\frac{3}{4}$, not $\frac{6}{8}$)
Seven time 1 2 (3) 4 (5) 6 (7)

Another dance of which I was too busy noting the tune to watch the feet was in slow tripleted seven rhythm.

Ex. 28.

It was full of grace notes of course, but as most of the performers chose their own graces, and their own moments to apply them, it was impossible to distinguish more than two which enjoyed a consensus of opinion.

Then followed an interval for putting rice on their *dhols*. These are barrel-shaped drums with terminal diameters of seven and eight inches respectively. Boiled rice mixed with wood-ash was applied to the larger end,[1] thereby giving more resonance to the tone and lowering the pitch by anything up to an octave. They did not tune the *dhols* to the same note by tightening the braces, nor did they aim at any definite interval between the two ends of the *dhol*,

[1] The lump so affixed is generally made of flour (*ātā*), and goes by that name. Iron filings are added when obtainable, for greater resonance.

by the application of the rice. They brought no wind or strings; they would have played the bamboo flute, but 'would have had to make one', and there was no time.

They then formed in a large circle, each with his drum slung, with two peacock feathers rising straight up from his *pagrī*, and a bunch that looked like grass with beans or pods at the end hanging down behind. Between man and man was a distance of two feet, which each kept accurate by touching his right-hand neighbour during the silent beats of the rhythm, beating in fact the silent beat on him. Rainu now danced amongst his men, shouting directions every now and then. He was distinguished not only by his absence of ornament, but by his abundant good humour and zest. The dance began with a wild prolonged shriek; this was followed by a steady monotonous beat on the drums as they walked round, apparently to settle themselves at their proper distances. Next they adopted a stealthy crouching step, all eyeing the centre, to a four-rhythm. The next dance, in three-rhythm, six beats, with the fifth and later on the sixth also omitted, or rather supplied only on a single drum, showed a limping gait. These were wedding dances, and without singing: the only sound beyond the pattering and shuffling of feet in the deep sand being an occasional whoop after the manner of Scotch reels. Then there was a funeral dance: nine men facing another row of nine and advancing as they retreated, and vice versa, with linked arms. This should have been at night; and they protested that it was 'a foolish dance' in the garishness of day. They chanted, without drums.

At Raipur a *Gond* played the bamboo flute (*bāṇsrī*), an instrument with the tone of the clarinet, and blown at the end but without reed: it had six holes covered by the left finger tips and right knuckle joints. A characteristic of these tunes was the very long crescendoed tonic. Assuming the C to be in tune the higher notes were all a little flat, the F most so, and the lower one a little sharp; the C itself sharpened a good deal under the overblowing of the crescendo.

Phonogram. *Allegro.*

Ex. 29.

Māria Gonds. Circular dance; central figure, Rainu

Gonds and Kanwars. Slow dance, with anklets

Malyas dancing

Malayan women dancing

Ex. 30.

A *Kanwar* also played the *singāra*, a sort of attenuated kit. It had two strings which the player tuned to C and F♯, and then began to play. I asked if they were right, and he altered them with a smile to C and G and said they were right now. The G was used as drone, so that the tune was below it; each section closed on two G's. They had also a slow dance with bells fastened below the knee like morris-dancers. (See illustration, preceding page.)

At Trichur (west coast) there was an exhibition of local industries, and tribal musicians had been brought in. The *Malyas*, from the spurs of the neighbouring hills, sang:

Ex. 31.

'A handsome girl makes her appearance with joy.'

and two of them alternately:

Ex. 32.

'A handsome maiden became a mother and had a son. She had a dream' —but it appeared to pass the wit of my interpreter to say what manner of dream it was.

In this there was one short passage in fourths which however only occurred once, and was gone before I could note it. It is impossible of course to get any particular passage repeated unless you know and can ask for the words of it: they repeated the whole song by request, but the passage did not recur.

In their dance the left foot, slightly advanced, came on the beat, and the weight of the body, a little bowed, was placed on it. Then the leg, and with a serpentine movement the whole body, straightened again.[1]

Ex. 33.

Towards the end there was more action; the feet flung higher, the right foot turned out, the body facing alternately right and left, and so on. Then a *pas seul.* The dancer could not get his accompaniment (a single singer) to his satisfaction for a long time, and they wrangled as to how the tune went. The *Kadars* who were to sing next were sitting by; and one of these broke in with a wildly different tune as a suggestion; but the *Malya* was not in the least put out, and got his way in the end, which was this,

Ex. 34.

sung alternately by himself and his accompanist.

It was now the *Kadars'* turn. One played the *kuzhal.*[2] He had great trouble in getting his reed to speak the tonic (C) properly, and cut several before he was satisfied; the *Malya* dancer did not fail to note his distress. It is curious how hard it was to arrive at the scale of this instrument. The player had no notion of playing a single note by itself, he invariably played a grace with it, showing how inseparable grace is from even the simplest phrase. It was achieved at last by my holding down his fingers in succession. A phrase which frequently occurred in his playing was:

Ex. 35.

[1] See illustration, p. 30.

[2] Pronounce, *kŭrāl. Kurāl* is the name in Tamil for the first note of the scale (Sa).

Two *Kadars* sang:

Ex. 36.

'A maiden chewed betel nut, and walked gaily round the streets of Coimbatore.'

Ex. 37.

A wedding song: the drum was the *maddale* of p. 42.

Next came the Boatmen of Ernakulam, called *Velans.*[1] First a long song with six variations—'seven ways' of singing, he called it,

Ex. 38.

the first four minor, the last three major. No. VII got faster at each repetition. The general sense was: Invocation to a deity to inspire the singer; description of a town; of a palace; of a temple;

[1] *Vel-* rhymes with 'pale'.

in praise of the Rajah of Cochin (who had opened the exhibition); rowing in a boat. Fragments of other boatmen's songs were:

Ex. 39.

Ex. 40.

Two *Pāṇans* now appeared. This tribe formed in old days the band of the Rajah, but has sunk now into the position of an inferior caste. They are recognized magicians. An astrologer settles what is the form (*mūrti*) of the demon, and the *Pāṇans* are called in to exorcise it. They perform the exorcism (*teyāttam*) with drum and pipe; occasionally they wear masks. Their pollution distance, that, namely, within which they may not approach a Brahman, is 36 feet. The usual time of year for exorcism is July and August, when demons are apt to be specially prevalent and malicious, when in fact the rains have developed a certain amount of malaria.

A man and his wife sang alternately with a *chakravādya*[1] and a triangle, which divided the eight quavers respectively as 3 + 2 + 3 and 2 + 2 + 4, thus:

Ex. 41.

Two other of their tunes are these:

Two Pāṇan men. (Phonogram.)

Ex. 42.

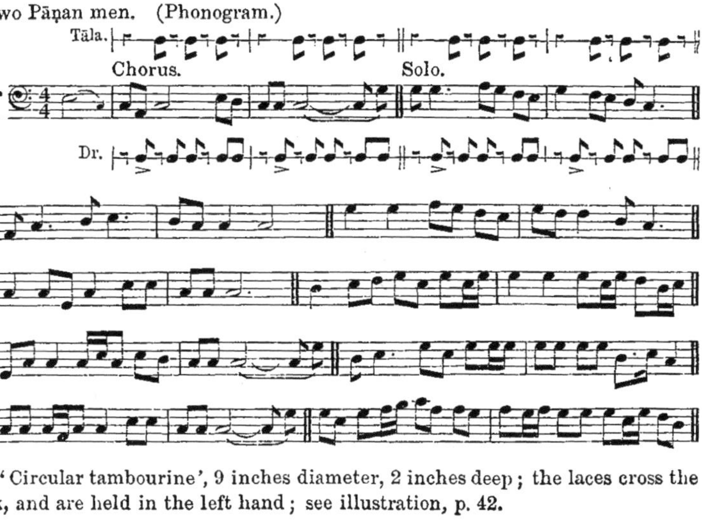

[1] 'Circular tambourine', 9 inches diameter, 2 inches deep; the laces cross the back, and are held in the left hand; see illustration, p. 42.

Chorus. Solo.

(Phonogram ends.)

Pāṇan woman. (Phonogram.)

Ex. 43.

They are quite different from the neighbouring tunes; both have a large compass, ten or eleven notes, and both oscillate from tonic to dominant, each section closing on the tonic. The woman also definitely closed her tune on the tonic, making a pause, which an Indian seldom does; and it is rare to find instances of such disjunct motion as in bar 4, where the dominant chord is distinctly formed twice. Lastly the arrangement of bars in Ex. 43 is elaborate—4 + 3 + 4 + 2 + 3 + 3 + 3 + 3; and the quick tripleted rhythm unusual.

Next day I started for Paddikad, ten uncomfortable miles by *ekka*. *Malayans* (different from *Malyas*) were to come in to the Traveller's Bungalow and receive their annual present from the *Sirkar* of cloth, rice, coco-nuts, coco-nut oil, chilis, and tobacco. They sang, with drum. First a boy of ten as solo with a chorus of men and women:

Ex. 44.

Ex. 45.

Ex. 46.

Ex. 47.

Then the men alone:

Ex. 48.

Ex. 49.

Lastly the women danced. Alternate feet were placed behind, the body inclined to that side, and the corresponding hand made a motion as if sowing paddy[1]: meanwhile the men sang

Ex. 50.

Of course all these skeleton themes were considerably varied. As to the thirds, though they oscillated a good deal between major and

[1] See illustration, p. 30.

minor, there was little doubt by the time the tune was finished as to which was intended. Most of the tunes quickened towards the end. The performers clapped the time; but as they differed from one another it was not easy, on one or two occasions, to make out whether they were beating 2 + 2, 2 + 3, or 3 + 3. Probably Ex. 44 was intended for 2 + 3, but the drag of the chorus soon settled it into a 3 + 3.

At Alleppey, further down the coast, there were Hindu boatmen landing Arabs at the pier. The boatmen sang:

Ex. 51.

The Arabs

Ex. 52.

Ex. 53.

Ex. 54.

quite a different scale. These were short phrases between the strokes.

From Quilon to Trivandrum is a series of lakes and canals formed by the silting, in early times, of the alluvium of five rivers. Alleppey is about half way; and the method of cultivation there is this. The fields, surrounded by low banks, are, during the rains, inundated, and coated with fresh soil. The water is then pumped out, and paddy sown. Practically a large part of the country is most of the year under water of shallow depth, and locomotion is almost entirely by boat. This lends itself to singing. I had two opportunities. Once, in an open boat with four men. I was innocent of their language and had no interpreter, so that I was unable to tell what view they were taking of their passenger, who is usually the topic of their song. I had merely armed myself with the *Malayālam* for 'sing' and 'repeat'.

Ex. 55.

Ex. 56.

Ex. 57.

Most of these began with a short colloquy in monotone between a soloist and a chorus. The abrupt ending of Ex. 58 was character-

Ex. 58.

istic. Sometimes, not always, the chorus would come in with the last phrase, snapped out with emphasis. In Ex. 59 the B and E

Ex. 59.

were distinctly flat, the D appreciably so. The whole gave the impression of three approximately $\frac{3}{4}$ tones, with tonic C. Other tunes were:

Ex. 60.

Ex. 61.

Ex. 62.

The other opportunity was on a night journey by *valam*[1] from Trivandrum to Quilon. A *valam* is a covered boat in which you may balance yourself during the day on a semicircular roof and watch a slowly moving panorama of palms, Chinese fishing nets, wheel pumps, and naked children, and at night recline inside making such account as you may with heat, smells, and mosquitos, or other inmates. There were two boatmen, punting; one in the bows with a bass, the other in the stern with a tenor voice. Each kept his own pitch accurately: their tonics were a fourth apart, though for readiness of comparison all are given here with the same tonic.

[1] Pronounce, *wŭllŭm*.

Ex. 63.

Ex. 64.

Ex. 65.

Ex. 66.

Ex. 67.

Ex. 68.

Ex. 69.

Ex. 70.

Ex. 71.

The songs were difficult to catch as they were seldom repeated, and were apt to be broken off suddenly and frequently with an 'illā!' as a boat loomed ahead in the darkness, or an 'irava!' as it glided past. In Ex. 66 the three D's, so marked, and these only, were distinctly sharp every time. The songs are given in the order in which they were scribbled down by candle light, the different voices being shown by the clefs.

Later on I heard two Negapatam boatmen. As I had succumbed to the climate I was obliged to have them to my bedside, in a railway waiting-room; the novelty of the place acted unfavourably on the singers, and the whistling and shunting on the listener.

Ex. 72.

Coda (in unison.)

When the sails are spread we pray to Allah and Mahomet.

There is an interest attaching to this. In Bourgault Ducoudray's *Mélodies de Basse-Bretagne* on p. 21 is a tune 'Le Sabotier'.

Ex. 73.

It seems possible that, since French sailors are chiefly Bretons, these boatmen may have heard this tune at the French port of Pondicherry which is not far from Negapatam; if so, their treatment of it is interesting; they have smoothed out the articulations of its rhythm, and bridged the leaps of the melody.

Ex. 74.

Lifting by derrick.

Ex. 75.

Carrying passengers through the surf.

Ex. 76.

Unloading cargo. The superfluous fifth bar in No. 76 which dislocates the rhythm was really there.

Ex. 77.

Sung in honour of the captain when he comes to Singapore. The streets of the town have been cleared for him.

Trivandrum. A caste of Trivandrum, the *Pāudarans*, sang the following, called Kavidachindu, in praise of the god Subrahmanya, otherwise called Skanda or Murga.

Ex. 78.

Ex. 79.

Ex. 80.

The two versions of Ex. 81, of which the first is like the overture to *Zampa*, were from the same lips. The three omitted bars, thirteen

Ex. 81.

instead of sixteen, gave a lift to the melody of Ex. 82. The two

Ex. 82.

Ex. 83.

versions of Ex. 83 were from different singers. They are probably in seven-rhythm, but in the absence of any clear indication only what appeared to be the time values of the notes has been given. The A♮ sounded more piquant than the A♭; as the flattening is obviously only a case of *Musica ficta* it does not appear in the signature.

Two *Pulaiyar* women, shy and tearful, sang

Ex. 84.

The second woman began invariably by skipping a beat. This was the only song they knew. It was what they sang when they were tilling paddy, to this effect:—'We were once slaves. There was a fire on the estate and the landlord stopped it with a spear. The fire got into the fort, and the landlord's men stopped it with their pistols and shields. His women came out and stopped it with their broomsticks.'

Next two Sudras[1] from the Maharajah's brass band sang

Ex. 85.

'in the Pulaiyar style', whatever that may have meant (the scale is tonal). They spoke English, and one of them gave me some information about 'two-four and six-eight' time. They also sang some *Sopānam* songs, i. e. those sung on the steps of the temple:

Ex. 86.

Ex. 87.

The *udukku* is a small drum, shaped like an hour-glass, held in the right hand so that the squeeze of the fingers tightens the braces and sharpens the tone within the limits of about a sixth. A pea at the end of a string swings from the middle and strikes either drum-head. The *tālam*, lit. time-instrument, was a pair of shallow cups of bell metal, about three inches in diameter. This song bears marks of genuineness, and the three rhythms and the suggestion of harmony are interesting; but the other is not very distantly related, except perhaps for its seven-bar rhythm, to the strains of the Salvation Army, which I heard that evening outside in the *bazar*.

A regular *Sopānam* singer also came. He sang in some of the five *Rāgams* peculiar to Travancore:

[1] The fourth of the four castes of India—Brahmans, Kshatriyas, Vaisyas, Sudras.

Ex. 88.

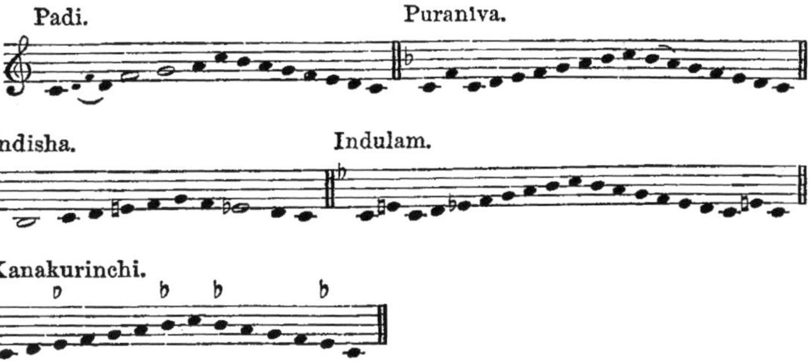

As far as the mere notes go, there is nothing in these that might not be heard elsewhere in the peninsula, except that, whether intentionally or not, he sang the F, G, and upper C (especially the F) decidedly flat. The 'predominant' notes (see Chap. IV) are distinguished by semibreves. The two commonest were said to be *Indisha* and *Padi.* This group of modes special to one place is interesting as proving, what the names of many *Rāgs* also bear witness of, the strictly local origin of all *Rāg*, just as the harmonic minor is very common in Swedish songs, the Lydian in Icelandic, and the Aeolian and Mixolydian in Irish songs.

The most primitive tribe I came across were the *Kānikas.* A company of fifteen or so had marched in over night from two villages twenty miles away in the Ghāts. Small, wiry, pictures of men. They had had no food since the previous morning, as the shops were all closed when they arrived late at night. They brought with them bows and arrows and *kokkaras.* This is a flat piece of metal, eight inches by six, with serrated edges, rolled into a cylinder with the edges turned up. Along these a tenpenny nail is rubbed furiously. I offered one of them four annas if he would hit a tree twenty-five yards off; he missed it by a yard. Apparently they shoot hares, not at such distances, but by lying in wait near the hare's form. They told me, 'we live among tigers and elephants. We are not afraid. We say "shoo" to a tiger, and he goes away. We speak the truth, there is no need to tell a lie.' They are loyal subjects of the Maharajah. They address him as 'thou', and would do anything for him. They live clean lives and treat their women well: there was not a degraded face amongst them.

After they had been fed they gave their performance. Seven of them took part, each provided with a *kokkara.* On this the tunes

Ex. 89. 

were accompanied in trochees. The headman of the village picked up his *kokkara*, bowed his head over it, and murmured a prayer. Another, likewise, and another followed, scraping them up and down with growing excitement. The leader recited a list of twenty or thirty divinities,[1] in no particular order, repeating some more than others. After five minutes or so one of the men began to tremble violently, and holding his *kokkara* with both hands straight out in front of him tapped it rhythmically on the ground. The leader was the next to tremble, and his access was more violent. He flung himself about, his *pagrī* fell off and his hair fell down. A third leapt, when the fit was on him, from his sitting posture about three feet into the air, and dropped again into his original cross-legged position. The whole service was interspersed with shouts and yells from individual performers. When it was over the *mantizomenoi* bent forward sobbing vehemently, and took a minute to recover. One felt ashamed to have been merely an interested spectator amongst so much sincerity.

At Tanjore I heard some 'bandy'[2] men. They sing at night, as they drive along, to let the dacoits, of which there are plenty there, know that they are awake (and in a position therefore to return blow for blow). One of them had been beaten, and showed a mark on his forehead in proof of it: the other said he had been stoned. The feature of their tunes (Exs. 90, 91) was the long note

Ex. 90. 

Ex. 91. 

of indefinite length; the words were not given, as unfit for publication. In the temple at Madura I heard the *nāgasāram* (N.

[1] Some of the names were Rāma, Hari, Harichandra, Shiva; and local deities, Sāsthan, Amman, Amcala.

[2] Covered cart.

India *shahnai*), a kind of oboe with a very loud tone; it was unbearable close, but sounded majestic and rather awe-inspiring at a little distance in the long galleries, as it did blown on the breezes from the top of the Trichinopoly rock. The illustration is of two players at Tanjore; they took it in turns to play chanter and drone. When the second was asked to surcease from droning, the first said he felt 'like a ship without a rudder'.

At Calcutta I heard a Maratha gipsy, from the Circus. He belonged to Tasgaoṉ in the Kolhapur district. These gipsies are the bards of the Maratha empire, now thrown out of employ. This man was an acrobat. He sang two *Povāḍas*:

Povāḍa (chivalric song of 1795).

(In tempo and style of Bonnie Dundee.)

Ex. 92.

Kashmīri bīn-player
(Taken by Ananda K. Coomaraswamy)

Nāgasaram-players, Tanjore

Povāḍa.

Tonic C.

Ex. 93.

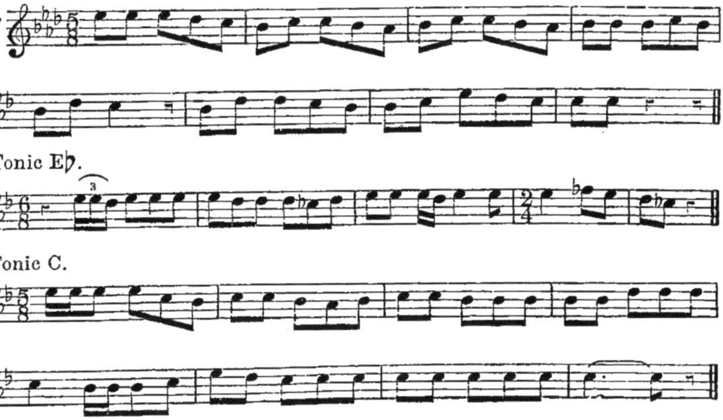

Concerning the expedition of Pendreh, military officer of Kolhapur, who marched against Pasgaoṇ and was defeated by a Brahman, Patwardhan.

This should be compared with Ex. 99. The change of key is most unusual, and does not appear to be recognized at all in the art-music. It is possible to suppose the tonic is the same throughout—E♭ in Ex. 93 and C in Ex. 99. But against this is the very definite close in C of Ex. 93, and the exact correspondence of the two sections of Ex. 99. They must stand, therefore, as rare instances of a change of tonic; in which case the mode also changes in Ex. 93 from Doric to Lydic,[1] but remains the same in Ex. 99.

[1] The terminations -ic and -ian are used here to denote the Greek and Ecclesiastical modes respectively. Appended is a list of them with their Carnatic and Hindostani equivalents.

As on the white notes of the piano.	From C, with	Greek mode.	Ecclesiastical mode.	Carnatic *Melakarta* (mode).	Hindostani *Thāṭ* (mode).
B—b	5 flats	[Mixolydic	Locrian]	(Sāman chant)	
E—e	4 ,,	Doric	Phrygian	Hanumatoḍi	Bhairavī
A—a	3 ,,	Hypodoric	Aeolian	Nāṭabhairavī	Sindhubhairavī
D—d	2 ,,	Phrygic	Dorian	Karahārapriya	Kāfī
G—g	1 ,,	Hypophrygic	Mixolydian	Harikambogi	Jhinjoti
C—c	0 ,,	Lydic	Ionian	Dehraśankarābharaṇa	Bilāval
F—f	1 sharp	Hypolydic	Lydian	Kalyānī	Imankaliān

The *Sāman* chant is discussed in Chapter XI. The Sāman may be sung in Hindostan too, but I could hear of no Sāmagās (singers) there. The place of other much more elaborate modes is discussed in subsequent chapters.

I got the singer to clap his hands—a thing it was generally impossible to persuade him to do, though he would sometimes do it of his own accord—so that there was no doubt about the changes of rhythm in both these songs.

On these seven dozen melodies some generalizations are possible.

1. The further we get from civilization the more limited the compass. In cities, seaports, and the like, the compass is anything up to, or even beyond, the octave. Among the *Gonds* and the west coast tribes it is not more than four or five notes; among the *Malayans* and the Travancore boatmen, and the *Toḍas*,[1] not more than three or four; among the remote *Kānikas* only two or three.[2]

2. The tonic is sometimes locally as well as logically central, i.e. the tune 'takes off' from some note below the tonic, and ranges through some two or three notes above it. Cf. Exs. 29, 44, 45, 47, 62, 66, &c.

3. But a larger number have the lowest note for tonic. Cf. Exs. 27, 31, 33, 36, 38, 80, &c.

4. There is a tendency for the melody to begin in the upper part of the voice, reaching it perhaps by a leap, and to settle down upon a tonic. Cf. Exs. 27, 28, 36, 38, 63.

5. A small number of the tunes employ conjunct motion exclusively. Cf. Exs. 17, 37, 56, 59.

6. In others, when two notes are taken by leap they have sometimes previously appeared as taken by step. Cf. Exs. 39, 48, 58, 61.

7. Real transilient scales are not found here; see, however, Exs. 44, 45, 46.

8. The pivot on which the melodies turn is the interval of a fourth with the lower note as tonic (see *passim*).

9. Imitation at different levels is rare. Cf. Exs. 47, 63, 66, 81.

10. Two-time is common, three-time rare.

[1] Collected by Mr. Thurston, whose phonograph records are at present in the hands of Dr. Myers of Cambridge.

[2] See Chapter XIII (by Dr. C. S. Myers) of Dr. Seligmann's *Veddahs of Ceylon*, where the melodies of two or three notes are classed as 'more archaic' than others of four or five.

11. A mixture of these takes three forms:

(*a*) Two counted as three, or three as two. Cf. Exs. 27, 37, 38 II–V, 92.

(*b*) Two and three, or three and four are alternated. Cf. Exs. 21, 24, 28, 36, 63, 67, &c.

(*c*) Cross rhythm of song (Exs. 58, 66) and drumming (Exs. 42, 48).

CHAPTER II

A MUSICAL DIARY (*continued*)

At Allahabad I came across some Garhwālīs who had been got down from Mussouri in the *Himālaya* for the Exhibition as *riksha-wālās* because they would be in good training, and because they were cheerful and honest. They said they could not sing in the day-time because they were thinking about their work, so we had a very merry evening in a hot tent from nine o'clock to past midnight. There was great competition to sing into the phonograph and have their performance given back to them; but unfortunately only one phonogram has survived the railway journey. The subjects of their songs are given for what they are worth; I was able to get them only at fourth hand. The men sang in Bālī; this was translated by one of them into bad Hindostani, retranslated into good Hindostani by a bystander, and from that a version was given me by a (most patient) English boy of fourteen who spoke Hindostani like a native; his actual words are given here.

Ex. 94. 

(He and she on opposite banks of a river).
She. If God gave me wings I'd fly to you.
He. If God made me into a bullet I'd reach you so.
She. Are your father and mother well?
He. How are all the village people, &c.

Ex. 95. 

Make me the best instrument in the world.
What will you give?
I will give you four annas a day and as much *dāl* (maize) as you like.

Ex. 96. 

A man had a daughter and sold her in marriage to an old man (aetat. 36) She protests:—

'Why did you marry me to such an old man?'
An old woman says:—'It was your fate; don't be sad about it.'

'Still, I'm not happy. I'll go away and get married to a young man.'—for she had many lovers.

But they say—'You have chosen an old, old man and now we won't have you'.

Tonic G.

Ex. 97.

(*He*). O give me those pret - ty eyes, And I'll
(*She*). And if I give you my pret - ty eyes, Oth - er
(*He*). Then O let me bor - row them And
(*She*). For six months you shall bor - row them; Pro - mise
(*He*). What word is this of a bar - gain-ing! I will

make you the gift in re - turn of my own, dear.
lov - ers 'll laugh and 'll leave me a - lone, dear.
keep them safe till you need them a - gain, dear.
tru - ly you'll give me them back then a - gain, dear.
keep your eyes and your heart and your soul, dear.

Ex. 98.

A Gurkha song. He deserts his sweetheart.

Tonic B.

Ex. 99.

1. Mo-ther, send to the *dho - bi* to bring back my li - nen.
2. Nev - er mind where I'm go - ing if you'll send to the *dho - bi*.
3. Oh I'm go - ing to get me a new wife, pret-ty Hi - ra.
4. Oh I'm wea - ry of Chhai - la as you know, lit-tle mo - ther.
5. For the love of your son, moth - er, my Hi - ra will leave him.
6. For five hun - dred ru - pees I can make good the de-ceiv - ing.
7. He shall cease from his griev - ing for I'll dou - ble the ran - som.
8. Some new ear - rings of pearl and a long neck-lace of ru - by.

Tonic G.

1. O where will you go if I get back your li - nen?
2. You must say where you go be - fore I send to the *dho - bi*.
3. Lit - tle Chhai - la is yours and will you mar - ry an - o - ther?
4. But her hus - band 'll kill you if you get pret-ty Hi - ra!
5. He will fol - low with fif - ty if you dare to de-ceive him.
6. For five hun - dred ru - pees he will not cease from his griev - ing.
7. And what gems will you get to a - dorn Hi - ra the hand-some?
8. You have said where you're go - ing and I'll send to the *dho - bi*.

Ex. 100.

A postman and his sweetheart.

'Since we were at school we have loved each other. I have spent all my money on you; and didn't you love some one else?'

'Up to now you haven't married me!'

'I'm so busy all day; I've no time to speak to you.'

'If you loved me you'd find time; you'd leave all your work.'

'I'm being transferred to another village; I hope you'll be well.'

'You're going? I feel lonely.'

Tonic F.

Ex. 101.

Jāgalī wanted to go to a flour mill. Her uncles and brothers said, 'Don't go, else the police will catch you, and pinch you, and kiss you, &c.' But she,—'Never mind, I want to be caught, and pinched, and kissed, &c.'

Ex. 102.

1st version.

2nd version.

Called Jonu's song: I could make no story out of the words. It was accompanied by a graceful two step, with a drag on the second.

Phonogram.

Ex. 103.

1. Two pret - ty boys there were Un - der a gu - ru's care.
2. One day the Ra - jah came, Asked of their house and name.
3. In days that are now no more They sojourned in Ab - bot - pur.
4. Their moth-er, Con-sī-la fair, To Das-rat their fa - ther bare.
5. The names of the chil-dren are Rā - ma and Laksh - ma - na.
6. Forth they were cast from home, Far in the woods to roam.
7. Mes - sen - gers came, but they Would not the word o - bey.
8. But when they grew to men Home they re - turned a - gain,
9. Marched to the Ra-jah's throne, Slew him that sat there - on.
10. Now by high God's de - cree, At their re - turn, I see.

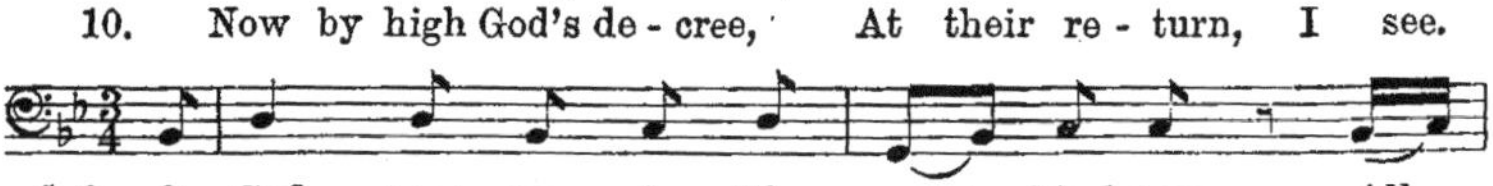

1-9. O God, hear me in Thy great kind-ness, All -
10. Thou God hear - est me in Thy kind-ness, Thou

- see - ing God light - en my blind - ness.
God hast light - ened my blind - ness.

Ex. 104.

No words available.

Ex. 105.

Bachhi married Dēvali; but she only bore him a daughter; so he expelled the former, and exposed the latter.

There was also a recitative song from Bhotan:

Ex. 106.

The long note was of indefinite length—as long as the breath lasted.

These Garhwālīs had come from the hills: I went next to Dehra Dūn, a few miles below Mussouri, and met with some more of the same tribe. Their songs follow below. Most of the words were, I was told, mere snatches of sentences, often in the wrong order, learnt by heart without understanding, interspersed with tags for the sake of the rhyme. The first half dozen were sung by a small boy. The intervals between the verses he occasionally filled up by a combined smack of the lips and clack of the tongue to represent the thud, or rather the squeeze (see Chap. IX) of the drum, which would at that place have a solo, in order to give the singer time to recover his breath. The other songs were given by men soli, or by women in chorus.

Tāra Padhāne.

Ex. 107.

Sovkin Biwāri.

Ex. 108.

Būji Dhānpuria.

Ex. 109.

Tānko.

Ex. 110.

Chhaila.

Ex. 111.

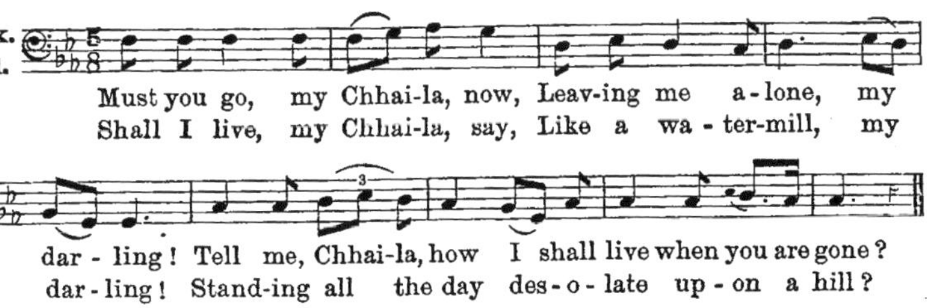

In this song two bars are taken as the unit, and the rhythm is 2+3+3+2; it would have been more correct to write it $\frac{10}{8}$, but more difficult to read. No method of writing it will reproduce the charm of the original. (*Chhaila*=darling.)

Hyun Pārio Gād.

Ex. 112.

Ranwain Bāja.

Ex. 113.

Biglitār.

Ex. 114.

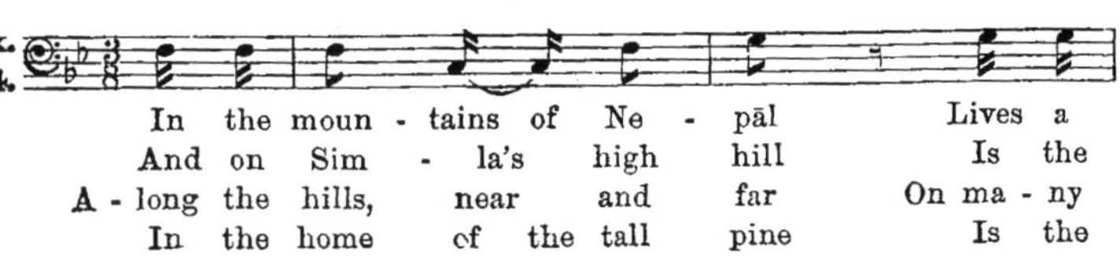

might - y king; And his peo - ple one . . and
Lāt Sahib's[1] camp; And when mount Me - ru . . is
poles hang wires; Is not that a fair . . Dar -
Lāt Sahib seen; But in Mat - tra's ho - ly

all . . . To his feet hom - age bring.
still . . . You may hear his Si - pa - his' tramp.
- bār . . . Lit by a thou - sand fires!
shrine . . Is Ne - pa - lī - ya queen.

Chhaila.

Ex. 115.

(The spelling of the titles in Exs. 107–115 is merely phonetic.)

Ex. 116.

Tonic C?

Ex. 117.

Ex. 118.

Ex. 119.

Ex. 120.

Ex. 121.

[1] Viceroy's.

These were sung by women, tile-layers. They clattered their wooden trowels on the floor, in an approximate rhythm, and 'felt shame' because there was no actual roof to work on.

Ex. 122.

Ex. 123.

Ex. 124.

This came from Dharmsāla[1]; and the *Rāg* was given me as Behāg. That its singer knew so much about it as that, not to mention its carefully balanced sections (the same as in our National Anthem), removes it from the category of folk-song proper.

In many of these Garhwālī songs, and still more in the Gurkha songs which follow, I noticed, instead of the usual slide or vibrato on the emphatic notes, a sort of luscious squeeze, a glutinous warble—quite incommunicable.

[1] An officer of the 1st Goorkha's at Dharmsāla gave me these two tunes that his men sung on the march.

Zakmi Dil (the wounded heart).

Ex. 125.

O Sādhu.

Ex. 126.

N.B.—The tonic of this is probably C, but may be F. The third bar begins with what may be the 'warble' noticed below.

To such tunes as

Ex. 127.

Ex. 128.

four men, A, B, C, D, danced, lifting the foot to the level of the knee, their movements corresponding to the four beats of the bar [0 stands for the silent beat].

(1) All clap hands.

(2) B, D touch right palm to A, C's left palm, the fingers pointing upwards.

(3) Clap hands.

(0) D, B touch left palm to A, C's right palm. All step backwards (instead of forwards) on this beat.

One night during my stay a sing-song was kindly organized for my benefit among the men of the 2nd Goorkhas. They were in more than their usual good spirits over a successful hockey match with the 9th. There was no *gêne* in the presence of their officers, and the performance was in no sense 'to order'. The songs followed in such quick succession that there was no time to get down any words: most of them were danced to. One man, or perhaps two, stood out in the midst of an admiring crowd, and whirled round and round; bent knees and elbows, palms of the hands upturned, arms extended. At regular intervals a couple of bars, or four, were danced in a crouching position. At the end of a chorus there was occasionally a grunted 'Ha! Ha!'

Ex. 129.

Ex. 130.

3rd version.

4th version.

Ex. 131. 1st version.

2nd version.

Ex. 132. 1st version.

2nd version.

Ex. 133.

Ex. 134. 1st version.

2nd version.

Ex. 135.

Ex. 136. 1st version.

2nd version.

Ex. 137.

The following two melodies were given me by an officer of the regiment.

Andante. ♩. = 100.

Ex. 138.

This is a Chitrālī dance (the regiment spends its time between Dehra Dūn and Chitrāl). It is played loud, soft, *staccato*, and *staccatissimo*. The final notes are blown with all the fingers off the holes, the *acciaccatura* being got by overblowing.

Ex. 139.

A Kāfir song. The three-crotchet cross-rhythm of bars 2, 3, 4 is noteworthy.

At Jhelum the station was entertained one evening by the 20th Punjabis with a Cuttack dance. About one hundred men grouped themselves in a double circle round a bonfire, which shot up into bright flame at intervals in response to libations of kerosene. They advanced towards and retreated from the fire with swoopings, punctuated by sudden crouchings, twirlings, and pirouettings; waving their arms, with handkerchiefs in their hands; sometimes pausing suddenly by bringing one leg sharply down on the ground. Later on some picked dancers substituted swords for handkerchiefs. Then two swords, one in each hand; and one man dangling a third sword held in his teeth by the sword knot. The *surnai* (or *shahnai*), a sort of oboe, or bagpipe chanter, and the *dhol* were employed. The dance tunes were:

Ex. 140.

Surnai. ♩ = 92.

Ex. 141.

Surnai. ♩ = 165.

Ex. 142.

At Achilgarh, near Mount Ābū, women climbing up to the temple, with waterpots, stopped by request and sang,

Ex. 143.

At Bhavnagar (Kāthiawār) some *khawas* (maidservants in the royal household) sang:

Ex. 144.

Ex. 145.

Ex. 146.

Ex. 147.

Ex. 148.

Ex. 149.

Ex. 150.

Ex. 151.

Ex. 152.

The first eight of these were danced to, the silent beat (the *khālī*) being marked by a retrograde step.

The last, *Sītājī na mahina,* is a well-known and popular song, describing the twelve sorrows[1] of Sītā, one for each month.[2]

Dasrat, king of Ayodhyā, had two sons, Rāma and Bharata, by two wives. Bharata's mother had a promise from Dasrat that he would give her anything she liked. She demanded nothing till Dasrat was on the point of abdicating, when she asked that Bharata should succeed, and Rāma go into retirement in the jungle with his father for fourteen years. Bharata was away at the time; the claim was honoured, and Rāma retired. Bharata on his return refused to accept the situation, and tried to induce Rāma to return; but he

[1] For other (*Bihārī*) forms of the 'Twelve Sorrows' see *J. R. A. S.*, xvi, New Series, pp. 203, 207, 213, 216, 218.

[2] The Indian months are:

Kartik	Nov.–Dec.	*Vaishak*	May–June
Magashir	Dec.–Jan.	*Jeth*	June–July
Posh	Jan.–Feb.	*Ashā'ī*	July–Aug.
Megh	Feb.–March	*Shravan*	Aug.–Sept.
Phalguna	March–April	*Bhadarva*	Sept.–Oct.
Chaitra	April–May	*Aso*	Oct.–Nov.

said he was bound by his promise. Bharata then placed his *padūka* (wooden shoes) on the *gaddi* (throne) and dressed like his half-brother in jungle clothes to show sympathy. Meanwhile Sītā, Rāma's wife, was carried off by Rāvaṇa, with a view to marriage. In her captivity she laments to her friend.

'O girl, with the month of *Kartik* my beloved went away. This month is the harbinger of winter, when cold is fierce like lightning. My beloved has left me, and the night which is my enemy begins to increase in length. I wonder why my soul does not leave my body. *Magashir* is full of emotion. It is difficult for a woman to pass her days apart from him who loves her; so her condition is very unhappy. The rooms of the house look empty, and Sītā is grieving with tears in her eyes. Will any one bring a letter from my beloved, or carry one to him? In *Posh*, here in the court of Rāvaṇa, my home comes to my mind: this Sītā says with tears. In *Megh* the wind from the Himālaya blows, and my body trembles. To whom can I open my heart, O friend, that heart which is attached to Rāma alone? In *Phalguna* the flowers bloom; but what are these to her who has not her lover. The Rāg Basant is being sung, but how can she care for such songs. In *Chaitra* my mind has become anxious and confused, and the absence of a letter from him pains me. All the leaves return to the trees, but not my lover to me. In *Vaishak* grapes and mangoes are ripe, and the hot wind is blowing, and the body of one who has not her husband breathes fire. In *Jeth* it is the custom to go to the tanks with friends to bathe; but he is not here, and my heart does not permit me to do so. Why bathe, or dress, or put on ornaments; I will none of them. In *Ashā'ī* when the rains have begun, and birds are singing in the trees, I envy them. In *Shravan* the tanks are full and the rain falls in streams. My gay clothes are wet with rain and tears. One who has once loved can never change; but for all this I must not lose heart. In *Bhadarva* all kinds of corn are ripe, but they please me not. It is now *Aso*, and I have heard, O friend, that Rāma has constructed a bridge to carry an army from India to Ceylon.'

[Rāma brought his army of monkeys from Rāmesvaram across 'Adam's bridge', Rāvaṇa was killed, Sītā was brought back to Ayodhyā (Oudh) to the great joy of her people, and Rāma embraced Bharata.]

'I Rāmayya, the poet, and whoever will sing my song, shall obtain heaven, and all his desires will be fulfilled by God, and all his accumulated Karmas will be exhausted.'

Cradle Songs.

There is one special class of song, lullabies,[1] of great interest and beauty. They seem not to be much known in the Punjab, where Mahommedan mothers croon only The Name, *Illāh-il-illāh,* over their babies. But in any part of the peninsula they may lurk

[1] Is it too daring to offer 'Lali', I rock, or cradle ('Lālo' in Kashmir), and 'Bai', baby, as an alternative to Skeat's not very convincing derivations of 'Lullaby'—brought from India possibly by gipsies?

Rāgi-grinding

Pāṇans

Schoolmistress, Tanjore

unsuspected, as the difficulty of persuading a woman, except of the lowest class, to sing before a man, and especially before a European, is almost insuperable. Those I got were chiefly in the south, and from 'enlightened' women.

At Trivandrum I obtained[1] the song with which His Highness the present Maharajah of Travancore is said to have been put to sleep as a child.

Ex. 153.

Is this sweet babe
The bright crescent moon, or the charming flower of the lotus,
The honey in a flower, or the lustre of the full moon,
A pure coral gem, or the pleasant chatter of parrots,
A dancing peacock, or a sweet singing bird,
A bounding young deer, or a bright shining swan,
A treasure from God, or the pet parrot in the hands of Īśvarī,
The tender leaf of the *kalpa* tree, or the fruit of my tree of fortune,
A golden casket to enclose the jewel of my love,
Nectar in my sight, or a light to dispel darkness,
The seed of my climbing fame, or a never-fading bright pearl,
The brilliance of the sun to dispel all the gloom of misery,
The Vedas in a casket, or the melodious *vinā*,
The lovely blossom put forth by the stout branch of my tree of enjoyment,
A cluster of *pichāka* buds, or sugar-candy sweet on the tongue,
The fragrance of musk, the best of all good,
A breeze laden with the scent of flowers, or the essence of purest gold,
A bowl of fresh milk, or of sweet smelling rose-water,
The field of all virtue, or an abode of all duty,
A cup of thirst-quenching cold water, or a sheltering shade,
A never-failing *mallika* flower, or my own stored up wealth,
The auspicious object of my gaze, or my most precious jewel,
A stream of virtuous beauty, or an image of the youthful Krishṇa,
The bright forehead mark of the goddess Lakshmī,
Or, by the mercy of Padmanābha, is it the source of my future happiness,
Is it, in this beautiful form, an Avatār of Krishṇa Himself?

The next five examples were obtained from a schoolmistress in Tanjore.

[1] The songstress wanted to accompany herself on the inevitable harmonium, until I pointed out that it would be much in her way when she pulled the string of the cradle, and that the sound of it might prevent the baby from going to sleep.

Rarāro. ♩=90. Phonogram.

Ex. 154.

Lālishrīta. Phonogram.
Adagio. ♩=70.

Ex. 155.

The rhythm of the first of these is obscure even on the phonograph; it was probably some $\frac{7}{4}$ rhythm, but the melody floated away so easily on a *tempo rubato* that it seems better to leave it barless. It is evidently a variant of Ex. 155.

Lāli Keshavuda. ♩=100. Phonogram.

Ex. 156.

Lāḷi pardare. Phonogram.

Allegretto. ♪. = 80.

Ex. 157.

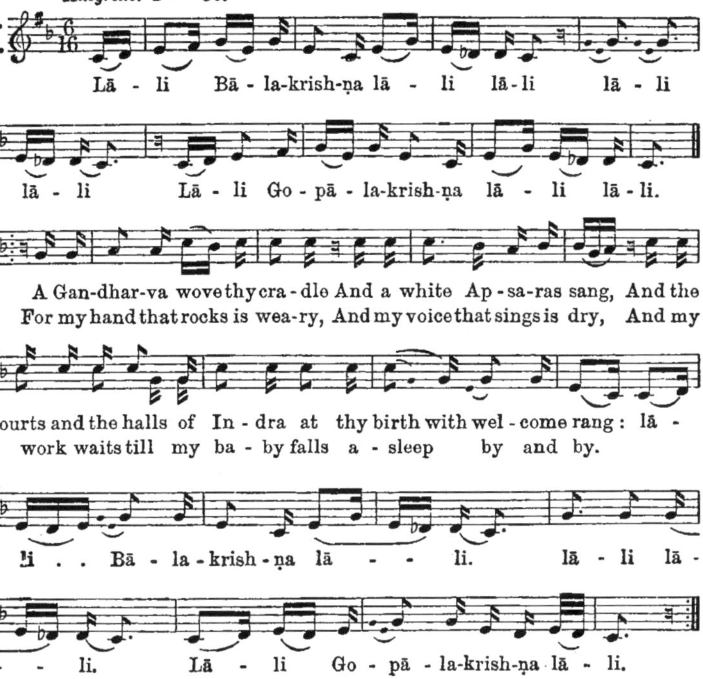

The words are borrowed from Ex. 162.

Ex. 158.

The next two examples

Andante. ♪ = 90.

Ex. 159.

Ex. 160.

were gathered from an unmusical ayah on board the steamer; she lost her key a good deal, and the songs were difficult to piece together. My interpreter could make nothing of her particular dialect (of Hindostani). Ex. 159 is evidently a distant variant of Ex. 156. The slide gave a wonderful 'value' to the close and the half-close of Ex. 160.

The three following are Maratha songs; the first two, lullabies, and the third, an epithalamium. They were kindly sung to me by a Hindu lady in Calcutta.

Rāma's lullaby.

Ex. 161.

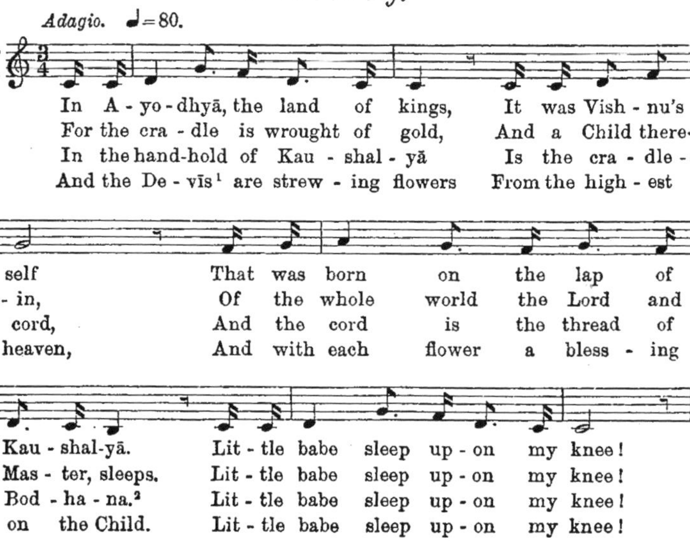

Nirguna's[3] lullaby.

Ex. 162.

[1] Goddesses. [2] Knowledge.

[3] The supreme being—'without qualification'.

Celestial carpenters have fashioned thy cradle. My hand is tired of pulling the string. My throat is dry with singing. I cannot go about my work because my baby is not yet asleep. The cradle is covered with flowers, &c.

Epithalamium.

Ex. 163.

In another class, not exactly Folk-song because conscious nor Art-song because unsophisticated, are children's songs. The following were sung to me at schools at Jhelum in the Panjab. The boys ranged from ten to eighteen, and one of those who sang was married.

Boys' songs.

Ex. 164.

There is no place like one's own country. If you would know, ask the inhabitants. The Bulbul knows. The wind blows purer there; the water is clearer; the very dust is an elixir. The name of our country refreshes us. Its mountains are higher than heaven. It is a garden of Eden. Every corner has deeds to tell.

Ex. 165.

Children must not wear ornaments. There is a fear of losing person or property. [Boys as well as girls wear ornaments, and are not infrequently kidnapped and robbed, possibly even murdered to prevent detection.] How can parents be at ease when their eyes are constantly riveted on their children, watching their necks or wrists.

Ex. 166.

No words obtainable.

The following is a love song, which the boy would not have sung before his father or elder brother for fear of being beaten:

Ex. 167.

Girls' song.

Ex. 168.

The song that women sing at marriage, speaking of the deterioration of women nowadays, how that they know nothing of the housewifely duties which made the name of Sītā famous.

In two particulars the Garhwālī and Gurkha songs here given (Exs. 94–128 and 129–139) stand out from the rest. They were in true intonation; the salient intervals, the Thirds and Fourths, unmistakably 'just'. And they are in transilient scales; even if the scale is complete the notes follow each other in such a way as clearly to show that the melodies have a pentatonic basis (cp. Exs. 117 and 139), and it is probably correct to regard such hexatonic (*shāḍava*) and heptatonic (*sampūrṇa*) scales as 'spoiled' forms of the pentatonic (*oḍava*), as in the more familiar Scotch songs.

The Gurkhas are Mongolians of Nepāl, and the Garhwālīs one of many Indian tribes of the Himālaya, and their use of this *oḍava* scale differs. The typical Gurkha form is GA—**C**DE (Exs. 129, 130, 137, plagal; and Ex. 135 authentic). The typical Garhwālī form is G**A**—CDE (Exs. 94–7, 103, 107–9, &c.), though there are instances also with C (Exs. 110, 127), D (Ex. 103), and E (Exs. 99, 123) for tonic. The Gurkha use is what the books represent as the typical Chinese scale; and it seems not impossible that the Garhwālī melodies present the form which that scale took on Indian lips, and that the transilient element of Indian song comes from the East (see Chapter IV).

The harmonic basis of this scale is of course the Fourth, and a melody is a succession of partly filled Fourths; the backbone of the song, what gives it its strength, is this leap of a Fourth through a passage note. In the Gurkha songs this passage note is adjacent to the lower note of the tetrachord,

,

in the Garhwālī to the upper

;

and this makes their general character very different. The passage note cleaves to the sound which is being left, not to the one which is being approached. We may see this in the melodic figure so common in the Cinquecentists

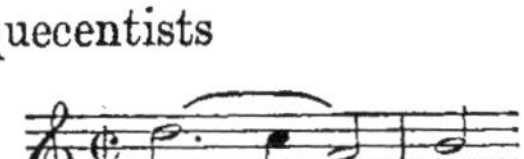

for instance, in the close of Palestrina's Motet, *Tribus Miraculis*:

Ex. 169.

That it should do so is natural because the leap of a Fourth is a leap to the known through the unknown, and the 'unknown' is taken primarily as a melodic, i. e. an adjacent interval. Hence the Garhwālī figure, even though taken in ascent, is essentially a falling figure, and the Gurkha, even in descent, essentially a rising one; and the character of the latter is accordingly more jovial and exhilarating. Added to this there is in the Gurkha songs a strong rhythm, recalling the Scotch 'jerk', and an absence of complicated cross-rhythm.

As we are upon the subject, another very common way of filling the tetrachord may be mentioned

There do not happen to be any instances of it in these chapters, but the scale which is taught to children as the 'easiest' is composed of two such phrases, and there is no doubt that it is a favourite and most characteristic locution. It has the appearance of being a transilient passage from G to C, but the origin is probably a different one; it will be discussed in Chapter IV.

A natural result of 'transilience' is the tendency to build harmonic phrases

Ex. 115. Ex. 117.

Ex. 170.

Ex. 94. Ex. 111. Ex. 103.

Ex. 98. Ex. 104. Ex. 99.

otherwise rare in Indian song; Exs. 115 and 99, indeed, get very near to implying a definite change of harmony, which would be quite foreign to the spirit of the music as a whole (cp. also Ex. 43).

Imitation at different levels may be seen in Exs. 117, 140, 141, 142, 163. Cross-rhythm occurs in Ex. 161 where the third line wavers between two bars of $\frac{3}{4}$ which suits the words of the first and third stanzas, and three bars of $\frac{2}{4}$ which suits those of the others: a device of frequent employment in the cadences of Handel's time. Another instance is in Ex. 167 where the 'throbbing and aching' is to be accented as triplets, but in strict time, not 'three in the time of two', giving a pleasurable shock analogous to that felt at the beginning of Brahms's third Symphony.

The Indian may be disposed to think these melodies too trivial to be dignified by the name of song; he will say his art begins where these stop, and will hardly recognize in them any of the real spirit of his music. The European may protest that they are too fragmentary to be of real use, and that there are too many gaps in the information about the occasion and the subject of each. Both charges are justified; but the object has been not so much to present complete and finished specimens, as to get close down upon those natural instincts of song-makers which, when followed out in the domain of art, cause their music to take one form rather than another; to get behind the conventions, of which all art is full, to the things themselves of which those conventions are the outcome.

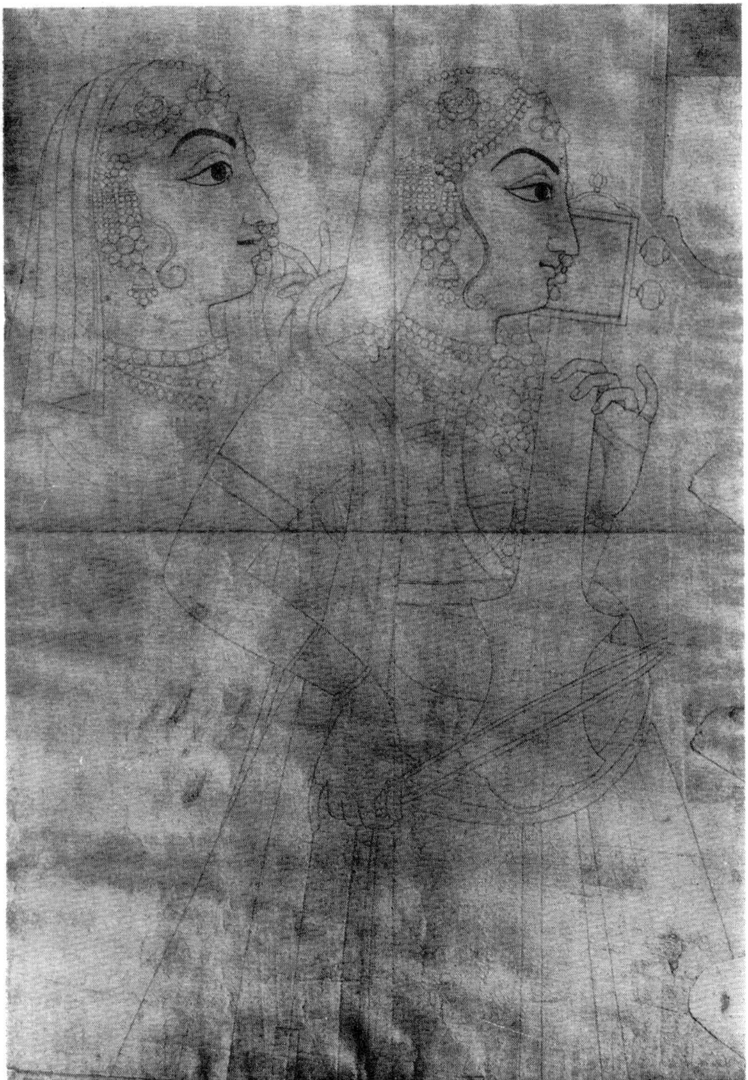

Musicians. Detail from an eighteenth-cenutry Rajput cartoon in the collection of A. K. Coomaraswamy

CHAPTER III

LEGEND, HISTORY, AND THE PRESENT DAY

> 'It is the most distant course that comes nearest to Thyself; and that training is the most intricate which leads to the utter simplicity of a tune.'—*Tagore.*

THE Indian does not make or read histories, and does not appreciate the value of chronological record. It is the custom to smile at this; but it would be well to understand his point of view first. A whole people is not generally mistaken about its real needs.

In the first place, Brahman philosophy draws no real distinction between what a thing 'is' and what it 'signifies'. Time and place, so integral a part for the Western of what a thing is, are for the Hindu accidents, not essentials. It is not that he cannot conceive or manipulate their divisions; astronomy, for instance, has been one of his strong points; but that they do not, for him, add to the significance nor therefore to the nature of the phenomenon.

Secondly, whereas chronologically ordered history enables us to compare the present of a nation with its past and so to predict its future, and to compare one nation at a given moment with another, neither of these motives appeals to the Hindu. His past is like his present and throws little light upon it. If we look at the sculpture of a thousand years ago from Ellora, or the painting from Ajanta, or the carvings of Amravati and Sanchi another thousand years earlier, we see the same mothers carrying babies on their hips, the same graceful little movements of the hands, the same methods of grinding corn, the same kinds and shapes of musical instruments, the same antimony for the same almond-shaped eyes, the same dress, the same symbols of rank. Life in Europe during such space of time has been subject to gusts of fashion or revolution, and we have looked up between the whirlwinds and gratefully murmured 'e pur si muove'. We thank God that we look before and after; the Indian contemns mushroom growths, and thinks methods of such recent origin and subject to such constant change hardly worth the trouble of acquiring.

And it does not interest him to compare one nation with another, or to take a side in or strike a balance between competing activities. His life is in the family rather than the state, in idea rather than fact, in the soul rather than the mind. His knowledge is of revelation more than of science; his truth contemplative rather than practical. Compromise is for him not so much the *media via* which emerges from the battle of two forces, as the philosophic calm which without despair can hold in solution two diametrically opposed statements.

Lastly, he is like Macaulay's Puritan, the man of a book. That he believes in his *Śāstras* may be argued from the surprising number of cases in which he is prepared to undergo inconvenience and unpleasantness in deference to them. That, further, he believes them may be seen from the way in which the typically Indian mind turns, courteously but peremptorily, from any attempt to impugn them.

For such reasons as these, and possibly others, the one conspicuous gap in an Indian library is the history shelf. We find it natural, therefore, in the Hindu to ascribe remote antiquity—in point of fact, eternity—to his earliest memories. He does not know any author for his Vedas, but speaks of such and such a *Rishi* as being allowed to 'hear' them the last time they were revealed. He does not discriminate between one antiquity and another, or take much interest in the development of ideas, for all development is potentially included in the original revelation, which was either 'heard' (*śruti*) or 'remembered' (*smṛti*) by the human agency to whom its record was entrusted. Thus he holds that four Vedas have existed from all time, although the Buddhist *Jātakas*[1] never speak of more than three. And what concerns us more particularly here, the *Nāṭyaśāstra* (circ. A. D. 500), the *Ratnākara* (1220?), the *Rāgavibodha* (1609), the *Sangīta Darpaṇa* (1625?), and *Parijāta* (early eighteenth century) are all quoted as 'scriptures' of practically equal value; while the undated *Nāradaśikṣā*, whose system shows a considerable advance on that of the *Nāṭyaśāstra*, is held, apparently on the strength of its name alone, to have been put forth by that mythical sage himself.

[1] Circ. 300 B.C. Stories of the former incarnations of the Buddha.

Legend

On the shore of this eternal past lie fragments of the living rock rounded into pebbles. History's *sic ibat, sic sedebat* is denied us; but in the legends we may gather some impression of what the reflective mind made of the daily happenings of the life around it.

'Once upon a time the great anchorite Nārada thought within himself he had mastered the whole art and science of music. To curb his pride the all-knowing Vishnu took him to visit the abode of the gods. They entered a spacious building the inmates of which were numerous men and women, who were all weeping over their broken limbs. Vishnu stopped short and inquired of them the reason of their lamentation. They answered that they were the *Rāgs* and *Rāgiṇis* of music, created by Mahādeva; but as one anchorite of the name of Nārada, ignorant of the true knowledge of music and unskilful in performance, had sung them recklessly, their features were distorted and their limbs broken, and that unless Mahādeva or some other discreet and skilful person would sing them properly, there was slender hope of their ever being restored to their former state of body. Nārada, ashamed, kneeled down before Vishnu and asked to be forgiven.'

So an unnamed Indian treating of undatable personages writes history and criticism in one. Believe, he says, in the divinity of the elements of your art, and know that your carelessness and ignorance will maim them, and you will not murder a song; and it may be doubted whether the well-weighed epithets and refined distinctions of musical 'appreciations' do the thing any better, or indeed achieve their object so well.

With Nārada, the *Rishi* who first 'heard' the laws of music, are associated Tumburu, the first singer, and Bharata, the first to draw up rules for the drama, of which music formed a large part. Of Tumburu it is said that he increased the scale in which the *Sāma-veda* was chanted from five notes to six or seven. The treatise which purports to record the doctrines of Nārada, the *Nāradaśikṣā*, is probably of late date[1] and gives no clue whatever to the achievement of the Nārada of legend. The treatise which bears the name of Bharata, the *Nāṭyaśāstra*, is similarly an eponym. One or other of these three names appears probably in every book on music that has been written, and the existence of the authors is held, though in complete absence of any specific doctrine attributed to them, as a pious belief; the belief is equal to that which the Greeks pro-

[1] The stage of the art which it describes is identical with that referred to in the *Pañcatantra*, the text of which may be dated circ. A.D. 1000 (see p. 82).

fessed in Olympos and Thamyris, the latter of whom some greatly daring philologist has connected with Tumburu, and the piety is something more than that which we accord to Jubal. The *locus classicus* for this posthumous fame is in Daṇḍin's *Mṛcchakaṭikā* (sixth century A. D.), where a servant says:

'I wish every one to take notice that the harder it rains the more thoroughly do I get ducked, and the colder the wind blows down my back the more do my limbs shiver. A pretty situation for a man of my talents—for one who can play the flute with seven holes and the *vīṇā* with seven strings, can sing like a jackass, and who acknowledges no musical superior except perhaps Tumburu and Nārada.'

The musical inhabitants of Indra's heaven were Gāndharvas,[1] Apsarāsas, Kinnaras, and Nāras. The original Gāndharva, in the singular, dwelt in the fathomless space of air and stood erect on the vault of heaven. He was the guardian of the nectar of the gods (*soma*). In later Vedic books the Gāndharvas[2] are many, and espouse the Apsarāsas, whose name describes them as 'moving in the waters' (sc. of the clouds). In still later Vedas these frequent the earth, and inhabit especially trees; their mission from Indra is to blunt the edge of human virtue which else, through abstinence and prayer, had grown too overweening; and one of them, Urvaśī, who hovers thus between earth and heaven, is the heroine of Kalidāsa's *Vikramorvaśī* (fifth century). The Kinnaras and Nāras, possibly the same, are classed with the Gāndharvas as celestial musicians. Their name[3] implies a superhuman form, said to have been a man's body with a horse's head. In company with them appear, in the Gāndhāra sculptures and elsewhere, Nāgas (snakes) with musical instruments, whose melodies are represented as coiling themselves about the hearts of men.

But music in its highest, most emblematic form moves to the sound of Krishṇa's flute (*muralī*) and dances to the pulsations of Shiva's drum (*ḍamaru*).[4] With Shiva, who enters the celestial

[1] An etymological connexion between Gāndharvas (who, besides being musicians, had to do with horses) and Centaurs (of whom Cheiron is said to have been a musician) is not impossible.

[2] In the second book of the *Rāmāyaṇa* there are summoned to Bharadvāja's feast the Gāndharvas, Hāhā, Huhū, and 'the sweet' Viśvāvasu, and the Apsarāsas Alambuṣā, Ghṛtāchī, Viśvāchī, Hemā, Bhīmā, and Nāgadantā, with Tumburu 'to lead the strain'. Alambuṣā is the Apsarāsa chosen out of 25,000,000 handmaids to 'make a breach in the virtue' of a Brahman of Kāśi.

[3] *Kim-nāra*, 'what sort of man?'

[4] See Chap. IX, *Udukkai*.

Detail from a picture of the Surrender of Kandahar in the collection of Sītarām Lal of Benares.
Seventeenth century

hierarchy in the Brāhmaṇas and wrests the supremacy from Indra and Brahmā, enters too the eternal becoming and ceasing to be of evolution, and to the woven rhythms of his dance the whole creation moves. And in the Rāmāyaṇa it is Krishṇa sporting with his Gopis 'qui fait le monde à la ronde'.

In Hindu legend other instruments can scarcely be heard for the din of the drum. It beats the night watches, heralds proclamations, and preludes the sentence of death. Porus (Purusha) posts the drummers with the infantry and archers behind the elephants, who are accustomed to the sound and not in the least alarmed by it[1]; and Dionysos in his turn uses cymbals and drums instead of trumpets in making signals, in order to deceive the Indians.[2] A king of Kanauj progresses accompanied by several hundred men with golden drums, called 'music-pace-drums', beating one stroke to each step.[3] Of another it is said 'When king Devānāmpriya practises righteousness the call of his drum (*bheri*) has become a summons not to war but to righteousness'.[4] There are many allusions to the 'five great sounds' (*pañca mahā śabdā*), an honour conferred by kings on the greatest of their servants, in which the drum (*nāgara*, *tammaṭa*, *ḍamaruka*) is associated with various forms of horn, gong, and cymbal. These were 'sounded in front of a chariot which is occupied, but behind one which contains no occupant. The car went solemnly round the palace and up the kettledrum road. They sounded the hundreds of instruments—it was like the noise of the sea.'[5] Brahmadatta finds a mountain hermit who is annoyed by elephants, and presents him with a drum: 'if you beat upon this side your enemies will run away, if upon that they will become your firm friends.'[6] The following remunerations are interesting:—'One *mattar* for the sacrificial vessel, two to the horn-blower, four to each of the five courtesans of the temple, twelve to the skilful Pollama who built the temple, and fourteen to the drummer.'[7]

In the Tamil *Pura-Nānnuru* (first centuries A. D.) the drum, kept

[1] Quintus Curtius, 1st cent. A. D.
[2] Polyainos, 2nd cent. A. D.
[3] Hiouen Tsang, A.D. 629.
[4] Aśokan inscription (circ. 250 B. C.), Western India.
[5] Mahājanaka Jātaka.
[6] Jātaka, bk. ii.
[7] Canarese inscription, A. D. 975.

in every chieftain's palace, was treated almost as a lesser divinity.[1] It reposed on a luxurious couch, was constantly cleaned, rubbed with perfumed earth, and garlanded. When used as the prelude to one of the ruler's proclamations it was carried on an elephant. The poet, Nośikaranār, relates how one day he had wandered into the courtyard of the palace and saw the ornamented and cushioned couch on which the royal drums were usually placed. The drums had gone to be cleaned and anointed, and he threw himself on the unoccupied couch and fell fast asleep. The king came by with his courtiers who expected to see the intruder meet with condign punishment. But the king took up a fan and cooled the sleeper's forehead with it till he awoke; and the poet's comment is:

> Surely 'twas not to win applause from earthly bards
> But that the deed might echo loud in higher worlds.

With the drum (*dundubhi*) of the Vedas are mentioned the flute (*vāṇā*), which is heard in the abode of Yāma (death), the lute (*vīṇā*), often called 'seven-stringed' (*saptatantrī*),[2] which, in the Sūtras, is played at the sacrifice to the Manes, and the cymbals (*āghāṭa*, lit. something struck), to accompany the dance.

In spite of the fame conferred upon it by Krishṇa's performance among his Gopis, the flute seems to fade out of Indian music; at least there are few references to it, and it is seldom to be heard nowadays. Perhaps its mellow tone is not of the kind which appeals to Indian ears; at any rate the *shahnai* and *nagasāram* (both reeds) which have ousted it are stridently nasal; and the buzzing of the *tambura* strings, effected by the insertion of a piece of silk (*jivala*), the jingling of the fifth string of the *satār*, called *laraz*, and made, for this very purpose, of twisted brass, and most of all the nasal tone of voice which is deliberately cultivated for singing, seem to show that so mild a sound as that of the flute-tribe is not thought to be piquant enough.

To the *vīṇā*, the national instrument, there are so many references, both direct and allusive, that it is difficult to choose. Perhaps one story, from the Jātakas, will be enough. A feeble musician, Mūsila of Ujjain, whose music on the *vīṇā* was 'like scratching on a mat', came to learn of Guttila of Banāras (the Bodhisatta in an

[1] See also Macdonell, *Sanskrit Literature*, p. 200.

[2] Cf. Pindar's *heptatonos phorminx*. The modern instrument also has seven, four on the fingerboard, three as the drone.

Mughal drawing, seventeenth century, of a bīn-player, from an original in the collection of G. N. Tagore

earlier birth). Guttila's parents when they heard him said, 'Shoo! Shoo! the rats are gnawing the *vīṇā* to pieces.' Guttila who, as Bodhisatta, was 'skilled in discerning from the lineaments of the body' said, 'Go, my son, this art is not for you.' But Mūsila got his way; and Guttila Bodhisatta, who 'did not stint his knowledge', at last pronounced his pupil perfect. Mūsila pressed to be taken into the king's service. This was done; but the king awarded Guttila twice as much as his pupil. Mūsila protested, and forced matters to a contest, of which proclamation was made to tuck of drum. The Bodhisatta reflected that he was old, and that 'if he beats me, death in the woods is better than the shame which will be my portion'. So to the woods he went; but 'kept returning through fear of death, and going back to the wood for fear of shame', so that 'the grass died as he walked and his feet wore away a path'. In his trouble Sakka, the king of the gods, appeared. Guttila was to break, in the contest, one string after another, beginning at the 'beestring', and the music should be as good as before. 'Then you shall go on playing with nothing but the body; and from the ends of the broken strings the sound shall go forth and fill all the land of Banāras for the space of twelve leagues.' All happened as was foretold, and the scholar, beaten out of the field, was stoned and torn in pieces by the populace.

The rest of the picture is filled with horns (*sṛinga*), conchs (*śankha*), gongs (*jayaghaṇṭa*, lit. bell of victory), cymbals (*jallali*), pipes (*kuṛāl*), and various other instruments not identified. We get a glimpse of the scale on which ecclesiastical music was planned from an inscription (A.D. 1051) on the Rājarājeśvara temple at Tanjore:

'Apart from the priests the following musicians and attendants are to have a daily allowance for the recitation of the Tiruppadiyam (a form of service) calculated in shares of 3 *kaṛuṇi* of paddy, as follows:

Number employed.	*Shares each.*	*Title.*
		ORCHESTRA.
66	·5	Men 'engaged in drumming'.
32	·75	Musicians.
1	1·0	Large drum.
1	1·0	Small drum.
2	1·0	Large drums (*koṭṭi mattaḷam*).
48	1·0	Musicians.
2	1·5	Small drums (*udukkai*).
3	1·5	Pipe players (*vaṅgiyam*).
2	1.75	*Vīṇā* players.

Number employed.	*Shares each.*	*Title.*
		CHOIR.
4	1·0	Singers (Tamil).
3	1·5	Singers (Sanskrit).
5	1·5	Singers (male).
		OTHERS.
10	·4	Parasol holders.
7	·5	Lamplighters.
8	1·0	Clerks.
5	1·0	Heralds.
400	1·0	Dancing girls.
6	1·5	Dancing masters.
2	2·0	Female superintendents.
4	2·0	Accountants.
		NOT ASCERTAINABLE.
4	1·5	?
2	1·5	?
4	2·0	?

About music and dancing there are two views, the puritan and the utilitarian. In the *Anugīta*, among the 'actions of the quality of passion' and ranked with the sins prohibited in the Ten Commandments are 'devotion to dancing, and instrumental or vocal music'. And in the laws of Manu,[1] 'a student of the Veda must . . . avoid ointments, collyrium for the eyes, shoes, carrying an umbrella; lust, anger, and greed, dancing, and music': and again, 'the sound of the Sāmaveda, which is said to belong to the Manes,[2] is impure.' In Cāṇakya's *Arthaśāstra* ('Politics'),[3] on the other hand, 'song, instrumental music, recitation, dancing, acting, writing, playing on the *vīṇā*, flute (*venu*), and drum (*mṛdanga*), knowing the mind of others, making scents, and garlands, shampooing, employing alluring words—those who know all these and can teach them to courtesans and actors should be provided with livelihood by the state.'

The power of song is a favourite theme; here is the story of the Indian Arion. The minstrel Sagga in search of Queen Sussondī came across certain merchants of Bhārukachha (Broach) who were setting sail for the golden land. He said, 'I am a minstrel (*magadha*). If you will remit my passage money I will be your minstrel.' They agreed. When the ship had set sail they called to him to make music for them. 'I would make music,' he said, 'but the fish would be so excited that your vessel would be wrecked.' 'Fish',

[1] Circ. A.D. 200.

[2] A strict Brahman purifies himself after seeing a dead body.

[3] Circ. 400 B.C.

PLATE 8

Dancing girl, South India

they said, 'will not be disturbed by what mortals do. Play on.' Then tuning his lute and keeping perfect harmony between the words of his song and the accompaniment of the lute-string he made music for them. The fish were maddened, and a certain sea-monster leaping up upon the ship broke it in two.

And again, purity of singing. A hunter of Banāras captured in the Himālaya a brace of fairies (*kinnara*). He presented them to the king, who said, 'Hunter, what kind of creatures (*kiṃ-nāra*) are these?' 'My lord, these can sing with a honey voice, they dance delightfully; no man can dance or sing as they can.' The king bestowed great reward on the hunter and commanded the fairies to sing and dance. But they thought, 'If we are not able to convey the full sense of our song, the song will be a failure, they will abuse and hurt us; and then, again, those who speak much, speak falsely.' So for fear of some falsehood or other they neither sang nor danced. Then the king said, 'Kill these creatures and cook them and serve them up to me, one for supper and the other for breakfast.' Then the fairy dame thought within herself, 'Now the king is angry, without doubt he will kill us. Now is the time to speak'; and she sang:

A hundred thousand ditties sung all wrong
All are not worth a tithe of one good song.
To sing ill is a crime; and this is why
The seeming-foolish fairy would not try.

Then the king commanded to let her go, but to have the other one cooked for to-morrow's breakfast. But the other fairy thought, 'If I hold my tongue surely the king will kill me; now is the time to speak'; and he recited a couple of stanzas to make it clear that they had been silent not from unwillingness to obey the king's word, but because they saw that speaking would be a mistake. And the king said, 'He speaks the truth; 'tis a sapient fairy.' And he had the two fairies put in a golden cage, and sending for the huntsman made him set them free in the same place where he had caught them.[1]

A fine appreciation of good singing is to be found in the *Mṛccha-catika* (sixth century). Two friends have just come from a concert; 'Excellent, excellent indeed; Rebhila sang most excellently.

[1] This and other stories from the Jātaka are taken from Prof. E. B. Cowell's translations. Cambridge University Press, 1905.

Smooth and sweet were the tones, articulate, full of emotion, delicate and mind-pleasing. What do I say? Some girl seemed to be hidden in the sounds. I can hear him still; his notes are well-ordered,[1] his song is soft, and the sound of the strings of the *vīṇā* is in tune with the voice. The upper notes which are introduced into the middle of the rise and fall of the Aria have a soft close.[2] He sings it as easily as a child plays with a toy. Although the music is finished, I seem still to hear it as I move.'

And this scene is relieved by one in Kalidāsa's *Mālavikāgnimitra* (fifth century) of a mediocre performance, where two musicians are rivals, and one brings forward a pupil who performs a great feat in singing—a piece in four-time (*caturpada vastu*) and Andante (*madhya laya*)—the 'young lady of Rio', in fact, fifteen centuries ago.

Pedants are dealt with in the *Pañcatantra* (fifth century) in the story of the musical ass, who gets out at night into the cucumber fields and joins the jackal in hedge breaking and other delights. Waxing fat and kicking, his joy takes a vocal form, and he asks the jackal in what *Rāg* he shall sing. 'Why sing at all?' said the jackal; 'people with coughs don't steal. Besides, your voice is about as good as ——'. 'What? I don't know how to sing? Listen to the theory of it. There are seven notes (*svara*), three scales (*grāma*), twenty-one modes (*mūrchaṇa*), forty-nine melodic figures (*tāna*), three time units (*mātrā*), three tempi (*laya*), three voice registers (*sthāna*), six ways of singing (*āsyāni*, lit. mouths), nine emotions (*rasa*), thirty-six *rāgs* (*varṣma*), forty languages (*bhāṣa*). This sort of singing when well performed embraces all the 185 (?) parts of song.' 'My friend,' said the jackal, 'if you must have your way I will take up my position at the gate and look out for the farmer and his boy.' They were not long in coming, and the musician learnt what it was to be an ass.

The mass of legend relating to music, of which this is a mere handful, does not perhaps prove anything very definite about the state of the art in past times. But we get, in reading, an impression that wherever we look the attitude of the writers and the storytellers towards song and instrument, towards the purpose of music and the general practice of musicians, has for a long time

[1] *Sankrama*; calculated to display the *Rāga*.

[2] He is speaking of the return from the Antara to the Astaï; see chapter on Form.

Portrait of Numa Khan Katawant, a musician of the court of Jahāngīr, from a picture in the collection of A. K. Coomaraswamy

past been much what it is now : and if datable documents were to come to light showing that music, in the form in which we read of it in *Bharata*, existed many centuries before his time we should not be at all surprised.

HISTORY

And now, leaving legend, the first musician we meet with who is anything more than a name is Jayadeva (circ. A.D. 1100) the author of the Gita Govinda. He was a native of Kindavilva in Bengal. He assigns to each of his poems a definite *Rāg* and *Tāl*,[1] which are named after the Bengāli fashion. There is no musical notation; and it is open to any musician, now as then, to make or mar them by his treatment. In a poem of such delicate texture as the Gita Govinda the musical scheme could hardly fail to be a thoughtful one. The names of *Rāg* and *Tāl* which would be full of association to a Bengāli may connote little to us; but we may see from the mere titles how they have been used as an element in the design. The song of 'one of Rādhā's maidens' in praise of love with which the Gīta begins is echoed by the 'Hymen o Hymenaee' at the close; both are in *Rāg Vasanta* and *Tāl Yati*. The voice of one 'fair, but not so fair as Radha' consoles and breathes hope which finds its fulfilment in Rādhā's triumphant song of reconciliation (*Ramagiri; Yati*). The slighted Rādhā and the flouted Krishṇa utter their sorrows in the same accents, and in these accents they afterwards forget them (*Gurjjari; Yati*). Krishṇa's assuring message is met by Rādhā's jealousy; and the messenger, who is persuading her to relent, draws forth only a pitiful plaint over his neglect, to which the 'chorus' gives a new turn after Krishṇa's home coming (*Deshivarāḍi; Rūpaka*). Again, Rādhā rebukes Krishṇa in the moving tones of *Bhairavi*, and his answer, when she has yielded, is in the ecstasy of *Bibhās*.

Akbar, late sixteenth century, is reported to have loved music as much as Aurungzeb, late seventeenth, hated it. He is said to have been a good player on the *Naqqārah* (a drum, used in pairs) and to have composed more than two hundred melodies. He invited Miyān Tānsen the pupil of Haridās Swāmi from the court of Rājah Rām

[1] The *Rāgs* are Gurjjari, Deshivarāḍi, Mālava, Bhairavi, Rāmagirī, Mālavagaṇḍa, Karnāṭa, Deshāga, Gondakirī, Vasanta, Varāḍi; and the *Tāls* Yati, Rūpaka, Ekatāli, and Aṣṭatāli. They are given here in the order of frequency of occurrence for the seventeen songs.

of Baghelkhand, and loaded him with honours and gold. The Mohammedan *Ain-i-Akbari* says of Tānsen, 'a singer like him has not been in India for the last thousand years.' The Hindus, however, hold him principally responsible for the deterioration of Hindu music. He is said to have falsified the *rāgs*, and two, Hindol and Megh, of the original six have disappeared since his time.

Of Tyagayyar or Tyagarāja or Thiaga Iyar of Tanjore (early nineteenth century) more is known. He was revered by his contemporaries as a perfectly sincere and selfless man; he was an ascetic in the original sense of the word, one who 'prepared' his heart for the reception of truth. In Mudaliar Chinnaswami's *Oriental Music* sixty of his songs (*Kritis*) are printed in staff notation, accompanied by adequate indications of scale, time, and tempo. There is a list also of eight hundred more, and this is probably not exhaustive. They are all in Telugu, the most musical language of the south, as Bengāli is of the north. They exhibit considerable sense of balance, as may be seen from the structure of the song, Ex. 379. They refrain from abusing the ear with excessive compass, and eschew cheap contrasts, both of which are to be found in the compositions of less able musicians. He signs his songs; that is to say, he ends them with words such as 'This is the last counsel of Tyagarāja' or 'You who are the treasure of Tyagarāja's heart'.

This is a common practice in the mediaeval songs of Germany, and may be compared with Dufay's signature 'Karissime Dufay vous en prye' or occasionally 'Du  y', and with Palestrina's incorporation of the titles of the 119th Psalm (Aleph, Beth, &c.) into his Lamentations. Two of the syllables of Tyagarāja's name (ga-rā) would have admitted of the same treatment; but there is no instance of his adopting it. It was also a practice of his time to set the syllables of the song to the notes which they name,[1] as as in the example quoted by Day, p. 72:

Ex. 171.

and the Indian form of 'Ut queant laxis' is (putting Ra, Ri, Ru for D♭, D, D♯, and Ga, Gi, Gu for E♭♭, E♭, E, and so on):

[1] These are called *Svarākshara's* (note-syllables).

Rāgam Dhīraśankarābharaṇa.
Tālam Maṭya. (4 + 2 + 4.)

Ex. 172.

But the practice does not appear to have attractions for Tyagarāja; he resists them at any rate in a song beginning *Nidāsānu*, a word which would have suggested four notes of the scale.[1] Neither does he seem to be particularly in love with *Svaras*. *Svara* in the South, *Sārgam* (i.e. Sa, Ri, Ga, Ma) in the North, means a rapid passage in which the notes are sung to the sol-fa names instead of to words as an amusing feat of skill. It takes the place of our cadenza, and like that was occasionally added by another hand. *Svaras* occur in only four of his sixty songs.

There is a pretty story about Tyagarāja's meeting with 'Shatkāla' Govinda Mārār, a fine musician of Travancore. *Shatkāla* means 'six-time', and 'time' is here used in the sense of 'diminutions', i.e. that a piece that had been in crotchets was now sung in quavers; and the point is that he could 'diminish' six times over, i.e. begin with his theme in semibreves and end with it in semi-demi-semi-quavers. He used to sing to a *Tāmbura* with seven strings—the ordinary *Tāmbura* has only four; and this instrument seems to have been a sort of bow of Ulysses to inferior singers; in token of which, apparently, it was adorned with a flag. They met at Tyagarāja's house at Tiruvaiyyar near Tanjore in 1843, where the

[1] B, A, C, H, to be accurate.

great man was sitting with his disciples. Mārār, after listening to the disciples, expressed a wish to hear Tyagarāja himself. 'Who is the man', said Tyagarāja in Telugu, 'that can ask me to sing?' Apparently the audience were to hear him only when he sang of his own accord. He asked who was the man, pointing to Mārār, who sat with a flagged *Tāmbura* in his hand; and was told that Mārār could sing a little. A *Pallavi* was then sung round, and when it came to Govinda Mārār's turn the other instruments had to be laid aside and his *Tāmbura* only used, so high was the pitch of the music. He sang it in *Shatkāla*, and Tyagarāja, after remonstrating with the understatement of Mārār's powers, improvised on the spot a song in the *Śrī Rāgam*, which is the *Ragam* sung at the close of performances, of which the burden was, 'There are many great men in the world, and I respect them all.' This contrasts well with the many stories there are of professional jealousy, which are too unlovely to repeat here.

The Present Day

A few notes may be added upon so much of the present-day music as a hurried traveller might hope to hear. In a land not blessed with concert advertisements or concert notices, it is difficult for a stranger in the first place to find the best music, and in the second to know what the inhabitants themselves think of it. He can only remember with gratitude some of the good things it was his fortune to hear. There was some beautiful *vīṇā*-playing at Mysore, where the general standard is high. The crisp and expressive touch and imaginative improvisation of Subbanna contrasted well with the smooth tones and solid technique and exact intonation of Seshanna, of whom it was said that he could 'put Sabbanna in his pocket and shake him about', a criticism the truth of which I was not in a position to gauge. They got by heart at my dictation 'Ye banks and braes', selected because it is in the *Mohanna Rāgam*, and were to improvise upon it next day, when a concourse assembled to hear the result. They quite entered into the spirit of the thing; Subbanna played the tune more as if he cared for it; Seshanna produced the more ingenious variations. Afterwards they played the following in unison with the utmost accuracy:

PLATE 10

Seshanna, vīṇā-player, Mysore

Aiknāth Vishnu Paṇḍit, vīṇā-player, Poona

Rāgam Mohanna (Rāg Bhupkaliān). Tālam Adi.

♩ = 120. *Allegretto cantabile.*

Ex. 173.

Rāmachandra of Trivandrum, who was suffering from rheumatism, could not play for long together. He had the expressiveness of Subbanna without his invention, and the smoothness of Seshanna without his execution. He used the lower strings more than either of them; his fingers went down firmly on the strings and gave a clear and precise tone. His favourite 'grace' was the 'Slide', whereas Seshanna's was the 'Deflect'.[1]

Next to the expressive *vīṇā* comes the dignified *surbahar*, which I heard only in Calcutta, where it was played by Sourendro Banerji. Its lower strings, which are freely used, have to be struck hard in order to produce the after effect of *gamak*

Ex. 174.

which is a favourite opening; and this gave it a rather ponderous sound. Its frets are but slightly, it at all, moved; and there are no 'settings' (*thāṭ*) for the different modes as on the *satār*. Consequently much more is left to be done by *gamak*, especially the 'Deflect' (*mīnḍ*, called in Bengal *mīrh*), and this contributes to its grave and dignified tone. There is also a mandolin stroke, double, with the forefinger and little finger each armed with a plectrum (*misrab*), which, though no less irritating as a continuance than the mandolin itself, provides a good occasional contrast. Banerji was fond of contrasting his gamakked and his fretted note, as a violinist likes to contrast his open and his stopped E. The *chanterelle* is away from the player's body, i. e. nearest his fingers (it is the other way on the *vīṇā*), and this seemed to give better opportunity for the Deflect. Altogether there was much more mystery in the sound of this instrument than in that of the rather commonplace *satār* or

[1] See Chapter VII.

the thin-toned North Indian *bīn*, although I certainly did not hear these so well handled.

Good drumming is commoner, perhaps, than any other form of music. It is said to take a lifetime to become a good drummer, but the comparative failures manage to give much pleasure. The most interesting exponents of this art I heard at Trivandrum. One was a boy of seven who had won a medal at Ernakulam for his skill, and who played on a drum bound with silver. He played with great solemnity, with funny little poses of the head to right or left as if he were thinking of anything else but what he was giving his whole attention to. His drumming was in the 'new style', which seemed to consist of flurry, silence, flurry, silence. After his performance he went to sleep during the rest of the music, and was ordered off to go and play in the verandah. The other was a man of sixty, Somaji Bhāgavatār, who ranks with Rāmachandra as a foremost musician. He was most careful about the tuning of his *Mṛdangam* (in two F's like the Scherzo of the Ninth Symphony, but an octave higher). The upper F (right hand end) was adjusted by wedge and hammer, and gave the most trouble; the lower, on the left, by application of more or less flour and water to form the *karane* (Hindostani *āṭā*). There were no antics; it was all pure drumming. A good deal of it was a quiet tapping of the time with the forefinger of the left hand; then little points appeared, and a climax, and a solo or two, and the general effect was that of reserve power.

The difference between Mohammedan and Hindu singing is more easily felt than described. One's general impression, which a longer stay would no doubt have corrected in detail, is that the Mohammedan prefers the more cheerful *Rāgs*—*Khamāj*, *Kāfi*, and the *Kalians*; and the simpler rhythms, such as *Titāla* and *Dādra*; and the Rondo to the Variation form. With these he takes a considerable amount of liberty, concealing the rhythm, especially, by interspersed rests, and broken phrases that run counter to it, so that it would be unintelligible sometimes without the drummer. He has the performer's instinct; he rivets the attention of the audience as a whole, and the less able singer is apt to tear a passion to pieces rather than not challenge their admiration. The performance of the best musicians (*Ustāds*) has a wonderful fascination in spite of the language difficulty. The phrases are finished off and fit so well into their place, there is so much variety and so much telling gesture, that the time goes quickly by, although you may find that, with the help of another singer perhaps, he has sung for at least half an hour continuously. All this the Hindu can do too, but he does it in a less vivacious way. He is at his best in the quieter *Rāgs* like *Bhairavi,* or the more characteristic such as *Vasant* or *Bilhās* or *Toḍi*, and in the more irregular rhythms such as *Surphakta* or *Aḍachantāla.* His singing is less broken up with rests, and he luxuriates in cross-rhythm. His song gives much more the impression of coming from the heart, and of reaching out for sympathy rather than for applause. You can more easily fancy him singing over his work, or her over her household duties; and, as has been mentioned, the Mohammedans have no cradle songs. There are some fine Mohammedan religious songs; they seem to treat religion more deeply and less imaginatively than the Hindus, and to produce it on occasions rather than as the natural expression of their daily life: the two songs, 'Hādi e illah' and 'Cherarāvade-mirā', Exs. 268, 379, seem typical of the two peoples.

The singing that appealed to me most was that of Chandra Prabhu at Bhavnagav. She compelled respect at once by refusing on any account to be phonographed; perhaps she thought, amongst other things, that if she committed her soul to a mere piece of wax it might get broken in the train—and my subsequent experience showed that this was only too likely. She sang for an hour, three songs. The most striking of them was in 'a sort of' *Bhairavi*, upon a theme of the Maharajah's:

Ex. 175.

(with the drum at E, of course, all the time). The others were in Imankaliān, to which the descending F♯ gives an indescribably light-hearted touch, and in Bageshri (a Dorian). She used *gamak* sparingly, and therefore effectively; she detached the notes cleanly without making them too staccato. There was something most satisfying in the sweep of the periods, apparently haphazard but really conforming to strict law. A voice with good tone, as we understand tone, is a rarity in India; but Chandra Prabhu sang with full round notes and variety of quality in addition to the extraordinary flexibility of all her nation. But the musicianship of her song was the most notable thing about it. She never seemed to come across technical difficulties—as that friend of

Assheton Smith's never could 'think where the young men found all these big things—*he* never met with them'.

It is impossible to measure this sort of song by any European standards, the problem is so entirely different. With us, as with them, a singer concentrates into a single song all his knowledge and past experience, and has taken years to learn what it takes a few minutes to sing; but he is only interpreting. It seems a fresher and more convincing thing when, after an equal or perhaps larger number of years training, the song is created there and then; when its message has never been given in quite the same terms before and never will be again. The greatest European singers are apt to be voice-producers first and musicians afterwards; the Indian singer is before all things a musician, who may happen to have a good voice, but seldom has a good tone. And it seems possible to overrate good tone; at any rate, it is surprising how much art can be heard behind a poor one. Then, too, in the absence of orchestration and of counterpoint—except such as the drum provides, and of harmony—and, with that, of a certain terseness of structure, the voice has unaided to supply all the interest and to spread it over a certain lapse of time.

To maintain this interest recourse is had to all those things of which a description has been attempted in the chapters on *Rāga* and Grace. The result is a kind of full-throated utterance quite unlike the elaborate tremolos of our singers, which often seem to resolve themselves into a battle between the voice and the accompaniment. The nearest analogy we have is perhaps Mr. Henschel playing his own accompaniment, where the whole is under the direction of one mind and it is difficult to say whether voice or instrument is contributing most to the result. Again, the form of the song is wholly diverse: we can hardly imagine a composition without a main climax and perhaps a coda: an Indian simply stops when he has sung enough. It seems as if climax too can be overrated as it certainly is sometimes overdone. Still, though there are plenty of minor crises in the course of the music, this absence of any convincing close remains a difficulty for us.

A different kind of interest and a still greater pleasure was afforded by a visit to Rabindranāth Tagore, the Bengāli poet. In accordance with the best Indian tradition he is poet and musician in one. His poetry is beginning to speak to us for itself: even in a few scattered translations it is possible to hear the voice of a man who thinks deeply and truly, who sees things as they really are, making invisible things visible as florescence does in optics, and touching them with tenderness and reverence. To hear him recite his poems is to be reminded of the way in which Tennyson is said by his biographer to have recited *Maud*; and indeed such a line as 'Laborious orient ivory sphere in sphere' has something of the ring of Bengāli verse about it, while the terseness, the inheritance of the Sutras, of a language which is the descendant of that compact wonder, Sanskrit, we could hardly parallel short of Horace. To hear him sing them is to realize the music in a way that it is seldom given to a foreigner to do. The notes of the song are no longer their mere selves, but the vehicle of a personality, and as such they go behind this or that system of music to that beauty of sound which all systems put out their hands to seize. These melodies are such as would have satisfied Plato. 'I do not know the modes,' said Socrates, 'but leave me one that will imitate the tones and accents of a brave man enduring danger or distress, fighting with constancy against fortune; and also one fitted for the work of peace, for prayer heard by the gods, and for the successful persuasion or exhortation of men.'

The portrait of Mr. Tagore which forms the frontispiece is by Mr. William Rothenstein, who has most generously lent the copyright of it for this book. It was drawn one afternoon while the words and the songs were being transcribed; and perhaps the sympathy and fidelity of it may be taken as some compensation for the limitations imposed by a foreign language and for the inability of musical notation to convey the tones of the living voice.

Mr. Tagore's translations of his own poems are given in Examples 176-180.

Rāg Bhairavī, Tāl Tevra (3 + 2 + 2).

♪ = 100. *Adagietto.*

Ex. 176.

Jibane jata.

The *pujas* that have not been finished in this life I know that they are not altogether lost. The flowers that have shed their petals on the dust before being full blown, and the rivers that hid their streams in the desert sand, I know, I know they have not been altogether lost. Those that lag behind in this life I know, I know that even they have not lived uselessly. All my unformed thoughts and all my unstruck melodies are still sounding on the strings of thy *vīṇā*, and I know that they have not been altogether lost.

Ba'ul tune,
Tāl Dadra. ♩ = 90. *Andantino.*

Ex. 177.

Jadi tor dāk.

If no one responds to your call then go on alone. And if there is no one to speak out, and if they turn their face and are afraid, then open your heart and speak only you. Speak alone, speak alone.

If every one goes back and none accompanies you in the difficult path, then tread the thorns with bloody feet alone. Tread alone, tread alone.

If there is no one to light the lamp, and if every one shuts his door in the stormy dark night, then burn the ribs of your heart with the thunder fire and burn alone, burn alone.

Rag Khambāj, Tāl Ektāla.
♩=60. *Andante.*

Ex. 178.

Āmār kara tomāra binā.

Make me thy *vīṇā*; lift me in thine arms. All the strings of my heart will break out at thy finger-touch. With thy tender hands touch my life, and my heart will murmur her secrets in thine ears. In happiness and in sorrow she will gaze on thy face, and cry; and shouldst thou neglect her she will remain silent at thy feet. None knows in what new strains her songs will rise up to the heavens and send a message of joy to the shore of the infinite.

Rāg Jhijhit, Tāl Ektāla.
♩. = 60. *Andante.*

Ex. 179.

Āmi chini go chini.

I know, I know thee, O thou Bideshini[1]; thou dwellest on the other shore of the ocean. I have seen thee in the autumn, I have felt thee in the spring night. I have found thee in the midst of my heart, O thou Bideshini. Putting my ear to the sky[2] I have heard thy music, and I have offered to thee my life, O thou Bideshini. I have roamed all through the world and have come at last into the strange country. Here I am a guest at thy door, O thou Bideshini.[3]

[1] O thou stranger lady; perhaps, Intellectual Beauty.

[2] *Ākāśa*, space; the source of all sound and speech.

[3] Mr. Tagore writes:—'I heard when I was very young the song "Who dressed you like a foreigner?" and that one line of the song painted such a strange picture in my mind that even now it is sounding in my memory. I once tried to compose a song myself under the spell of that line. As I hummed the tune I wrote the first line of the song "I know thee, thou stranger", and,

Rāg Kāfi. Tāl Ektāla.

♩ = 80. *Andante.*

Ex. 180.

if there were no tune to it, I don't know what would be left of the song. But under the spell (*mantra*) of the tune the mysterious figure of that stranger was evoked in my mind. My heart began to say, "There is a stranger going to and fro in this world of ours; her house is on the further shore of an ocean of mystery. Sometimes she is to be seen in the autumn morning, sometimes in the flowery midnight; sometimes we receive an intimation of her in the depths of our heart, sometimes I hear her voice when I turn my ear to the sky. . . . One day, long afterwards, some one went along the road singing, "How does that unknown bird go to and away from the cage? Could I but catch it, I would put the chain of my mind about its feet!" I saw that that *Ba'ul* song too said the very same thing. Sometimes the unknown bird comes to the closed cage and speaks a word of the limitless Unknown. Then the mind would keep it for ever, but cannot. What but the tune of a song could report the coming and going of this unknown bird? Because of this I always feel hesitation in publishing a book of songs, for in such a book the main thing is left out. To set forth the music's vehicle and leave out the music itself is just like keeping the mouse and leaving out Ganapati himself.'

Mama jaubana nikunje.

In the bower of my youth a bird sings, 'Wake, my love, wake! Open thy love-languid eyes, my love, and awake.' There is a tremor in the midnight darkness to-night, and the air is resonant with the praise song of spring. O timorous maiden, thrilling with the mysteries of first love, listen; in my grove of paradise a bird sings in a repeated rapture, 'Wake my love, wake!' Wake in the first fullness of thy youth, wake in the lonely stillness of starry night, fanned by the ardent breath of spring drunk with the perfume of *bakula*. Wake in my arms my love, a-tremble with a tender shyness, decked in a wreath of blushing rose. O listen to the sweet piping in my heart, 'Wake, my sweet love, wake.'

The rhythm of Indian song is more fluid than that of European. It seems to cost us more, so to say, to be perpetually altering the accent; it produces a certain instability which has to be made up for in other ways. But there is no feeling of instability in these songs. Such a line as,

Ex. 181.

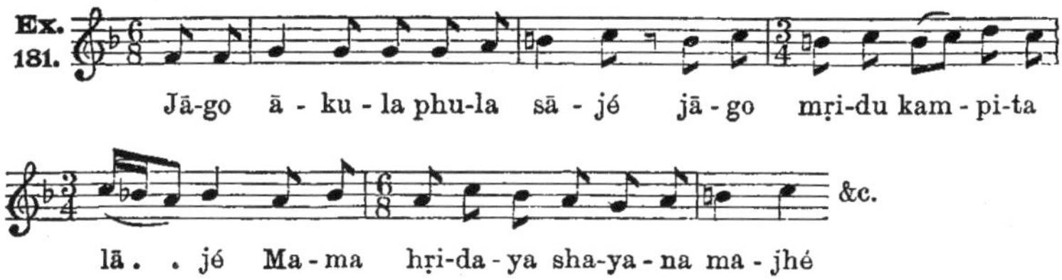

flows quite as naturally as the close of Brahms's *Minnelied* :

Ex. 182.

These, and some others of his, show a securer balance and a stronger sense of rhythmical proportion than many Hindostani songs, and, without doing violence to the principles of the music, bind it in a closer grip.

CHAPTER IV

THE SCALE

You can work it out by Fractions or by simple Rule of Three,
But the way of Tweedledum is not the way of Tweedledee.

The Jungle Book.

THE subject now to be discussed is complex. To do justice to the problems which it involves would require a large book; all that is attempted here is to state them, and to give a possible reading of the available data.

Scales are a tabulation of the facts of song. In a country of the size of India these facts are very various, and that there should be one parent scale is hardly to be expected. From the facts given in Chapter I for the south, and in Chapter II for the east of that country, we should perhaps draw the following conclusions:

(1) that the compass increases with the state of civilization;

(2) that there are two broad tendencies in scale-building: to step melodically to the 'next door' note, and to leap harmonically to one which is not 'next door';.

(3) that the 'steps' are of various sizes, viz. anything up to, not as a rule beyond, a whole tone—although the means of defining the exact intervals was not at hand;

(4) that the 'leap' from a given note is to a note which is consonant to it—for instance, an upward leap through F would generally be to A if the preceding note was E, to A♭ if the preceding note was E♭;

(5) that the 'steps' seem to prevail in the south, the 'leaps' in the east;

(6) that whether 'step' or 'leap' is in use, the melody pivots on two notes which are a Fourth apart, much more rarely a Fifth.

It may be observed in passing that this distinction between step and leap, between a 'melodic' and 'harmonic' scale, lies at the bottom of all music. It appears in our music in the form of 'passing' and 'substantive' notes; in two successive chords[1] the constituent notes of the second of them can be, and can only be, justified as melodic steps or as harmonic leaps from those of the first, however much the current conception of what is melody and what is harmony may grow. But, just as in our music the two

[1] Chords are compressed arpeggios, and arpeggios are, or may be, skeleton scales.

ideas were held apart to some extent and ticketed as Counterpoint and Thoroughbass respectively, but afterwards fused in Harmony, so,

(7) together with the 'melodic' and 'harmonic' scales, we find everywhere in India the 'complete' scale—a scale, that is, which extends beyond the small gamut of adjacent notes, or which fills up the gaps left by the sparse notes.

No melodies have been noted in India until quite modern times, so that we have no direct means of determining what those songs were of which the scales were later tabulations. But we may perhaps take remoteness of local origin to be an efficient substitute for antiquity of record; and these seven 'conclusions' may therefore not be without value as a guide to the constitution of the early forms of scale. At any rate no reading of the theory would be satisfactory if it did serious violence to the practice.

Another guide is to be found in the tunings of local instruments. These are, if we can interpret them, a record of the essential notes of the melodies of the district to which the instrument belongs. Essential, because other subsidiary notes are got, or are always there to be got, by special fingerings and by varying pressure of lip or finger. We will examine some of these Ludwig Riemann[1] has given, from observations made on Indian stringed and wind instruments, with the help of an *Appunn's Tonmesser*—scales correct to an eighth of a tone. His results for stringed instruments may be neglected because the frets undoubtedly shift by lapse of time, by handling, and by the shaking of the journey, and also because such instruments as those of the *vīṇā* aud *satār* tribes, from which his examples are mainly taken, belong to civilized, i. e. modern, music. There is more help to be got from the wind instruments, because niceties of intonation obtained by fingering and overblowing belong rather to a fully developed art, whereas these rustic flutes would tend to be pierced in accordance with the accepted local scale, so as to save trouble in performance.

The following table divides the Semitone into four parts. It will be useful to remember that the Tone[2] is here 8 of such parts, the minor Third 12, the major Third 16, the Fourth 20, the Tritone 24, the Fifth 28, and the Octave 48:

[1] *Über eigentümliche bei Natur- und orientalischen Kulturvölkern vorkommende Tonreihen.* Essen, 1889, pp. 3, 27–30.

[2] The true relations of major Tone, minor Tone, and Semitone would be best expressed (in single figure integers) as 9, 8, and 5.

Flute scales.

	No.	Intervals	Riemann's numbering.	Name and origin of instrument.
Approximate European Just scale.		0 8 16 20 28 36 44 48; intervals 8 8 4 8 8 8 4; C D E F G A B C		
Fourth.	1.	2 5 3 5 5	77*a*	Flute, Lahore.
	2.	4 3 5 8	74	Flute, Lahore.
	3.	4 6 4 6 6	77*b*	Flute, Lahore.
	4.	6 6 4 4 7	78*a*	Flute, Lahore.
	5.	4 4 3 4 8 8	76	Oboe, Ceylon.
	6.	4 4 4 6 4	75	Double flute, Ludhiāna.
	7.	4 4 4 5 6	66	Flute, Jaipur.
	8.	13 6 (Fourth) 8 10 9 4 (Tritone)	81	Reed flute, South India.
Tritone.	9.	6 8 10	67*b*	Bansri flute, Mathura.
	10.	13 8 (Fourth) 9 15	80	Flute, Kandha.
	11.	8 7 8 8	67*a*	Bansri flute, Mathura.
	12.	10 1 7 8	76*b*	Bansri flute, Ludhiāna.
Fifth.	13.	1 9 8 10 12 10 4	95	Bansri flute, Sovala.
	14.	6 8 6 8	76*a*	Bansri flute, Ludhiāna.
Fourth and Fifth.	15.	8 8 8 4 8½ (♯A) 8	65	Flute, East Bengal.
	16.	8 8 8 4 10 8 10	73	Thumri double flute, Lahore.
	17.	8 8 4 8 8 (A) 8 10	70*b*	Nai flutes, Kashmīr.
	18.	8 4 8 8 8 (A) 8 9	70*a*	Nai flutes, Kashmīr.

We have no hint as to which note is to be regarded as the tonic, though it would be a reasonable guess to consider the lowest note to be so as a rule, because the large majority of Indian melodies are authentic, not plagal. Ignoring any suggestion of that sort, the arrangement adopted here is to group together those scales which respectively make (1) the Fourth, (2) the Tritone, (3) the Fifth, or (4) the Fourth and the Fifth, their basis, placing between the groups those which show approximations to these intervals. Where there might be doubt as to which interval was intended, a slur, or if an approximation a dotted slur, has been added.

We must not argue from these eighteen scales to any preference for a particular size of interval, for neither do we know how representative this list, a mere handful of the flutes of India, may be, nor can we hope to base anything upon the sporadic list of 'origins'. But a given scale tends to consist, on the whole, of one size of interval, showing that there was an average feeling, varying of course locally, of the sort of distance it was to the 'next door' note. We see, however, that in no scale is this distance uniform. The scale is conceived 'diatonically', that is to say, mixing up large and small intervals. This throws light incidentally on a statement of Aristoxenus that 'it is impossible to hear three next door notes in succession'.[1]

The interest of this table centres in the basic intervals (Fourth, Fifth, &c.) and the way they are filled up. So far as this small list may be considered to be representative, we find in it the largest group based on the Fourth, the next largest on the Fourth and Fifth together. This corroborates the conclusions from the Folk-songs given above. But more interesting is the appearance of the Tritone as a base, and of the various approximations to it. There was a fairly large number of songs which employed this interval in Chapters I and II; so that it must be taken as an important factor of scale.

[1] His name for them is 'passage-note' (*diesis*). Gevaert (*Musique de l'Antiquité*, vol. i, p. 285) thinks that there is a tinge of exaggeration in this statement; but it is possible to believe that Aristoxenus meant what he said. He always subscribes to the musical not the acoustical view, and his words must be taken to mean not that the mind cannot think these intervals in the abstract, but that the voice will not sing them in the concrete; that they are what we should call 'unvocal'. This may be observed whenever a village choir wrestles with three or four semitones in succession.

Also, in no case (until the last four examples, where the scale is thoroughly established) is the basic interval filled in in exactly the same way. There are signs, indeed (especially in Nos. 1, 3, 4, 7, 8, 9, and 12), that the process was to supplement a chosen melodic interval by a residue. In No. 1, for instance, the general scheme involves large semitones (5, 5, 5). But the tetrachord begins with a quarter-tone (2), and to this there is a residue in a larger quarter-tone (3).

There are also signs of a practice which is familiar to us,[1] of sharpening the higher intervals. In No. 7 the semitones get larger as they ascend; in No. 13 the tones. In Nos. 8 and 13 the octave is sharp; in Nos. 16, 17, 18 the eighth note is considerably sharp on the octave. In No. 10 the octave is the first harmonic. In no other case is the octave true. This shows that the octave was not considered a basic interval in the sense in which the Fourth, Tritone, and Fifth were; and this again accords with what we find in the songs.

There is no accounting for this Tritone: it must be accepted as a fact.[2] It may have been arrived at by a series of Tones, as Nos. 9–12 would seem to suggest; or it may be the result of a shift of tonic—e.g. B–E becoming C–F, with a resultant interval B–F—in support of which view some arguments will be adduced later. But in any case it is a fundamental fact of Indian music. The Carnatic system classifies the *Rāgams* into those which employ the Fourth and those which employ the Tritone as basic interval (*Śuddhamadhyama* and *Pratimadhyama*), and it will be seen that the same principle underlies the *Rāgs* of Hindostan. It might be supposed that F♯ (in C–F♯ G) was felt as a leading note to G merely, were it not that it is used in many *Rāgs* with obvious pleasure in descent also; and we must conclude that Indians value the Tritone for its own sake.

We turn now to the theory. There are in all about three dozen Sanskrit musical works which may be dated with varying degrees of confidence; they are, with the exception of half a dozen (marked with an asterisk), as yet unpublished, and the MSS. are scattered

[1] Pianoforte tuners have found by experience that the English public likes to have the upper octaves tuned sharp, as being more brilliant. The rise in pitch since Handel's time is said to be due to the desire to secure greater brilliance by tuning brass instruments sharper than normal.

[2] Cp. the *Kanwar's* tuning on p. 31, and the progression of the bass in Debussy and Stravinsky.

about in various Indian and a few European libraries. A list, extracted from Aufrecht's and other catalogues, is here given, in case it should be of use to future students of the subject:

List of Sanskrit Authorities

Title.	*Author.*	*Date.*
Nāṭyaśāstra*	Bharata	First seven centuries of our era; there is a slight probability that it belongs to the late 5th cent.
Sangītaratnākara*	Śārṅgadeva	1210–1247.
Sangītopanishad	Sudhākalāśa	1324.
Sangītopanishadsāra		
Rāsikapriyā	Rāna Kumbhakarṇa Mahimendra	circ. 1450.
Sangītamīmānsā		
Sangītarāja		
Sangītaratnākaratīka*	Kallinātha	1460 (or 1560).
Sangītasāra	Harināyaka (?)	1500, or earlier.
Anandasanjīvana	Madanapāladeva	1528.
Rāgamāla	Kshemakarṇa	1570.
Svaramelakalānidhī*	Tīmamatya	Second half of 16th cent.
Sangītaratnākara	Bhanuraka	
Nartananirṇaya	Paṇḍarīkaviṭṭala	
Rāgamañjarī		
Cighrabodhinināmamāla		
Ṣaḍrāgacandrodaya		
Rāgamāla		
Sangītavṛttaratnākara		
Rāgavibodha*	Somanātha	1609.
Hṛdayaprakāśa	Hṛdayanārāyaṇa	Early 17th cent.
Sangītānūpānkuśa	Bhavabhaṭṭa	circ. 1640.
Sangītadarpaṇa*	Dāmodara Miśra	1560–1647.
Sangītasārasangraha*	Rājah Jagajjyotirmalla	circ. 1650.
Sangītabhāskara		
Anūpasangītavilāśa	Bhavabhaṭṭa	circ. 1680.
Muralīprakāśa		
Nasṭoddiṣṭaprabhodakadhraupadatīka		
Sangītamakaranda	Veda	End of 17th cent.
Sangītadāmodara	Śubhankara	Before 1700.
Sangītanārāyaṇa	Purushottama Mishra	1730, or before.
Sangītanārāyaṇa	Nārāyaṇadeva	Before 1765.
Sangītaparijāta*	Ahobala Paṇḍit	18th cent.
Sangītasārāmṛitā	Rājah Tulajī	circ. 1770.

These catalogues contain references also to thirty-eight more of which the author and the locale of the MS., but not the date, is known; fourteen of which the author only is known; and seventeen of which the locale of the MS. only is known. Total 103. The twenty-eighth *adhyāya* of Bharata which is concerned with music (the subject of the work being the drama) has been translated into French by Jean Grosset. Mr. Clements's *Introduction to the Study of Indian Music,* 1913, gives extracts from Bharata and Śārṅgadeva.

The *Rāgavibodha* of Somanātha is in course of translation in the *Indian Musical Journal,* Mysore.

It will not be possible to speak with confidence about Indian theory until all the important books have been adequately translated. What is here said is taken from Grosset's translation of Bharata.

We begin with the explanation of a few technical terms.

Grāma, lit. 'village', as opposed to jungle (*araṇya*), means a civilized as opposed to an unsophisticated scale.[1] The name has been applied specifically only to three scales—the *Sa-grāma,* our major with a sharpened Sixth, the *Ma-grāma,* our major C–c, but intended presumably to be used as an F–f scale with a sharpened Sixth, and the *Ga-grāma,* possibly intermediate between these two, long obsolete.

Thāṭ, lit. 'array', is used in Hindostan for the setting of the frets of a string instrument (especially the *satār* or *surbahar*) for the purpose of playing in a given mode. But, as one setting will do for several modes, *Thāṭ,* which takes the name of one typical mode—e.g. *Bhairavī Thāṭ,* or *Kāfī Thāṭ*—has a classifying sense. The South Indian term for this classificatory sense is *Melakarta,* lit. 'group maker', because it groups together several *Rāgams*; though it does not seem to be applied to 'setting', and, indeed, I never met with a *Satār* in the south.

Mūrchaṇa (Sanskrit), *murchhana* (Hindostani), from a root *mūrch,* 'to increase', means primarily the 'swelling of sound' and seems to have been applied originally to high and low pitch and to have meant the rise and fall of the voice in song. Then it came to have the technical sense of (1) a rise and fall from and to a particular note of a specific scale, and in this sense is accurately translated by 'mode'. (It may be worth mentioning that the *mūrchaṇas* are always given as a descending series.) But since the note on which they started was the most important and was generally ornamented with a grace note, *murchhana* has come to mean (2) grace note as applied to a particular *Rāg.* When grace is otherwise applied, i.e. not to single out the predominant note of a *Rāg,* it has either the general name *Gamak* or the particular names *Mīnḍ* or *Ghasīt.* These are treated of in a later chapter. In the old sense of the word the 'mode' consisted of seven notes, i.e. two tetrachords, so that

[1] The usual explanation is that the notes are arranged in a scale as mankind are in a village, which gives rather a poor sense.

mūrchaṇa may (3) be held also to translate the Greek *harmoniā* (heptachord).

Rāga, from a root *rañj*, 'to be dyed, to glow', means 'colour'; hence colour of mind, i. e. emotion. Its European analogue will therefore be whatever gives colour to a piece of music; and since this may be according to circumstances melody, harmony, counterpoint, or instrumentation, but most of all harmony, we have no real equivalent for a word which applies technically only to melody. *Rāga* is connected with *Rakti*, 'affection'. *Rāga* is Sanskrit, and is used in this book when the general sense is intended; *Rāg* is North Indian, and *Rāgam* South Indian. The same is the case for *Tāla*, *Tāl*, and *Tālam* (time). Its usual translation is 'melody-type', or 'melody-mould', or even 'tune'. If it must be translated, perhaps 'Mood' would convey as much as is compressible into one word. Its definition is rather long, and will not mean much until the chapter on *Rāga* has been read:—An arbitrary series of notes characterized as far as possible as individuals, by proximity to or remoteness from the note which marks the *tessitura*, by a special order in which they are usually taken, by the frequency or the reverse with which they occur, by grace or the absence of it, and by relation to a tonic usually reinforced by a drone. Although Indians never confuse the masculine *Rāg* with the feminine *Rāgiṇī*[1] the attributes of these are indistinguishable.

Saptaka, a 'set of seven', takes the place of our word 'octave'; the *saptaka* contains seven *svaras*, i. e. not notes, but intervals between them; and all Indian notations assume three *saptakas*, a higher (*tāra*), middle (*madhya*), and lower (*mandra*), arrived at as the average compass of the human voice (in their art songs).

Svara, from root *svṛi*, 'hear', is also a degree of the scale, or a diatonic note. It may be natural (*śuddha*) or chromatic (*vikṛta*). 'Natural' means not a 'white' note, but 'proper to the scale', whatever the scale may be. *Vikṛta* notes are sharp (*tīvra*) or flat *komala*), very sharp (*atitīvra*) or very flat (*atikomala*). F is the only note which is sharpened, and it has three degrees of sharpness —$\overset{\sharp}{F}$ (*ma tīvra*), $F\sharp$ (*ma tīvratar*), $\overset{\sharp}{F}\sharp$ (*ma tīvratam*).[2] $\overset{\sharp}{F}$ being

[1] '*Rāg*' means strictly one of the Six Original *Rāgs*; all others are considered to be descendants of these, and are called *Rāgiṇīs*.

[2] -tar and -tam are the Greek -teros and the Latin -timus (e.g. finitimus, optimus, &c.).

rarely used the names are more often moved on one place, so that F♯ is *ma tīvra* and $\overset{\sharp}{F}\sharp$ *ma tīvratar*. Three degrees of flattening are sometimes wanted for D, E, A, B: $\overset{\flat}{D}\flat$ is *Ri atikomal*, D♭ *Ri komal*, and $\overset{\flat}{D}$ is sometimes called *Ri madhya* (middle).[1] *Tīvra* and *komal* are, literally, 'strong' and 'tender'. Divine attributes are assigned to all the *svaras*. Their full names are—C, *ṣaḍja*; D, *ṛśabha*; E, *gāndhāra*; F, *madhyama*; G, *pañcama*; A, *dhaivata*; B, *niśāda*; and their abbreviations *Sa*, *Ri*, *Ga*, *Ma*, *Pa*, *Dha*, *Ni*. In South India D♭, D, D♯ are called *Ra*, *Ri*, *Ru* (as the Tonic Sol-fa system names them *Ra*, *Ray*, and *Re*) and the others analogously. In old music the *svara* names the interval; when it names the note it names the note above the interval; thus, *Ga* means the interval E–F, and in old books the note F, in modern parlance the note E.

Śruti, from root *śru*, 'hear', is the (smallest) 'audible sound'. Like the *svara* it names both the interval and the note. The twenty-two *śrutis* have special names, and specific attributions of divine qualities lie no doubt concealed in these. The first of them, i. e. C–$\overset{\flat}{D}\flat$, is called *Tīvra* (sharp); the other names are obscure.

Vādī, *samvādī*, *anuvādī*, *vivādī* (translated 'sonant', 'consonant', 'assonant', 'dissonant') are survivals of a theory of consonance (*samvāditva*) now forgotten. *Samvādī* definitely means the consonance of Fourth or Fifth, as we should say 'Perfect consonance'. *Vādī* is the note to which it is so related. *Vivādī* is applied by Bharata to the Semitone. He speaks (verse 24) of notes being *vivādī* to one another when they are at the distance of twenty *śrutis*. This is the same thing as two *śrutis* (22–20), which reading actually appears in another manuscript. *Anuvādī* is the name for 'all other relations which are not *vādī*, *samvādī*, and *vivādī*'. These three relationships belong to the tetrachord, and presumably *anuvādī* does too. Current tradition makes *anuvādī* the major Third. But Bharata says 'all other' (*śesha*), as if more than one relationship was *anuvādī*. If it is possible to suppose that in the term *anuvādī* he included the major and minor Tone (which together make up the major Third) all the determining elements of Bharata's scale (see below) would be accounted for.

In discussing the scale (*grāma*) the first difficulty which confronts

[1] 'Intermediate' between *Ri śuddha* and *Ri komal*, D and D♭.

us lies in the double meaning of *svara*, 'note' and 'interval'.[1] Does the *Sa-grāma*, for instance, begin with the Sa-interval, or on the S-note? In the former case it will begin on what we should call C (the Indian N), in the latter on our D (the Indian S). Bharata gives some colour to the latter view in verse 25, where he says the arrangement of the *śrutis* in the *Sa-grāma* is 3, 2, 4, 4, 3, 2, 4—i. e. that they begin with the *svara* Ri, which is of three *śrutis*, and therefore on the S-note (our D).

But if we reflect that the scale is always spoken of as a 'set of seven' (sc. intervals), whereas it consists actually of eight notes, that these seven are always given as beginning with Sa, and that a scale so taken (from N-note or Sa-interval) satisfies the demands of the practice (in Chapters I and II), we shall not be disposed to attach too much importance to this *obiter dictum* of verse 25, even supposing that were the only way in which it could be interpreted. We assume, therefore, that the *Sa-grāma* begins with the Sa-interval, on the N-note (our C).

But there is a second difficulty, which Mr. Clements's recent book raises. Was the *grāma* a scale beginning on a definite note at all, or was it not rather a gamut, a continuous series, which might be started at any point, but which differed from some other *grāma* by having one place where the series diverged? But there is the difficulty of the names. Why were they called *Sa-grāma*, *Ma-grāma*, unless they had some obvious connexion with Sa and Ma? And what could that connexion be except that they began there? The distinction between *grāma* (scale) and *mūrchaṇa* (mode) may well be, essentially, that between *genos* and *harmoniā* (scale and mode), only that the Indian *grāma* did and the Greek *genos* did not begin on a particular note.

In assigning the *śrutis* thus, for the *Sa-grāma*,

Sa	Ri	Ga	Ma	Pa	Dha	Ni
4	3	2	4	4	3	2

Indian theory is indicating the relative sizes of the major Tone (4), the minor Tone (3), and the Semitone (2) with accuracy sufficient for its purpose. Complete accuracy would demand 4·08, 3·64, and

[1] Bharata speaks of two *svaras* (notes) being *saṃvādī* when they are nine *śrutis* (a Fourth) or thirteen *śrutis* (a Fifth) apart. Again, he speaks of Sa (one of the *svaras*) as 'of' four *śrutis*, meaning the interval from the note N to the note S. [Sa is hereinafter used for the interval, S for the note.]

2·24 respectively.[1] The *Ma-grāma* is formed from this by the interchange of the *śruti*-values of Pa and Dha; 'Dha takes one *śruti* from Pa'—thus:

	Sa	Ri	Ga	Ma	Pa	Dha	Ni
Ma-grāma	4	3	2	4	3	4	2

But the *Ma-grāma* is so called, we must think, because it begins on the note Ma. Hence the scale intended is:

Ma	Pa	Dha	Ni	Sa	Ri	Ga
4	3	4	2	4	3	2

But there is a third scale, the *Ga-grāma*, which is not mentioned by Bharata. It is said by Śārṅgadeva to have 'retired to Indraloka' (heaven). In spite of this, however, he knows how it was formed.

When (*a*) Ga takes one *śruti* from Ri and one from Ma,
(*b*) Dha takes one *śruti* from Pa,
(*c*) Ni takes one *śruti* from Dha and one from Sa,
then this arrangement is what Nārada taught us as the *Ga-grāma*.

The process is as follows:

		Sa	Ri	Ga	Ma	Pa	Dha	Ni
Sa-grāma		4	3	2	4	4	3	2
	(*a*)	4	**2**	**4**	**3**	4	3	2
	(*b*)	4	2	4	3	**3**	**4**	2
	(*c*)	**3**	2	4	3	3	**3**	**4**
Ga-grāma beginning on Ga		4	3	3	3	4	3	2

The three *grāmas*, put for comparison together, are:

Sa-grāma	4	3	**2**	**4**	4	3	2
Ga-grāma	4	3	**3**	**3**	4	3	2
Ma-grāma	4	3	**4**	**2**	4	3	2

and the notes of which these are composed may be represented by:

Sa-grāma	C	D	E	F	G	A♯	B	C
Ga-grāma	C	D	E	F♯	G	A♯	B	C
Ma-grāma	C	D	E	F♯	G	A♯	B	C

[1] That the numbers 4, 3, and 2 do represent these intervals is usually taken for granted. It appears to depend ultimately on the current tradition that *anuvādī* means the major Third; that is to say, that early theory recognized the major Third and not the Ditone, i.e. the major and minor Tone and not two major Tones.

In favour of this explanation, which is in principle that adopted in Mr. Clements's book, it may be said (1) that the *Ga-grāma* is thus made a true *grāma* and differs from the *Ma-grāma* (as that did from the *Sa-grāma*) by the alteration of one *śruti* only; and (2) the difference between the three *grāmas* lies in the treatment of the F, and this is just the difference we were led to expect by the Folk-songs, and still more by the flute tunings.

Against it, however, it must be said (1) that this explanation is based on a solitary passage of a thirteenth-century writer, and that the scheme of the other two *grāmas*, given in full by a writer of the fifth century A.D., the principle of which can be traced to the fifth century B.C., makes no mention of a third *grāma*; and (2) it is difficult to imagine so much prestige[1] as belongs to the *gāndhāra* scale attaching to a series of notes which makes the principal interval (the Fourth) break the law of consonance by consisting of ten *śrutis* instead of nine. The *Ga-grāma* must, one would think, have been some series of notes which is as fundamental a part of Indian music as the other two *grāmas* are.

But the directions of the *Ratnākara* may be taken in another way. The *Ga-grāma* may be intended there to be derived not from the *Sa-grāma*, but from the *Ma-grāma*. Thus:

Ma-grāma	4	3	2	4	3	4	2
(*a*)	4	**2**	**4**	**3**	3	4	2
(*b*)	4	2	4	3	**2**	**5**	2
(*c*)	**3**	2	4	3	2	**4**	**4**

This is the scale $\overset{\sharp}{\text{A}}$ B C D E F G $\overset{\sharp}{\text{A}}$, which is open also to the objection of having the Fifth $\overset{\sharp}{\text{A}}$–E consisting of twelve instead of thirteen *śrutis*. But in an early, i.e. a vocal, scale the Fifth is not nearly so important as the Fourth; and that is perfect ($3 + 2 + 4 = 9$). We notice also that, though derived here from the *Ma-grāma*, it is a mode of the *Sa-grāma* (and *not* a distinct *grāma*), and with that we leave it for further discussion in Chapter X.

[1] The *Harivaṃśā* (fourth century A.D.) speaks with enthusiasm of music composed in the *āgāndhāragrāmarāga*, 'the scale which comes down to *gāndhāra*,' i.e. which, if taken upwards, begins on *Ga*. The Mahābhārata speaks of 'the sweet *Gāndhāra*', and this implies a mode or scale, since no note is sweeter than another until it has a context.

The $\overset{\sharp}{A}$ of the *Sa-grāma* and *Ma-grāma* differed from A by the Comma of Didymus ($\frac{\text{Major Tone}}{\text{Minor Tone}} = \frac{81}{80}$ = 22 Cents). Bharata calls this comma the 'indicative' (*pramāṇa*) *śruti*. He uses it for the tuning of the *vīṇā*.

Take two *vīṇās*, he says, **alike in all respects, and tune them both in the Sa-grāma. On one of them diminish Pa** [i.e. lower the note P so as to form our A$\natural$ instead of $\overset{\sharp}{A}$] **by this** *pramāṇa śruti*, **but in such a way that the Pa of the Sa-grāma can be put back again. This is the diminution of one** *śruti*. **By a second diminution Ga** [on one *vīṇā*] **becomes Ri** [on the other], **and, similarly, Ni becomes Dha.** [The second *śruti*, then, is the difference between the *pramāṇa śruti* and the Semitone, and the *śrutis* were therefore not equal in size.] **By a third diminution D and R of one** *vīṇā* **coincide with P and S of the other; and by a fourth diminution P, M, and S coincide with M, G, and N. This scheme shows the twenty-two** *śrutis* **of the two grāmas.**

The only thing this establishes is that the *śrutis* were not equal in size. They are of three sizes: (1) the difference between the major and minor Tone, the *pramāṇa śruti*, twenty-two Cents; (2) the difference between the minor Tone and the Semitone, seventy Cents; and (3) the difference between the Semitone and the *pramāṇa śruti*, ninety Cents. He does not tell us in what order these diminutions are to be made; and if we took him literally, and made them successively downwards from each note we should get quite a wrong idea of his scale.

What that scale is we discover from his account of the *jātis*. There are seven modes (*mūrchanā*) of each of the two *grāmas*, i.e. fourteen in all; but only seven of these fourteen are in practical use under the name of *jātīs*, species. In the following table each mode is given as from a common tonic. The constituent units of the *Sa-grāma* (4 3 2 4 4 3 2) are successively added, and each *mūrchana* begins on a different one of these notes. The same is done for the *Ma-grāma*, giving another set of seven *mūrchanas*, each of which differs in one note, and only one, from some mode of the *Sa-grāma*.

Bharata's *Mūrchanas* and *Jātīs*.

Mūrchana.																									*Jātī.*
Abhirudgatā	D mode	**0**	...	...	**3**	...	**5**	...	...	...	**9**	...	...	...	**13**	...	...	**16**	...	**18**	...	...	...	**22**	*Arśabhī.*
Aśvakrāntā	E mode	0	...	2	...	...	...	6	...	...	...	10	...	...	13	...	15	...	...	...	19	...	...	22	
Matsarīkṛta	F mode	0	...	...	...	4	...	...	...	8	...	...	11	...	13	...	...	...	17	...	...	20	...	22	
Śuddhaśaḍjā	G mode	0	...	...	...	4	...	...	7	...	9	...	...	...	13	...	...	16	...	18	...	...	...	22	
Uttarāyatā	♯A mode	**0**	...	...	**3**	...	**5**	...	...	...	**9**	...	...	**12**	...	**14**	...	...	...	**18**	...	...	...	**22**	*Dhaivatī.*
Rajanī	m ode	**0**	...	**2**	...	...	...	**6**	...	...	**9**	...	**11**	...	...	...	**15**	...	...	...	**19**	...	...	**22**	*Niṣādinī.*
Uttaramandrā	(C mode) *Sa-grāma*	**0**	...	...	...	**4**	...	...	**7**	...	**9**	...	...	...	**13**	...	...	...	**17**	...	...	**20**	...	**22**	*Ṣaḍjī.*
		C	♭D♭	D♭	♭D	D	♭E♭	E♭	E	♯E	F	♯F	F♯	♯F♯	G	♭A♭	A♭	A	♯A	♭B♭	B♭	B	♯B	C	
Śuddha-madhyamā	*Ma-grāma*, i (C mode)	0	...	...	...	4	...	...	7	...	9	...	...	...	13	...	...	16	...	...	...	20	...	22	
Kalopannatā	D mode	0	...	...	3	...	5	...	...	...	9	...	...	12	...	...	...	16	...	18	...	...	...	22	
Harinaśvā	E mode	**0**	...	**2**	...	...	...	**6**	...	...	**9**	...	...	...	**13**	...	**15**	...	...	...	**19**	...	...	**22**	*Gāndhārī.*
Sauvirī	F mode (*Ma-grāma*, ii)	**0**	...	...	...	**4**	...	...	**7**	...	...	...	**11**	...	**13**	...	...	...	**17**	...	...	**20**	...	**22**	*Madhyamā.*
Hṛśyakā	G mode	**0**	...	...	**3**	...	...	...	**7**	...	**9**	...	...	...	**13**	...	...	**16**	...	**18**	...	...	...	**22**	*Pañcamī.*
Pauravī	A mode	0	...	...	...	4	...	6	...	...	...	10	...	...	13	...	15	...	...	...	19	...	...	22	
Margī	B mode	0	...	2	...	...	...	6	...	...	9	...	11	...	...	...	15	...	...	18	...	...	...	22	

We will now digress for a moment to record an important date in this connexion.

The scheme as a whole is much earlier than Bharata. The theory of consonance (*samvāditva*), or at least the terminology which that theory uses (*samvādī*, *anuvādī*, *vivādī*), is alluded to in the *Mahābhārata* (14, 14, 19). The date of the *Mahābhārata* is generally considered to be 400 B. C.–200 A. D., and the fourteenth is a late book. The author gives as the 'ten elements of sound' the seven notes of the scale (Sa, Ri, Ga, &c.), and three others, *iṣṭa*, *aniṣṭa*, and *saṃhata* (lit. 'agreeable', 'disagreeable', and 'struck together'). These last are described as 'classificatory' (*pravibhāgavān*); and it is tempting, therefore, to see in them the terms 'assonant', 'dissonant', and 'consonant' with which we are familiar.

But a much more important passage is to be found in the *Ṛkpratiśākhya*, which is probably not later than 400 B. C. It is there said that there are twenty-one notes in all, seven for each voice register (*sthāna*)—the lower (*mandra*), the middle (*madhya*), and the upper (*uttama*).[1] These seven notes (of the octave, or of course twenty-one of the three octaves of the gamut) are described as twins (*yama*). 'Each twin is separated from its fellow by such a small distinction that from one point of view the difference is hardly perceptible; yet, from another, the two are distinct things.' The metaphor of 'twins' describes so accurately the pairs of scales we have been discussing, which are identical in six notes and differ in the seventh by an almost imperceptible interval, and puts the finger so unerringly upon the salient point of the system, that there can be little doubt as to the reference. This highly elaborate system may, then, be dated back beyond the time of Aristoxenus, to the fifth century B. C., and, like his, points to a long antecedent period of development.[2]

It appears from the table of *mūrchanas* that all the twenty-two *śrutis* except the first and twenty-first are accounted for. These two are inserted, by analogy, in the next diagram in square brackets as consonant notes from the eighth and tenth *śrutis* respectively. If we take account of the *jātis* only, we find that these two, the eighth and the tenth, are not in use; they are accordingly placed in

[1] The modern name for the upper register is *tāra*.

[2] See Weber's *Indische Studien*, the eighth volume of the *Beiträge für die Kunde des indischen Altertums*, pp. 262 and 271.

round brackets. No. 11 is arrived at in two ways, with different results.

In the following diagram column I gives the constituent elements of each note in terms of the major Tone ($a = \frac{9}{8}$), the minor Tone ($b = \frac{10}{9}$), and the Semitone ($c = \frac{16}{15}$). Columns IV and V give the representative fractions, distributed into 'quintal' (those derived from the Fifth ($\frac{3}{2}$) alone), and 'tertian' (those derived jointly from the Fifth and the Third ($\frac{5}{4}$)). Column II gives the equivalent of these in cents,[1] and Column III their differences (or, speaking

[1] Cents are a set of slightly modified logarithms of fractional ratios between 1 and 2, and represent musical intervals within the compass of an octave ($\frac{2}{1}$) correct to the hundredth part of a semitone. The system is explained in Appendix XX of the second edition of Ellis's Translation of Helmholtz's *Sensations of Tone.* (This appendix is not in the first edition.)

For the following statement of the theory, and of practical rules for finding cents, the writer is indebted to the kindness of Mr. T. B. W. Spencer, of Wellington College:

The number of cents corresponding to any musical interval must satisfy two conditions, namely, that the addition and subtraction of cents should correspond to the product and quotient of the intervals they represent; and also that 1200 cents should correspond to the interval $\frac{2}{1}$, that is the interval between a note and its octave.

The first condition is satisfied by representing any interval by its logarithm to any base; the second, by multiplying these logarithms by some factor.

Using common logarithms, the logarithm of $\frac{2}{1}$ is ·3010300. As the number of cents corresponding to this interval is 1200, the factor that the logarithms must be multiplied by is $\frac{1200}{3010300}$ that is by 3986.

The rule, then, to find the number of cents corresponding to any interval is as follows: Find the common logarithm of the ratio, and multiply the result by 3986.

Example. If the ratio is $\frac{9}{8}$, the logarithm of $\frac{9}{8}$ is ·0511525. Multiply this by 3986, and the result is 204 to the nearest whole number.

The above is the only accurate rule, but as it is intelligible only to those who are acquainted with logarithms, we proceed to obtain a rule for calculating cents by means of elementary arithmetic.

The common logarithm of any fraction $\left(\frac{m}{n}\right)$ is given by the formula

$$\log \frac{m}{n} = 2 \times {\cdot}43429 \left\{ \frac{m-n}{m+n} + \frac{1}{3}\left(\frac{m-n}{m+n}\right)^3 + \frac{1}{5}\left(\frac{m-n}{m+n}\right)^5 + \dots \right\}$$

which is proved in every book on Higher Algebra. The number of cents is 3986 times this expression, that is, number of cents corresponding to $\frac{m}{n}$ is

$$3986 \times 2 \times {\cdot}43429 \left\{ \frac{m-n}{m+n} + \frac{1}{3}\left(\frac{m-n}{m+n}\right)^3 + \frac{1}{5}\left(\frac{m-n}{m+n}\right)^5 + \dots \right\}$$

$$\text{that is, } 3462 \times \frac{m-n}{m+n} + 1154 \times \left(\frac{m-n}{m+n}\right)^3 + 692\left(\frac{m-n}{m+n}\right)^5 + \dots.$$

in ratios, their quotients). Columns VI and VII are adjustments proposed by Mr. Clements on the strength of observations taken by Mr. Deval of Poona on a dichord: his two tertian intervals are a Fourth apart, and his two septimal, a Fifth. [Septimal intervals are derived from the septimal seventh; $\frac{7}{4} = 969$ cents.]

If we take $\frac{m}{n}$ less than $\frac{4}{3}$, $\frac{m-n}{m+n}$ is less than $\frac{1}{7}$ and $692\left(\frac{m-n}{m+n}\right)^5$ is less than ·04; therefore this term and all those after it may be neglected. Also $1154 \times \left(\frac{m-n}{m+n}\right)^3$ is less than $1154 \times \frac{1}{7^3}$, that is, less than 3·4; hence to the nearest whole number this term is either 0, 1, 2, or 3.

It is therefore simpler to calculate the number of cents, corresponding to $\frac{m}{n}$, from the formula $3462 \times \frac{m-n}{m+n}$, and add 1, 2, or 3 as required.

No simple rule can be given which will always give the correct result. The following, although slightly more complicated than that given by Ellis in his article on 'The musical scales of various nations' in the *Journal of the Society of Arts* for March 27, 1885, has the advantage of being more accurate.

(*a*) If the ratio is less than $\frac{4}{3}$, multiply 3462 by the difference of the numerator and denominator, and divide by their sum, obtaining the quotient to the nearest whole number. If this quotient is

over 262 add 1,
,, 378 ,, 2,
,, 448 ,, 3.

(*b*) If the ratio is greater than $\frac{4}{3}$ and less than $\frac{3}{2}$, multiply the larger number by 3 and the smaller by 4 and proceed as before, and finally add 498 to the result.

(*c*) If the ratio exceeds $\frac{3}{2}$, multiply the larger number by 2 and the smaller by 3 and proceed as in (*a*), and add 702 to the result.

Examples:

(*a*) The ratio is $\frac{10}{9}$. Multiply 3462 by 1 and divide by 19. Result, 182.

(*b*) The ratio is $\frac{45}{32}$. Multiply 45 by 3 and 32 by 4, giving $\frac{135}{128}$, difference 7, sum 263. Then

$$\frac{3462 \times 7}{263} = 92.$$

Add 498 and the result (in cents) is 590.

(*c*) The ratio is $\frac{7}{4}$. Multiply 7 by 2 and 4 by 3, giving $\frac{14}{12}$, i.e. $\frac{7}{6}$. Then

$$\frac{3462}{13} = 266.$$

Since 266 is more than 262, add 1 as well as 702. The result is

$$266 + 1 + 702 = 969,$$

the cents required.

		Constituents. I.	*Cents.* II.	*Differences.* III.	*Fractional ratios.* *Quintal.* IV.	*Tertian.* V.	*Adjustments.* *Cents.* VI.	*Ratios.* VII.	
Ni.	22.	$3a+2b+2c$	1200	90	2	2	...	...	C
	21.	[Samvādī to No. 8]	[1110]	22	...	[243 : 128]	1108	256 : 135 (tertian)	$\overset{\sharp}{B}$
Dha.	20.	$3a+2b+c$	1088	70	...	15 : 8	...	...	B
	19.	$3a+b+2c$	1018	22	...	9 : 5	...	...	B♭
	18.	$2a+2b+2c$	996	90	16 : 9	...	...	...	$\overset{\flat}{B\flat}$
Pa.	17.	$3a+b+c$	906	22	27 : 16	...	...	...	A
	16.	$2a+2b+c$	884	70	...	5 : 3	...	...	A
	15.	$2a+b+2c$	814	22	...	8 : 5	...	...	A♭
	14.	$a+2b+2c$	792	90	128 : 81	...	787	63 : 40 (septimal)	$\overset{\flat}{A\flat}$
Ma.	13.	$2a+b+c$	702	22	3 : 2	...	...	...	G
	12.	$a+2b+c$	680	70	...	40 : 27	...	...	$\overset{\sharp}{F\sharp}$
	11.	$a+b+2c$	610	20	...	64 : 45	610	64 : 45 (tertian)	F♯
		$2a+b$	590	70	...	45 : 32			
	10.	$(2a+c)$	(520)	22	...	(27 : 20)	...	...	$\overset{\sharp}{F}$
Ga.	9.	$a+b+c$	498	90	4 : 3	...	...	...	F
	8.	$(2a)$	(408)	22	(81 : 64)	...	...	...	$\overset{\sharp}{E}$
Ri.	7.	$a+b$	386	70	...	5 : 4	...	...	E
	6.	$a+c$	316	22	...	6 : 5	...	...	E♭
	5.	$b+c$	294	90	32 : 27	...	...	...	$\overset{\flat}{E\flat}$
Sa.	4.	a	204	22	9 : 8	...	...	...	D
	3.	b	182	70	...	10 : 9	...	...	$\overset{\flat}{D}$
	2.	c	112	90	...	16 : 15	...	...	D♭
	1.	[Samvādī to No. 10]	[22]	22	...	[81 : 80]	85	21 : 20 (septimal)	$\overset{\flat}{D\flat}$
N.	0.		0		1	1	...	...	C

It may be noticed that since the *Ma-grāma* (4 3 2 4 3 4 2), which is identical with our major scale, can be treated in the same way, it would have been open to Europeans to divide the octave similarly into twenty parts. Having a different object in view we have preferred to do two things. First, we have 'merged' nearly identical intervals; that is, we have made one note do duty for two. Thus, E♭ is $204 + 112 = 316$, and D♯ is $386 - 112 = 274$; and we have made 316 do duty for both notes. And secondly, since we wished to have all the relations of the successive notes of the key the same, on whatever note the key began, we have 'tempered'; that is, we have made the major Tone, minor Tone, and Semitone expressible in terms of each other by adopting a compromise. Thus 204, 182, and 112 have been altered to 200, 200, and 100. With these particular intervals the falsity of intonation does not seriously matter; but since it involves reducing the Fifth, 702, to 700, and increasing the major Third,[1] 386, to 400, the falsity on some instruments and in certain connexions is very apparent. There are purists who regret this, and others who do not appreciate the reason for it—that we have an ample compensation in Harmony, which it alone makes possible. If India were ever to adopt Harmony it would be driven eventually to the same or a similar device; there is not, permanently, any half-way house.[2]

Bharata's is the North Indian theory of *grāma*, though, as we have seen, it touches the South Indian theory also in one point, the division of *Rāga* into two classes, those which have the Fourth and the Tritone respectively for basic interval. But in other points the South Indian theory diverges.

First, the Carnatic system 'merges'; it recognizes not twenty-two, but only sixteen nominal and twelve real sub-divisions of the scale:

Modern Carnatic Scale.

C	Sa (śuddha)	
B		Ni kākali
A♯ B♭	Dha shatśruti	Ni kaiśiki
A B♭♭	Dha catuḥśruti	Ni śuddha
A♭	Dha śuddha	

[1] The ear perceives these relations immediately, but those of the Tone, &c., mediately.

[2] See Appendix.

G	Pa (śuddha)	
F♯	Prati-madhyama	
F	Śuddha-madhyama	
E		Ga sādhāraṇa
D♯ E♭	Ri shatśruti	Ga antara
D E♭♭	Ri catuḥśruti	Ga śuddha
D♭	Ri śuddha	
C	Sa (śuddha)	

N.B. Śuddha, natural, normal.
Catuḥśruti, of four *śrutis*.
Shatśruti, of six *śrutis*.
Antara, interval.
Sādhāraṇa, twilight.
Prati-, mock-, counter-.
Kaiśiki, hair's-breadth.
Kākali, low, quiet.

The Hindostani system ran :

śrutis	4	5	6	7
		♭		
	D	E♭	E♭	E
	204	294	316	386

The Carnatic system, by calling the D♯–E♭ note *shatśruti*[1] (6–*śruti*), selects the 316 rather than the 294.

The second point which is peculiar to the Carnatic, or Dravidian, system is the designation *śuddha* as here applied. It will be seen that the *śuddha* notes taken by themselves form the scale

C D♭ D–F G A♭ A–C

whereby each tetrachord is filled by two semitones and a 'residue'. This is identical in form with the ancient Greek chromatic. Not only is this chromatic scale apparent in the nomenclature, but *Rāgams* in this mode (or scale) were once popular, though now somewhat neglected. In the scheme of *Grāmarāgas* in the *Ratnākara* and the *Svaramela-kalānidhī* (both of the sixteenth century) the first on the list, by name *Mūkhārī*, is in this scale, and is plentifully filled with *Rāgams*, showing that it was popular and was

[1] The nomenclature of this scale has a long history behind it, much of which will be found in Mr. Clements's book. Some of the names are transferred from the Hindostani system, e.g. *Kākali*, *Kaiśiki*, *Sādhāraṇa*, *Antara*, where they had a precise meaning which they have here lost.

considered the natural one to put first.[1] [*Grāmarāga* is an early name for *melakarta.*] Popular favour has now, however, been transferred to another scale, *Māya-Mālavagaula*:

C D♭–E F G A♭–B C

It looks as if the second of these two scales had developed from the first by way of modal shift of tonic. These five notes

Māyamālavagaula.

Ex. 183.

Mūkhārī.

show the characteristic tetrachord of each chromatic scale. The two complete scales compare thus:

Authentic Māyamālavagaula.

Ex. 184.

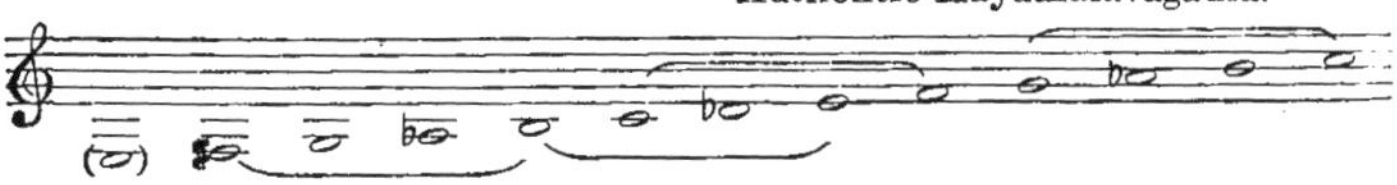

Plagal Mūkhārī.

This would sound too ingenious to be true were it not that a strictly analogous thing has happened with Greek music. The modern form of Greek chromatic is:

C D♭ E F G♭ A B♭[2]

and the two, ancient and modern, complete scales are therefore

Modern Greek (plagal).

Ex. 185.

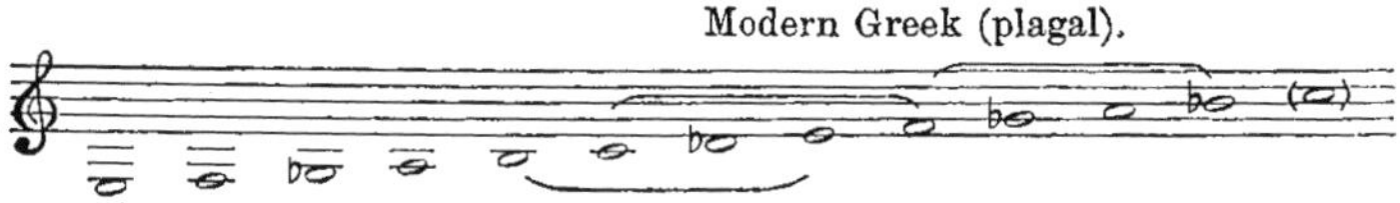

Ancient Greek (authentic).

The Carnatic scale has, then, a chromatic basis; and the Greeks held that the chromatic preceded the diatonic.[3] The latter we found in Hindostan taking shape in three, according to one explanation, but at any rate in two *grāmas* which differed from each other by one *śruti*, precisely as the 'hard' and 'soft' varieties of the Greek diatonic differed by one *diesis*. Here we have analogues,

[1] It is still put first in the modern system under the fancy name of *Kānakangi* (part of an elaborate *memoria technica*, see Mudaliar's *Oriental Music*, p. 17).

[2] See the examples in Pachtikos, *Aismata Hellenica*, Athens, 1905, passim.

[3] South Indians claim that the Dravidian system (that of the Carnatic) is older than the Hindostani. It may be remembered also that Tamil (the prevalent language of southern India) has the oldest datable literature of any Prakrit.

therefore, for two of the Greek *genera.* We may even trace the third *genus*, the enharmonic, in *Rāgs* like *Toḍi*, *Multāni*, and others.

The Greek enharmonic scale, expressed in *śrutis*, appears thus

Ex. 186.

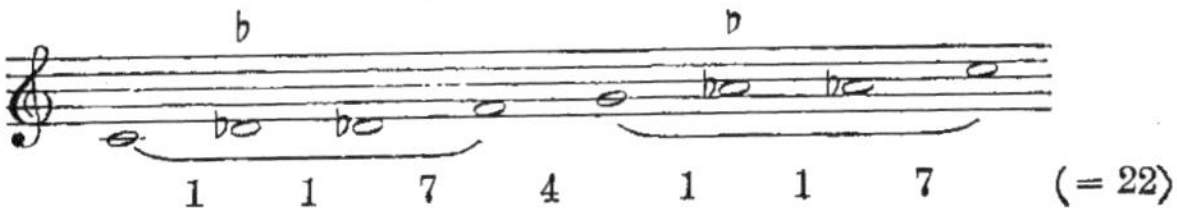

The scale of *Toḍi* is:

Ex. 187.

They meet, like the old and new South Indian chromatic scales, in two overlapping tetrachords:

Ex. 188.

The Greeks called the three notes which are separated by one *diesis* (*śruti*) the cluster (*pyknon*), and recognized three forms of tetrachord according as the lower note (*barypyknon*), middle note (*mesopyknon*), or upper note (*oxypyknon*)[2] of the cluster was made the tonic, i. e. the terminal of the tetrachord. If this ever formed a part of Indian theory, no trace of it has as yet been discovered; but the fact is here —the Greek enharmonic with the *barypyknon* and the enharmonic *Toḍi* with the *oxypyknon*. Further, *Toḍi* and its congeners are really distinct from other *Rāgs*, because, as has been seen, there is no place for them in Bharata's *jātīs*, which do not provide for the first and twenty-first *śrutis* which *Toḍi* involves. They may therefore point to a different basic principle of scale.

It is not suggested that the three *genera*, to borrow the term, are confined respectively to different parts of India, although the enharmonic seems to be opposed in principle to the Carnatic system.

[1] These notes are given for the sake of clearness one quarter tone higher than they stand in Ex. 187.

[2] Aristoxenus did not recognize the latter two; he held that the *pyknon* must always be at the lower end of the tetrachord.

The diatonic is ubiquitous (though the sharp Sixth is not found in the South), and the chromatic is quite as popular in the North under the name of *Bhairau* as it is in the South as *Māyamālavagaula*.

Neither is there any suggestion that Greece borrowed from India, or vice versa; their musical systems, like their languages, were no doubt part of their common Aryan inheritance—with enough likeness and unlikeness to make the comparison convincing.

We turn now to the other class of scale, the transilient, which proceeds by 'leap' to the Fourth, with a bridge note. It might seem at first glance as if these were not very different from the chromatic scales, since in both there is as a rule a leap of a minor Third. But there is a great difference in the melodies which embody them. A 'chromatic' melody tends to centre in the cluster of semitones, and to treat the leap as an occasional excursion. A 'transilient' melody moves more freely, and the leap is the most important material of the song.

We found a hint in the Gurkha and Garhwālī songs that these transilient scales had their home in the east of India. Although they are to be found everywhere, they seem to be especial favourites in Bengal; and the Bengāli system especially insists on heptatonic (*sampūrṇa*), hexatonic (*shāḍava*), and pentatonic (*oḍava*) as a primary division of *Rāga*, whereas the other systems, while recognizing these, draw no special attention to them. Of these names there is something to be said about *oḍava*. It is always understood to mean 'a set of five'; but the word is neither Sanskrit nor Prakrit. What the connexion is, if any, with *Auḍavī* (an unlocated place-name) or the *Oḍras* (who inhabited Orissa = *Oḍra-desha*) or with *oḍrapushpa* (the Chinese rose) must be left to others to determine. No Indian language owns *oḍava*, and, if the name is foreign, the scale may have been imported. That it is foreign is further suggested by the form *shāḍava*, 'a set of six,' formed on analogy, for which the proper Sanskrit would have been *shashtaka*.

Indian theory, which is nothing if not complete, has names also for scales of fewer notes. Scales of one note, which seems a little Irish, are called *Arcika* (i. e. belonging to the *Rigveda*). This is curious since the *Ṛk* was by common consent chanted to three notes. Of two notes, *Gāthika*; *Gāthas* were religious non-Vedic songs. Of three notes, *Sāmika*, belonging to the *Sāmaveda*.

(Incidentally, the *Sāman* chant involved from five to seven notes.) Of four notes, *Svarāntara* (= hiatus); this seems to be a confession that the tabulation had broken down. Still, the list as a whole may be read to mean that a small compass connotes antiquity, as we found it connoted also remoteness of locality. No one doubts, either, that pentatonic scales precede, what indeed may be considered 'spoiled' forms of them, hexatonic and heptatonic. They are, logically, older because they are innocent of the Semitone, which comes into the scale only when the ear can appreciate the major Third. ($\frac{\text{Fourth}}{\text{Major Third}}$ = Semitone). Melodies in these scales have extraordinary strength and sweetness, but not much variety.

It remains to bring these different scale formations into relation with acoustical fact, on the one hand, and with musical fact on the other.

When primitive man—and he is to be heard in London streets as well as in Otahiti or in the glacial epoch—begins to articulate his upward whoop or downward wail, he uses his 'musical ear'. It is this ear which is in a low state of development when he 'loses his key' or 'sings out of tune'. What is it, then, to sing in tune? It is to be able to hear, *with* a given note, certain other notes which are present in it at various pitches and intensities. 'The' note is known as the 'fundamental', and the 'other' notes as 'upper partials': the latter diminish in intensity as they rise in pitch. Intensity of sound has not yet been measured, and the amount of average diminution is not known. The following series omits octaves (as mere replicas), and hints at the average diminution by time-values:

Ex. 189.

&c.

1 3 5 7 9 11 &c.

The 2nd, 4th, 6th, 8th, 10th upper partials are omitted as duplicates. The B♭ is $\frac{1}{8}$ tone flat, the F is $\frac{1}{4}$ tone sharp on notes of the same name which are derived from lower partials, and which therefore in certain connexions have precedence. Human powers of hearing vary a good deal, and still more the power of defining and naming what is heard; so that individuals and tribes may be classified according as their powers extend to the 3rd, 5th, or even 7th upper partial; there is no certain record of powers that have exceeded that. These upper partials are present on all sound-producers; poorest on the tuning fork and flute, richest in the human voice. But they are present in different intensities,[1] and this fact gives its 'character' to each sound-producer.

But, secondly, it seems to be a law of music (not of acoustics) that no tonal fact can be realized at all without its entering at once into all the relationships of which it is capable; and we must now consider this series in another way:

1 2 3 4 5 6 7 8 9 10

Ex. 190.

&c.

$\frac{2}{1}$ $\frac{3}{2}$ $\frac{4}{3}$ $\frac{5}{4}$ $\frac{6}{5}$ $\frac{7}{6}$ $\frac{8}{7}$ $\frac{9}{8}$ $\frac{10}{9}$ &c.

Each partial forms with its neighbour in the series an interval represented by a 'super-particular'[2] fraction, and these intervals are the ultimate facts of music. They immediately combine to form new intervals as quotients: thus, $\frac{2}{1} \div \frac{3}{2} = \frac{4}{3}$, that is, the power of hearing the Octave and Fifth carries with it the power to hear the Fourth as well. Further, $\frac{3}{2} \div \frac{4}{3} = \frac{9}{8}$; that is, the hearing of the Fourth and Fifth involves the appreciation of the major Tone. This means that in order to discriminate the major Tone it is not necessary to have an ear fine enough to hear the 8th and 9th partials, which also give it (because they are partials of the 2nd and 3rd partials), but it can be apprehended directly as the 'difference' between (strictly, quotient of) an Octave and two Fifths.

The power of hearing up to the 3rd partial provides a scheme of notes which is known as 'quintal' harmony; and since this is infinite, it would be possible to plot a scale in this harmony alone of twenty-two or any other desired number of degrees in the octave. But the relationships would begin soon, after the first half-dozen or so, to be remote and practically unintelligible. For instance, the obvious relationship of C to B♭ is that B♭ is a minor Third (316 cents) from G, and G is a Fifth (702) from C; total 1018. It is possible in quintal harmony also to reach B♭ from C,

[1] The 2nd partial is prominent in the flute, the 3rd in the clarinet, the 3rd and 5th in the human voice, the 7th in bells, the 11th in the trumpet. Pianoforte makers cause the hammer to strike the string at a place which eliminates the 7th, which is not wanted.

[2] Of the form $\frac{a+1}{a}$.

but only by calculating upwards in major Tones ($5 \times 204 = 1020$), and this process confuses the ear. It does not matter that 1020 is not the same as 1018; for the difference is only $\frac{1}{56}$ of a semitone, and it requires a good ear to distinguish even tenths of Semitones in an interval which, like C–B♭, is derived, and not a matter of immediate perception like, for instance, C–G, or C–E. What matters is that the ear cannot make so elaborate a calculation as five successive major Tones—as, indeed, Aristoxenus, quoted above, suggested.

The ear, therefore, takes by preference the intervals derived from the 5th partial, the major Third, which form 'tertian' harmony. As 'quintal' harmony was derived from the Octave and Fifth, so tertian harmony is derived from the Octave, Fifth, and Third; and 'septimal' harmony, if it is ever used, is derived from these three and the 7th partial. In tertian harmony the series is again infinite, as indeed any of these series must be, since no basic interval is an exact power (or root) of another basic interval. But since there are three basic intervals instead of, as before, two, it is found by experience that a larger number of derived intervals, about eight, are easily intelligible in tertian harmony. We have no experience of septimal harmony, and it is impossible to say what intervals the ear would here accept. And this is important. With the acoustical material available, many and diverse scales might be constructed, and they would all look equally well—or ill—on paper. Whether Indians have modified the ancient Hindu theory of strictly quintal and tertian intervals by the introduction (due, Mr. Clements suggests, to Mohammedan influence) of septimal intervals, can only be established on evidence. If any people hears septimal intervals, the Indians and Greeks, with the fine ear which practised and the fine discrimination which recorded the niceties of the *genera* and the *grāmas*, would have been among the first to do it; but to establish the fact it requires, in the complete absence in their theoretical works of any hint that they did so, a broader basis of observation than is provided by the performance of a single singer.

With regard to the transilient scales, I received from the melodies sung in them a strong impression that they were in just intonation —that a major and minor Tone made a major Third, that the Sixth was just and not sharp. There is no reason, however, why tertian intervals (which this implies) should not have been accepted in pentatonic scales later, and yet the origin of these have lain originally in pure quintal harmony. An argument may be found to support this.

Quintal pentatonic scales are based on a series of five Fifths—say, C–G–D–A–E. Reducing these within the limits of an Octave, and relating them to a common tonic, we get the following scheme for the five pentatonics:

	Cents.	Ratios.	Scale on 'white' notes, as from C	G	D	A	E
C	1200	2	C	C	C	C	C
♭ B♭	996	16 : 9	...	...	♭ B♭	♭ B♭	♭ B♭
♯ A	906	27 : 16	♯ A	♯ A	...	...	...
♭ A♭	792	128 : 81	...	...	...	...	♭ A♭
G	702	3 : 2	G	G	G	G	...
F	498	4 : 3	...	F	F	F	F
♯ E	408	81 : 64	♯ E	...	...	...	...
♭ E♭	294	32 : 27	...	...	...	♭ E♭	♭ E♭
D	204	9 : 8	D	D	D	...	...
C	0	1	C	C	C	C	C

The worst scales—the least euphonious, those which involve the more abstruse fractions—are those of C and E; that of D is the best. This D scale

Ex. 191.

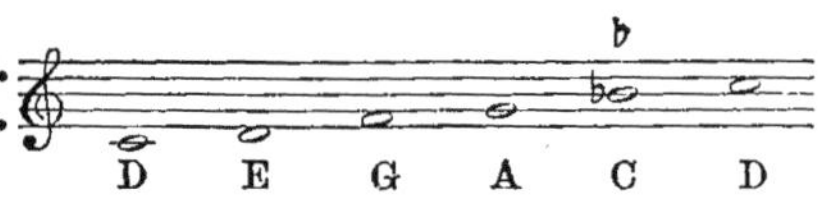

is the type, which goes under the name of *Sārang*, of a favourite form of pentatonic *Rāg*. We saw also (p. 70) that there was a decided preference in the Garhwālī songs for the A scale:

Ex. 192.

though not to the exclusion of the C and E scales.[1]

[1] In the *Journal of the English Folksong Society* (vol. xvi), Miss Gilchrist records her belief that the typical Scotch pentatonic is the G scale. A cursory glance at the first hundred or so in Petri's collection suggests that the Irish favourites are the G and A scales. (A song may be in a pentatonic scale although more than five distinct notes are touched in it, if it has only five *substantive* notes and the other one or two are used as passing notes.)

But the D and A scales (and G) are the best of the five only if the intervals are taken as strictly quintal; if tertian intervals are substituted, i. e. if 'merging' takes place, the five scales are equally 'good'. If, therefore, these particular scales are found to be the favourites in a country, it is an argument that all the pentatonics were in that country taken as strictly quintal, at any rate originally, though tertian intervals may have crept in later.

The *śruti* enters into music as one of three definite intervals. Just as there are three diatonic intervals (*svaras*), so there are three enharmonic intervals (*śrutis*). The diatonic intervals we have seen to be

Major Tone, $\frac{9}{8}$, 4 *śrutis*
Minor Tone, $\frac{10}{9}$, 3 *śrutis*
Semitone, $\frac{16}{15}$, 2 *śrutis*

and the enharmonic intervals are such intervals as correspond to a difference of one between the *śrutis* of the *svaras* (or are the various quotients of the fractions which answer to those *svaras*). The numbers 4, 3, and 2 may be handled in three ways so as to produce a difference of one; thus:

(*a*) $4-3 = 1$ *śruti*
$\frac{9}{8}\cdot\frac{9}{10} = \frac{81}{80} = 22$ cents.

This is the 'indicative' *śruti*, the 'Comma of Didymus'.

(*b*) $3-2 = 1$ *śruti*
$\frac{10}{9}\cdot\frac{15}{16} = \frac{25}{24} = 70$ cents (strictly, 70·6).

This is the 'small semitone'.

(*c*) $3+2-4 = 1$ *sruti*
$\frac{10}{9}\cdot\frac{16}{15}\cdot\frac{8}{9} = \frac{256}{243} = 90$ cents.

This is the 'Pythagorean Limma'.

But these intervals as such remain theoretical. They are actually sung only as increments of other larger intervals.[1] There is no case in any *Rāg* where two notes are separated, for instance, by the Comma of Didymus. That interval represents the difference between the two major Sixths (A and $\overset{\sharp}{\text{A}}$), or between the major and minor Tone (D and $\overset{\flat}{\text{D}}$). But both notes (A and $\overset{\sharp}{\text{A}}$, &c.) do not appear in the same *Rāg*; the *Rāg* contains the one or the other.

[1] 'Heterotone' would be a better name for *śruti* than the usual translation 'microtone'.

We may notice in passing that this principle extends to the *svaras* also. A *Rāg, Pilu* for instance, has an E and an E♭ with a D and a F on either side of them; but in a given passage either E or E♭ will occur, but not both as a rule. And the principle, though not so strictly carried out, may be traced with tones as well as semitones. It is not at all uncommon for a *Rāg,* especially in southern India, to omit a note in ascent, but its next door neighbour in descent. Two notes, A and B♭, being 'in' the scale an ascending passage will employ by preference G A–C, a descending C B♭–G; though quite possibly both notes will be used occasionally. The same thing is common enough in our own Folk-song:

Abroad as I was walking.[1]

Ex. 193.

Here the salient notes are clearly C, F, and B♭,[2] and it is interesting to see how the tetrachords C–F, F–B♭ are filled. In bars 1 and 13 we have the equivalent of

Ex. 194.

though both notes (D and E♭) are present in ascent and descent in bars 2 and 3. In bar 7 occurs

Ex. 195.

and in bars 9 and 11

Ex. 196.

[1] From the *Journal of the Folksong Society,* vol. iii, p. 124, No. 40.

The reader may wish to add G. But 'modes' are tetrachordal; the tetrachord hangs about them like the 'shame of the swaddling-clothes'; and the tetrachords are certainly not D–G, G–C.

In these instances a non-modal writer would be more likely to have employed

Ex. 197.  and Ex. 198. 

and he would probably have sharpened the F's. The principle is, then, broadly that between two salient notes modal melody tends to employ only one of two alternatives, and, for choice, that alternative which is nearest to the note which is being left, not to that which is being approached.

It is difficult to show this convincingly with regard to the *śruti*; but it may be seen in the grace-notes which occur like 'enclitics' in many Indian melodies, i.e. they belong to the note which is being quitted, not to that which is being approached:

Ex. 199. 

They are on the principle of the violinist's slide. In passing from C to G he does not use all the intermediate notes, but only the first few:

Ex. 200. 

Hence comes no doubt the statement that for southern India the quarter-tones (*śruti*) are 'confined to *grace*' (Day, p. 30). But that is not the usual acceptation of the word in the South. *Śruti* there means keynote. A singer has 'lost his *śruti*' when he sings out of tune; the drone strings of the *vīṇā* are called the *śruti*, and so on. This is clearly a transference of meaning from 'a nice distinction of pitch' to 'that which determines the pitch'.

But in the North *śruti* has retained its original meaning, nice distinction of pitch. There, however, its nature has been sometimes misapprehended. Stress has been laid on there being twenty-two of them, and the scale has come to be regarded as an octave with twenty-two stopping places. Consequently theoretical musicians are to be found who are prepared to sing from C to C, stopping at twenty-one places on the way. We have seen that this is wrong artistically, because melodies rarely use two of these, and never three, in succession. But it is wrong scientifically also. For the *śruti* did not arise as a division, equal or unequal, of the semitone. It has no independent existence. It is only a difference between two intervals considerably larger than itself. Thus the $\overset{\sharp}{A}$ which we reach from C through D, and the A reached through F or E differ by the interval $\overset{\sharp}{A}$–A ($\frac{27}{16} \times \frac{3}{5} = \frac{81}{80}$) the 'Comma of Didymus'.

Ex. 201.

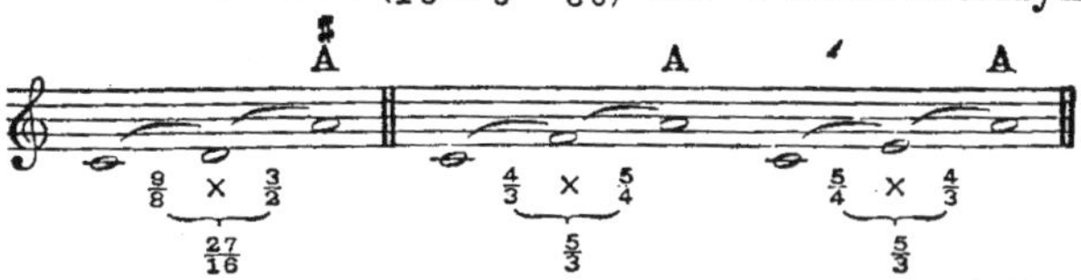

So also with

Ex. 202.

the *śruti* is not an independent interval, but an increment of, or a defalcation from, some larger one. We get in this a suggestion which will reconcile the North and South Indian connotations of the word. A *śruti* is not, as it has hitherto been understood to be, the *smallest* audible sound, but the *accurately* audible sound—that which is 'heard' in accurate relationship to some other. This position throws some doubt on Helmholtz's[1] account of the Greek quarter-tone (following Plutarch[2]) as a division ($\frac{32}{31} \times \frac{31}{30}$) of the semitone ($\frac{16}{15}$). It seems possible, at least, that as the Greek and Indian systems were alike in so many other respects, they were alike also in deriving their 'enharmonic' tones from a persistence in just intonation and a refusal to compromise, i. e. to temper.

It is hard for Europeans to realize the state of things here described; but we have occasional glimpses of it. The major Sixth,

Ex. 203.

for instance, tends to be sung as a larger interval (since the B is forced up by the harmony to be a major tone from A) than that in

[1] *Sensations of Tone*, English translation, 1875, p. 407.

[2] *De Musica*, chap. viii. He says the old players 'took the semitone as simple (A–B♭), not a compound interval (A $\overset{\sharp}{A}$ B♭). Later the semitone was divided.'

Ex. 204.

where the interval E–F♯ is a minor tone. The first of these is, in fact, what we have been speaking of as the interval C–$\overset{\sharp}{A}$, the second the interval C–A. The distinction between these two is also made use of in Schubert's *Ganymed* for a particular effect:

Ganymed. SCHUBERT.

Ex. 205.

Here the harmonies of the third and fourth bars wrench the melody up a major tone,[1] whereas the scale would demand in the third bar a minor tone; so that for two whole bars—the words 'strebt's hinauf! hinauf'—the voice is travelling at a pitch a fraction higher than normal, and admirably illustrates the meaning of the text, while at 'es schweben' it drops back (again owing to the harmonies) to normal pitch.

This example shows also the other two *śrutis*. The Comma of Didymus and the Pythagorean Limma are correlatives; the two together make up the diatonic semitone (22 + 90 = 112). The latter occurs, therefore, in the fifth bar of Ex. 205. The 'small semitone' appears also in the accompaniment of the next bar. The *locus classicus* for this interval is the Elizabethan madrigal, in which a minor Third is frequently, and with beautiful effect, substituted for a major Third, as a deliberate 'False Relation':

WEELKES, 1598.

Ex. 206.

or, by the reverse process, constitutes the peculiar charm of the 'Tierce de Picardie'.

There are also other '*śrutis*' in European employ. (1) The difference between an Octave and three major Thirds (1200 – 386

[1] C, the sixth of the scale, is normally a minor tone from B♭, the fifth. But the basses E♭ and F in the third and fourth bars are a major tone apart. And therefore the melody which they bear (the B♭ and C) must here be separated by a major tone. Similarly, in the fourth and fifth bars, where we have modulated to F minor, the F and the G (and therefore the C and the D) are a major tone apart.

×3 = 42 cents). It is present wherever, for instance, G♯ is taken as A♭. A fine example of this forms the climax of the introductory bars to the second Act of the *Walküre*. (2) The difference between four minor Thirds and an Octave (316 × 4 − 1200 = 64), of which a rather wooden example is to be found leading up to an entry of the C major subject in the overture to Smetana's *Bartered Bride*. (3) The difference between twelve Fifths and seven Octaves (702 × 12 − 1200 × 7 = 24). This occurs in a descending form in the six bars which follow Wotan's words 'So küsst er die Gottheit von dir' at the end of the *Walküre*, and, ascending, in the five bars which close the first of Vaughan Williams's *Five Mystical Songs*:

Ex. 207.

And the same fact is present, of course, whenever the whole tone scale is played (204 × 6 − 1200 = 24), the musical effect of which is closely comparable to that of the *Pratimadhyama* scales of India. Then there is that magnificent mounting bass which compasses a Fifth in seven semitones (112 × 7 − 702 = 82) towards the close of the Finale of Schubert's C major Symphony; and there are no doubt instances of other such intervals. The point is that we use enharmonic intervals for precisely the same reason as the Indians—for their jubilant or pathetic effect; only we do it in a different way. Equal temperament has nothing to do with this matter—we hear the effect in the orchestra and imagine it on the piano; though it has a great deal to do with the vocalization of a melody.

CHAPTER V

MODE

The terms 'scale' and 'mode' are frequently used as synonymous, because it is often unimportant to insist on the distinction between them. But in their essence they name two primary musical instincts. Scale is the expression of the melodic impulse, mode is ultimately the outcome of the rhythmic impulse. They are relative, not absolute terms; and in two ways. First, any given series of notes may be in a scale, or it may be in a mode, according to the moments of it which we are taking to be important. And, secondly, it can seldom be said that at any given point in a melody a change of mode or scale has taken place; the change requires to be 'established', and that is a matter of degree. There is a sense also in which scale 'is' established mode. We propose shortly to discuss these points.

A change of scale is a change in a prescribed order of notes brought about by the melodic impulse. It is a more or less violent change in pitch of some one note which results in musical 'effect', exhilarating, pathetic, &c. In the following Song of Somerset, 'Sovay, Sovay,' the pathetic flattening at (*a*) is a purely melodic

Sovay, Sovay.

Ex. 208.

effect. It causes the melody to droop a little at that point, and so to give value to the F♯ when it is restored later on. The ear has been cheated for the moment of the major scale it expected, and has been presented with another, the major scale with the flat seventh. It is owing to this species of deception which they involve that such devices are known as *Musica ficta*, feigned music. They come in the first place as vocal accommodations, but they stay as musical effects. They do not establish, they only suggest a new scale. If in this song the F♮'s had been the rule and the

F♯'s the exception, we should have said the melody was in another scale (of G) or in a mode (of C). For our present purpose, since we are discussing G not C, it is a change of scale.

A change of mode is a change in the relative importance not of one note, but of all, brought about by a shift of the rhythmic centre of gravity. The following Folk-song,[1] 'A sailor's life,' shows in its three versions a change both of scale and of mode. We may take the germ of the song to be contained in the pentatonic form marked I, which is placed for comparison between two derivatives, II and III.

A sailor's life.

Ex. 209.

I is a pentatonic 'Dor-aeolian' on D. II and III are only slightly veiled pentatonics, but two important changes have taken place. In II the notes of the scale have not been altered, but, by the rhythmical stress which is thrown upon it, G has become the tonic, and the mode is now a *Mixolydian on G*. In III, though the rhythmic points are not quite the same as in I yet they are not vitally different; but the addition of an F♯ implies a change of scale, which is now a *Mixolydian on D*.[2]

It is the custom to consider the C–c scale to be the primary

[1] From the *Journal of the Folksong Society*.

[2] A really beautiful instance of the musical process here involved is a shifting 'Ground' of Purcell's quoted on p. 176 of E. Walker's *History of Music in England*, 1907.

series of notes from which others (D–d, E–e, &c.) are derived, and of which they are modes. But it would be logically as defensible, and historically more correct to consider C–c as a mode of the D–d scale. The fact is that a mode when it is thoroughly established anywhere becomes the scale of that country, or countryside; thus, some of England sings by preference in the Mixolydian, some of it in the Dorian, and so on, Ireland in the Mixolydian and Aeolian. There can be little doubt that the difference between the *Sa-grāma* and the *Ma-grāma*, though it figures as a difference of scale,

Sa. C D E F G A♯ B C } or C D E F G A♯ B C }
Ma. C D E F G A B C } or C D E F♯ G A♯ B C }

was originally a difference of mode

Sa. C D E F G A♯ B C
Ma. F G A B C D♯ E F

Thus when mode is thoroughly established it comes to be regarded as scale.

This distinction between mode and scale is commonly thought to apply only to an antiquated style of music. But the thing is perfectly well known to us in modern music whenever modulation[1] takes place, as a familiar melody from Brahms's First Symphony shows:

Ex. 210.

The modulation comes at (*a*) in the form of a pathetic flattening of the obvious note, and at (*b*) as a heightening of the meaning by a shift of the melodic centre of gravity. Every musician feels the effect at (*a*) to be quite different from that at (*b*); the first is a difference of scale, the second of mode, and both involve a temporary change of key; the first is like a mechanical, the second like a chemical change. Without some such connecting link as this with our own music we are apt to look on unusual scales and modes, especially when they display such intricacy as the Indian scale (*grāma*) and mode (*mūrchaṇa*) and individualized mode (*rāga*),

[1] i.e. modification, taking another 'mode', or way of doing things.

as merely weird and fanciful. They are, however, formulas which are doing all they can to express the facts of unharmonized melody, if we will let them ; and we should approach them in that spirit if we were not hindered by our harmonic preconceptions. For we have to forget a good deal before we hear the beauty in such as this :

Ex. 211.

My heart rejoiced, seeing the locks on the forehead of Rāma wave, when he with ease and grace put down the pride of the giant, Mārīcha, and broke the bow of Śiva at the beck of the sage, Viśvamitra.

If we could treat it as in D minor, with a mere D drone without harmonies, we should be happier ; the last bar would then have finality. But the drone is G, and for us this leaves the tune in the air. It takes a long time before we become accustomed to this queer way of looking at things, and can take it as it presents itself. We keep wishing to accommodate the tune by appropriate harmonies at this or that point, and do not easily realize that these introduce subsidiary modes (which we can, however, in virtue of those harmonies, subsume under the main one), but that a change of drone (without harmonies), by introducing a subsidiary mode, merely destroys the principal mode.

As a preliminary to the consideration of Indian modes we may review our own (omitting the F–f and B–b modes as obsolete) :

Ex. 212.

They all consist of similar tetrachords ; those on C, D, and E being arranged as disjunct to one another, those on G and A as conjunct.[1]

[1] This is not a mere piece of theory. It will be found that melodies in the G and A modes (the Mixolydian and Aeolian) throw much emphasis on the seventh note, the terminal of the second tetrachord, which those in the other modes do not, at any rate to the same extent.

The mode of D was, we said, the historically prior of all these modes. Its tetrachords are disjunct and similar. We may keep them disjunct, but make them dissimilar; in which case we get, for instance, the A mode transposed down to D:

Ex. 213.

Also in these two forms of the D scale we may sharpen the leading note, in which case we get respectively the 'ascending' minor:

Ex. 214.

and the 'harmonic' minor:

Ex. 215.
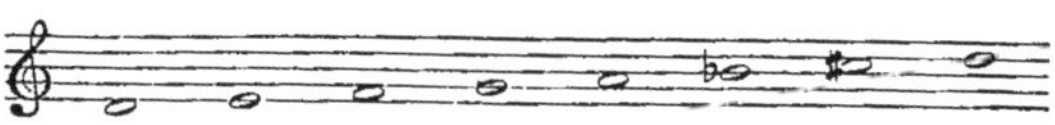

By these three methods, (1) similar tetrachords, (2) dissimilar tetrachords, and (3) scalar alteration, we can account for all the modes we know. There are of course other ways of accounting for them, but this is the plan on which the Indians have worked; only they have carried it further and included every practicable combination of both tetrachords.

With them modes are 'pure' (*śuddha*), or 'mixed' (*mishra, sankīrṇa*), or 'altered' (*chāyālaga, sālanka*).

They are 'pure' when the two tetrachords of which they are composed are similar. In theory every note of a *Rāg* should be consonant (*samvādī*) to some other, and the effect of this would be to make the tetrachords similar, as we have seen that they are in the European modes. But they are similar in others also, such as

Bhairau.

Ex. 216.

where every note is consonant to some other, and C doubly consonant; and

Toḍi.

Ex. 217.
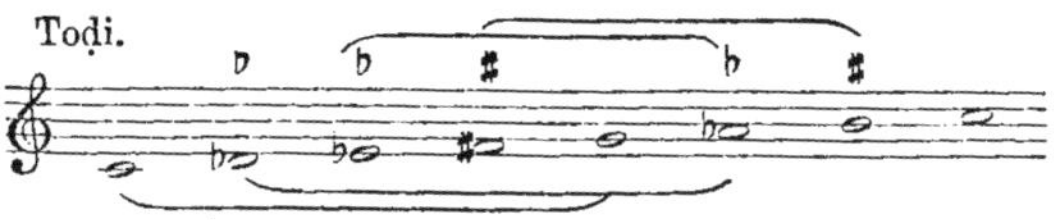

in which not C, but A♭ is doubly consonant. Modes are 'mixed' when the tetrachords are dissimilar, as in

Bilāskhānī Toḍī.

Ex. 218. 

in which C and A♭ are doubly consonant, but B has no consonant. The Greeks also knew these modes, called them by the same name, *tonoi miktoi*, and defined them in the same way.

'Altered' modes. The words *chāyālaga* and *sālanka* mean different things. *Chāyālaga*, lit. 'shadowy', is used in the Panjab, and probably elsewhere, to mean a mode in which the B has been flattened (or the B♭ sharpened). *Sālanka* is not a Sanskrit word at all. It is a piece of *memoria technica*.[1] The seventy-two *melakartas* are divided into thirty-six with F♮, *Śuddhamadhyama*, and thirty-six with F♯, *Pratimadhyama*; and *Sālanka* is the first *melakarta* of the *Pratimadhyamas*. It therefore came to be used as a general term for any *Rāg* that had the F sharpened. At present *Chāyālaga* seems to be used in Hindostan for both the adventitious B♭ and F♯, and *Sālanka* similarly in the Carnatic. Simple instances would be:

Jhinjoti.

Ex. 219. 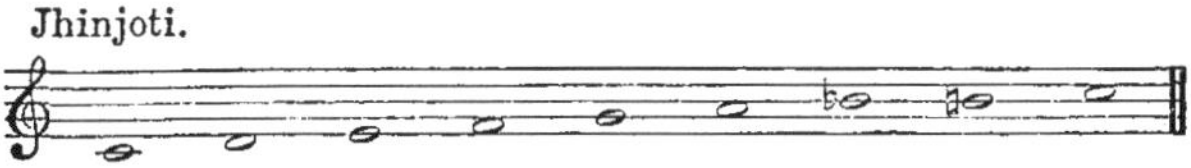

Behāg.

Ex. 220. 

in these the B♭ and F♯ are alternative, not additional. The principle is extended to other notes, E♭, for instance, in

Desh.

Ex. 221. 

This does not account, however, for all the varieties, and the subject needs more investigation; still it carries us some way. All three kinds ('pure', 'mixed', and 'altered') are known to Bharata, though he names them differently. The 'mixture' of dissimilar tetrachords he calls the 'twilight of the *Rāg*' (*jāti-sādhāraṇa*). For the 'altered' *Rāg* he gives no name, but he

[1] The high-sounding names of the seventy-two South Indian *melakartas* are arranged on a plan so that those who know the key of it can tell at once from the name what the constitution of the particular *melakarta* is.

explains[1] that the *Ma-grāma* can be formed *directly*, as we should say 'modally', from the *Sa-grāma*

C D E | F G A♯ B C
| F G A B C D♯ E F

and also *by reckoning* (*saṃkhyena*), as we should say 'by scale',

C D E F G A♯ B C
C D E F♯ G A♯ B C

He speaks also of the lower tetrachord (*mandragati*, lit. low-going) and upper tetrachord (*tāragati*, high-going), but he does not explain, apparently, how the 'twilight' *jātīs* were put together. He tells us, for instance, that the compound (*vikṛta*) *jātī*, *ṣaḍjakaiśikī*, is made up of

Ṣaḍjī.

Ex. 222.

and

Gāndhārī.

Ex. 223.

but he does not explain which elements of the simple *jātīs* were taken to form the compound. A knowledge of this would contribute a good deal to the history of *Rāga*.

Students of ancient Greek music agree in this, that there came a time when the *Harmoniā* was replaced by the *Tonos*. The change may have taken centuries; it was placed on record by Ptolemy (A.D. 150). The *Harmoniā*[2] (lit. joint, union, apposition), which was a section of the gamut consisting of two conjunct tetrachords, was not associated with any definite pitch, but adaptable according to the singer's needs. The *Tonos* (lit. tension, pitch) was likewise a section of the gamut, but consisted of two tetrachords *plus* the disjunctive tone (which might be between them or beyond them) and formed a complete octave, each *Tonos* being calculated from the same pitch. There seems to be no record in the ancient writers of the *Tonoi* having been sung upon a drone-note; Gevaert makes no

[1] *Nāṭyaśāstra*, adh. 28, śl. 35.

[2] Monro explains this as 'adjustment' in the sense of 'tuning'. It seems not impossible that it names the 'joining' of two tetrachords to form a heptachord.

mention of it, and *to ison*, the modern word for drone, is not in Liddell & Scott. But Pachtikos[1] speaks of the drone as being 'an indisputable relic of the original musical system'. And though the silence of so observant a people as the Greeks is difficult to get over, it is just possible that they took so obvious a thing for granted.[2] In the *Harmoniā* the notes were related according to their 'functions' (*kata dunamin*); the extremes of the tetrachord were 'fixed' (*hestēkotes*), the intermediate notes were 'movable' (*kīneisthai pephūkotes*, or *kīnoumenoi*) and were distributed within a certain prescribed 'locus of variation' (*topos tēs kinēseōs*). The 'functions' of the intermediate notes meant therefore, apparently, their relations to the extreme notes (of the tetrachord). In the *Tonos*, on the other hand, we see a segment of a stereotyped scale (of two octaves) in which the 'functions' of notes within the tetrachord are, though they still exist, no longer of importance, but the individual notes of the scale are related according to their 'position' (*kata thesin*) with regard to some one of the notes of this scale taken as tonic and, in India certainly—in Greece perhaps—supplied with a drone.

Unfortunately it is not possible at present to give such a detailed account of the Indian *Mūrchaṇa* (the equivalent of *Harmoniā*); more will perhaps be possible when Bharata's *Nāṭyaśāstra* has been adequately translated. He speaks of the Predominant (*aṃśa*) as the foundation and source of musical charm (*rāga*), as determining the tetrachord (*aṅga*) above (*tāra*) and below (*mandra*), as distinctly perceptible in a combination of different notes, as a prominent (*balin*) note provided with consonances (*samvādī*) and assonances (*anuvādī*), and as giving birth to the initial (*graha*) and final (*nyāsa*) and to three other notes of which the meaning is not given[3] (*vinyāsa*, *apanyāsa*, and *samnyāsa*), but which help in some way to constitute the tetrachord. The initial and final are definitely said to begin and end the tetrachord, and the initial is always a Predominant. Finally, the Predominant may, according to the particular mode, be any one of five notes; and this seems to fix the meaning of Predominant definitely as 'the note of conjunction of

[1] *Aismata Hellēnica*, Athens, 1905, Introd., lviii. *To ison touto, hoper anantirrētōs einai bebaion leipsanon prohyparchousēs harmonikēs mousikēs, ēcheitai*, &c.

[2] There is no mention of the drone in the Sanskrit theorists either.

[3] But at least it is clear that they named relationships to the terminal (*nyāsa*), and are therefore analogues to the Greek *kīnoumenoi*.

two tetrachords': for if modern Indian *rāgas* are analysed they will be found, if 'pure' or 'mixed', to contain from one to five possible points of conjunction; if 'altered', more.

So that the *aṃśa* [1] seems to take exactly the place of the *mesē* in Greek music, and has the same sort of satellites round it. *Madhyama*, 'middle,' accurately translates *mesē*, and it is on the face of it likely that they named originally the same musical fact. We must digress for a moment to discuss *madhyama*.

It is noticeable that only two notes of the scale have names with an assignable meaning—*madhyama*, middle, and *pañcama*, fifth. *Ṣaḍja* ('born of six') might make a similar claim; but the explanations of it have hitherto been fanciful.[2] *Madhyama* and *pañcama* are next door neighbours, and of these *madhyama* appears to be the older name, i.e. to be applicable to an earlier state of the scale; for (1) they can hardly be contemporaries, otherwise they would have been called *caturtha* (fourth) and *pañcama*, and (2) since no other note is named by an ordinal number this particular note *pañcama* appears to be so named for distinction, possibly from the *madhyama* (with which it constantly disputed the hegemony). From the earliest times the scale is quoted as consisting of seven notes, the eighth being a repetition; and the *madhyama* divides these seven, in the same way as the *mesē*, into two tetrachords. It may be added that as the other four notes of the scale (*Ṛśabha*, *Gāndhāra*, *Dhaivata*, and *Nishāda*) are all apparently place names, they may have been adopted into the scale as the local way of passing from one end of the tetrachord to the other, and hence are of the same nature as the Greek *kīnoumenoi*; and this survives also in the modern scale, for it is these notes, and no others, which are liable to be made flat (*komal*) and very flat (*atikomal*).

But by Bharata's time all the eight notes are clearly defined; they are, as we should write them, (C) D E F G A B C, because the old theory names the upper extremity of the *svara*. The *madhyama* is the note G in a scale C–C, not, as before, in a heptachord D–C; and he has a great deal to say about it. It is the 'eldest' (*pravara*), the 'imperishable' (*anāśin*), the 'note fixed by the singers of the *Sāmaveda* in the *Gandharvakalpa*' (musical treatise), the 'note

[1] The word means a 'part' of a whole. Since it appears in manuscripts indifferently with *aṅga* ('part'), which is a name for the tetrachord, *aṃśa* may originally have meant tetrachord (i.e. 'part' of the whole *mūrchaṇa*), and later the note on which the tetrachord started.

[2] See Chapter X.

which would still subsist though all the other notes of the mode should disappear'. This last delightful hyperbole could not have been applied to the *aṃśa*, which, though it regulated the notes in its tetrachords, was itself liable to be shifted, and the tetrachords with it.

In modern music *Pa* is the 'imperishable' note, i. e. it is never sharpened or flattened as are the other notes, with the exception of *Sa*. So that we see here perhaps the transition from the heptachord consisting of two conjunct tetrachords meeting at the *madhyama*, to an octachord based on the Fifth-relationship of *Sa* and *Pa* (the new *madhyama*) with the movable *aṃśa* doing the work of the old fixed *madhyama*. In other words we have the transition from the *Harmoniā* to the *Tonos*.

An instance will make this clearer:

Ex. 224.

is a *mūrchaṇa* with two similar tetrachords and with its *madhyama* at A. A, then, is the note of greatest emphasis. Songs sung in this mode came to have a certain character whatever it might be; let us say, sombre. They would then lie on the whole in the upper part of the compass of the mode—not necessarily in the upper register of the voice, for the mode might be taken at any pitch—and the Predominant note (early *madhyama*, later *aṃśa*) would consequently lie low in the song. In order that the low position of the A, on which the character of the song depended, should be effectively felt, a note about the position of F, let us say, assumed the character of fundamental note—the *mūrchaṇa* had of course, as such, no fundamental—and if instruments were used, this fundamental was furnished with a drone. Thus the *mūrchaṇa* (*Harmoniā*) passes into the *Rāg* (*Tonos*):

Ex. 225.

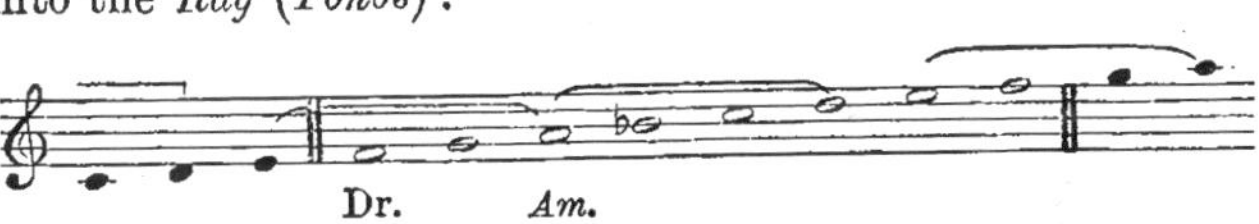

and the *madhyama* (A) of the *mūrchaṇa*, the meeting point of two similar tetrachords, becomes the *aṃśa* of the *Rāg*, the central note of the *tessitura*, while a new note, C, is now the 'imperishable', &c., *madhyama* of the *Rāg*. But in the new *Rāg* there was no need to have the *tessitura* always in one place, since the character of songs that might be sung in it varied; and it might be moved, without doing much violence to the *Rāg*, to any note except B♭ and E (of this particular *Rāg*), because at neither of these points could the *aṃśa* be the meeting point of two tetrachords. If it *was* moved to either of these points, B♭ for instance, there was a tendency to flatten the E and so to develop a different *Rāg*.

Let us try to realize this in a melody:

Shardula-vikridita.[1]

Ex. 226.

If we put away all thoughts of a tonic as we understand it and simply pick out the most prominent notes of this tune, we should probably say that in the first eight bars they were:

Ex. 227.

in the next six:

Ex. 228.

and in the last six:

Ex. 229.

i. e. G and A twice, and D, E, F, and high and low C once each. The scale therefore might be written:

Ex. 230.

It is difficult for us not to attach more importance to the low C than is here shown; both because the tune appears to end there, and

[1] *Shardula-vikridita* is the name of a Sanskrit metre; and the rhythmical aspect of this melody is discussed in Chapter VIII.

because, if we emphasize that note, the tune is in our major mode, i. e. in one of the only two that we know. But the tune is, like most Folk-song, circular; after the end it goes back to the beginning and finishes there—in this case probably with the phrase,

Ex. 231. 

though the D is not thereby made the tonic either; in fact, there is no tonic exactly in our sense. Also, we do not easily put ourselves into the frame of mind of a person who knows not two modes, but from 62 to 162, and are not so easily content to leave off up in the air, so to say.

But though there is no tonic as we understand it, there is a Predominant (G at the beginning, A in the middle, and either G or A at the end of the song). So that the song is conceived as in one of two modes (*mūrchaṇa*).

I

Ex. 232. 

or

II

Ex. 233. 

Now Indian songs, and probably other non-harmonic songs, are seldom sung twice in the same way, however small the variation each time. Some singers would tend to give prominence to the G of I, some to the A of II. There would also be many songs similar to this one which might be considered to be in mode I or mode II according to the particular singer. These would form a class; and the class would depend largely on the character of the words—sad songs in one class, merry in another, and so on. The words of this particular song are of a reflective nature. And reflection is associated with a low 'lie' of the voice. So that songs in these modes might well keep the G, or the A, for their Predominant if jubilant, but if reflective might drag it down to the consonant (*samvādi*) note D, or E.

Next, if we suppose that with the progress of music this general tendency to have a high Predominant for some songs and a low one for others becomes more defined and scientific, the need would arise to determine precisely how high or how low; and a note would be taken and enforced from which to measure the height of the Predominant. This would be done solely for the musical reason of giving more decided character to the tune, of making explicit what was before implicit. If then a low 'lie', such as D or E, was required by the character of the song, and C was chosen as the measuring note or drone, its 'mode' would now become a *Rāg* (particularized mode) of the form

Ex. 234. 

or

Ex. 235. 

The *Rāg* of this particular song is stated to be *Manḍ*, a *Rāg* used in the late evening (a possible time for reflection), and it will be seen on turning to the list on p. 151, No. 12, that the Predominant of *Manḍ* is given in one part of India as D and in another as E.

A musical purpose of importance is served by this Predominant and its consonant. One of the most effective resources of melody is appoggiatura, i. e. the delaying of a note, the raising of pleasing expectations. This melody from Tristan, for instance,

Ex. 236. 

owes almost its whole force to the enhancement by appoggiatura of some simple scheme such as:

Ex. 237. 

The essential condition of appoggiatura is that the delaying note should be felt to be only transitory and the delayed note to be relatively final or permanent. This is effected in our music by the harmony, expressed or implied, which moves on from substantive to passing chord and forces the delaying note to yield. Thus (substantive chords (*a*) and passing chords (*b*)):

Ex. 238.

And the same is true when the harmonies are only implied, as in the first four bars of this passage from the Ninth Symphony:

Ex. 239.

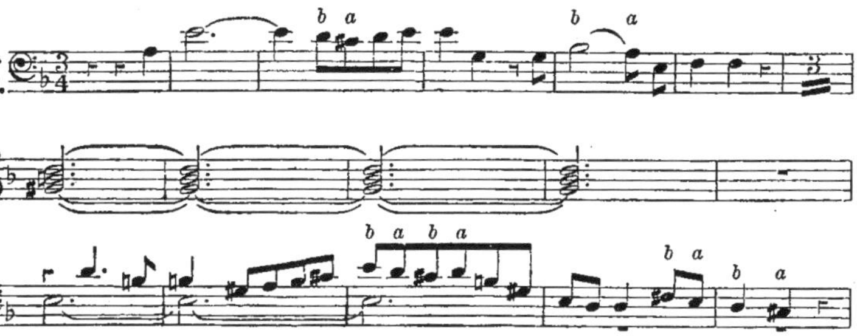

Here the harmonies, implied in the first five bars and expressed in the last five, are:

Ex. 240.

and at every place marked *b* the melody gets a purchase on one of the constituent notes of these.

But when there are no chords at all in question the substantive nature of the delayed note has to be established in some other way. In Indian, as no doubt in ancient Greek and probably (see Chapter VI) in the ecclesiastical melodies, this is done by the Predominant (*aṃśa*, *mesē*, *reciting note*); notes receive the force of appoggiaturas as they delay this. Thus, in the melody with which we are dealing, D being Predominant and G its consonant (both established by long association) and C the drone (generally expressed), we have appoggiaturas (*b*)

Ex. 241.

leading to a substantive note (*a*) which is either the *aṃśa* (D), or its consonant (G), or the drone (C). This is a particularly easy *Rāg* for us, because C, G, and D are notes we should have no difficulty in feeling to be important; but when, in other *Rāgs*, D and A, or E♭ and A♭, are *aṃśa* and *saṃvādī* it is not so easy to feel the musical impulse, though it is not hard to understand the principle.

As we have been tracing points in common between Indian and Greek music, we may notice two more. One, that the salient distinction between the two *grāmas* is found in the four notes, F G A B of the *Sa-grāma* and F G A B♮ of the *Ma-grāma*; and this was precisely the distinction between the Greek 'lesser complete' and 'greater complete' systems. Only the problem presented itself differently. In Greece the scales were:

Ex. 242.

and

Ex. 243.

and in India

Ex. 244.

and

Ex. 245.

The other point of resemblance lies in an apparent recognition of absolute pitch. The lowest note of the Greek systems (the *proslambanomenon*) was of the pitch,

Ex. 246.

and the lowest note of the *vīṇā*, the oldest instrument of India, is that same A. It is difficult to say how far Indians were ever, or are now, conscious of absolute pitch. There is an interesting comparison of the notes of the scale to the cries of animals. *Sa* is the note of the peacock. *Ri*, of the *chātaka*, the bird of the rainy season. *Ga*, of the goat. *Ma*, of the crane. *Pa*, of the *koïl*, generally translated cuckoo, but bearing no resemblance in its vocal achievement to our bird; it hammers out a single note when making love in the spring, and its mate joins in, invariably at the distance of a tone, and perhaps a rival lover at the distance of a semitone. *Dha*, of the frog. *Ni*, of the elephant. This has been quoted as showing that the scale was conceived as a matter of absolute pitch; and there is some evidence that the cries of animals always keep the same pitch. It may be so: it would require special knowledge to decide this point. On the other hand, the musicians of to-day have no name for and no means of determining absolute pitch; and they are not usually backward in coining names for, or in devising simple methods of putting into operation, any ideas they may possess.

The theory of *grāma* has remained barren, just because it was a mere scientific tabulation and did not sufficiently take account of the whole musical fact. It is true that the system of the Carnatic is arranged in accordance with it, and that the musicians of Hindostan hold it as a pious belief. But the musical science of South India is sadly over elaborated; and that of the North has followed quite another classification (see Chapter VI). The essence of the modern music lies in its numerous and intricate *Rāgs*, which, being modes calculated from one tonic and having the compass of an octave, correspond in so far to the *Tonoi*; but which again are very unlike them on account of their being sections not of one scale common to all, but of a variety of scales which practically refuse to be coordinated in Northern India, though not so much so in the South. Indian music has in fact retained in full force what, after the introduction of the *Tonoi*, Greek musicians only faintly felt, that distinctive *ēthos* of which Plato and Aristotle spoke so enthusiastically.[1]

Broadly speaking this transition from the heptachord (*mūrchaṇa*,

[1] This may explain why, even to a foreigner, the *Rāgs* in the North seem to have more individuality, and why the tone of voice in which natives of Hindostan speak of Carnatic music sounds a little apathetic, whereas Southerners, though for the sake of association they like their own *Rāgams* best, always seem interested in a Hindostani singer.

harmoniā) to the octachord (*rāg*, *tonos*) is the passage from the domination of the Fourth to that of the Fifth, from vocal to instrumental music. The voice discovers the consonance of the Fourth before that of the Fifth. Its upper notes are the more powerful, and the overtones accordingly more audible. Consequently it is in singing the upper notes that the desire to reach a consonant note chiefly makes itself felt. A bass voice, for instance, is singing . The E above it sounds clearly in his ear: but it is beyond his compass; he therefore takes the lower E as the most obvious consonance. With instruments, however, the case is reversed. It is the lower notes that are the most powerful and yield the clearest overtones; and with these the Fifth comes to be appreciated more than the Fourth. In this respect, besides that mentioned above, the music of the Carnatic shows signs of greater age—of having begun earlier that is, and lived longer, and reached a further, not necessarily a higher, point of development. The *aṃśa* is there less a vital element of *Rāgam*; musicians often cannot tell you which note is *aṃśa*, and the songs make little account of it. This shows that the consonance of the Fourth, which the principle of *aṃśa* emphasizes, is less keenly felt there. And again the songs tend to close on the tonic or the Fifth, whereas in the North there is no such preference; they may end anywhere, but do, for choice, on the first note or with the first phrase of the song, on whatever note it may bring them to rest. Here, for instance, is a typical Carnatic phrase (cp. Ex. 379):

Ex. 247.

with the tune ranging down and up and down again over a Fifth and closing with some pomp on the drone note; as against this Hindostani phrase (cp. Ex. 380):

Ex. 248.

&c.

which closes, it is true, on the same drone, but seems to pretend that it has reached it by an accident, and strongly emphasizes the Fourth (C) of the mode which is in this *Rāg* (*Mālkos*) the Predominant.

CHAPTER VI

RĀGA

I'll take my pipe and try
The Phrygian melody;
  Which he that hears
  Lets through his ears
A madness to distemper all the brain;
  Then I another pipe will take
  And Doric music make
To civilize with graver notes our wits again.

RANDOLPH.

THE *Rāgs* of Hindostan vary[1] so much with the locality (those of the Carnatic less so) that there seemed to be no better way of showing them than to place in parallel columns the *Rāg* as given by different authorities (see the Table of *Rāgs*, opposite). In the first column appear sixty-three *Rāgs* as given me by Ashreka Ganga Rām, whose teacher was Balwant Rao of Gwālior, a state which has a high reputation for music. Ashreka seemed to be particularly sure of his knowledge; and from no one else was I fortunate enough to get any certain information about the *Rāgs* which employ quarter-tones (see Nos. 2, 26, 33, 35, 36, 40, 41, 49 in App. II). The second column is taken from the *Bālsangīt-bodh* (Juvenile Singing Tutor) of T. B. Sahasrabuddhe, of the Poona Gayan Samāj (singing school). The third column is extracted from a list of eighty-three *Rāgs* in B. A. Pingle's *Indian Music* (Bombay, 1898);

[1] All the same, a *Rāg* is one thing, not several. It is, as will be seen, so sharply characterized that although in this or that respect one *Rāg* trenches on the domain of another, yet it never does so in all respects, and therefore a change of one of its constituent notes does not obscure its individuality; just as a man through all sorts of not easily definable varieties of vocabulary or pronunciation, or even grammar, may yet be speaking pure English. This is what an Indian believes, although he will tell you in the same breath that the *Rāgs* are to be found in their purity only in the school of music to which he belongs. The true *Rāg*, of which all those with which the traveller meets are manifestations, is stored up in the heavens—or in the bosom of the most educated musician, whoever he may be.

the mordents show where he places the *mūrchhaṇas* (grace notes), and the *mūrchhaṇa* comes as a rule on the *aṃśa*; as these *mūrchhaṇas* are generally a Fourth or a Fifth apart the list confirms the view that the *aṃśa* was placed at the limits of the tetrachords. The list in the fourth column was given me, in response to a request for the thirty *commonest* and most popular *Rāgs*, by Upendrakisor Ray of Calcutta; and of these he named Nos. 2, 10, 11, 14, 32, and 60 as quite the commonest of all. 'This list', he writes, 'was obtained by analysing a collection of more than one thousand songs. But its value is somewhat impaired by the fact that most of these songs were popular, not classical. Writers of popular songs are not always good musicians, so their opinion as to the *rāgas* has to be accepted with some reserve; the "popular" Behāg, for instance, is C D E F G A B♭ C, popular Lalit is C D♭ E F G A♭ B C, popular Multān is C D E♭ E♮ F G A♭ A♮ B♭ B♮ C' (as compared with Nos. 60, 42, and 41). With regard to the descriptive epithets, which are interesting to compare, and which on the whole agree with those of the second column, he says—'I give them with a good deal of diffidence; in fact I am not very sure about the majority of them. The quality of restraint is a predominating feature of Indian music, and this precludes any free exhibition of the emotions. Our gaiety and sadness often merge into each other: our most impassioned passages fail to stir anybody up. There is any amount of enjoyment of the deepest kind, but it is undemonstrative and reposeful; it leads not to action but to abstraction.'

In these lists the notes shown by a crotchet head are those which are comparatively lightly touched; which are (1) used in ascent only or descent only, as the B♮ and B♭ in No. 11, or (2) are more or less optional, as the F and F♯ in No. 63. In this *Rāg* the usage is E F E and G F♯ G, never, as a rule, E F♯ E or G F G; while in the passage from E to G, or the reverse, either an F or an F♯ may be used, but F♯ more commonly is used. This is very much the same as the mediaeval *Musica ficta.* And (3) some *Rāgs* are on their way from being transilient to being complete; though all the notes are potentially there, some of them are as a rule jumped. This is the case in No. 60, where the D and the A are occasionally heard, but never dwelt upon. It did not seem worth while to go into the details of each *Rāg* in this matter, even if sufficient and accurate knowledge had been forthcoming; but these three principles throw a good deal of light on the conception of *Rāg*.

The ♭ or ♯ over a note means the lowering or raising by some kind of *śruti*, see p. 117.

The mark [=] under a note shows the Predominant (*aṃśa*).

Graha [Gr] and *Nyāsa* [Ny] are respectively the notes on which a melody is supposed to begin or end; this rule seems not always to be obeyed.[1] The final note has nothing like the importance it has in harmonized music.

Śuddha [Shud] means 'pure'; *Chāyālaga* [Chāyā] means 'transitional' (from *Chāyā* shadow); *Sankirṇa* [Sank] means 'mixed'; and *vakra* [vakr] is literally 'crooked' and means that the notes are taken not in direct order from *Sa* to *Sa*, but that the *Rāg* has certain melodic figures as characteristics.

The twenty-four hours are divided into eight watches, beginning at 6 a.m. The Hindus attach much importance to, and are wonderfully unanimous as to, the ascription of a *Rāg* to a particular hour of the day or season of the year,[2] although 'advanced' musicians may be found among them who say it has no meaning. A musical distinction, however, may be extracted from the *Rāgs* themselves, independently of the melodies sung in them or of the words to which these are set. Taking column 4, an analysis shows that if we may divide the *Rāgs* into 'sad' and 'merry', the 'sad' have an average of three flats to an average of two flats in those which are 'merry'. Again, if we divide them into morning and evening *Rāgs*, the morning have an *aṃśa* ranging about G, the evening about E. And the same thing, though in a less marked degree, may be deduced independently from the second column.

[1] And this makes it probable that it is not the true explanation. There is another, quite different. The *Graha* is the note which an individual singer chooses for his *Sa*. Thus if a bass voice chooses C, a tenor would take F, and a soprano B♭. The *Graha* is therefore the 'clef'. And this seems to be in complete agreement with the statement in Bharata that the *Graha* is identical with the *aṃśa*. It seems probable that *graha* originally meant the upper and *nyāsa* the lower extremity of the tetrachord (*aṅga*), and that these meanings have been forgotten.

[2] The first thing, sometimes the only thing, that an Indian who is not very familiar with the science of music can tell you about a particular *Rāg* which is being performed is that it is a morning, or that it is an evening *Rāg*—though this perhaps does not prove more than that the *Rāgs* are as a matter of fact confined in their performance to the appropriate time of day.

So that there is a real musical basis for this ascription of time of day and of *ēthos*. The ascription of time of year is possibly more fanciful.

But the truer explanation of this deep-seated feeling is more likely to lie in the history of *Rāga,* as far as we may hope to know it. What is antecedently probable, and, indeed, is evident from the data in the first two chapters of this book, is that songs were sung long before *Rāga* as such was formulated. The Hindu account is that there were four sources of *Rāg*: (1) local tribal song, (2) poetical creations, (3) the devotional songs of the mystics, and (4) the labours of the scientific musicians. The principal ground for this belief is, no doubt, that all four causes are in full operation in India to-day, and are evolving the *Rāgs* of the next thousand years; a secondary reason for thinking it to be the case is to be found in the names of *Rāgs* such as (1) *Kānaḍā*, the Carnatic; (2) *Hindol,* a swing; (3) *Jogi,* a mystic; (4) *Sārang,* from Sārañgadeva, a musician of the thirteenth century. The most important of these sources, because the most constant and widespread and unconscious, is the first—tribal song. Unfortunately, we do not yet possess nearly sufficient data to enable us to trace the actual formation of *Rāga* from this source, for India; but we may get an idea of it from our own Folk-song.

The fourteen versions of a song variously called 'The seeds of love', 'The sprig of thyme', &c., given in the annexed example, have been taken from the volumes of the *English Folk-song Society's Journal,* and one of them from Sharp's *Folk-songs of Somerset.* When the English counties have been thoroughly explored, there will prove to be not fourteen, but very likely forty or four hundred of such versions. The first seven of these are, however, enough to show how a melody may take various shapes and yet centre in a common mode; and also how by a slight shift of the centre of gravity, brought about by the battle of its several phrases for supremacy, the melody slips from one mode to another. At the end of each melody is set the scale in which it appears to lie, with the strong (*balin*) and weak (*alpa*) notes marked, and after these the name of the *Rāg* to which in principle, though not, of course, in detail, this scale corresponds.

Supposing a variety of scales to have been brought into use by tribal song from various sources, next comes the poet and weaves his mythology round them. He speaks of six original *Rāgs* which were *śuddha* (pure). The six are variously given. The six of the *Rāgavibodha*, as authoritative as any, are, though under other names, Nos. 13, 26, 37, 47, 49, 51. Of these, modes were taken, sometimes called *mūrchaṇa* (rise and fall), sometimes *jāti* (species). The next step was to cross the *jātis* and produce hybrids[1] (*Chāyālaga, Sankirṇa, Sālanka, Miśra*, &c.). The poet speaks also of the six original *Rāgs* having wives (*bhārya*) and sons (*putra*), and it seems hardly worth while to translate these into the plain prose of 'mode' and 'hybrid'. The exact pedigree of the *putras* seems to be irrecoverable: their names are all there (though no two lists give them alike), but not a trace of form or feature.

Meanwhile the philosopher has been at work upon the psychology of the music, and, without any special theories as to the emotional value or the 'mental effect' of this or that note or combination, determines on general grounds the *ēthos* of the *Rāg*, its appropriateness to occasion or to circumstance, or its effect upon the body, or its affinities with the various affections of the spirit or aspirations of the soul. These views linger in some of the names of the *Rāgs*: *Dīn-ka-(pūria)*, 'of the day', *Shām-(kaliān)*, 'evening', *Basant*, 'spring', (*Gaurī-)mano-hāri*, 'pleasing to the mind'; or in the legends about them, as of *Dīpak* (= *Māravā*, No. 49), which enflamed not only the mind, but the body of the singer so that even the Jumna could not put out the fire. Descriptive names of this kind were commoner and more elaborate in old days. The famous *Mahā-vyut-patti* (Sanskrit-Tibetan vocabulary, seventh century or later) has a list of sixty *Rāgs*, the translations of a few of which are—'with a voice like the thunder-cloud', 'like the trumpeting of the elephant', 'like a sparrow', 'like the serpent king', 'like Indra', or again, 'smooth', 'refined', 'making fully to comprehend', 'not puffed up', 'delighting every organ', 'having the chief voice in all sorts of sounds', and so forth.

Last of all, when by these three processes the number of *Rāgs* had reached hundreds or thousands, came the mathematically-minded musician who tabulated the scales as deviations from a normal scale (*grāma*), calculated the departures in quarter-tones (*śruti*), and rung the 13678 changes (*prastāra*) on the seven notes

[1] I have been unable, however, to find any explanation of the way in which this was done.

(*svara*); reduced the 108 traditional ways of counting time by syllable (*akṣara*), i.e. a development from the longs and shorts of poetry, to thirty-five ways of counting it by time-unit (*mātrā*,[1] lit. syllable) which are rhythms (*tāla*); and provided both *Rāg* and *Tāl* with an intricate *memoria technica* to which not every one possesses the key.[2] This kind of musician is commoner in the Carnatic than in Hindostan, where theory has reared a less imposing edifice.

The aesthetic effect of the *aṃśa* is important. Whatever may have been its origin—and there is every probability that it was the tonic in the same sense as the Greek *mesē*—its present function is to define the *tessitura*. With harmonized melody we are not accustomed to think much about this—until perhaps we have to consider what sort of song we shall be able to sing when we are tired.[3] But in unharmonized music very much, more than anything else, depends on the general level in which the song lies. A song with a high *tessitura* has quite a different character from a song with a low one. It was in this very point that in Greece the 'plaintive' modes (e.g. the Mixolydic) were distinguished from the 'soft and convivial' (e.g. the Lydic), according to Dr. Macran (*Harmonics of Aristoxenus*, 1902, pp. 39–81). An example of the plaintive kind of Greek song with a high *tessitura* (and the Mixolydic fifth) may be seen in Pachtikos (*Aismata Hellēnica*, Athens, 1905, No. 133), a funeral dirge circling about B, B♭, and A, and descending to a tonic E. There is no doubt also of the low position of the *aṃśa* in the convivial *Kaliāns* (Nos. 50–59), or of its high position in the serious *Bhairavī* (32) and *Bhairav* (37). Similarly, the theme of Mozart's Clavier Sonata in A major owes perhaps some of its alertness to its high, and that of the Choral Symphony something of its restraint to its middle *tessitura*; but we can hardly be said to have erected this into a principle of our art.

An English-speaking Indian habitually chooses the word 'tune' to translate *Rāg*. And the fact is he does not attach much importance to *the* tune of a song. A song may be sung in many ways—the more the better, as a rule—so long as it is within the well-

[1] It is noteworthy that both *mātrā* and *akṣara* are terms of prosody. Cp. the early reckoning of musical time in Europe, *Oxford History of Music*, vol. i, p. 168 seq.

[2] See Chinnaswami Mudaliar, *Oriental Music*, pp. 16 and 25.

[3] Aristotle spoke of modes with a low *mesē* as 'old men's scales'.

defined limits of the *Rāg*; on the other hand, the least departure from the prescribed notes surprises us, not always pleasurably. This has one advantage, at any rate, that it is unnecessary to record Indian tunes in notation. The names of the *Rāgs* to which the *Gīta-Govinda* (eleventh century) was sung have been preserved, and even in the absence of a notation it is open to any musician of to-day of sufficient skill to sing them as expressively as Jayadeva himself.

On the other hand, the absence of definite melody precludes concerted music. Several rehearsals are necessary in order to get a dozen people to sing a hymn in unison, and to overcome the lust for 'grace' and *contrappunto alla mente.* When some years ago *Bande Mātaram* was being sung there were probably six different versions at half a dozen different street corners of Calcutta, of which the following, taken down from the lips of a blind man in Dalhousie Square, and sung at the top of his voice without causing a single passer by even to turn his head—so little did the mere tune convey anything—is one:

Ex. 250.

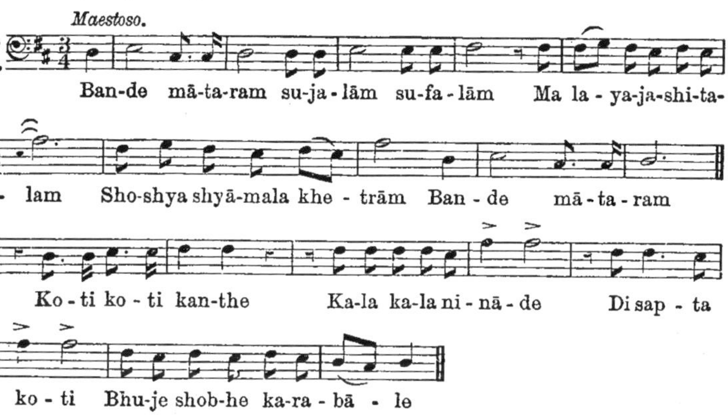

I bow before thee, O mother, who art washed clean by rivers, by rain-drops, by oceans. By the help of thy life-giving waters and the free breezes born in the Malaya mountains thy crops yield and thy fruit-trees bear. A thousand thousand nurtured on thy lap are making prayer to the Almighty Father and to thee. O mother Durga, in your ten hands you have as many weapons always ready to protect your children. But because we have lost our devotion therefore you have no sympathy for us.

We have seen nothing in the facts of *Rāga* so far with which to meet a possible suggestion of the frivolous, that if you were to put the phonogram of an Indian melody on to the cylinder fore part behind and hear the tune backwards it would sound just as well. One answer to this would be that in that case all the ascending passages would come out as descending and vice versa, and that many (not all) *Rāgs* have a distinct form for ascent and descent. And this in two ways, or at least as two manifestations of the same instinct. The pentatonic (*oḍava*) and hexatonic (*shāḍava*) modes are often pure (as in Nos. 1 and 24), but sometimes mixed (as in Nos. 4 and 11): in the pure mode the 'leap' is taken absolutely; in the mixed mode it is taken with a subsidiary grace-note, or in a sort of tentative way. In descent the 'leap' is bridged by a passing note:

Ex. 251.

in ascent, if it is not taken absolutely, the voice climbs up to it, as it were

Ex. 252.

If we refer back to Ex. 226 (*Śardula-vikridita*) for a moment we shall find an example of this. The scale is

Ex. 253.

and the weak note is B; the gap A–C has to be negotiated, and this is done thus:

Ex. 254.

Behāg (No. 60), for instance, is divided into tetrachord (B C–E) and pentachord (E F G–B) with the gaps occasionally filled. We will take the tetrachord

Ex. 255.

The B usually, but sometimes the E, is given as *aṃśa*; they are at any rate about equally prominent notes. Next in importance is the C, and least important the D. In effecting the passage from B to E such phrases will occur as

Ex. 256.

while the descent from E to B may be by leap, but will generally be by step:

Ex. 257. 

In most *Rāgs*, even if heptatonic (*sampūrṇa*), there is still a feeling that some notes are strong (*balin*) and others weak (*alpa*), and these weak spots tend to be negotiated in this 'crooked' (*vakra*) way. And if the *Rāgs* are actually transilient (*varja*) they are apt to be *vakra* in ascent, and to have the gap filled in descent—rather than the other way. So that to turn ascent (*ārohaṇa*) into descent (*avārohaṇa*), or vice versa, would be completely to falsify the *Rāg*. Other answers to the 'frivolous' person could be made on the grounds of Time and of Form (see Chapters VIII and XI).

Similarly other *Rāgs* have typical phrases:

58. *Kaliān.*

Ex. 258. 

54. *Yaman-kaliān.*

Ex. 259. 

55. *Kamod-kaliān.*

Ex. 260. 

59. *Hamir-kaliān.*

Ex. 261. 

57. *Shām-kaliān* is not *vakra.*

But it must not be thought that every melody necessarily contains the typical phrase of the *Rāg*. In India, as in Europe, the rules are 'the obedient humble servants' of the composer; he obeys them, of course, but in the spirit, not the letter, just as the best sculptor's work approximates most nearly to, but never exactly coincides with, the nine-unit or ten-unit or other system which the case may require; or, as we ourselves should maintain, while a given chord has its typical resolution, yet that music is chiefly to be prized which in obeying this 'rule' manages still to say something new that, when closely examined, really disobeys it.

What surprises us most in this music is its predominantly conjunct motion.[1] Leaps of all sorts are taken, including those which do not appeal so much to us—the tritone and the augmented second. But if small they still have the character of being *a*, if not *the*, next door note; if large, they seem to be merely a means of getting quickly to some other contrasting register. They do not seem to be used for the pure pleasure of the interval itself, as in many examples we might quote from our music:

Ex. 262.

Contrast with these such a melody as the following:

Ex. 263.

[1] So little is there any idea of the possibility of disjunct motion that there seems to be no distinctive name for it. The leap of a Third is called *Abhyucchraya*, 'pressed together'; of a Fourth, *Prastāra*, 'extension'; and of a Fifth, *hiṃkāra* (making the sound *Hiṃ* or *Om*, the syllable of the sacred name; the application is obscure). A singing exercise in mixed leaps is also called *vārida* (?). The old words *nigraha*, 'subduing' (sc. suppressing the intermediate note), and *praveśa*, 'binding together' (sc. the neighbouring notes)—disjunct and conjunct motion—seem now to be forgotten.

[2] A *Jhil* is a *Rāg* without grace-notes.

Upendrakisor Ray's translation.—Day by day shall I sing thy sweet song. Give thou me the words, give thou me the tune. If thou abidest in my heart in the full-blown lotus seed,[1] if thou makest my soul overflow with thy love, if thou hearest my song, seated in my heart, if thy noble and beautiful eyes lend me the nectar of their glance, if thou on my sorrows placest thy hand pitifully, if thou from my happiness chasest away pride—give thou me the words, give thou me the tune.

It is true this is a Folk-song, to which words have been added by Rabindranath Tagore, and a *Jhil* (i. e. without grace-notes); but it will do as well as one in a formal *Rāg* to show the general preference for step over leap.

Another thing which completely baffles our ears is the way even the conjunct motion is taken. The following hymn of the Brahma Samāj:

[1] God abides in the innermost recesses of the heart in the form of a lotus seed. The lotus is the type of purity; it may be offered, even when not fresh (as other flowers may not) unless previously offered to another. Hence 'lotus lips', 'lotus feet', &c.

Brahma Samāj hymns. Rāg Sohani; Tāl Surphākta.
'Prathama ādītāla.' ♪ = 130. Music and words by RABINDRANATH TAGORE.

Ex. 264.

N.B.—Crotchets or minims would have been more appropriate; quavers are used in order to suggest the rhythm better.

Upendrakisor Ray's translation.—Thy power is from all time; from all time is thy supreme radiance in the skies. Thine is the first word. Thy joy lives in each new year afresh in the heart. In the firmament of thy mind glisten the sun and the moon and the stars. The wave of life vibrates in the atmosphere. Thou art the first poet; the master of poems art thou. Thy deep-voiced utterances find voice in praise and prayer which ascends from all the world.

sung as I heard it on their anniversary (January 25) with a choir of twelve voices supported, in unison, by a small organ and two violins, with drum, was extremely impressive. In particular the phrase marked (*a*) at the end of each section seemed to give it that sort of sublimity which we recognize in those chords that smote on Samuel Butler's ear on his entrance into Erewhon.

Both these peculiarities, a preference for conjunct over disjunct motion, and unusual sequences in conjunct motion, are made possible and almost demanded by the absence of harmony. They are demanded as a means of contrast. Motion through the notes of a chord, when there is no idea of forming chords at all, does not give enough contrast; E and G say more or less the same thing as C. And again, when the ear has become accustomed to the sound of F♯ G A♭—a note with an upward and downward leading note—to pass direct from F♯ to A♭ is a very striking divagation from the normal, and gets a high value from the consciousness of the norm behind it.

The claim is occasionally made that this music has harmony, or a 'sort of' harmony, in it. Such feeling for harmony as is involved in the construction of a scale at all, especially of such an elaborate and balanced scale, or in the appreciation of the greater sonority of C G C over the simple C in the drone, it has. But of harmony, in the sense either (1) of the sequent intervals in melody being chosen for their consonance, or (2) of two notes being sounded simultaneously for the sake of the consonance, there is none; there is less even than among the North American Indians whose music,[1] as far as at present investigated, is at a very early stage. And it seems impossible that there should be any. Hindu music, though it has enormously refined the detail, has not advanced beyond the principles of Greek music. This may not seem an inducement to deny them harmony to those who still think that the Greeks had harmony. But at least this is true that harmony in the sense of the Organum and of Dufay did not become possible till the Greek modes had long lost any feeling of the *mesē* (*aṃśa*) and of the functions (*dunameis*) of the other notes.[2] And the first thing that harmony would do, if now applied even tentatively to Indian music, as some advocate, would be to get rid of that feeling and those functions, and with them of the grace-notes and all that makes *Rāg* worth having. As the *Rāg* now is, its notes are like the pieces on the chess-board; harmony, by investing them all equally with powers of its own, would make them like the pawns. Hence the serious menace to Indian music of the harmonium, which has penetrated already to the remotest parts of India.[3] It dominates the theatre, and desolates the hearth; and before long it will, if it does not already, desecrate the temple. Besides its deadening effect on a living art,

[1] There is one curious point of contact, the more curious that any direct connexion is unthinkable: the Chippewas draw a picture of a tune, by the help of which another man can sing it, and the Hindus set store by their *Ragmālas*, sets of paintings of gods or men affected by the passion which the particular *Rāg* expresses. See also Ex. 457.

[2] That in virtue of which they took their part in the mode as *vādi*, *samvādi*, &c.

[3] I was present for an hour at a concert in Trivandrum at which this appalling instrument never ceased, and I found in the Salt Range (Northern Panjab) a 'Teacher of Song and Harmonium'.

it falsifies it by being out of tune with itself. This is a grave defect, though its gravity can be exaggerated; it could also be lessened by a revised tuning. A worse fault is that it is a borrowed instrument, constructed originally to minister to the less noble kind of music of other lands. It has taken a century to invent and perfect the pianoforte; if she must have the fatal facility of a keyed instrument, India could well spare a century or two for inventing something that should do justice to her music.

The question as to what foreigners are to make of this music is still more difficult. To add harmony to it is to kill it; and yet it is impossible for Europe to understand melody except in terms of harmony. Harmony has been successfully added to songs whose musical thought is nearer our own in Stanford's *Irish Songs* or Bourgault Ducoudray's *Chansons de la Basse Bretagne.* But are the *Chansons de la Grèce et de l'Orient* a complete success? And is the problem quite so simple as Herr Polak[1] supposes; though he exhibits the curiosities of Indian music, does he convey the art? It is quite possible to select, as Lady Wilson[2] and others have done, those songs which have definite cadences—and there are a few—or even to invent cadences for those which have none, to give them a frankly European dress, and to suggest the kind of mood in which a foreigner listens to Indian music. That is a definite thing well worth doing; but it does not bring one any nearer to an understanding of the indigenous art. The best authorities on Bengāli say that it is untranslatable, and one has heard the same of Sanskrit; and there seems to be no way of understanding the music except to set to work and learn its language.

We now examine a *Rāg* in practice, and for this purpose take one of the commonest—*Yamankaliān.* Of the three instances here given:

Yamankaliān.

Ex. 265.

[1] *Die Harmonisirung indischer, türkischer und japanischer Melodien*, Leipzig, 1905.

[2] *Five Indian Songs*, Paterson & Sons.

(2)

(3)

the first is a *Svarāvarta*, an exercise sung to the *Svaras* (Sa, Ri, Ga, &c.) used as a teacher's model of the *Rāg;* the other two are simple songs for children. We learn that the E is made prominent by the melody circling about it, or stopping there; that the passage E–G or G–E may be taken as a leap, but that if the movement is slow an F♯ is inserted as a grace-note (not an F♮); on the other hand, an F between two E's is always made natural. Of the following songs, 'Dukhera beshe' is a hymn of the Brahma Samāj; I do not know why the mode is called *mishra* (mixed). 'He mora debatā' is a poem. Both are *Khyāls*, and by Rabindranath Tagore. 'Hādi e illah' is a *Thumri* from Benares. It was sung to me by a Mohammedan in Bombay with very genuine feeling. The words are Hindostani. The *Rāg Kalyānī* does not differ much in this particular melody from *Imankaliān*, except that occasion might arise, but does not, for F♮'s.

Brahma Samāj. V. 40. Mishra Imankaliān. Jhampa.
Tonic D. (3 + 2.) ♪ = 125.

Ex. 266.

(The translation of 'Dukhera beshe', by Upendrakisor Ray.)—Though thou comest in the garb of war, yet shall I not fear thee; rather shall I hold thee tight to the place where it hurts. Though thou hidest thy face in darkness, yet shall I know thee. If thou comest as Death I shall clasp thy feet and die. In whatever manner thou showest thyself to me, I shall not fear thee. Tears fall from my eyes to-day: let the tears fall from my eyes. My hurt aches in thy hard embrace: let it ache. Let that pain tell me thou hast me held to thy breast. Nothing shall I want, nothing shall I say, but simply keep my gaze fixed on thy face. Tears fall from my eyes to-day: let the tears fall from my eyes.

Imankaliān (Tonic F). Ektāla. ♩ = 70.

Astaï.

Ex. 267.

sf
Ki am-ri-ta tu-mi . . . chā-ha ka-ri-bā-re pān . .
Antara.
he mo-ra de - ba-tā . . . Ā - mā-ra na - ya-ne
f
to-mā-ra bī - sa chhā - bi De-khy-a la - i - te . . . .
sadh jai ta-ba ka - bi Ā - mā-ra mu - gdha . . .
sra-va-ne ni-ra-be ra - hi Su-ni-ya la-i - te chā - ha
ā - pa-nā - ri gān . . He mo-r(a) de - ba-tā . . .
Sanchari.
Ā - mā-r(a) chi - tte to-mā-ra sri - shti khā - ni
Ra-chy-a tu - li-chhe bi-chi - tra e - ka ba - ni
Abhog.
Tā - ri sā-the pra-bhu mi-li-ya to - mār prī - ti
Jā-gā-ye tu-li-chhe . . . ā-mār sa-kal-(a) gī - ti
Ā-pa-nā - re tu - mi de-khi-ccha ma-dhu-ra ra - se

(The poet's, and composer's, own translation.)—What divine drink wouldst thou have, my God, from this overflowing cup of my life! My poet, is it thy delight to see thy creation through my eyes, and to stand at the portals of my enchanted ears silently to listen to thine own eternal harmony? Thy world is weaving words in my mind, and thy joy is adding music to them. Thou givest thyself to me in love, and then feelest thine own entire sweetness in me. (*Gītāñjalī.* No. 65.)

Kalyānī. 𝅗𝅥 = 40.

Ex. 268.

Mighty is God the Lord. O Lord God, from thee cometh salvation. Mighty, Almighty, All-knowing, All-loving! Day by day thy holy presence is nearer to us: in the darkness thou art near us.

The melodies 'Dukhera beshe' and 'Hādi e illah' do not lose so much as some others in notation: if they are sung with a little faith and goodwill some impression at least will be conveyed of their sincerity and quiet fervour. 'He mora debatā', is perhaps more difficult; the melody will strike a European at first as running up hill only in order to run down again. There is a great temptation to regard the close as in A minor and to supply a G harmony to the fourth bar; and these temptations must be firmly resisted. The fourth bar rises to the tonic (not the seventh of G) through the 'strong' notes A and E (not C); and an F pedal must be held on in order to get the plaintive character of the close

Ex. 269.

(not at all unlike that of the Sixth Ecclesiastical Tone) which is on the 'strong' note and therefore in a sense a 'full' close, but which is not the tonic, and therefore points away, as it were, to something beyond it. Also the rhythm of the ninth bar is difficult. The eighth and ninth bars are taken as one sweep of melody and in strict time, but with the prosody of the words crossing this time in the ninth bar, as if it were

Ex. 270.

&c.

It offers just that sort of pleasure which we get in lines of blank verse

—Dúncan is in his gráve;
After lífe's fítful féver he sleéps wéll;
Treáson has done his wórst; nor steél, nor poíson,
Málice doméstic, fóreign lévy, nóthing
Can toúch him fúrther.—

where the assertiveness of the individual words fights against and yields to the compelling calm of the metre.

The next thing is to consider the list of *Rāgs* as a whole. We notice that they are re-entrant: that is, they return upon themselves after making the full circle as, by an accepted adjustment, our keys do, but as our modes do not.[1] The order here adopted is to show this; it is not the order of the native treatises. Any point might have been, and the simplest form of our major scale is, taken as the point of departure. Nos. 1–5 are transilient, and modes of

[1] These refuse to admit the Locrian, so that there is a gap between the Lydian at one end and the Phrygian at the other.

each other. Nos. 6–8 transitional. No. 9, the major scale. Nos. 10–14 substitute B♭ for B♮. Nos. 15–21 flatten the E as well. Nos. 22–5, the B♭ and E♭ are fully established. No. 26, anomalous. Nos. 27, 28, A flattened. Nos. 29–31, though they seem to show a good deal of licence, are really transitional between the two-flat and the four-flat scale.[1] Nos. 32, 33, D♭ (of some sort) established. At this point the European circle of modes stops, because the next modal shift would flatten the G. This mode with a flat Fifth will be discussed later under *Sāman* chant. The *Rāgs* proceed, after reaching four flats, by sharpening the leading note to the tonic and then the leading note to the Fourth as well.[2] No. 34, B♮. Nos. 35–8, B♮, E♮. No. 39, a tentative sharpening of F, as the leading note to the Fifth. Nos. 40, 41, the F sharpened instead of the E♭. Nos. 42–8, all three leading notes sharpened. Nos. 49–52, after a little remaining hesitation over the A♭ and D♭ we get back in Nos. 52–63, through the *Kaliāns*, to the place we started from. These sixty-three are only the best known out of some hundreds of *Rāgs*; but to have shown them all would only have taken the principle of re-entrance to another place of decimals, as it were.

The *Rāgs* have been arranged in this way not merely to obtain a symmetrical system, but also to bring out an essential point. They fall, in the first instance, into nine or ten groups, of which the centres are perhaps:

1. *Bhūpkaliān.*	32. *Bhairavi.*
9. *Shankarābharaṇa.*	37. *Bhairav.*
14. *Jhinjoti.*	44. *Basant.*
23. *Kāfi.*	50. *Pūriakaliān.*
28. *Āsāvarī.*	53. *Kaliān.*

But secondly, each group consists of an average of seven *Rāgs* (out of a total of sixty-three; out of a total of 500, an average of fifty or sixty). And a *Rāg* gets its special flavour not so much from its being just what it is, as from its not being something else, closely allied to it, which is present all the time in the musician's con-

[1] There is the same sort of hesitation about our Aeolian mode which frequently shows a Dorian sixth and a Phrygian second.

[2] What has hitherto been described as successive flattening might, of course, have been taken in reverse order and described as sharpening. The two are the same thing looked at from different points of view.

sciousness. Any one can hear the difference between, say, *Jhinjoti* and *Bhairav*; but the more of a musician a man is the more he can hear and enjoy the subtler distinction between, for instance, *Jhinjoti* and *Desh*, or the still subtler between *Jhinjoti* and *Tilang*. It might appear that as a given *Rāg* is taken so differently (see Nos. 27–9, 46) in different parts of the country these distinctions do not much matter; but it must be remembered that the distinctions are accurately adhered to in any one district, or by any particular school; and that it is of no use to test the songs of Bengal, for instance, by the system of Gujarāt. And some of these characteristics are so strikingly beautiful as not easily to be missed, or to be forgotten, even by a foreigner: the strong legato from F♯ to E in *Imankaliān*, for instance, or the pentatonic suggestion of *Behāg*, or the plaintive alternation of the two B's in *Khamāj*, or of the two E's in *Kāfi*, or the old-world sound of the scale of *Kānaḍā*.

In No. 59, *Hamīrkaliān*, the sharp Sixth (A♯) appears. It is sounded very likely in others, but I could get no certain information. Similarly, the eight *Rāgs* with exceptional intonation given in Appendix II is probably not a complete list; they are merely those of which the true intonation has been preserved in one part of the country, Gwālior; at Calcutta, for instance, I heard of *Āsāvarī* (No. 28) as being of exceptional tuning, but of none of these; and Mr. Clements gives other instances from the Deccan.

Express mention is seldom if ever made in the books of the Drone. It is taken for granted of course; though, to those who have never heard it, it is not at all an obvious concomitant of melody.

In fact, at first it is a little confusing, even irritating; but one gets to discount it as readily as one does the hammering of the pianoforte keys or the scraping of the violin bow. It is there not only because without it, especially with quarter-tone scales, the singer would feel, as a Benares musician said, 'like a ship without a rudder,' but in order to consolidate the melody. Not that a song cannot be sung without it; a ryot returning from his work, or a mother nursing her baby, does not have first to go and fetch a *tambura*; but, as the boy said when asked why he had godfathers and godmother at his baptism—'because, I suppose, it makes it a sweller thing'. The drone may be a drum, carefully tuned, or two drums, in unison or at the octave, or the drone strings of the *vīṇā*; but is as a rule, and with the best singers, a *tambura*, a large *vīṇā*-shaped instrument, with one gourd (sound-board) instead of two, and with open strings—two or three Sa's and one Pa. The drone strings of the *vīṇā* and *satār* or of the *surbahar*, a large *satār* common in Bengal, often have amongst them one tuned to Ma, and there is, curiously, no objection to the Pa and the Ma sounding together. The effect of this may be heard in the 'wilderness' part of Granville Bantock's *Omar Khayyám*.

Ex. 271.

But they avoid putting either of these notes on the drone if the *Rāg* which is being sung omits it. Thus, for *Bibhās* they would tune the Ma to Ga, in spite of the 'thick' effect of a major Third so low in the compass; for *Malkos*, in which there is no Pa and the Ga is an $\overset{\flat}{\text{E}}$, and neither this nor E would be available on the drone (which must be as consonant as possible), the Pa string would be tuned in unison with the Ma string; and it is only for the European that the re-inforced Fourth of the scale upsets the tonality. The strings of the *tambura* are long and sonorous, and the Fifth overtone (Ga) comes out very clearly from the fundamental whatever the other strings may be; and this still further adds to the dissonance of the Fourth. It is curious, too, that the B♮ and D♭ of *Bhairav*, and the $\overset{\sharp}{\text{B}}$ and $\overset{\flat}{\text{D}}$♭ of *Todi* should be sung, and evidently with special pleasure, against a C drone[1]; it recalls the cadence of the Organum:

Ex. 272.

(except that it is the C which is stationary, and the D comes down to it); and the dissonance upon a strong beat of Descant:

Ex. 273.

(except that it is much more common than that apparently was). Thus the drone is of considerable use too in forcing a strong appoggiatura, which is the peculiar, perhaps the only, melodic point of the snake-charmer's pipe:

Ex. 274.

About the simultaneous presence of Ma and Pa in the drone a word more may be said. It is interesting that the 'consonance' of the whole tone which appeals to the Hindus was one which the Greeks recognized too,[2] and we see that it is the logical outcome of quintal harmony. That the appreciation of the whole tone is historically prior to that of the major Third may also be gathered from the form of the pentatonic scale which may be pronounced typical. This is not

[1] Cp. the last chord of the *Matthew Passion.*

[2] See Gevaert, *La Musique de l'antiquité*, vol. i, p. 98, and Westphal's edition of Plutarch's *De Musica*, p. 46.

Bhūpkaliān Ex. 275. 

but *Sārang* Ex. 276. 

or *Arabhī* Ex. 277. 

and these entail no harmony except that of the Fourth and its derivatives, among which the whole Tone. Indeed the construction of the *Sa-grāma* and *Ma-grāma* (see pp. 109 foll.) point to a stage of Indian music when the Pythagorean Third (derived from the Fifth) was being exchanged for the harmonic Third (heard directly) which has left its impress in this and other ways on the national art. There is of course no hesitation about this interval (the harmonic major Third) nowadays. A singer when preluding often touches the common chord of the key note, and will do this even when the Third of the *Rāg* he is about to sing is minor.

What, then, are the main differences, if we consider melody alone without rhythm for the moment, between this music and ours? First of all the song is cast in one definite mood throughout. This mood calls up associations, unnameable, but yet distinct, of similar song heard under similar circumstance; so much so that to tell an Indian what *Rāg* a singer chose on such and such an occasion is to tell him a good deal about the song. We have no similar classification. We have plenty of 'mood' in our music, but we use it to articulate the balance of the song, not to differentiate one song from another.

Secondly, in the chosen 'mood' (*Rāg*) the notes stand out from each other as clearly as the faces of our friends do to the mind's eye. One of our systems describes the Third of the scale as the 'restful' note, the Fourth as 'awe-inspiring', another note as 'desolate', another as 'enterprising'. But in this music any given

[1] Miss Gilchrist also (*Folk-song Society Journal* for 1911) makes out the original Scotch pentatonic to be

On the other hand, Frances Densmore (*Chippewa Music*, Bureau of American Ethnology, 1910, p. 9) shows the typical North American Indian scale to be what is here called Bhūpkaliān, and next to that Miss Gilchrist's form. (These two are Helmholtz's 'Fourth' and 'Second' form of the pentatonic.)

note of the scale may be any or all of these according to the 'mood' in which it occurs. Its character depends not on its pitch relation to a tonic only, though it does so depend partly, and on its relation to the *tessitura* of the song, which we also feel to be part of its essence (though the, to us, more important distinctions of harmony largely cut across this), but also on the extent to which it is *ex officio* a substantive or a passing note. The whole scale is made up of a hierarchy of notes; so that the passage from G to A♭, let us say, is not merely an exaltation of pitch, nor merely an exchange of the perfect consonance C–G for the imperfect C–A♭, but a passage from a stable to an unstable note of the scale (for A♭ may under certain circumstances become A♮) and from a permanent to a temporary (for the A♭ may be altogether omitted, or omitted in certain conditions), or from a note of universal application to one which requires special treatment (for the A♭ may be used in descent, but not in ascent).

An instance, *Rāg Kedāra,*

Ex. 278. 

as used in the following melodies, slightly different from the version given in the list of *Rāgs*. The A is lightly touched, the E still more so. The F is predominant (*aṃśa*), the F♯ is used in *Musica ficta*, i. e. between two G's. In the first melody the B♭, in the second the B♮, is adopted. In both the E has a special treatment; it is used only as a pendant to the F. The scale is seen to be a filled up *Sārang,*

Ex. 279. 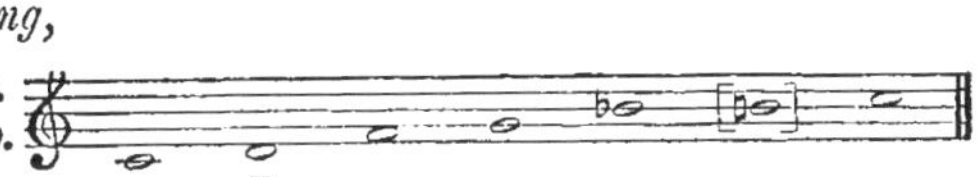

but with the *aṃśa* at F instead of D.

Rāg Kedāra. Metre, Vasantatilaka

Tāl. Mānt. – – ⏑ – ⏑ ⏑ ⏑ – ⏑ ⏑ – ⏑ – ⏑

Andantino. ♩ = 92.

Ex. 280. 

Rāg Kedāra. RABINDRANATH TAGORE.

Ex. 281.

N.B.—Basanta = spring; Megha = the rains.

It seems possible that closer investigation may one day discover in the European mediaeval modes, i. e. in the melodies which were sung in them, the counterpart of this distinction between 'strong' and 'weak' notes. When Luther, discussing the Church tones, said 'Christ is a gentle Lord and His words are lovely; therefore let us take the sixth Tone for the Gospel; and since St. Paul is a grave apostle, we will set the Epistle to the eighth Tone', we can hardly believe that the peculiar flavour which he was conscious of in these tones proceeded merely from the substitution of the notes

Ex. 282.

for

Ex. 283.
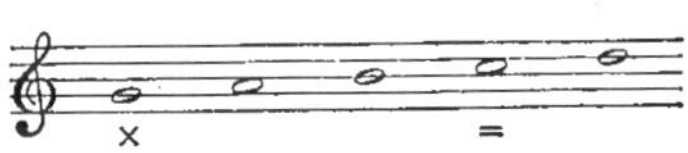

Each tone, or mode, must have had its individual notes characterized far more than appears from the mere formal statement of them. In this statement the relation of the *aṃśa* (Reciting note), marked (=), to the drone note (Final), marked (×), is the only discernible characteristic. But the other notes must have had felt relationships analogous to those of Indian *Rāga.* Amongst these one or two may be mentioned. It is common to find Dorian melodies with the sixth of the mode flattened; a common beginning was

Ex. 284. 

This is, of course, *Musica ficta,* a B flattened between two A's. But why did *Musica ficta* confine itself to one or two special positions of the scale like this? We should not find, for instance,

Ex. 285. 

or

Ex. 286. 

It can only have been because in the Dorian the B was felt as a 'weak' note, one which was touched lightly, or was alterable, or alterable under certain conditions. Again, modal melodies will be found to slip easily into the C major triad, making C a 'strong' note. Many Dorian melodies drop accordingly one place below the tonic at a close:

Ex. 287. 

or Aeolian melodies begin naturally with a minor third:

Ex. 288. 

and Phrygian substitute a C for a B as the 'dominant':

Ex. 289. 

Of course the theoretical rules about Dominants and Participants state all this, but they do not make the point clear that the underlying feeling of the mode proceeds from the fact that each individual note has a character of its own and that a melody takes a certain tinge or flavour from the cumulative effect of these.

We can see also why the C major mode was out of favour: it did not supply what was most valued in a mode, the antithesis of the Final (in this case C) with the 'strong' note (which was, in all the modes, C). It is interesting to find that in India the major mode pure and simple is at a similar discount. Still the Indian *Rāgs* are not so closely parallel to the Ecclesiastical modes as to the Greek; for the former lay much more stress on the Fifth, whereas in the latter the Fourth is the principal factor of consonance: in the Ecclesiastical a rather firm line is drawn also between authentic and plagal modes, a distinction which is on the whole foreign to Indian music.

Thirdly, as a result of this individualizing of the several notes of the scale to form a *Rāg*, repetition at different levels, 'imitation', is rare. Exact imitation can only take place in similar tetrachords. And though the majority of *Rāgs* are composed of tetrachords of which the constituent notes are similar in *pitch*—both are of the form tone, semitone, tone, or both of the form semitone, tone and a half, semitone, and so on—the two tetrachords are seldom identical in the *character* of their constituents. In the instance just given, Ex. 281, if the A is touched lightly its corresponding note, E, is touched still more lightly; the F is a substantive note and the F♯ a passing note, whereas the B♭ and B♮ which correspond to them are equipollent alternatives. A piece of imitation, therefore, in the two corresponding parts of the scale would not really be correspondent; hence we meet with only a very limited use of imitation at different levels.

Again, our melodies tend to circle round the notes which are harmonically related to a tonic, as we see if we take melodies which have more or less the same motive—here, a downward passage through the scale:

Ex. 290.

Allegretto ma non troppo. BEETHOVEN.

Andante con moto. SCHUBERT.

Largo ma non tanto. BACH.

Adagio. THOMÉ.

Allegro vivace. MENDELSSOHN.

Allegro. MENDELSSOHN.

An Indian melody sets no store whatever by any progress through notes which suggest harmony; on the contrary, it moves as far as possible by step, and notes which are harmonically related come quite indifferently upon the strong and the weak places of the rhythm.

Another point in which the tunes just given would be un-Indian is the progression through the whole octave. An Indian melody confines itself to one part of the scale, and 'establishes' that—generally the lower part—first, and follows this by a passage in the upper part of the scale. Ex. 12 (1 and 2) is exceptional enough to prove the rule.

On the whole, then, Indian *Rāg* and mediaeval mode are interesting, as human beings are who consist of 'strong' and 'weak' points, so that we often do not know which we like them best for, or whether it is not rather for the interplay of both.

CHAPTER VII

GRACE

Bot. That will ask some tears in the true performing of it: if I do it let the audience look to their eyes.

Midsummer Night's Dream.

MUSIC has been called a universal language, and no doubt, in the deepest sense, it is. But just as no one language can really be common to all peoples because it will be pronounced differently in different mouths, so the very same notes will be sung by different throats in such a way as to be unrecognizable to us. This is conspicuously the case with Indian singing, in which all the distinctions of colour which we should get from notes in simultaneity has to be extracted from notes in succession. A note, G, has for us hundreds of different colours according to its harmony, such as, for instance:

Ex. 291.

&c.

not to mention the cases where E♭ is not the bass, or G not the treble, or the parts are more or less than four; while the passage from G to F admits of only a few variations,

Ex. 292.

and the like, singly or in combination. In Hindu, and probably in all purely melodic music, the single note as such is itself and nothing else, while the passage from one note to the next has a number of possibilities by way of grace-note.

We think of grace-notes as something which may but need not be added to the note, not as something actually inherent in it. If cultivated for their own sake or used at all in excess they are regarded by us as meretricious. We remember with a smile Mendelssohn's trombone-player who announced the theme of the *Lobgesang* Overture as

Ex. 293.

or we laugh with Spohr at his Italian horn-players who supplied obvious omissions in his score by their *contrappunto alla mente*, or on our own account at an occasional festival singer who ornaments penultimate notes into consecutive Fifths with the bass. The trills of the voice leave us cold, the 'turn' in 'Rienzi's prayer' spoils a rather dignified tune, and the family of double appoggiaturas in harpsichord music enjoys at best a sort of *succès d'estime*.

Indian 'grace' is different in kind. There is never the least suggestion of anything having been 'added' to the note which is graced. The note with its grace makes one utterance. The object of grace is, of course, to add importance to the particular note; but there are such varying degrees in which this may be done that the whole system of *gamak*,[1] the general term for the thing, becomes an elaborate vehicle of light and shade. It brings the notes of a melody, as surely as the various light and shade of a picture brings the contours of the face, from the flat into the round; which again is precisely what harmony does for them, by assigning to the successive notes varying degrees of consonance.

There are nineteen[2] forms of *gamak*, or, omitting minor distinctions, a dozen. For practical purposes these may be referred to two main types, on stringed instruments.

The first sort is formed by sliding (*gharsaṇa*, 'rubbing') the finger along the string, in either or perhaps in both directions. It differs from what we are accustomed to on the violin only in being more frequent and more spontaneous. The other sort is unknown to us and is not possible nowadays on our instruments.[3] We set store by a rich, full-bodied tone; and for that and other reasons we prefer a comparatively thick string at a high tension to produce a note which in India is produced on a thin (and longer) string at a low tension.[4] A lateral deflexion of any appreciable extent would set one of our strings out of tune by forcing the tuning peg

[1] Pronounce 'gummuck'.

[2] See the Ragavibodha in R. Simon's *Notationen des Somanātha*, Munich, 1903.

[3] Except on a small scale on the practically obsolete clavichord.

[4] A long thin string is divisible into a large number of nodes, and the corresponding upper partials give, incidentally, to a note which is somewhat deficient in body a peculiar glitter and brilliancy.

from its position; indeed, we often see a violinist taking advantage of this fact when tuning his instrument. But an Indian string can be deflected a good deal without disturbing the peg. The stopping finger of the left hand 'makes' the note, which the right hand then plucks; and while it is still vibrating the left hand deflects it and, of course, sharpens the note. If the note is stopped near the nut, only a slight sharpening, a semitone or two, is possible; but if it is stopped in the middle of the string, a sharpening of as much as four or five or even seven semitones may be got. A good *vīṇā*-player prefers to get his notes in this way, much as a violinist would rather play in the third position than in the first. To get an E, for instance, he will 'stop' at the B or the C or the C♯ fret and instantly deflect the string, so quickly, in fact, as almost to deceive both the eye and the ear of the listener. The 'deflect' as we may christen it (the Sanskrit word is *dolana*, 'swinging') imparts a wonderful flexibility to the execution, and demands, of course, an accurate ear for its successful performance. The 'slide' and the 'deflect' are known in Hindostan as *Ghasīṭ* and *Mīṇḍ*, in Bengal as *Āsh* and *Mīrh*, in the Carnatic as *Dhara* and *Varek*, and by other local names.

But the *vīṇā*, with its congeners the *satār* and *surbahār*, is only a younger brother of the '*vīṇā* of the body', the voice. It cannot rival the voice in one notable respect, the passage at will from loud to soft or from soft to loud. It is true that Indian singers do not make so much use of this advantage as they might, or rather they do it in a different way from what we might have expected. *Crescendos* are but seldom spread over several bars so as to lead to a climax; they are used rather to assist the grace-notes in their work of rounding the edges of the notes of the melody. In this, as in other ways not confined to music, Indian art aims rather at elaborating detail than at corroborating the lines of structure.

It is in the grace-note that the unusual intonations, which were once no doubt commoner in the *Rāgs* than they now are, still survive. A grace seldom consists of the diatonic notes of the *Rāg*, as is obvious from the description just given. Consequently it is impossible without a very elaborate notation to give a true picture of it. There is the less need to do so since, even if it were faithfully presented, it would be impossible for European throats or fingers to perform it. Still an attempt has been made to hint at it. In the following example the crotchet heads representing the grace are attached to the substantive note by a slur. They are, indeed, placed upon a definite space or line, but must be taken only to suggest the place where the auxiliary notes begin and the sort of course they take. The heads without the tails of the notes are given because the time is variable and entirely at the will of the singer, which is influenced by the context in which they occur; but also in order to remind the reader that they are subordinate in a special sense to the substantive note. They occur after the note as well as before it:

Rāg. Bhairaū. Tal. Tevra. (Seven crotchets, 3 + 2 + 2.)

RABINDRANATH TAGORE.

Lento. ♩ = 70. (Hymn.)

Ex. 294.

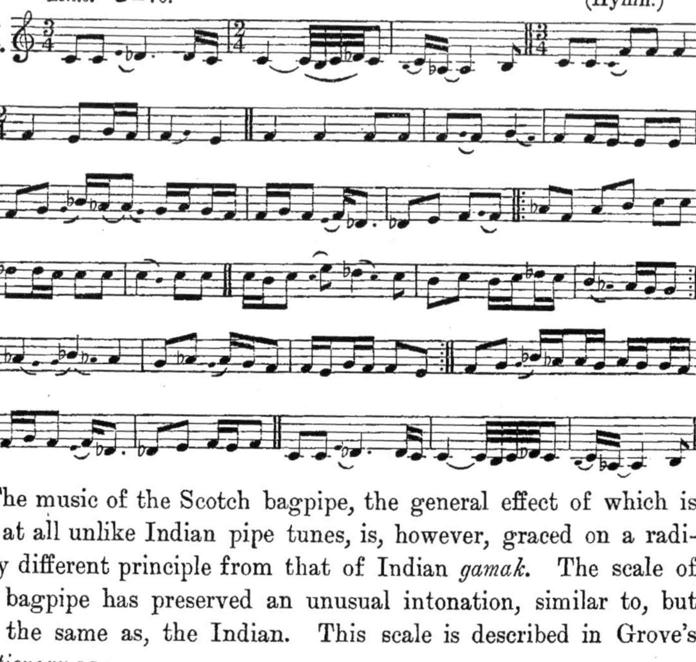

The music of the Scotch bagpipe, the general effect of which is not at all unlike Indian pipe tunes, is, however, graced on a radically different principle from that of Indian *gamak*. The scale of the bagpipe has preserved an unusual intonation, similar to, but not the same as, the Indian. This scale is described in Grove's *Dictionary* as:

Scotch Bagpipe scale.

Ex. 295.

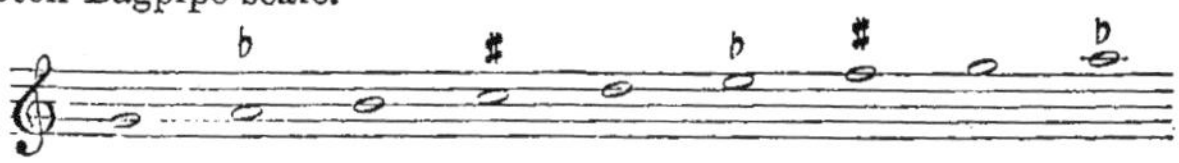

i.e. as, practically, a three-quarter tone scale (which is decidedly rare in India, and as Ellis[1] points out is very nearly the same as,

[1] 'Musical scales of various nations,' *Journal of the Society of Arts*, March 27, 1885.

and is probably intended for, the Arabian Zalzal's scale, *Meshaqah*). But its grace-notes are entirely diatonic; and, what is more significant, they are used not to soften the transition from note to note of the melody, but, principally, to intensify them by a rudimentary harmony. This may be seen in the 'Cock o' the North', taken from McKinnon's *Collection of Pipe-music*:

The Cock o' the North.

Ex. 296.

More accurately, for those who are interested in such matters, the bagpipe scale may be given in cents (i.e. $\frac{1}{100}$ths of a semitone).

					C C♯			F F♯	
From G	Just scale	0	204	386	498, 590	702	884	996, 1088	1200
	Bagp. scale	0	191	388	532	686	894	1044	1200

		G	A	B	C	D	E	F	G	A
From A	Bagp. scale		0	197	341	495	703	853	1009	1200
	Just scale		0	204	316, 386	498	702	814, 884	996	1200
					C C♯			F F♯		

The true representative of the Indian instinct is found, in Europe, amongst the Magyars, as we should expect, of course, from the close connexion between the Romany and Hindostani languages. And if the Magyar grace-notes have, in their native purity, the microtonic intonation, some of their figures

Ex. 297. 

might, with a little less insistence on the rhythm, pass for Indian; and their favourite metre,  , is quite in the Indian style, and an example of it is to be seen in the song 'Akla chalo' on p. 93, Ex. 177.

At the end of the *Ragavibodha* are given fifty examples of the use of *gamak* in fifty separate *Rāgs*, and with the help of Herr Simon's book (p. 182, note) and a knowledge of the Hindostani *Rāgs* it is possible to decipher these. The time, however, presents difficulty. The indication, and the only indication, for all the examples is the word *dinmātrā*, which means 'general time', and refers, no doubt, to the *Alāpa* or 'preluding in the *Rāg*'. But timeless music is unappetizing and difficult to read; so bars have here been added, and the crotchets and quavers arranged on the assumption that a graced note is longer than one ungraced. It must be clearly understood, however, that these time-values have no warrant in the original. The example chosen is in the *Rāg Vasanta* (=spring). This *Rāg* is endeared by its associations, which, whether they arise from it or not, are those of its name. It has also a strongly marked character. It is the F–f scale with the G flattened: the C is lightly touched, and the salient notes are A and E, which it will be noticed alone bear the trill; the D of this *Rāg* is generally held to be natural, but is sometimes given as flat (see the list of *Rāgs* on p. 151, though it differs in some particular from each of the versions there given). Perhaps it may be possible to realize some of its strange beauty by playing over the notes without the graces three or four times till they are familiar, and then singing or whistling it with the graces; but until it is heard in its native land the strangeness will probably remain more credible than the beauty:

Vasanta. (i.)
Tonic F.

Ex. 298.

The example of *Vasanta* was selected mainly because this particular one was curiously misinterpreted in Sir William Jones's article in *Asiatic Researches,* and has been so reprinted by others. It was written out in an ordinary major key (A major); no hint was given of a *gamak* from beginning to end; and on the strength of its rhythm (as *not* given in a book of 1609) it was suggested as the melody of three of the songs in the *Gīta Govinda* of the eleventh century (whose musical rhythm was *not* established by the poetic metre). Thus:

(*Pseudo-*) Vasanta (ii).

Ex. 299.

The typical form of composition which exhibits 'grace' in all its glory is the Mohammedan *Tappa,* in which melodic flow and rhythmical structure are so veiled that it has seemed worth while to give them in a simpler statement in the stave below:

Tappa. Rāg Khamāj. Tāl Tintāl.
Andante con moto. ♩ = 70.

Ex. 300.

Tappa. Rāg Kāfī. Tintāl.

Ex. 301.

The numbers over the bars of the skeleton tune represent the beats (see *Tāl*). The graces are here written out in full, because abbreviations would have been confusing, and on the diatonic notes so as the better to be taken in at a glance. But if the grace of bar 3, for instance, were put, as it were, under an aural microscope the real sounds would appear something like this:

Ex. 302.

with other passage notes in between which can be mentally supplied.

Grace is so natural an accompaniment of any non-harmonic music that it may seem idle to search for a reason for it. Yet in the music of India it is so elaborate and so integral a part of song that it is tempting to try to account for it in some way. It seems as if the language may have been at least a contributory cause. When two vowels meet in Sanskrit, except in a few special cases they coalesce; and the compound thus formed was marked in the *Rigveda* with the circumflex accent called *Svarita* ('sounded'), which had half a dozen or more names according to the particular vowels which were in question. When the *Rigveda* accents (there were two others) were employed in the *Sāmaveda*, that is, in the chants to which the *Rigveda* was sung, they took the form of musical notes; and the *Svarita* in particular was a high note with 'grace' attached to it. It is natural to conclude, therefore, that the 'deflect', as we have called it when it appears in instrumental music, represents that 'grace' and is traceable to this peculiar treatment of the vowels.

When two consonants meet one is assimilated to the other so as to slide into it almost imperceptibly. Accommodations such as those in *orthodok-sy* and *dog-ma*, *younk-ster* and *blag-guard*, *Sut-ton* and *Sud-bury*, *eks-tra* and *egz-ample*, and the like, have their counterparts in Sanskrit, not only in the interior of one word, but quite as commonly between the end of one and the beginning of the next. It is the tendency to weld words together in these and other ways that gives perhaps its importance, as between notes, to that other class of grace, the 'slide'.

CHAPTER VIII

TĀLA

Language, Verse, Musical Time

From Helicon's harmonious springs
  A thousand rills their mazy progress take:
The laughing flowers that round them blow,
Drink life and fragrance as they flow.
GRAY.

Musical time is in India, more obviously than elsewhere, a development from the prosody and metres of poetry. The insistent demands of language and the idiosyncrasies of highly characteristic verse haunt the music like 'a Presence which is not to be put by'. The time-relations of music are affected both by the structure of the language, and by the method of versification which ultimately derives from it. Without pretension to any minute acquaintance with these, a sketch of their bearings upon musical time is here attempted.

I. Language

Those who spoke and speak Sanskrit have shown the delicate appreciation they had of minute phonetic changes. They have introduced modifications of the word to suit every emergency of context, and have recorded these with a precision to which Europe is a stranger. We may acquaint ourselves theoretically with the characteristics of the language, but it requires an effort to feel their effect and therefore to realize the force of the music which suits it. What we find difficult is to make a syllable long without putting a stress on it, or to put a stress at will on any short syllable; we do not easily imagine the effect of a language which is quantitative and not (or only slightly) accentual. In setting such a word as *Ălăkălāllă*, an Englishman would certainly put the fourth syllable on the musical accent, because he would think at once of *Abracadábra*, confusing duration with stress. It has been set in an Indian song:

Tāl Rūpak.

Ex. 303.

and could no doubt have been set in other ways provided the fourth syllable were *longer* than the others; and we notice that it does not disturb the singer that the first syllable, which is short, comes on the accent, while the two long syllables (*lā*) come one of them off and the other on the accent; but both are kept long, and all the short syllables are kept short in the music. It is moreover set not in $\frac{6}{8}$, as the sound of the word would have suggested to us that it should be, but in $\frac{3}{4}$, which further throws a slight emphasis on the syllable *ka-*, because, as we shall see, the beat comes there. Not that a long syllable invariably has a long note, especially if two or three of them come together; but it does as a rule.

In our poetry we do not know long and short, only stressed and unstressed syllables. When Keats writes:

> Upon the sodden ground
> His old right hand lay nerveless, listless, dead,
> Unsceptred;

there is hardly a syllable that we can call longer than the others, unless perhaps 'ground'. But there are several places where we pause between the words, making up a kind of imaginary musical time. We lengthen out the last syllable of 'sodden' because of the next word. If that word had been 'earth', 'sodden' would have gone quicker. As it is, a little more emphasis is laid on 'sódden ground' than would be the case in 'sodden earth'; and the same thing happens with 'nerveless, listless', where the difficulty of pronouncing one word after the other makes us pause a little at the termination and so throw a slightly greater emphasis on the root of the word.

All this is unlike Sanskrit. If we could imagine these syllables to occur in their poetry they would all be long by position— sōddēn groūnd. 'Nerveless, listless, dead' would be altered to 'nerveleh, listleh, dead', the whole idea of the line being to run smoothly on as if it were one word, and not to aim at what we prize, the variety imported into it by the irregular stresses. Consequently rests are seldom written (except in order to break up the metre intentionally in a dramatic way) in any of their songs, at any rate not, as we should, on account of the words:

Tāl Ādi.

Ex. 304.

A European would probably have put a rest at the end of each word. They appear to take breath when they want it, not at the end of words; but it would require an intimate knowledge of the various languages to be sure of this.

II. Verse.

Sanskrit metres fall into two main classes: (1) those which consist of quarter-verses (*pāda*) of a given number of syllables, and (2) those which consist of verses of a given number of feet, each foot having a given time-length which is reached by equivalence. The first are called 'syllable-fixed' (*varṇavṛtta*), the second 'time-unit-fixed' (*mātrāvṛtta*).

In the first class (*varṇavṛtta*), when the *pāda* does not exceed eight syllables most of them are of optional quantity; when it exceeds eight the quantity of every syllable is fixed. The typical metre of this class with an eight syllable *pāda* is the *śloka*, the 'flowing' measure. The following lines constitute the first two *ślokas* of Bharata's *Nāṭyaśāstram* (28th *adhyāya*):

tătāṃ caīvāvănāddhām că | ghănām śŭṣirăm ēvă că
cătūrvĭdhām tŭ vījñēyăm | ātōdyām lākṣănānvĭtăm (1)
tătāṃ tāntrīkṛ̆tām jñēyam | avanāddham tŭ paūśkărăm
ghănām tālās tŭ vījñēyăḥ | śŭṣirō vāmśă ēvă că (2)

The first two lines make a verse marked off into quarter-verses. Though the normal verse is a distich, an occasional tristich or three-line unity is, as in Scott's ballad metre, not excluded. The sense ends with the couplet, which includes, as in Pope's heroic metre, both the subject and the predicate of the sentence. Out of the sixteen syllables in the line only four are fixed by rule as regards quantity. These are marked below the words in the example; the quantity of the other syllables is optional; and the two lines of the *śloka* are independent of one another as regards this distribution.

But it is difficult to realize the prosody of a language which is not familiar. The scansion may therefore be illustrated in any language which, like Latin, distinguishes quantity. The quantity of these particular lines is accordingly reproduced in the following rule for the versification of the *śloka*:

> Hăbēnt pērnīcītātēmquĕ : pĕdūm mŏdūmquĕ cārmĭnă.
> Mŏdīs brĕvēsquĕ lōngīquĕ : mīscēntūr vērsĭpēllĭbŭs.
> Brĕvīs quīntūs lŏcūs, sūmmo īn : pĕdĕ dūplēx ĭāmbŭs ēst.
> Brĕvī lōngāvĕ mōmēntă : sŏnāntūr vōcĕ caētĕră.[1]

Even this, however, is not quite satisfactory, as Latin does not convey the sonority of the ubiquitous *ā* sound in the Sanskrit, or the final thud of such a word as *lakṣananvit*am, which is more heavily stressed than the final of, for instance, *pedum*.[2]

The *śloka*, or *anuṣṭubh* ('with regular stops') is the most famous of all Sanskrit metres. There are two other typical examples of a *pāda* with 8, or less, syllables—the *gāyatrī* ('singing') of 3 × 8 = 24 syllables, and the *uṣṇiḥ* ('hymn') of 4 × 7 = 28, which like the *śloka* have a large number of optional quantities and only a few fixed.

When the *pāda* is of more than 8 syllables—as in the *triṣṭubh* ('with three stops') and the *jagatī* ('lively'), of 11 and 12 syllables respectively, and various others up to 21 or more syllables—*all* the quantities are fixed. Couplets of these greater lengths are usually written in stanzas of four lines, and the lines are in modern poetry rhymed. Here is an instance of the *triṣṭubh* genus (11 syllabled); it has the poetical name of 'the thunderbolt of Indra' (*Upendravajra*), and is in Marathi (rhymed):

> Nă-hēṇ năbhō-māṇḍălă, vārī-rāśī,
> Nă tārăkā, phēnsăcī hā tăyāśī,
> Nă cāndrăhā, nāvăcī cālătāhē,
> Nă ānkă tō, tīvără śīdă āhē.

Metre, Upendravajra.

⏑̱ – ⏑ – – ¦ ⏑ ⏑ – ⏑ – ⏑̱

Not this the sky-vault, ¦ but a li-quid o-cean;
Not stars we see span- ¦ gle, but flecks of sea-foam;
No moon a-loft glides, ¦ but a ship; and those spots
Masts, that the wind bends ¦ as she runs be-fore it.

Ex. 305.

[1] 'The verses contain feet which are at once measured and flowing. Longs and shorts are mingled by chameleon-like measures. The fifth place is short; there is a di-iambus in the last foot. The other syllables are sounded either long or short.'

[2] When sung, the note to which it is set is hummed on the *m* and not vocalized on the *a*.

It will be noticed that the line is composed of the first half of an Alcaic (◡ – ◡ – –) and the second half of a Sapphic (◡ ◡ – ◡ – ◡). And there is a pretty story of Alcaeus having sent Sappho a line which began, similarly, in his metre and ended in hers :

Alcaic.

Ĭ - ō - plŏk' āg - nā mēl - lĭ - chŏ - mēi - dĕ Sāp - phōi[1]

Sapphic.

which, but for the fifth syllable, is exactly the metre *Upendravajra*. It does not spoil the grace of the valentine if we fancy that its metre was one of many Aryan memories that lingered on in the Hellenic consciousness.

Upendravajra is read thus :

Nă-hēṇ năbhō- | māndălă | vārī-rāśī

as the arrangement of the words in the four lines of Marathi shows This is of the form $a+b+a'$, in which a' is a taken backwards, and b is a well-contrasted member of the line. This suggests an interesting reading of the scansion of Alcaic and Sapphic stanzas, both of them forms about which it is difficult to make up one's mind :

Sapphic.

Iam satis ter	rīs	: nĭvĭs	atque dirae	$a+b+a$
Grandinis mi	sīt	: Pătĕr,	et rubente	$a+b+a$
Dextera sa	crās	: iăcŭ	latus arces,	$a+b+a$
		Tĕrrŭĭt	urbem.	$b+\frac{a}{2}$

Alcaic.

Vides ut alta	stĕt nĭvĕ cāndĭdŭm	$c+d$
Soracte, nec iam	sūstĭnĕānt ŏnŭs	$c+d$
Silvae laboran		$c+c$ overlapping
antes, geluque		
Flūmĭnă cōnstĭtĕ		$d+c$ overlapping
stiterint acuto.		

[1] Dark tress'd, chaste, dimpled Sappho !

where the masculine element, as it were (in the Sapphic – ◡ – –, in the Alcaic – – ◡ – –), balances the feminine (in the Sapphic one dactyl, in the Alcaic two). The *caesura*, shown in the Sapphic by the dotted line, and coinciding with the other division in the Alcaic, is at the corresponding place after the fifth syllable in the true Sanskrit form of *Upendravajra*,

– – ◡ – | – ⁝ ◡ ◡ | – ◡ – ⏓

and it is this clash between the formal and the free manner of reading it that gives it much of its charm.

Meanwhile, Indians themselves scan the lines on a different plan. They have a useful *memoria technica*:

Yă-mā-tā-rā-jă-bhā-nă-să-lă-gām.

Taking these syllables in threes they arrive at names for all feet of three syllables composed of longs and shorts:

Yămātā	bacchic.
Mātārā	molossus.
Tārājă	antibacchic.
Rājăbhā	cretic.
Jăbhānă	amphibrach.
Bhānăsă	dactyl.
Năsălă	tribrach.
Sălăgām	anapaest.

The first syllable of each word is all that is generally used. The last two syllables of the line (not necessary for that purpose) represent the words *laghu* (short) and *guru* (long). Accordingly four more feet of two syllables can be named:

Lălă	pyrrhic.
Lăgā	iambus.
Gālă	trochee.
Gāgā	spondee.

and the line

Nă-hēṇ năbhō-māndălă, vārīrāśī,

is scanned

Jăbhānă, Tārājă, Jăbhānă, Gāgā.

or, for short,

jatajagau[1]

[1] *Gau* is the dual of *ga*. There is a similar *memoria technica* for the $2^4 = 16$ varieties of four-syllable feet, ◡ – – –, – – – –, &c., used in the *śloka* and elsewhere.

There are many dozens of metres with fixed length of syllable like *Upendravajra.* Here are two or three more which are in common use:

Vasanta-tilaka. 14 syllables. Caesura not given.
(ta-bha-ja-ja-gala)

– – ⏑ – ⏑ ⏑ ⏑ – ⏑ ⏑ – ⏑ – ⏑
Ha chandra ma ugavalā gaganā pradīpa
A - he - ta shukta, guru, mangala jya samipa
Tya cha prakāśa bharata gagano daranta
To andha kara lapala giriga - bharanta.
(Cp. Ex. 280.)

Śikhariṇī. 17 syllables.
(ya-ma-na-sa-bha-laga)

⏑ – – – – – ⋮ ⏑ ⏑ ⏑ ⏑ ⏑ – – ⏑ ⏑ ⏑ –
Bhalyacya sangenen ⋮ avaguna ase toguna dise
Khalyacya sangenen ⋮ suguna tari to lopata ase
Jaseṇ khareṇ pani ⋮ piuni ganateṇ goḍa kariti
Phani dugdha teṇci ⋮ piuni garala teṇci vamati.

Metre, Śikhariṇī.

⏑ – – – – – ⋮
1 A good man's our firm friend, ⋮
2 A bad man's our false friend, ⋮
3 For so clouds drink salt brine ⋮
4 And so snakes drink sweet milk, ⋮

⏑ ⏑ ⏑ ⏑ ⏑ – – ⏑ ⏑ ⏑ ⏑
1 and ev - 'ry lit - tle fault soon will be for - got;
2 and ev - 'ry bud - ding vir - tue will droop and die.
3 from ev - 'ry lit - tle wave - crest, and make it sweet;
4 and ev - 'ry drop be - comes poi - son at the last.

Rāg Bhūp. Tāl Tevra. (3 + 2 + 2.)

Ex. 306.

Śārdula-vikrīḍita. 19 syllables.

Dolyaṇṇiṇ baghatoṇ dhvani parisatoṇ	kaniṇ padoṇ calatoṇ
Jivheneṇ rasa chakatoṇ madhura hi	vace amhi bolatoṇ
Ha taṇṇiṇ bahusala kama karitoṇ	viśranti hi dhyāvaya
Ghetoṇ jhompa sukheṇ phiromi uthatoṇ	hi iśvara cadaya.

Metre, Śārdula-vikrīḍita.

1. Ḍō - lyaṇ - niṇ ba - gha - toṇ dhva - ni pa - ri - sa - toṇ
Sweet these sounds in our ears, and sweet the ma - ny sights

1. ka - niṇ pa - doṇ ca - la - toṇ
that greet our eyes voy - a - ging.

Ex. 307. (Cp. Exs. 226, 253, 254.)

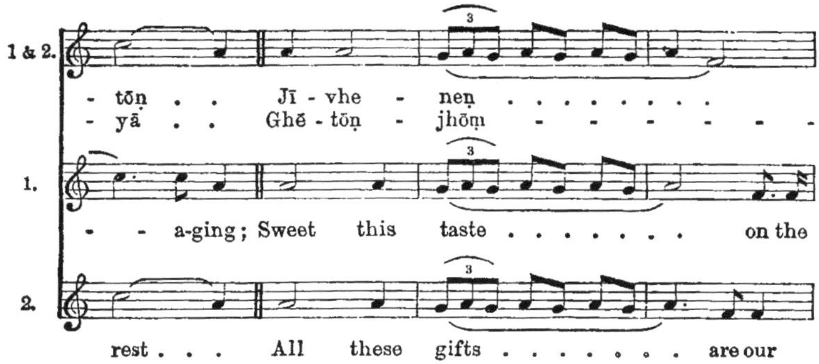

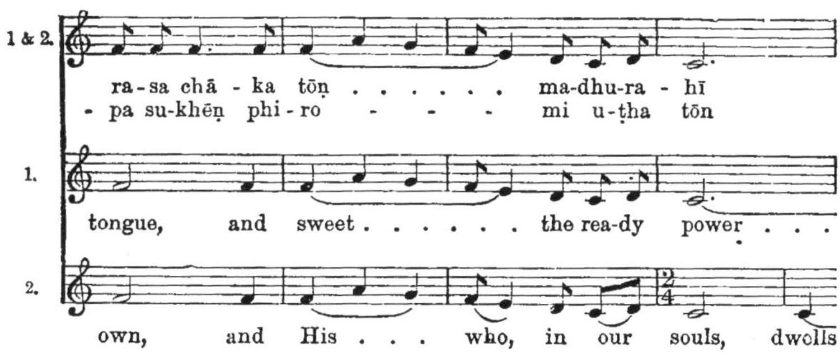

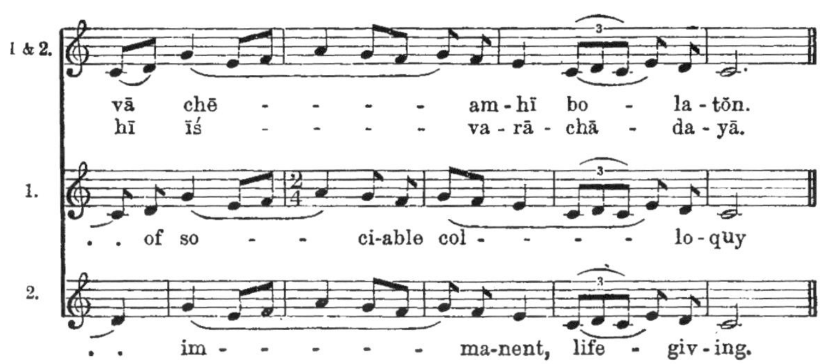

The characteristic of the other great class of Sanskrit metres, those measured by time-unit (*mātrāvṛtta*), lies in the principle of equivalence, that is, in the fact which we are familiar with in the hexameter, that two shorts take the time of one long. *Mātrā* means instant, or unit; what the Greeks called 'Chronos prōtos', the 'first' or smallest 'duration' from which you start reckoning. Each foot contains four *mātrās*, and its prosodial possibilities are:

Proceleusmaticus	ᴗ ᴗ ᴗ ᴗ
Amphibrach	ᴗ – ᴗ
Dactyl	– ᴗ ᴗ
Anapaest	ᴗ ᴗ –
Spondee	– –

The general effect of the *Āryā*, which is the typical metre of this class, is much that of hexameters or elegiacs, though the details are very different.

Poetry, then, bases the verse on the unit of (1) the syllable (*akṣara* [1]), less or more fixed, and (2) the time-length (*mātrā*) treated as the basis of equivalent combinations. Music similarly has two clearly defined stages, when time was reckoned (1) by *akṣara* and (2) by *mātrā*.

Reckoning by **akṣara**, that is, by the number of notes in a period (*parvan*). The *parvan*, as we shall see in the chapter on the Sāman chant, is the amount that can be conveniently sung in a breath, and the *akṣaras* which fill it are there of two kinds—long (*dīrgha*) and short (*hrasva*)—and occasionally the long note is intensified or lengthened, or both of these, in which case it is called *vṛddhā* (increased). Secular music similarly starts from a long (*guru*) and a short (*laghu*) note, and adds on one side the prolate note (*pluta*) and on the other the quick note (*druta*, from *dru*, to run). The *laghu* is then taken as the unit (*mātrā*), and the four notes have relative value, thus:

o	Druta	½ mātrā	♪
ı	Laghu	1 mātrā	♩
ऽ	Guru	2 mātrās	𝅗𝅥
ऽ̆	Pluta	3 mātrās	𝅗𝅥.

To these is added the rest (*virāma*), which is the equivalent of the *druta*,[2] and is marked thus: o̊, and ı̊. It does not occur with the *guru* (ऽ) or the *pluta* (ऽ̆).

[1] Lit. 'imperishable', in the sense perhaps of the 'irreducible minimum'; Sanskrit syllables are, of course, one consonant (simple or compound) plus one vowel (simple or diphthong). Cf. Aristot. *Met.* xiii. 1. 7, p. 1087 b, *Basis hē syllabē*. Aristoxenus knows nothing of the syllable as a unit of rhythm.

[2] Day says that its value was not definitely stated by his authority. It seems

The *Ratnākara* gives 120 examples of such periods as may be formed by combinations of these four values, varying in length from one note to nineteen notes. Another authority gives 108. It is clear that this list is not meant to be exhaustive, for it does not reach a millionth part of the possibilities; and it is also clear that the four measurements of music (or five including the *virāma*) cannot directly represent the two dimensions (long and short) of poetry. So that not all of these can represent poetical metres (though some may) and that for others there must be some other explanation. A list of forty-two specimens is given in Day; but as that book is now scarce a few typical ones taken at haphazard are given here:

No. of syllables or notes.	*Name.*	*Indian and European notations.*
1	Ekatālī	
3	Pratāp [illegible]	
5	Rangapradīpakaḥ	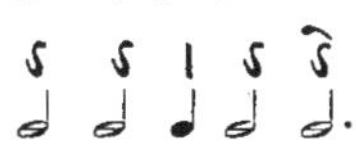
10	Layaḥ	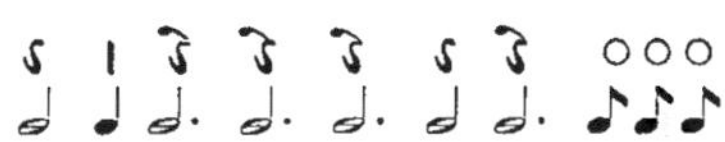
19	Miśravarnaḥ	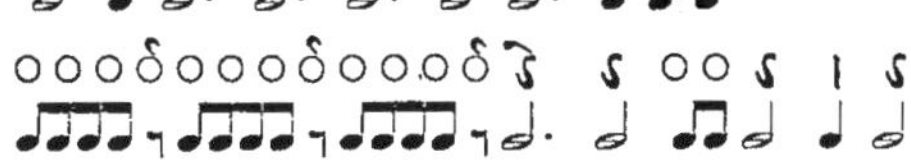

(An instance of  is not included here because its value is not certain.)

The names do not help us. They are often merely picturesque appellations. Where they have a recognizable meaning it is sometimes refuted by the accompanying signs; thus *Jhampa tāla* and *Marnt tāla* both occur, but the signs show them to be quite different from the modern *Tāls* of those names. Possibly the explanation, but it can only be a guess, may be that the longer *tālas* represent the rhythm of good recitation of well-known verses or *mantras*. It is clear that in our own poetry, for instance, longs and shorts do not represent

to be defined in the *Ratnākara* where (adhy. 5 śl. 258) ' a *druta* followed by a rest is a detached *mātrā* ' (i. e. *laghu*); though if this can be held to imply that the *laghu* followed by a rest is a detached *guru* the value of the rest is relative to that of the note which it follows.

all the distinctions we make in good reading. When we read aloud:

1. Of man's first disobedience, and the fruit
2. Of that forbidden tree, whose mortal taste
3. Brought death into the world and all our woes
4. With loss of Eden, till one greater man
5. Restore us and regain the blissful seats,
6. Sing heavenly Muse.

our voice travels somewhat as follows:

and such clusters of notes have a sort of family resemblance to those we are discussing.

This may account for the longer groups given in our list, but not for the short ones; it may account for *layaḥ*, for instance, which is much like the cadence of a Sāman (or of one of our mediaeval hymns), but not for *ekatālī*. We will examine some of these shorter ones. The first five in the list given in the *Ratnākara*, and these alone, are named by the first five ordinal numbers—*Adi*, *dvitīyaḥ*, *tṛtīyaḥ*, *caturthaḥ*, *pañcamaḥ*—just as the notes of the Sāman chant were named *prathamaḥ*, *dvitīyaḥ*, *tṛtīyaḥ*, *caturthaḥ*. It is possible that they were felt to represent more fundamental distinctions than those *tālas* which have what we may call a fancy name. They are:

Name.	*Indian symbol.*	*European symbol.*
āditālaḥ	I	♩
[1] dvitīyaḥ	O O I	♪ ♪ ♩
[1] tṛtīyaḥ	O O δ	♪ ♪ ♪ 𝄾
[1] caturthaḥ	I I O	♩ ♩ ♪
pañcamaḥ	O O	♪ ♪

[1] These are given differently by Day. But the *Ratnākara* is a good authority, and there is no doubt as to the meaning of the text.

If the explanation of the longer groups as typical examples of recitation was correct, the time-values of the several notes may well have been somewhat indefinite; we do not feel in the example from Milton that the musical notes present our style of reading more than approximately, nor that we should invariably read it so. In reciting a whole sentence the structure of one word reacts imperceptibly on the pronunciation of the next and interferes with the time-value. But these short groups cannot be sentences; they can at most be single words, and there is every probability that they represent exact time-values. And in passing from those to these we may be passing from the Cola, Commata, Membra, Incisiones, Distinctiones, &c., of the tenth century in Europe to the Modi, Proprietates, Perfectiones, and so forth of the fourteenth—from music which regulated its time-values by the words, to music which evolved its own values.

What makes these five groups interesting is that they offer a connecting link between the prosodial feet given on p. 196 (*ya-ma-ta-ra*, &c.) and some of the fundamental principles of Indian musical time. In the second, third, and fourth of them we have all the eight three-syllable feet. *Dvitīyaḥ* represents, according to the note you begin upon, three of them, ⏑ ⏑ –, ⏑ – ⏑, – ⏑ ⏑; *tṛtīyaḥ* two more, ⏑ ⏑ ⏑ and – – –; and *caturthaḥ* the remaining three, – – ⏑, – ⏑ –, and ⏑ – –. *Pañcamaḥ* similarly represents ⏑ ⏑ and – –; and, according as one or other note is dwelt upon, ⏑ – or – ⏑ also. That this is the true view is made more likely by the position of *pañcamaḥ* after the others; for the two-syllable feet follow the three-syllable in the *memoria technica*. *Aditālaḥ* is placed first, as much as to say 'this *laghu* (crotchet) you are to take as your unit (*mātra*) throughout the list'. We see also the genesis of the rest ('): for, stress-accent being foreign to this versification, there would, without it, be nothing in a series of *tṛtīyaḥs* to mark that they were to be taken in sets of three. This is borne out also by the comparative rarity of genuine Hindu songs which are in three time (it is commoner with Mohammedan); what we should call $\frac{3}{8}$ and $\frac{6}{8}$ are not unknown, but they are not favourite rhythms.

But *caturthaḥ* introduces us suddenly to a five rhythm, instead of, as we should have expected, a three rhythm. It is interesting to see how this comes about. Since the earliest, and by far the most prevalent metre is the *śloka*, which primarily counted the syllables and only secondarily weighed them also, the number of syllables in a unity of any sort came to have a greater importance than we should naturally have attached to it. Hence, when only three syllables were taken together (leaving aside ∪ ∪ ∪ and – – – which we have already disposed of), the trisyllabic forms – ∪ ∪ and – – ∪, for instance (of four and five *mātrās*), seemed to be more nearly related to each other than the trisyllabic – ∪ ∪ and disyllabic – – (each of four *mātrās*). Similarly, it being possible to proceed from – ∪ ∪ (four *mātrās*) to – – ∪ (five *mātrās*) or to – ∪ (three *mātrās*), the former step which kept the number of syllables seemed more natural than the latter which changed it. This may give a hint as to the hitherto unexplained delight of the Greeks in five rhythm; but it would be going too far to assert that it is the origin of five rhythm in general; for this appears quite independently in places as remote, in more than a geographical sense, as Finland and the Malay Archipelago, and others.

Reckoning by mātrā, that is, by the time unit and its multiples, or the principle of 'equivalence', launches us into the domain of

III. Musical Time.

The simplest unity after the solitary beat (*āditālaḥ*) is, as we saw, *dvitīyaḥ* (∪ ∪ –, ∪ – ∪, – ∪ ∪). This gives us the three ordinary distributions of the longs and shorts (crotchets and quavers) within the four-unit foot (beat), a certain number of which, generally four, make up the bar (*āvard*) or section of common time. The name *Ādi* is used for common time (transferred from the solitary beat). Further development within the beat takes place by resolving any long or short into any one of these feet. Thus:

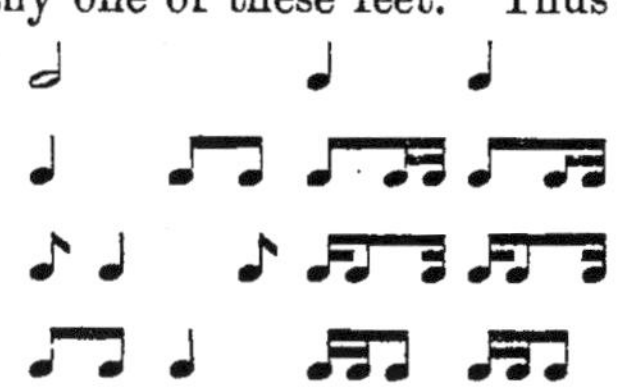

and similarly with

and

So that such a combination of notes as

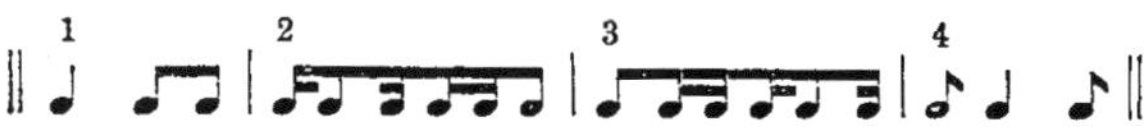

the look of which frightens us and the sound of which does not particularly appeal to us, appears to an Indian as quite an ordinary distribution of his accepted metrical units

$$\Big\|\overset{1}{-}\smile\smile\Big|\overset{2}{\smile}-\smile\,|\,\smile\smile-\Big|\overset{3}{-}\smile\smile\,|\,\smile-\smile\Big|\overset{4}{\smile}-\smile\Big\|$$

in an *āvard*[1] of *Ādi tāla.* In fact, the main difficulty of realizing and enjoying the nice distinctions of Indian rhythm is that we have not acquired the habit of resolving mentally every unit into any distribution of its constituent elements so that we could sing them at a moment's notice or that they would instantly appeal to us when we heard them sung.

Here are some instances of *Ādi* :

Tāla Ādi. Rāg Jhinjoti.

(1)

Ex. 308.

(2) Rāg Dhīraśankarābharaṇa.

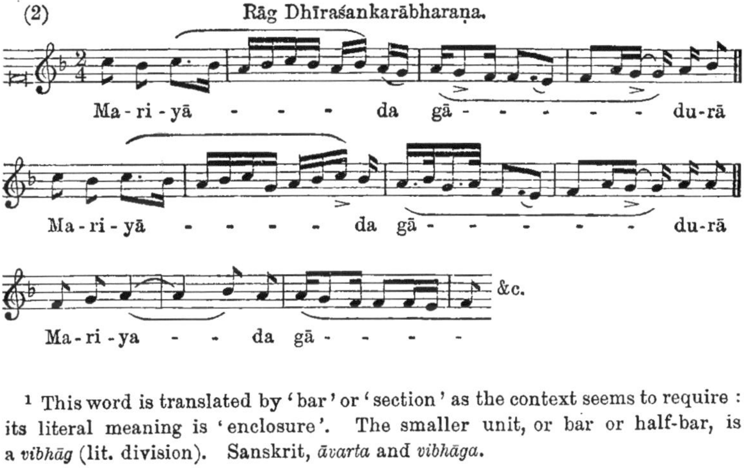

[1] This word is translated by 'bar' or 'section' as the context seems to require : its literal meaning is 'enclosure'. The smaller unit, or bar or half-bar, is a *vibhāg* (lit. division). Sanskrit, *āvarta* and *vibhāga*.

(3) Rāg Dhīraśankarābharaṇa.

(4)

Tālam Ādi. This Rāgam has E and A omitted in descent.

(5) 𝅗𝅥 = 72. *Vivace.*

But the section (*āvard*) need not synchronize with the bar (*vibhāg*); it may begin in the middle of the *vibhāg*, though, as with us, it seldom does. A more usual place for it to begin is on the last unit of the four. This kind is called *Deśādi* (foreign *Ādi*):

Deśādi Tālam.

(1)

Ex. 309.

(2)

Or it may begin on the second unit of the four, and is then called *Madhyādi* ('middle' *Ādi*). As the *Āvard* of *Deśādi* beginning on the fourth unit ended on the third, so here beginning on the second it will end on the first:

Madhyādi Tālam.

Ex. 310.

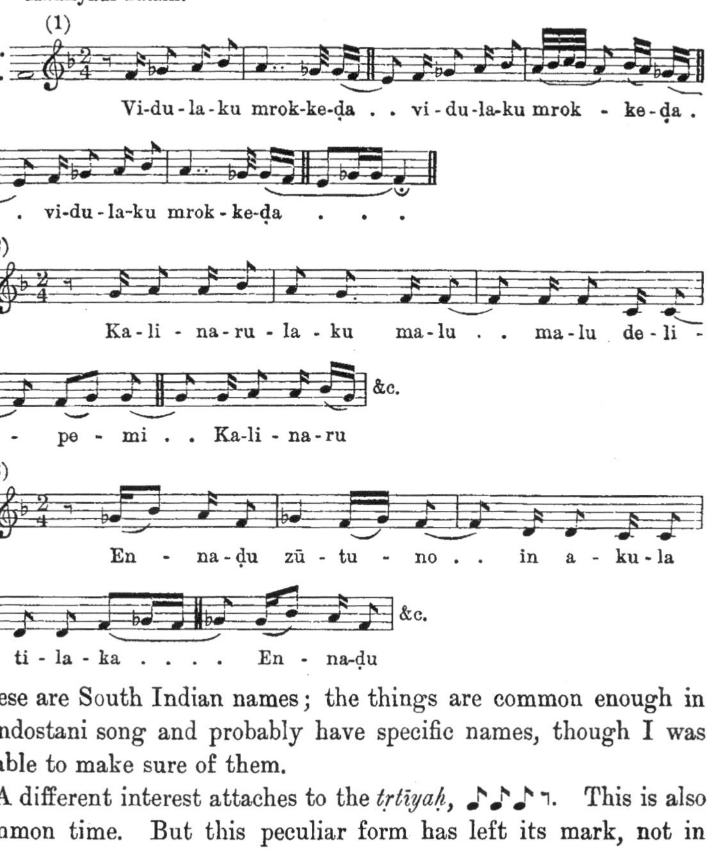

These are South Indian names; the things are common enough in Hindostani song and probably have specific names, though I was unable to make sure of them.

A different interest attaches to the *tṛtīyaḥ*, ♪♪♪𝄾. This is also common time. But this peculiar form has left its mark, not in any special metrical form, but in the way a bar of common time is counted, in whatever metre. A short explanation is necessary first.

When three notes of neighbouring *pitch* and no more are sung without any particular emphasis on any one of them, the voice tends of itself to emphasize and the musical consciousness to give pre-eminence to the middle one. Thus in the scale of the Andaman islands, which (in some parts at least) consists only of three notes separated by some very small interval, it is recorded that the middle note is made the tonic. Again, in the snake-charmer's pipe (see Ex. 274) the middle note of three is made the drone. Similarly, if three equal units of *time* are repeated and an accent is put on one of them, it will gradually determine to the middle one of the three: ⏑ ⏑́ ⏑, ⏑ ⏑́ ⏑ (or, if the commas between them represent rests:

$\frac{2}{4}$ ♪ | ♪ ♪ 𝄾 ♪ | ♪ ♪ &c.).

It is difficult to prove this, because it is so hard to make the experiment fairly. But, for some reason best known to the builders, the wheels of railway carriages commonly beat out a tripleted rhythm, and the reader may have noticed that if he is not particularly attending to them (and so making the experiment a fair one) these take the form ⏑ ⏑́ ⏑, and not ⏑́ ⏑ ⏑ nor ⏑ ⏑ ⏑́. However that may be, here is Indian verse on the one hand employing three equal syllables in succession followed by a rest ♪ ♪ ♪ 𝄾, and Indian music on the other counting a bar of common time with three equal beats (*tāl*) and a blank, or empty (*khālī*) beat; and the curious fact that this blank beat comes invariably on the third of the bar which gives the exact effect of prosodical feet: | ⏑ ⏑́ ⏑' | ⏑ ⏑́ ⏑' |[1] Common time is, accordingly, called in the North invariably 'three-beat' (*tīntāl*), the fourth beat being 'empty'. The first of the bar, which bears the musical accent, is called *sam*[2] ('complete', or 'total'), because at that point the two independent rhythms of

[1] Cp. the first four bars of Tristan, of which the main accent is on the second bar and the fourth is blank.

[2] Pronounced like, and accidentally having the same meaning as, our word 'sum'. It is important to be clear about this conception. The *sam* has no such stress as we place on the first of the bar. It gets its pre-eminence over the other *tāls* (beats) owing to the cross-rhythm (either with some other instrument or in the melody itself) being adjusted at that point. Or if there is no cross-rhythm, still the *sam* is pointed out by its distance from some typical or recurrent phrase elsewhere in the *āvard* (or *vibhāg*); as the quaver triplet of Tschaikowsky's Scherzo tells us how far we have got each time in the series of crotchets. It is true that when singer and drummer coincide at that point their united triumph at having got it right after all does result in a little more tone, i. e. in stress, but this in no way necessary to the rhythm of the music.

singer and drummer from time to time coincide. Time is ordinarily beaten with the hand upon the thigh (the singer is invariably seated), emphasizing the *sam* slightly, and beating in the air with upturned palm for the *khālī*. This method of beating is also applied to other times besides common time in a way which will appear presently.

These other times, various forms of three, five, and seven rhythm for the most part, are often regarded as intricate and unaccountable; but in the light of prosody they have a simple explanation. They are best summarized in the Carnatic system, which enumerates thirty-five different kinds as typical; but the principle which underlies them is of indefinite application, and as a fact I saw a book at Bhavnagar which enumerated some hundreds of them. It will be unnecessary to give the names of these thirty-five rhythms, because their names are only a piece of *memoria technica*,[1] or the picturesque ruins of titles whose meaning is long forgotten, and would only confuse us. It will be enough to arrange them in seven ranks and five files, lettering the ranks and numbering the files.

Counting by mātrā (Carnatic).

	I.	II.	III.	IV.	V.
A.	3	Eka. **4**	5	7	9
B.	3 2	Rūpaka. **4 2**	5 2	7 2	9 2
C.	3 1 2	4 1 2	5 1 2	Jhampa. **7 1 2**	9 1 2
D.	Triputa. **3 2 2**	(Ādi). **4 2 2**	5 2 2	7 2 2	9 2 2
E.	3 2 3	Mātya. **4 2 4**	5 2 5	7 2 7	9 2 9
F.	3 2 3 3	Dhruva. **4 2 4 4**	5 2 5 5	7 2 7 7	9 2 9 9
G.	3 3 2 2	4 4 2 2	Āta. **5 5 2 2**	7 7 2 2	9 9 2 2

N.B.—Rank A is usually given in the order 4, 3, 7, 5, 9; the point being that 4 and 3 make 7, and 4 and 5 make 9 (9 is never treated as 3×3). 6, 8, and 10 are obviously omitted as being multiples of three numbers which are already there, and 9 is, as we saw, *not* considered to be a multiple. Those in heavy type are in common use. The names refer to the whole rank (*Eka*, for instance, to the whole of rank A, *Triputa* to D, &c.), but are confined in practice to those files to which they are here assigned.

[1] See Mudaliar's *Oriental Music*, p. 25.

In rank A are the different values (in *mātrās*) given to the bar (*vibhāg*) when it is counted as a complete whole, that is, when it is not composed of various beats (*tāl*).[1] This merry little tune is an instance of the five-unit bar. Four bars make a section, as usual:

Khaṇḍajātī Laghu. Rāgam Mohāna (= Rāg Bhūpkaliān).

♩= 96.

Ex. 311.

A common way of counting the uneven numbers is by continuous syncopation:

The name of this is *Chapu Tāla*. File V is rarely used.

Rank B has two beats to the bar, C, D, and E three beats, and F and G four. It is not difficult to see in these the two, three, and four-syllable feet of poetry. B gives various forms of the trochee (– ◡) and iamb (◡ –), according to the beat with which the rhythm begins. The five files allow for different proportions between the long and the short beat. We may arrange the ten possibilities of iambs and trochees in a graduated proportion to a scale of 100, and it will be seen that a large number of ways of dividing a bar into two beats has been reached by very simple means:

[1] In this chapter *Tāl* is used for 'time' and *tāl* for 'beat'.

RANK B.

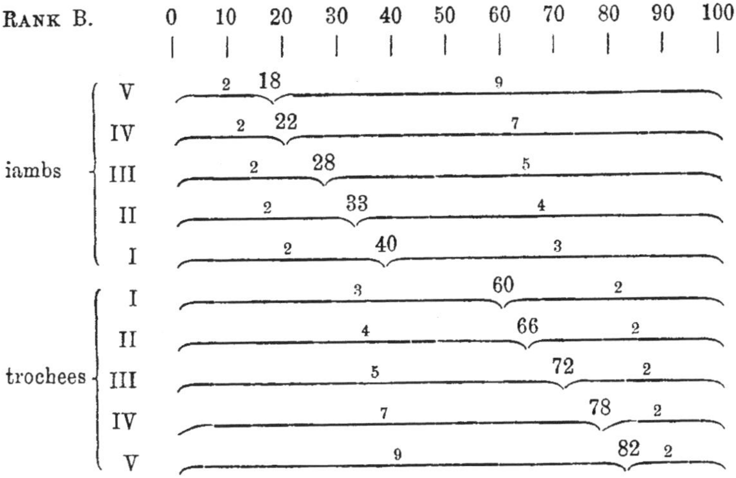

We see from this diagram that just as the scales took account of *śrutis* of different sizes, so here the rhythms take account of different sized units (*mātrā*) and embody them in a system; and it is characteristic of Hindu practice to tabulate ten species of a thing and to make practical use only of one of them. The other ranks may be taken in the same way, and these thirty-five are seen to include by implication one hundred varieties of *Tāl*:

A	B	C	D	E	F	G	
5 +	10 +	15 +	15 +	15 +	20 +	20	= 100

To continue: C and D give five varieties of dactyl, amphibrach, and anapaest (– ᴗ ᴗ, ᴗ – ᴗ, ᴗ ᴗ –). D. II is the normal dactyl, &c.; the rest of D lessens or increases the proportion of the long to the two shorts. C is our old friend the 'cyclical' dactyl[1] which modern theory has criticized out of existence, for Greece at any rate, but which made a considerable stir in its day. Here at any rate it has five separate values of its own. E gives the cretic (– ᴗ –), bacchic (ᴗ – –), and antibacchic (– – ᴗ).

Of the four-syllable feet (four beats in the bar—F and G) there are sixteen possibilities (for two things taken four together). Only eight appear here. Thus: F. I gives 3 2 3 3, and implies 2 3 3 3, 3 3 3 2, and 3 3 2 3. G. I, similarly, four more.

[1] The cyclical dactyl is one in which the middle syllable is shorter than the last.

The other possibilities are:

2 2 2 3 2 2 3 2 2 3 2 2 3 2 2 2	rare in the *śloka*.
2 3 2 3 3 2 3 2	C. IV is used if wanted.
3 3 3 3 2 2 2 2	already accounted for by *ādit̄ālaḥ*.

So that ranks F and G fairly represent the chief possibilities of the *śloka*.

But it will be more interesting to see how the most characteristic of these work out in practice. We will take:

B. II. 2+4 *Rūpaka* (iamb).
D. I. 3+2+2 *Tripuṭa* (dactyl).
C. IV. 7+1+2 *Jhampa* (cyclical dactyl).

and as a curiosity

G. III. 5+5+2+2 *Āṭa* (ionicus a majore).

Rūpaka Tālam. (2+4.)

(1)

Ex. 312.

(2)

(3)

Rūpaka is in idea Saraband rhythm. It is quite one of the commonest *Tāls*, and presents no difficulty, as, in practice, it is a simple $\frac{3}{4}$.

Tripuṭa is harder. The secret of all these *Tāls* is that the units are taken as sums, not multiples. And though seven is not a multiple of anything, yet the European having counted three, finds it very difficult not to expect another three. The only way is to take a fresh lease of counting with each beat. It will be found quite easy to realize all these *Tāls* if one does as a native does—count out each beat 1, 2, 3, &c., and tap at every '1'.

Tripuṭa Tālam. (3 + 2 + 2.) (Telugu words.)

Ex. 313.

Jhampa Tālam. The 'bar' (*Āvard*) is from one double bar line to the next. The single bar lines show the beats. Though it is *counted* 7 + 1 + 2, it is *thought* as 2 + 3 + 2 + 3 quavers.

Ex. 314.

Āṭa Tāla. 5 + 5 + 2 + 2. (The Rāg omits E and A in ascent).
Molto vivace. 𝅗𝅥 = 160.

Ex. 315.

Āṭa is one of the more difficult rhythms. This particular example seems to us almost impossible. We lose our bearings in the course of fourteen crotchets divided into semiquavers, especially at such a tempo as this, and with all sorts of cross-rhythms in the 'bowing'. The slurs really represent the syllables of words; and this tune is actually sung, and sounds very puzzling but very interesting. The *Āvard* is divided into four groups (marked I, II, III, IV), and the phrase, which is the same length as the *Āvard* but does not coincide with it, begins and ends at the third beat of the first group. (Mind the flat!)

Later on in the *Svaras* of this song another sort of rhythm is induced upon this. Every second crotchet of the melody ends on the note *Sa*, which occurs in the words at the same moment. This would have the effect of combining

Tripuṭa	1 2 3	1 2	1 2
Āṭa	1 2 3 4 5 1 2 3 4 5	1 2	1 2

But the last two *Sa*'s come one unit late. The original tune began, we saw, on the third beat, and the *Svaras* begin on the first beat; as there is a *Da Capo* at the end of them back to the tune, there will be two beats to make up; and this is the ingenious and effective way in which it is done.

N.B.—The slurs represent the syllables of the words. The *āvard* finishes at the end of each line. The phrase begins on the third of the fourteen beats.

Svaras (patter words).

Ex. 316.

The Hindostani *Tāls* are very much the same in practice as those of the Carnatic. The usage in different parts of Hindostan varies a good deal, as it does with the *Rāgs*, and it is difficult to be at all sure of more than the commonest. But as these are remarkably like those described as the commonest in the Carnatic, there is little doubt that the underlying idea is the same in both—the poetical metre. The following table gives them as corresponding to the Carnatic list:

Counting by mātrā (Hindostan).

	I.	II.	III.	IV.	V.
A.		4 Ekka } Ektāl }			2 4 3 [Madhyamāvati] 2 3 4 [Matta] 4 2 3 [Khaṭṭ tāl]
B.	2 3 [Rūpak]	2 4 Rūpak			
C.				2 3 2 3 Jhampa or Jāp	
D.	3 2 2 Tevra	4 2 2 Titāla } Tīntāl } Tritāla }			
E.		2 4 4 } 4 2 4 } Surphakta } Sulaphakata } Manṭ }			
F.		4 2 4 4 } 2 4 4 4 } Āḍa-chautāla			
G.	3 3 2 2 [Jhampa]	4 4 2 2 Chautāla 2 2 4 4 [Farodast]	5 5 2 2 Dhamār		

Amongst these the only *Tāl* which is commoner than in the Carnatic is G. II *Chautāla* (i.e. *Char-tāla*, 'four-beat'). It is used especially for *Dhrūpads* (see Chapter XI). The three names of *Titāla* (D. II) all mean 'three-beat'. Some of the other names are descriptive—*Jhampa*, 'jumping'; *Surphakta*, 'zigzag'; *Aḍa-chautāla*, 'crooked four-beat'; *Dhamār* (for *dha-mātrā*), 'having a high number of time-units'.

But there is one *Tāl* peculiar to Hindostan which entered it apparently with the Mohammedans—*Dādra*, $\frac{6}{8}$. It is the only rhythm which is treated as a multiple (and therefore cannot be Hindu), and it is in very common use.

Most of these *Tāls* which give the rhythm of one bar (*vibhāg*) can be taken in pairs of *vibhāgs*, and are then counted as one bar of common time (*Tīntāl*), thus:

3 + 2 + 2 3 + 2 + 2

two bars of *Tevra* 

counted 1 2 0 3 like *Tīntāl.*

Or even a single *Tāl* is so counted :

2 + 3 + 2 + 3

Jhampa 

counted 1 2 0 3

Surphakta, however, has two blank beats (*khālī*) :

4 + 2 + 4

Surphakta 

counted 1 0 2 3 0

and *Chautāla* has four beats (*tāl*) and two blanks (*khālī*) :

4 + 4 + 2 + 2

Chautāla 

counted 1 0 2 0 3 4

Aḍa-chautāla, again, four beats and three blanks :

2 + 4 + 4 + 4

Aḍa-chautāla 

counted 1 2 0 3 0 4 0

Indian rhythm, then, moves in *āvards* broken up into *vibhāgs*, each of which contains one or more *tāls.*[1] We can equally say of ours that it moves in sections broken up into bars each of which contains one or more beats. In what does the difference between the two systems consist ?

It may be answered that theirs is derived from song, ours from the dance or the march. That both are based on the numbers 2 and 3, but that they add and we multiply in order to form combinations of these. But the answer which goes deepest is that their music is in modes of time (as we saw also that it was in modes of tune), and that ours changes that mode at will by means principally of the harmony.

In order that rhythm, an articulation of the infinite variety of sounds, may be upon some regular plan, the plan must have some recognizable unit of measurement. India takes the short note and gives it for a particular rhythm a certain value as opposed to the

[1] It is unfortunate that the word is also used in the sense of *vibhāg* to mean the 'time' of the music.

long; Europe takes the stressed note and gives it in a particular rhythm a certain frequency as against the unstressed, and graduates its force. We find the unity of the rhythm in the recurrent bar (which is always in duple or triple time, just as our two melodic modes are either major or minor), and have to look elsewhere for the variety; they find variety in the *vibhāg* whose constitution is, as we have seen, extremely various, and must look elsewhere for unity. Both of us find what we want in the larger spaces of time; they find unity in the *āvard*, we find variety in the sections.

The *āvard* is a constant. In slow time there may be only two *vibhāgs* in it, in quick time there will certainly be four. And this series of four is unbroken, except at the end of the verse or the song, that is, where the singer breaks off temporarily or altogether. We can see why this must be so. Suppose the song is in *Rūpak* (♩ 𝅗𝅥 | ♩ 𝅗𝅥 |, &c.). Unless there were some accepted number of *vibhāgs* to the *āvard* it would be impossible to know that the music was not in the larger *āvard* (i.e. in fewer *vibhāgs*) of *Tevra* (♩. ♩ ♩ | ♩. ♩ ♩ |, &c.) or of *Jhampa* (♩ ♩. ♩ ♩. | ♩ ♩. ♩ ♩. |, &c.).

Ex. 317.

If the length of the *āvard* were not certain, the rhythmical 'mode', which has a connotation of its own just as the melodic 'mode' has, would not be clear, and all cross-rhythm, a corner-stone of this music, would become impossible; for this presupposes a constant against which something else is inconstant.

The 'section' in Europe is often, too often, also of four bars; it is this fact that makes much of our church services musically unattractive. But the section can have, and in the best music it has, a varying number of bars. Its length is altered, either really or apparently; it is either actually shortened or lengthened, or else two equal sections are made to overlap so that one seems shorter than the other. Any work on large lines will supply examples of this; here, for instance, in the passage for flute and bassoon out of *Leonora*, No. 3:

Ex. 318.

in which the sections are twice shortened from four bars to two, and the phrases twice overlap so as to produce the effect of two three-bar sections. It would be clearer if our music were printed as Handel wrote (though not consistently) his *Messiah*, with bar-lines running all through the staves at each new section, and between these places only through the single staves; it would have the effect which punctuation has upon the written word (and would be as difficult to get right). An instance of the judgement he exercised in this matter may be seen in the two versions, given in the autograph score, of the opening symphony of 'But who may abide'.

There is one case, however, which puts the thing in a nutshell. In 1893, when $\frac{5}{4}$ rhythm was less familiar to Europe than it now is, Tschaikowsky felt it necessary in his Sixth Symphony to do two things. He kept the metre free from complications; the Scherzo is almost entirely based on the crotchet, and the Trio on the minim. He also kept the sections uniform; they are in four-bar rhythm throughout except in two places—at the return from the Trio to the Scherzo, and at the Coda—the very places in which, as we saw, liberty was allowed in the *āvard.* It was only there, in fact, that he felt his rhythm so securely established that he could play with it. But now that it no longer piques our curiosity to see how $\frac{5}{4}$ is 'beaten', and that the problem of counting it accurately no longer provides us with a painful pleasure, the monotony of the sections comes back upon us with fatal force. But the four-bar section would not have this effect if, like the Hindus, we had a large assortment of variously characterized rhythms to fill it.

It is harmony which puts it in our power to prevent this frequently changing length of the phrase or section from upsetting the unity of the rhythm. In this Adagio from Haydn's First Quartet:

Ex. 319.

the phrases are made to stand out from each other by means of the harmony: *a* and *d* taper towards the end, *c* steals in unawares, and *b* contrasts firmly with its neighbours *a* and *c*; and that such insistence upon the rhythm was necessary is shown by the base form into which the melody has relapsed by the constant use which has ignored it.

In the Menuetto which follows it:

Ex. 320.

the harmonies by their postponement to the second bar clearly mark the beginning of a section there, and tell us that the phrase of the first bar is to be regarded as *extra sententiam*. Then by entering at the normal place in the sixth bar they proclaim that that phrase is now taken into the sentence. They are not responsible for the assertion that bars 6, 7 and 8, 9 each make a section; that is made clear by the balance of the phrases they contain—the phrase of 8, 9 is an inversion of that in 6, 7. But the harmonies again compel us to take bar 10 as a section all to itself, for they exactly repeat those of bar 9, only a place higher. This somewhat intricate arrangement of sections would be confusing but for the fact that they make up in all a period of twelve bars—that is, the time length of three normal sections—and so their excessive variety is unified.

Very similarly in Chopin's Sixth Nocturne a twelve-bar unity is reached by a different distribution :

Ex. 321.

and this is the work of the harmony, more especially of the tenor part :

Ex. 322.

But these two examples are the opening phrases of two several compositions where a certain clearness of balance is necessary and some general unity (here twelve bars) is indispensable: in the course of a composition (as we may conclude from Ex. 318) no such higher unity need be or is aimed at; the sections may be as various as the composer pleases.

It is needless to give instances where the harmony graduates the stress of the rhythm, as every page of music is full of them. This is a distinction which Indian music is also fully alive to, as we shall see in the next chapter.

It is sometimes thought that these uneven times—5, 7, 10, 14, and so on—are full of suggestion for European composers. This on the whole may be doubted, because duration is not the same thing as stress. All these Indian rhythms have their *raison d'être* in the contrast of long and short duration, and to identify these with much and little stress is to vulgarize the rhythms. The only genuine instance we have of their method is Saraband rhythm, and we see instantly how in

Ex. 323.

the effect is lost if the second minim in addition to being lengthened is also emphasized. Stress pulses, and demands regularity; duration is complementary, and revels in irregularity. In order to get the true sense of duration we have to get rid of stress, and this would mean that we must find some other means (as the Hindus do) of marking the beginning of the bar than by accenting it. Tschaikowsky's Scherzo and Trio do this. The Scherzo is in elongated trochees (7 + 3 instead of 6 + 3):

Ex. 324.

[1]

instead of

Ex. 325.

Both these phrases are characterized; the first by crotchets with an incidental triplet, the second by the dotted minim. This rhythm pervades the whole, although the units are afterwards slightly varied. The Trio is a truncated Saraband, and by its figuration appears as a contracted iamb (2 + 3 instead of 2 + 4):

Ex. 326.
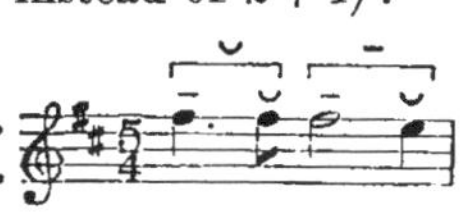
[1]

instead of

Ex. 327.

The way the composer has defeated the stress is by a variety of devices; in the Scherzo by the cross-bowing, running quavers, and syncopation of the accompaniment, in the Trio by the crotchet drone bass. And if the conductor would now lay down his stick for this passage there would be nothing to distinguish it from Indian rhythm.

But the fact remains that we feel these things as elongations and

[1] The two movements (Exs. 324 and 326) correspond practically to C. IV (7 + 1 + 2) and B. I (2 + 3).

truncations of rhythms which are familiar to us, and they could hardly be naturalized. Perhaps this is why in his variations on a Hungarian air in $\frac{7}{4}$ (*Tevra*) Brahms drops in the fourth variation into common time beginning on an off-beat, in the fifth and sixth into $\frac{3}{4}$ beginning on an off-beat, in the seventh into overlapping phrases, and continues from the ninth onwards frankly in $\frac{2}{4}$ and $\frac{6}{8}$. Perhaps he felt that he could best explain the nature of this rhythm by showing that it was like all these things which we have, but was not the same as any one of them.

But considered as forms of our rhythms gone mad they have a definite use, as, for instance, in Tristan's delirium (Act III, sc. ii), where fragments of melodies, his whole past in fact, come thronging disjointedly into his mind. Only these are not Indian rhythms. They are European rhythms distorted to suit the state of his bodily pulse; it is precisely the pulsation of them that is insisted upon.

The modern use of these unusual rhythms is again different. The constant changes of time—some half dozen perhaps, $\frac{7}{8}$, $\frac{5}{8}$, $\frac{2}{4}$, $\frac{7}{8}$, $\frac{1}{8}$, $\frac{3}{4}$, &c., occurring in not more than twice six bars—are part of the striving of the last twenty years after realism and away from formalism. Composers aim at substituting the rhetorical accent of prose for the metrical accent of verse, at imitating in instrumental music the broken accents of the speaking voice. As such their music has nothing in common with the systems we have been discussing where metrical law prevails. They appear to defy law; and they are justified, but only by success in the particular instance. Thus, of two such instances, we may say that Cyril Scott's Sonata, Op. 66, is less convincing rhythmically than Stravinsky's *Petrouchka*. For the latter has large tracts of uniform time which enable the vagaries to be felt as contrast, whereas in the former there is no such contrast—because it is all contrast.

'Tin'. The second finger rises as the first falls — 'Ke'

'Nan' — 'Ga'

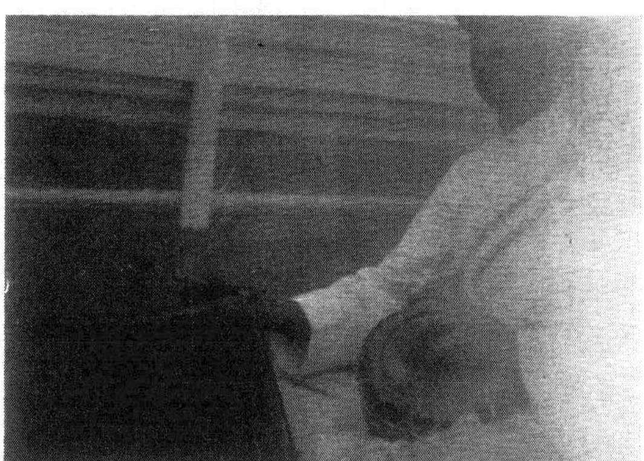

'Nan' — 'Ghe'

Ranganna, Mysore

CHAPTER IX

DRUMMING

> Monsieur le Grand knew only a little broken German, only the really important words—Bread, Kiss, Honour—but he could always make his meaning clear on the drum. If I wanted to know, for instance, what was meant by 'Liberté' he would drum the *Marseillaise* —and I understood. If I did not know the meaning of 'Égalité' he would drum *Ça ira, ça ira . . . les aristocrats à la lanterne*—and I understood him. If I did not know what 'bêtise' was he would drum the Dessau march—which we Germans, as Goethe records, used to drum in the Champagne—and I understood him. He wanted once to explain to me the word 'L'Allemagne', and he drummed that old, old tune, simplicity itself, the tune that you can hear on fair days outside the booth where the dancing dogs are—*Dumb, dumb, dumb*. It made me very angry, but I understood him.—HEINE.

THE drum is used not, as with us, to assert the accent at special moments, or to reinforce a crisis, but to articulate the metre of the singer's melody, or to add variety to it by means of a cross-metre. There are four main elements in drumming: the quality, the intensity, the pitch of the sounds, and the time-intervals between them. We do not, on the whole, use percussion much. When we do, we value it, perhaps, chiefly for the graduated intensity with which it points the rhythm. We look a little askance at varieties of quality; we recognize the drums (*grosse caisse* or *tympani*), the cymbals, and the triangle; but we are not quite sure how far the tambourine, castanets, and Berlioz's flannel-headed drumsticks are legitimate music. Of the pitch we only demand that it should not clash with the pitch of other sounds, it is in no way a vital constituent of the harmony, which is almost invariably complete without it. The time-intervals of the drum-notes reinforce as a whole those of the other instruments; they seldom cross them, and only produce a certain amount of confusion when they do, which, however, may be a useful resource upon occasion.

In Hindu music the graduated intensity of the sound is very little regarded, either in singing or playing or drumming, because their whole scheme is not accentual, but quantitative. It is true that the first of the bar (the *sam*) is louder than the rest often, not always; but this is not in order that it may, as with us, stand out against other accents, but because two quantitative schemes are apt to coincide there, and two sounds are louder than one. The time-intervals are with them all-important, and show great variety; it is seldom that more than a few bars, out of hundreds, are drummed in exactly the same way. And the drumming is practically continuous; it is only occasionally silenced for special contrast. The pitch, again, is all-important, for it is invariably the keynote, and frequently the drum is the singer's only accompaniment. Lastly, a maximum of variety is got into the quality; and this not mainly by the variety of the instruments. For though there are scores of shapes for drums, tambourines, cymbals, triangles, and so forth, they are not usually assembled together, because concerted music is the exception, not the rule. The variety is got out of the drum, or the pair of drums themselves. They are played with the full hand and the fingers, rarely with sticks; there are half a dozen strokes for the right hand and three or four for the left. Of these Lady Wilson's[1] drummer said, 'The beat (with the left hand) is like the seam of my coat—that must be there; the other notes (with the right hand) are like the embroidery I may put according to my own fancy over the seam.' These 'notes' are differentiated not by pitch, but quality. They are also articulated by great intricacy of time-interval. For neither of these two things has our music any real analogues; and the Bengalis do not overstate the case in their saying '*Yantrapatir mṛdānga*' (the drum is the father of instruments). It is proposed now to examine Indian drumming under these two aspects: quality and metre.

TONE-QUALITY. Under a multitude of names there are two main types of drum. The *mṛdānga* played at both ends with the hands (or if with sticks, called *dhol*); and the pair of drums, *tabla*, the right hand *daina* and the left hand *bayan*. Both kinds are tuned in the ordinary way by braces (*dīwal*), between which and the wall of the drum (*chattu*) tuning blocks (*gaṭṭa*) are wedged. In the

[1] *A Short Account of the Hindu System of Music*, by A. C. Wilson, 1904.

PLATE 12

'Ta' 'Na' (borrowed from the right-hand strokes)

Both hands, 'Dha'; Ghe + Ghe

'Ta' 'Ka'

Bhai Santu, Amritsar

mṛdānga the driving in of these wedges sharpens both ends simultaneously. When, as in the better class music, it is desired to have both drumheads (*warka*) in tune with each other, another device is adopted. A mixture of flour (*āṭa*) and water is worked on to the middle of the larger drumhead to lower the tone to the desired amount. The two heads are commonly tuned an octave apart. The plaster also adds to the resonance, and seems to be valued for that reason. It is therefore retained in the *tabla*, although it was not necessary here for the tuning, because each drum has only one head, and the braces do all that is wanted. On the *mṛdānga* the plaster is fresh made whenever the drum is used; on the *tabla* it is applied once for all, and has frequently been mixed with iron filings to add to the resonance, and is then black. It is called *sīyahi* (blackness) or *āk* (eye); the rim of the drum-wall over which the skin is passed is called *kanar*, and the drumhead, which is visible between that and the *ak*, is known as *warka* (lit. leaf of a book). On the left drum the 'eye' is in the middle; on the right it is eccentric, in the 'north-west' corner, lying under the tip of the forefinger.[1] The different tone qualities are obtained by striking with the full hand, or the several fingers at different places, and by damping or releasing. They are distinguished by names (*bol*). The *tabla* are generally tuned in unison, occasionally at a Fifth from each other; but there is no idea whatever of 'dominant-tonic' in this tuning. The alternation of sound between the two drums is incessant and instantaneous, so that the two notes merge; and they are obviously there for the same reason as they are upon the drone strings of the *vīṇā* or *tambura*, only as an enrichment of the tone. The note of the drum is also altered by way of 'grace'. There is a special hour-glass-shaped drum, especially in South India, small enough to be held in the hand, which can then squeeze the braces and sharpen the note. On the *tabla* too there is a special stroke (called *ghe*) which can be made with either hand; after a blow from the full hand the ball of the thumb is slid forward across the drumhead. This raises the pitch slightly and produces a sound like a galosh leaving the mud, curious, and by no means unattractive.

The *mṛdānga* and *dhol* are respectively barrel-shaped and cylindrical. The *tabla*, left and right, are of the shape of a giant tea-cup and coffee-cup respectively; the left is tucked into the crook of

[1] Sometimes the 'eye' of the right drum is called *sīyahi* and that of the left *āk*.

the knee, the right is propped against a cloth. For the other varieties of percussion, any one who has not access to Captain Day's excellent illustrations may get a rough idea of them from the photograph opposite of some South Indian specimens. The *karadivadya, udukkai,* and *budubudike* are three sizes of the same make, the smallest being squeezed in the hand, the longest under the arm. The *karadivadya* is beaten with a padded drumstick. Against it leans a *kokkara,* a metal tube with serrated edges, which are rubbed, to produce a grating sound, with the metal pin on a chain, which hangs down over the tambourine (*kanjari*) below it: it is used by pariahs, especially by the Pulaiyars of Travancore, for casting out devils. The goblet-shaped *udupe* is used by Lingayets in temple worship. Below are the *nāgari,* seventeen inches in height and diameter, for use on an elephant and in the temple, with seventy turns of lacing: the *maddale* (*mṛdāṅga*-shape) hollowed out of a tree, and the Mohammedan *dolu* (*dhol*) of copper. The *dhol* is played with hands or sticks; if open at one end, as occasionally, it is played with sticks at the other end. In a Panjabi regiment a drummer (Miranbaksh, see p. 237) was pointed out to me who sometimes wielded his sticks till his hands bled.

Confining ourselves now to the *tabla*—the *mṛdāṅga* is played in the same way—we will examine the different strokes (*bols*) given with either hand or both hands; singly, successively, or simultaneously; with one or more fingers or with the whole hand; upon the 'black', or the 'rim', or upon the 'white' between them; damped, or partly damped, or undamped. Indian fingers are extraordinarily supple. The forefinger, as pianoforte players know, is one of the weakest; but its stroke as it comes down flat with a whang on different parts of the drum is curiously powerful, and inimitable by Westerns. It is said to take half a lifetime to make a good drummer, and it will be seen in the following pages that there is much to learn.

There is considerable difficulty, short of the only true way—by learning to drum oneself—in finding out what these strokes really are. Not only do both strokes and names vary in the North and the names differ entirely in the South, but the drummer regards his strokes as a synthesis, and is not accustomed to analyse them. Also if too many questions are asked, the victim begins at last in sheer desperation to say the first thing that comes into his head.

PLATE 13

Udukkai Udupe Udukkai Karadivādya

Budubūdike Tambourines Kokkara

Tambourines

Maddale Nāgarī Dolu

(From the collection in the Museum, Bangalore)

NANNE KHAN'S *bols* (BHAVNAGAR).

Bol.	Hand.	Degree of complexity.	Fingers.	Part struck.	Damping.	Remarks.
Ta	Right	Single	{ 1st on { others on	rim } white }	damped	The normal right-hand stroke.
Na	,,	,,	1st	rim	released	Gives a short, matter of fact sound, easily recognizable.
Nan	,,	,,	1st	rim	4th damps	Gives the upper octave as overtone when the stroke dies away.
Tin	,,	,,	1st	black	3rd damps and releases	Metallic.
Ti or *Tiṇ*	,,	,,	1st	black	released	The 2nd and 3rd damp lightly.
Di	,,	,,	1st three	black	released	Heavier than *Ti*, more resonant.
Ka	Left	,,	whole hand	black	damped lightly	The normal left-hand stroke.
Ga	,,	,,	finger tips	white	released	Struck lightly; dully resonant.
Ghe	,,	,,	whole hand	whole surface	moderately damped	The ball of the thumb follows across the drum, pressing and sharpening. This stroke is also used by the right hand.
Ke	,,	,,	whole hand	whole surface	completely damped	The hand rests on the surface after striking.
Titi	Right	Successive	{ 4th on { 1st on	black } rim }	released	= *Ta* + *Ta*. The 1st follows the 4th quickly.
Gidi	Both	,,				= *Ghe* + *Di*.
Gina	,,	,,				= *Ghe* + *Na*.
Dhā	,,	Simultaneous				= *Ghe* + *Ta*, or *Ghe* + *Ghe*. The normal stroke for both hands. It occurs generally at the '*sam*', though not exclusively.
Dhi	,,	,,				= *Ga* + *Di*.
Dhin	,,	,,				= *Dhi* + *Na* = *Ga* + *Di* + *Na*.

Nor is much help to be got from the books; the author takes for granted that a thing which he sees and hears every day will be familiar to his reader, and accordingly omits to differentiate the strokes in words, and he does not always state their duration, which is of vital importance for the normal drum-phrases (*ṭheka*) and their variants (*parand*) which we shall examine later. The list on p. 231 was obtained from the court drummer, Nanne Khan, at Bhavnagar (Gujarāt), and is supplemented by statements of various others at Calcutta, Bombay, Allahabad, Lahore, Jhelum, and other places, and checked by the list in T. B. Sahasrabuddhe's book (in Marathi) and A. B. Pingle's *Indian Music,* the only full account of the matter in English.

The list is not complete, although the most important *bols* are probably there. Those of the right hand begin with dentals, those of the left with gutturals,[1] and those of both hands simultaneously with aspirated dentals. There are a variety of other 'successive' and 'simultaneous' strokes. A few of the 'single' *bols* are shown in the photographs of two drummers (at Mysore and Lahore) facing pp. 225, 227.

TIME-INTERVAL. These drum-words (*bol*) are distributed in drum-phrases (*ṭheka*), which constitute the drummer's *memoria technica* for the particular *Tāl*, and in drum-variants (*parand*)[2]; the former's duty is to 'keep up' the *tāl*, the latter's to 'swell' it (Pingle). In the next diagram are exhibited *ṭhekas* of *tīntāl* from different localities.

The first six of these are genuine *ṭhekas*: the alteration of *d* to *t* in the first *ṭhekas* and the *trikara* in the sixth is intended to distinguish the blank (*khālī*) section of the bar (marked 0) from the others. The eighth (from Jhelum) is an instance of four bars of *Surphakta* treated as one of *Tīntāl.* The seventh (from Calcutta) is of the nature of a *parand,* that is, the drumming of the various beats is contrasted.

The six *parands* from Bombay are continuous. At the end of the fourth line, at 'ta ta ghinna' begins a new rhythm in three time, which comes to an end just as the singer, going on in four time, reaches his *sam* at the beginning of the seventh line. This is a simple instance of a thing which is often enormously complex,

[1] We use *k* and *t* for double tonguing on brass instruments similarly, because of their distinctness.

[2] Pronounce 'pŭrrŭnd'.

Tīntāl.

The ordinary *ṭheka.*

1				2				0				3				
dha	dhin	dhin	dha	dha	dhin	dhin	dha	dha	tin	tin	ta	dha	dhin	dhin	dha	Lahore (Degambur).
na	dhi	dhi	na	na	dhi	dhi	na	na	dhi	dhi	na	na	dhi	dhi	na	Jhelum.
na	dhin	dhin	na	na	dhin	dhin	na	na	tin	tin	na	na	dhin	dhin	na	Gujarāt (Pingle).
na	dhin	dhin	na	na	dhin	dhin	na	ta	tin	tin	na	na	dhin	dhin	na	Amritsar.
ta	dhin	dhin	na	ta	dhin	dhin	na	dha	tin	tin	na	ta	dhin	dhin	na	Allahabad.
na	dhi	dhin	na	na	dhi	dhin	na	na	trikara	dhin	na	na	dhi	dhin	na	Pind Dadan Khan, Punjab.
det	det	dene	nag	drege	tete	kete	tag	greden		tage	dage	tete	kota	gadi	gene	Calcutta.

Compound time; 4 bars (*vibhāg*) of 5 units (*mātrā*) to make one section (*āvard*) of *Tīntāl.*

dhag	dhag	din	dhag	dhag	din	dhag	dhag	din	dhag	dhag	din	Jhelum.

Six *parands.*

dha	trika	dhikata	dhatri	ka	dhikita	dhage	tita	kiridha	tita	gadi	gina	diga	diga	naga	naga	Bombay.
na	krita	dhagina	dhage	trika	dhikita	dhan	na	dha	ta	na	dha	ta	dha	gadigina	dha	
dhi	ta	gan	dhit	dhit	krita	dhita	kri	dhit	ta	dhit	dhit	dita	tita	giga	tita	
giga	dhin	dhin	krita	dhikita	ta	ghin	dhage	dhin		ghitira	kitataka	ta	ta	ghin	na	
dhī	ta	kita	dha	kita	tutu	kitataka	gadigina	dha	ta	ghin	na	dhi	ta	kita	dha	
kita	tutu	kitataka	gadigina	dha	ta	ghin	na	dhi	ta	kita	dha	kita	tutu	kitataka	gadigina	
dha	trika	dhikita	dhatri	(&c. as in the first line.)												

which is very common, and which gives great pleasure to an Indian audience, who invariably greet it with appreciative *acchcha*'s ('good'), It is rare in our music, though instances are to be found, as of most things, in Bach; here, for instance, is one from the first movement of the Violin Concerto in E major:

Ex. 328.

in which the violin breaking into three bars of $\frac{3}{4}$ arrives at the reprise of the theme simultaneously with the piano, which continues in common time. Another instance is the common Handelian close:

Ex. 329.

which, though a still simpler device, is used for the same purpose of clinching the final note. (Cp. *Int. Mus. Monthly Journal*, Oct. 1913, pp. 3–7.)

What appear in the *parands* given above to be a number of new *bols*, are really those we have already met with subjected to phonetic decay. Thus (in alphabetical order):

dene = dhi + na
det = dhi + ta
dhāg(e) = dhā + ghe
dhān = dhā + na
dhikita = dhi + ka + ta
gadi = ga + di
gidi = ghe + di
gina = ghe + na
ghitira = ghe + ti + ta
greden = ghe + ta + dhi + na
kiridha = ka + ti + dhā
krita = ka + ti + ta
trika = ta + ti + ka
trikara = ta + ti + ka + ta
tutu ?

The time-value of the stroke is not implied in its name, though the compound *bols* naturally take longer than the simple. These values have to be learned by watching and noting performance; and those given here have no more authority behind them than a few mornings devoted to that rather tedious occupation.

But without inducing a climax, *parands* in a different rhythm are often introduced just for fun. The singer and drummer like to play hide and seek with each other; and the audience watch the contest with amusement. The drummer is worsted in the contest in the following (phonographed) passage:

Rāg Sārang.
Tāl Āḍachautāla. Phonogram.

Ex. 330.

B ♩ = 150.
C
D
♩ = 170.
E

in *Aḍachautāla*,[1] between *shahnai* (oboe) and *tabla*. They were asked to begin with four *ṭhekas* and go on with *parands*. The section (*āvard*) is marked off by the double bar. Down to the first double bar, however, is *ad libitum*. It is the *Ālāp* (prelude) with which the music always begins, in order to establish the *Rāg*, and it is not in strict time. But the drummer is trying over his *Tāl* too, and though he gets the same number of beats as the singer they did not, as a matter of fact, exactly synchronize. From A onwards it is in strict time, and after the four *ṭhekas*, the *parands* begin at B. Here the drummer breaks into an eight-rhythm (instead of seven) for variety. The oboist also varies. His phrase should have ended at C, but it ends a bar before. He ends the

[1] Properly one bar of 14 crotchets; here given for convenience as two bars of 7.

next one, however, correctly at D. Then he has a short one of two bars; and then, at ♩ = 170, a long one of six bars and an extra minim. At this point the pace becomes furious, and, shortening his phrase by that extra minim, he ends it up with *Haṇ* (yes) at G. Meanwhile the drummer, about D, has dropped his cross-rhythm, and seems to be plotting something a little more interesting. When the oboist begins his six-bar phrase, the drummer varies the little figure with which he started at B; thus:

Ex. 331.

{ The figure is dislocated to give a subsidiary cross rhythm.

which now becomes three-quaver rhythm:

Ex. 332.

and so through an orgy of triplets, accented on the middle note, to the end.

Whatever the reader may think of the melody, he will not deny the oboist a firm grip of a difficult rhythm. (His name was Panna, and he was said, incidentally, very likely with truth, to be the 'best Shahnai player in Hindostan'; the axis of the earth sticks up, however, in every city of India just as visibly as Heine said it did in Germany.) It is probably not accidental that the *tempo* ends up at ♩ = 260, exactly twice as fast as it began, and the phonograph leaves no doubt about the fact. The drummer is not so strong. He drums throughout in *Tīntāl*; and there is nothing in his *parands* which shows that he feels the rhythm of *Āḍachautāla* at all. He ought to arrange to meet the player at one or other of the *sams* (A, B, C, &c.), and he does not do so in any case, although he manages to get a general sense of climax towards the end.

The next is a Panjabi *ghazal*, on two *Shahnais* (Havildar Rashu and Naik Nawab) and *dhol* (Sipahi Miranbaksh):

Ghazal (Dorian).

Tāl Dhamār, 5 + 5 + 2 + 2 quavers. 33rd Punjabis.

Two Shahnais in unison. 𝅗𝅥. = 140. Phonogram.

Ex. 333.

The two oboes, always nearly and never quite in tune with one another, produced 'beats' which in the phonograph are heart-rending. Afterwards the Havildar played alone these two bars of *Chautāl*, which the drummer ornamented at different places:

Rāg Sindora (Dorian, hexatonic).
Tāl Chautāl. (4 + 4 + 2 + 2 quavers.) 𝅗𝅥 = 80. Phonogram.

Ex. 334.

These give but a slight idea of the intricacy which is sometimes attained by a really good drummer. They are given because the phonograph guarantees their accuracy. Unfortunately it is difficult to get both player and drummer into the phonograph, and I could only manage it when both, as in these cases, were very loud. In the case of song and drum, the song, and in the case of *vīṇā* and drum, the drum alone is audible. In this last specimen at the places marked 'inaudible' the drum was quietly tapping the regular beats of *Chautāl*.

Drumming of this kind is in fact the substitute for counterpoint; it serves the same purpose as that does of carrying on the interest of the music over the 'dead' points, or of converging on a crisis. We are familiar with just such cross-rhythms in fugues; in the following example the voices are never all in the same rhythm, and throughout bars 80 and 81 they are all in different rhythms:

The 46th of the forty-eight Fugues.

Ex. 335.

N.B.—The numbers are placed at the end of the bar to which they refer.

A few *ṭhekas* of other *Tāls* than *Tīntāl* may be added in order to give an idea of the kind of thing; the one or two new *bols* they contain will not offer any difficulty:

Ex. 336. *Rūpak.* 2 + 3 = 5 units.

1 2 (no *khālī*)
Tin trikad dhī nana

Rūpak. 2 + 4 = 6 units.

1 2 0 1 2 0
Dhīga nana tunna | dhinna nana tunna

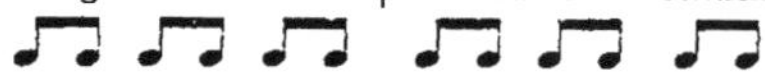

Tevra. 3 + 2 + 2 = 7 units.

1 2 3 1 2 3 (no *khālī*)
Kadhina dhina dha | katina tina ta

Gajala. 4 + 5 = 9 units.

1 2 (no *khālī*)
Tin taka dhin nana

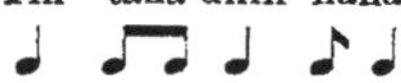

Surphakta. 4 + 2 + 4 = 10 units.

1 0 2 3 0
Dhagi tita dhagi dhagi tita

Jhampa (*Jhap*). 2 + 3 + 2 + 3 = 10 units.

1 2 0 3
Dhin dhatuna katta dhatuna

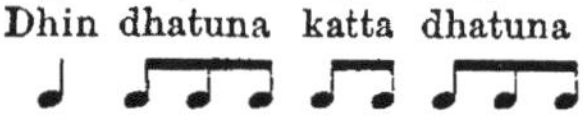

Chautāl. 4 + 4 + 2 + 2 = 12 units.

1 0 2 0 3 4
Dhadhadhinta kiṭadhadhinta tiṭakita gadigina

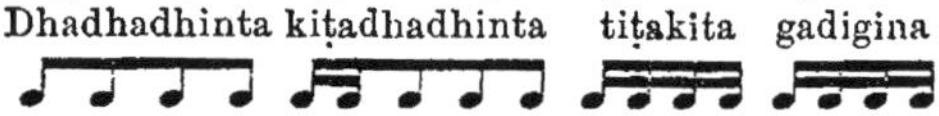

Āḍachautāl. 2 + 4 + 4 + 4 = 14 units.

1 2 0 3 0 4 0
Dhitrik dhinatuna kattadhindhin nadhindhinna

Dhamār. 5 + 5 + 4 = 14 units.

1 2 3 (no *khālī*)
Tadhe dhe dha takita kitataka

The above is the method, or it would be better to say a method, at Poona. The last two contain a cross-rhythm. They end respectively

dhindhinna dhindhinna

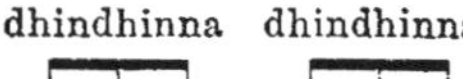

and

taka takita taka

PACE (*lāya*) AND 'SPEED' (*kāla*). There are three degrees of *tempo*; slow (*velambit*), moderate (*madhya*), and fast (*druta*). In whatever *tempo*, the music has a normal speed-unit, i. e. it is in crotchets, as we should say, or else in quavers, and so on. Doublings and halvings of this unit (*mātrā*)—as we say, augmentation and diminution—are common, and have names. The normal speed is called the 'time of the time' (*bārobārī*), or it is named *dhā* from the average length of the principal drum-beat of that name. The alterations of this speed are, taking the crotchet as the unit:

𝅗𝅥 *Thā* (lit. a loud sound).

♩ *Dhā*, or *Bārobārī* (the time of the time).

♪ *Dviguni* (*Dūni*, *Digan*), 'twofold'.

𝅘𝅥𝅯 *Caturguni* (*Chaugan*), 'fourfold'.

A 'sixfold' speed is known; but this generally not the 𝅘𝅥𝅰, but the triplet-semiquaver as in 𝅘𝅥𝅯𝅘𝅥𝅯𝅘𝅥𝅯 (3). We need only concern ourselves with *Dūni* (twofold). This principle of doubling the speed is at the root of the curious form the *ṭhekas* have assumed; it results in 'convergence' of the *Tāl*, either (1) in itself, or (2) with some other *Tāl*.

CONVERGENCE of one *Tāl*. A bar of a *Tāl* is beaten with one hand while two bars of its *Dūni* are beaten with the other. Using *Ta* for the right-hand stroke, *Ka* for the left, *a* for the empty beat, and *Dhā* for both hands, *Tīntāl* may be converged:

1	2	0	3	1	2	0	3	Right, Ta
1		2		0		3		Left, Ka
Dha	ta	ka	ta	ta	ta	ka	ta	

or Surphakta.

1	0	2	3	0	1	0	2	3	0	Ta
1		0		2		3		0		Ka
Dha	a	ta	ta	ka	ta	ka	ta	ta	a	

or Chautāl.

1	0	2	0	3	4	1	0	2	0	3	4
1		0		2		0		3		4	
Dha	a	ta	a	dha	ta	ta	a	dha	a	dha	ta

or Tevra

1	0	0	2	0	3	0	1	0	0	2	0	3	0
1		0		0		2		0		3		0	
Dha	a	a	ta	a	ta	ka	ta	a	a	dha	a-	ta	a

(♩. ♩ ♪♪ | ♩. ♩. ♩)

Similarly one *Tāl* may be 'converged' with another:

Tīntāl	1	2	0	3	1	2	0	3	1	2	0	3	Right
Chautāl	1		0		2		0		3		4		Left
	Dha	ta	a	ta	dha	ta	a	ta	dha	ta	ka	ta	

or,

ıtāl	1	2	0	3	1	2	0	3	1	2	0	3	1	2	0	3	1	2	0	3
rphakta	1	0	2	3	0	1	0	2	3	0	1	0	2	3	0	1	0	2	3	0
	Dha	ta	ka	dha	ta	dha	a	dha	dha	ta	ka	ta	dha	dha	a	dha	ta	dha	ka	tı

We have confined ourselves to three *bols*—*ta*, *ka*, and *dha*. But when all the *bols* are used we see that the application of this principle of convergence might, if we happened to know the details of the process, result in the concrete examples of the *ṭhekas* already given. We see, at any rate, that *dha* comes to be a long beat (*dhā*) because it is generally succeeded by *a*; and the prevalence of *tirakira* (*trikara*, *trikad*, *trika*, *trik*) in the *ṭhekas* is accounted for there by the prevalence of such forms as *takata* and *tatakata* here.

CUMULATION. There is one other principle of disposing the beats and silences which accounts for a few out of the way *Tāls*, and which must be mentioned for the sake of completeness. It consists of *cumulating* the beats and punctuating these by blanks. Thus:

one one two two four
(*a*) 1 0 | 2 0 | 3 4 0 | 5 6 0 | 7 8 9 10 0 |

one one two three four
(*b*) 1 0 | 2 0 | 3 4 0 | 5 6 7 0 | 8 9 10 11 0 |

one two three four five
(*c*) 1 0 | 2 3 0 | 4 5 6 0 | 7 8 9 10 0 | 11 12 13 14 15 0 |

In all these the cumulative element tends to throw stress upon the final beat (in *a*, 10; in *b*, 11; in *c*, 15). This, accordingly, becomes the first of the bar, and these three *Tāls* are received into music, with special names, as follows:

[=10] one one two two four
(*a*) *Savāri* 1 0 | 2 0 | 3 0 | 4 5 0 | 6 7 0 | 8 9 10 . . |
>

[=11] one one two three four
(*b*) *Brahma* 1 0 | 2 0 | 3 0 | 4 5 0 | 6 7 8 0 | 9 10 11 . . |
>

[=15] one two three four five
(*c*) *Rudra* 1 0 | 2 0 | 3 4 0 | 5 6 7 0 | 8 9 10 11 0 | 12 13 14 15 . . |
>

The striking thing about these *Tāls* is their length: 15, 16, and 20 units respectively. There may be a reason for this. It will be noticed that *a* is in geometrical, *c* in arithmetical progression. (On those principles the cumulations might have been variously arranged, but it will be found on trial that other arrangements are not so satisfactory.) We are told that *Savāri* (*a*), 15 units, in this its true form, is no longer in use, and that in its modern form it is simply taken as *Tīntāl* (16 units); and we can see that fifteen units is difficult to count, and that *Brahmatāla* (*b*) of sixteen units is an adulteration of it and a substitute for it. It was clearly necessary in these progressions to take a reasonable number of cumulations in order to display the principle; but there are other reasons for not taking a lower number of them than has been taken.

In (*a*) 'one, one, two' would not have shown the progression, and 'one, one, two, two' would have been too symmetrical, and Hindu *Tāl* loves variety.

In (*c*) 'one, two, three' produces nine units, which is seldom wanted; and 'one, two, three, four' produces fourteen units, which there are quite half a dozen other ways of counting. However, no doubt both these could be used, and probably are somewhere, and under some name or other.

Indian drumming, then, varies the quality rather than the quantity of the tone. It practically ignores accent for its own sake. Such accent as there is on the first of the bar is due to the fact that two rhythms diverge from that point and converge at the beginning of the next or a later bar. It is the accent induced by the juxtaposition of opposing metres, as in the Rondo of Beethoven, Op. 22

Ex. 337.

that pleases the Indian; not the accent which is sought for its own sake as a means of contrast, as, in the same movement, between the subject and the episode:

Ex. 338.

Here is a piece of rhythm that he would delight in (Brahms, Second Symphony):

Ex. 339.

N.B.—The small numbers refer to crotchets, the large to bars.

He would not have devised it exactly in this way, since, in the absence of harmony (which he does not mentally supply, as we do) and in the disregard (**4** + **4** + **5** + **4** + **5**) of the fixed section (**4** + **4**, &c., or **5** + **5**, &c., which he demands), there is nothing to hold it together. But he would be in sympathy with the metrical scheme:

$$\left.\begin{array}{c} 3 + 3 + 2 + 2 + 2 \\ 2\tfrac{1}{2} + 2\tfrac{1}{2} + 2\tfrac{1}{2} + 2\tfrac{1}{2} + 2 \\ 2 + 2 + 3 + 3 + 2 \end{array}\right\} = 12 \text{ crotchets } (\mathbf{4} \text{ bars}).$$

$$\left.\begin{array}{c} 2\tfrac{1}{2} + 3\tfrac{1}{2} + 2\tfrac{1}{2} + 3\tfrac{1}{2} + 3 \\ 2 + 2 \quad 3 + 3 + 3 + 2 \end{array}\right\} = 15 \text{ crotchets } (\mathbf{5} \text{ bars}).$$

It is this kind of variety which he gets from his drumming (*dardara*).[1] He uses the drum ornamentally, and not as we do (with the exception of certain dramatic passages) structurally.

[1] *Dardara* = *da-ḍa-da-ḍa*, a word formed from the name of the principal drum-beat, *dha*. *ḍ* and *r* have practically the same sound.

CHAPTER X

THE SĀMAN CHANT

It is a bemoanable pity to consider how few there are who know, but fewer who consider, what *wonderful-powerful-efficacious Virtues and Operations* Musick has upon the *Souls* and *Spirits* of *Men Divinely-bent.*

THOMAS MACE.

AN inquiry into the ethos and structure of some of the oldest music of which there is any record is not a mere piece of antiquarianism; it throws that sort of light on the music of modern India which a knowledge of the geology of a country throws upon its scenery.

Before coming to the *Sāmaveda* itself it will be necessary to glance at the recitation of the other Vedas, especially the *Ṛgveda.* For the *Sāmaveda* has borrowed the large majority of its text from the *Ṛgveda,* only altering or expanding the actual words so as to make them suitable for chanting; and much of the grammatical and prosodical determinations of the *Ṛgveda* has been given in the *Sāmaveda* a musical meaning.

The *Ṛgveda* is recited now, as it has always been, to three tones; for the accent was originally a mark of musical pitch, and became a mark of stress only after the beginning of our era. The 'raised' (*udātta*) and 'not raised' (*anudātta*) sounds represent the two main pitches of the speaking voice; this is the prose accent of the *Brāhmaṇas*; and there is nothing to show whether these two prose accents had any musical relationship. In addition to these two there was, for the reciting voice, the 'sounded' tone (*svarita*), which is shown on philological grounds to have been originally between the two others in pitch, but which is in the *Ṛgveda* above the *udātta.* No explanation is given as to what is exactly meant by 'sounded',[1] although it seems clear from the treatment of *svarita* that it means 'graced'. The *svarita* is in effect 'a falling accent of a dependent nature, marking the transition from an accented to a toneless

[1] Haug (*Ueber das Wesen,* &c., p. 74) appears to accept the view that *svarita* from *Svara* (like *getönt* from *Ton*) means 'accentuated'. But (1) this looks like a false analogy from the double meaning of *Ton,* and (2) *svarita* must surely be connected with *svāra,* which meant, technically, a downward slide through the *svaras,* i.e. the *svarita* was that note to which this slide was attached.

syllable. It regularly follows the *udātta*, to the rise of which its fall corresponds in pitch.[1] But also, 'the first part of the *svarita* sounds higher than the *udātta*' (ibid.), so that the *svarita* is practically an ornamented *udātta* falling to an indefinite pitch below it. This indefinite pitch is called *pracaya* ('throng'), in allusion to the number of unaccented syllables which occur there in succession; the *pracaya* is toneless, as distinguished from the *udātta* and *anudātta*, which are toned.[2] Before the rise from the *pracaya* to the next *udātta* or *svarita*, the voice descends to a 'lower' (*sannatara*) or 'more lowered' (*anudāttatara*) note, which is below the *anudātta*.

That is the original theory of the recitation; it will be seen, however, that it is modified in practice. This example, from Haug, p. 52, shows the *svarita* marked with a perpendicular line over the syllable, the *anudātta* with a horizontal beneath[3]; the *udātta* and *pracaya* are unmarked:

Ex. 340.

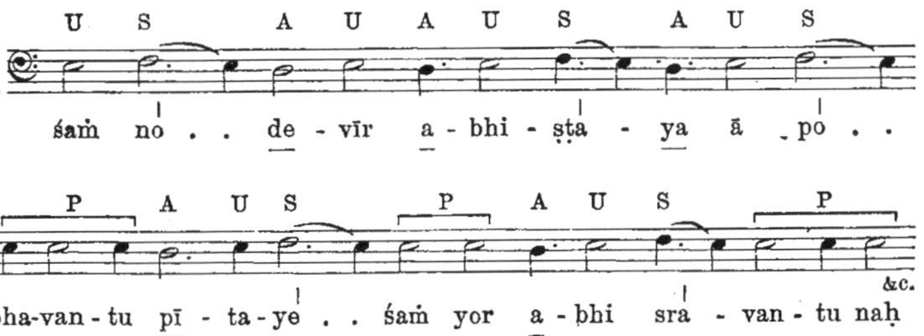

This is the Poona form of recitation taken down by Haug from the lips of Maratha Brahmans.[4] Only one form of the *svarita*, the

[1] A. A. Macdonell, *Vedic Grammar*, p. 77.

[2] It is tempting to see in the *pracaya* the counterpart of the *pyknon*. The *pyknon* was the cluster of three notes at intervals of a *diesis* (quarter-tone) which occurred in the Enharmonic genus (or of a semitone in the Chromatic). Thence there was a leap to the *mesē* just as there was a leap from the *anudātta*, or *pracaya*, to the *udātta*. But the *pyknon* was not an amorphous cluster; one of its three notes stood out from the other two, was in fact of the nature of a tonic. This is closely analogous to the toneless *pracaya* in which the toned *anudātta* stood out. And this 'toneless tone' may, further, be in principle the forerunner of the drone, frequently relegated to the drum, which might be called from one point of view toneless, from another, toned. The formation of the *svarita* tells us that the interval which was taken as a leap in ascent was bridged in descent; and this is borne out by the practice of modern *Rāga*, which prefers on the whole disjunct motion in ascent and conjunct in descent.

[3] *Devanāgari* letters are surmounted by a continuous horizontal line. A perpendicular line stands out well against this, and a horizontal line against the tails of the letters below.

[4] Haug (loc. cit.) gives four more of these stanzas.

appoggiatura F͡E, is here employed. But the noticeable thing is that the *pracaya* (marked P) is the same note as the *udātta,* not as the *anudātta;* if in a chant of only three notes it is to be distinguished from the *ānudātta,* it could not well have any other place; still, this change appears to await explanation.

In the following specimens[1] from Madras the *svarita* appears as a single note (F) and as an upward appoggiatura, E͡F.

Ex. 341.

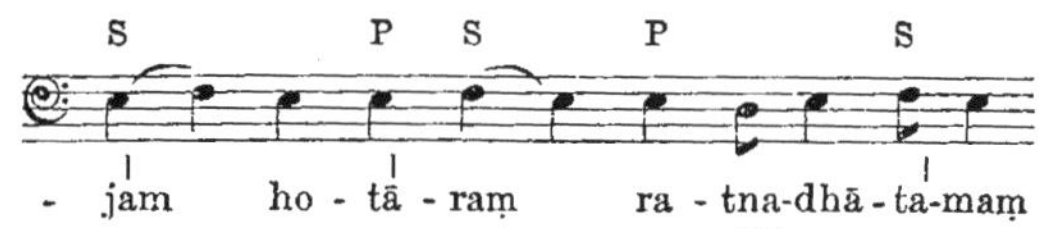

Ex. 342.

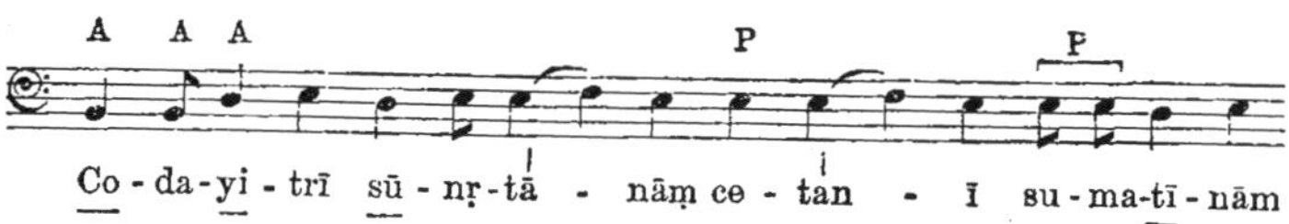

In the second of these examples the syllables *Co-da* obey a rule that 'when more than one *anudātta* precedes an *udātta,* all but the last are sounded lower'. Dr. Erwin Felber's book, which has lately appeared, *Die indische Musik der vedischen und der klassischen Zeit,* contains (p. 106, No. 433) an example of recitation of the *Ṛgveda* 'in the style of the old *Ṛṣis*', which is more florid and of larger compass than any of these.

The *Yajurveda* is also recited on the notes D, E, F; although in the half dozen times I heard it D, E, F♯[2] was quite as common. The following is from a Mysore singer:

Ex. 343.

[1] See M. Śeṣagiri Śāstrī, *Descriptive Catalogue of the Government Oriental MSS. in the Madras Library,* vol. i, pt. 1, pp. 3, 4.

[2] Noted here for convenience as C, D, E; I made no note of the absolute pitch.

but the passage is too short to show the compass. At any rate, Dr. Felber[1] gives two specimens of *Yajurveda* on pp. 108, 116, which show a compass of a Fourth and a Fifth respectively; his example (p. 106) of the *Ṛgveda* reaches a Sixth. This is perhaps only one more instance of what is so common in music, the 'official' rules lagging decades or centuries behind the practice. His three examples (of both Vedas) show a foundation scale D, E, F, though one of them begins in E, F♯, G, and continues in E, F, G.[1]

The *Atharvaveda* does not appear to be recited, at least not in accordance with rules. But all reading of the *śāstras* is recitation. Students read, i. e. recite, in the same room. Children are taught to read so. A boy read me some of the *Ṛgveda*, employing the accents correctly, but stopped when he reached a certain page 'because he had not learned any further'.

It will be noticed in these examples that with the exception of an occasional grace-note or appoggiatura—and a great many more grace-notes are put in than appears in the text, for seldom is a note ever sung, as we should say, clean—the syllables are allotted one note each; there are no melodic figures like the ligatures of Gregorians. For these we turn to the

Sāmaveda. The symbol round which the elaborate ritual of the *Sāmaveda* gathers is that sacrifice of which the drinking of the juice of the *Soma* plant was the central point. The virtues of this juice are recapitulated in the ninth book of the *Ṛgveda,* from which mainly the words for the *Sāman* chants are taken.[2] *Soma* is translated 'moon-plant'; and the *Sāmaveda* is specially connected with the worship of ancestors, whose abode was the moon. Great care was taken not to deviate from the original melody-types and rhythms, and the religious efficacy of the hymns was held to depend largely on the right application of directions contained in the Brahmanic explanations (*Brāhmaṇa,* not later than the sixth century B. C.) of the Vedic text (*Saṃhitā*). The expense of the full

[1] The names of the notes throughout this chapter indicate relative pitch only. They are chosen at any absolute pitch which is suitable, as fragments of the Sāman scale, which is explained, or at any rate discussed, later.

[2] There is nothing to show that the chants are later than the words; in fact, since *Sāmans* are often mentioned in the *Ṛgveda* there is a probability, beyond the intrinsic likelihood, that they are older.

ceremonial was not small; the *Soma* sacrifice involved days in performance and months in preparation. A full description of its elaborate and gorgeous ritual is to be found in the *Aitareyabrāhmaṇa* of the *Ṛgveda,* translated into English by Martin Haug, 1863, and its close connexion with the fire-worship of the Zoroastrians is there detailed. Other creeds have now swept across India and buried that of the Vedas in oblivion. The memory of the words and chants, and possibly of parts of the ritual, lingers chiefly in the South. Even there the true *Sāma*-singers are few, and impostors are beginning to flourish.

The body of hymns is divided into two sections, which may be centuries apart—the early, according to the latest authority,[1] the *Uttarārcika,* and the late, the *Pūrvārcika.* The early hymns are divided into (1) the 'investigated' (*Ūha*), and (2) those which are 'to be investigated' (*Ūhya*) or which are 'secret' (*Rahasya*). The later hymns are in three divisions, addressed to Fire (*Agni*), the Rain-god (*Indra*), and *Soma Pavamāna.*[2] These are arranged internally according to their metres, and according to the 'jubilations' (*stobha*) and the doxologies (the parts of the hymn which are genuine *Sāman*). Only seventy-five verses, out of many hundreds, are not borrowed from the *Ṛgveda* or other source; such borrowings are known technically as *yoni* (womb). A distinction is also made between those verses of the *Ṛgveda* which have one melody (*ekasāmi*) or many (*bahusāmi*), showing that *Sāman* is, properly speaking, music, not music and words, nor words for music. In fact the conception is the reverse of ours. We speak of setting words, that is, putting music to them; but the *Sāman* is a melody for which words were found (chiefly in the *Ṛgveda*). This is the case too with modern poets; Rabindranath Tagore says that when the general idea of the poem comes into his mind, he first thinks of the melody (generally his own) and then writes words to it. We are reminded of Burns's two manful attempts to find words for that 'crinkum-crankum tune, Robin Adair', with its 'cursed, cramp, out of the way measure', and of his better success with Duncan Gray, 'in Scots verse'.

The rhythm is, as in Plain-song, determined by the words, which decide where it will be appropriate to take breath. The two versions of the first hymn of the *Sāmaveda* which follow are from A. C. Burnell (*Ārṣeyabrāhmaṇa,* Introd., p. xlv) and Śeṣagiri Śāstrī (loc. cit.); and

[1] Caland, *Jaiminīya-saṃhitā,* p. 4.

[2] *Pavamāna,* clarifying.

the notation is in accordance with the directions of the *Gānas* (the *Sāmaveda* text as actually sung) as they understood them, checked in the first case by the verification of a musician, and in the second by the usage as the writer knew it:

Burnell, *Ārṣeyabrāhmaṇa*, p. xlv.

Ex. 844.

Here, and elsewhere, a long mark over a vowel sometimes represents musical, not prosodic, length.

The actual words of the hymn are:

Agná āyāhi vītaye gṛṇāno havyadātaye |
Ni hotā satsi barhiṣi || [1]

The bar-lines (given by Burnell only) are breath marks. The last note of each 'bar' (*parvan*) is accented (*vṛddha*).[2]

The next two examples have no such authority. They are merely the versions of two *gurus*, whom I heard in Mysore and Bangalore, of an identical verse, and represent possibly two different sects

[1] Translation: 'Come, Agni, praised with song, to feast and sacrificial offering; be seated as Hotar on the holy *Kuśa* grass.'

[2] Lit. augmented. It appears to be occasionally augmented in time-length also, counting 3 to the 2 of the long (*dīrgha*) and the 1 of the short (*hrasva*). Later theory (see p. 256) has added lengths between these. We are reminded of the Greek time-unit (*chronos prōtos*), 'two-time long' (*disēmos*) and 'three-time long' (*trisēmos*).

(*śākhā*). The tonic is D in both cases; that of Mysore 'closes' by means of an unusual leap (C, E, C, D), and that of Bangalore by the device of an 'Alleluia' (*stobha*):

Ex. 345.

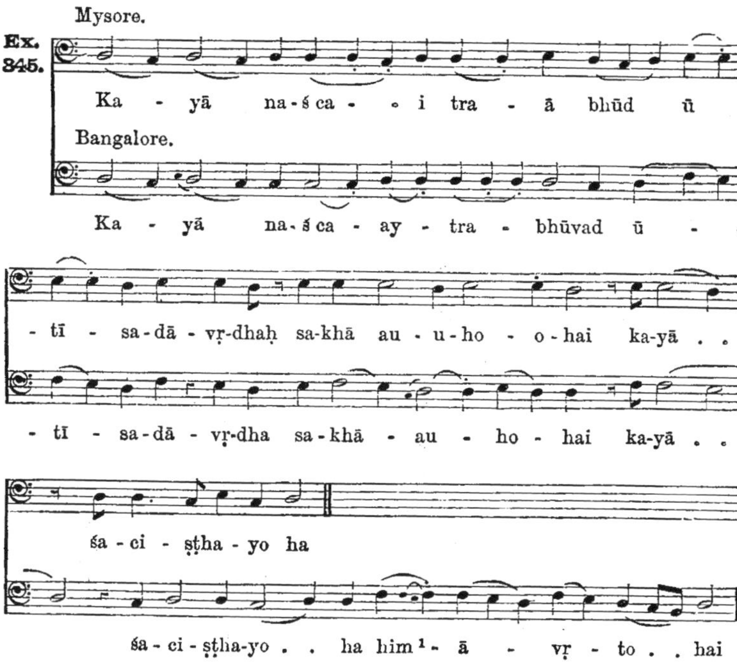

There was, not unnaturally, great difficulty in inducing priests to sing these chants, and one man, at Bangalore, offered in lieu thereof 'Sanskrit in the style of *Sāman*'. But the unusual content of the words shows its influence in the more or less rhythmical phrases induced by the prosody, which take the place of those vocal phrases and melodic figures which flow naturally from the liturgical use of the words in the *Sāmaveda*:

Ex. 346.

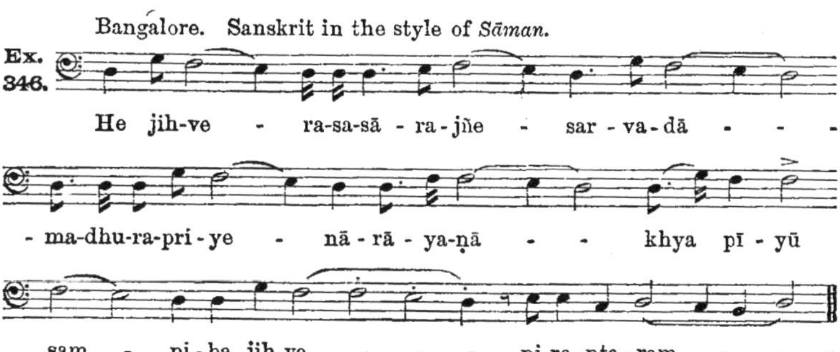

On the other hand, at Tanjore a man got up of his own motion and sang *Sāman* before a roomful of people, and, what was more surprising, before a European in their presence. It appeared that he had a theory of his own as to how *Sāman* should be sung, and was seeking converts. He has evidently taken the scale of the *Nāradaśikṣā* (see below, p. 259) as if it were in the modern notation, F–G, instead of the ancient, G–A, and the mode is therefore changed. Further, the essence of the *Sāman* chant is that it circles about one note, F (or E, or D), and only leaves that to form a downward cadence. His version draws attention away from the E to the A below, which in the true *Sāman* is quite a subsidiary note, and it begins, therefore, to be in a regular *Rāg*, which *Sāmagās* assert positively that their chants are not. Moreover, he has forgotten after the first line to put in those characteristic prolongations of notes by vocalizing syllables which add so much to the solemnity of the chant:

Tanjore.

Ex. 347.

The words are spelled phonetically ; his original text is not available.

Form. The *Sāman* is divided into five parts:

(i) *Prastāva,* introductory ascription of praise, preceded by the syllable *huṃ,* sung by the *prastotṛi,* or assistant priest.

(ii) *Udgītha,* preceded by *om,* sung by the *udgātṛi,* or priest.

(iii) *Pratihāra,* the joining in, preceded by *huṃ,* sung by the *pratihartṛi,* who 'joined in' at the last syllable of the *udgītha.* Sometimes the *pratihāra* is divided into two, in which case there is—

(iv) *Upadrava,* the recession, formed out of the last few syllables of the *pratihāra,* sung by the *udgātṛi.*

(v) *Nidhana,* the coda, consisting of one or at the most two syllables, sung by all three priests, followed in some cases by *om.*[1]

The following are the first two sections of the first hymn of the *Sāmaveda*:

Burnell, *Ārṣeyabrāhmaṇa,* p. xiv.

Ex. 348.

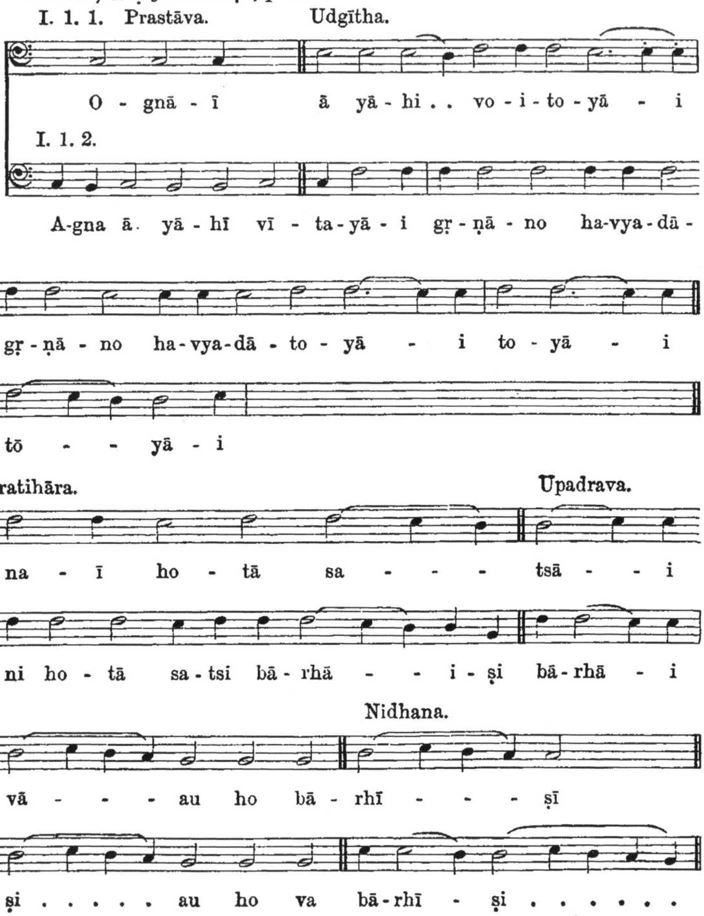

[1] These five *bhakti* (see p. 255) are the subject of Dr. Simon's latest work, *Das Pañcavidhasūtra,* Breslau, 1913.

The verse, *āgna āyāhi* (*.gveda* VI. 16. 10), is sung three times over to form a *stoma* (group); Burnell only gives two of the three, and they are arranged here under one another for comparison. Of the remaining nine verses of this particular hymn, eight are from the *Ṛgveda*, and the last, which forms a doxology, belongs exclusively to the *Sāmaveda*. Besides the first verse, the fourth and fifth also form *stomas*; the sixth, seventh, and eighth are sung twice, and the other four only once[1]; in all, nineteen sections (*bhakti*). The usual number was fifteen. Mention is also made of nine and twenty-one *bhakti*; so that a basis of three or five or seven *stomas* is implied, varied probably in any particular case.

The practical directions for the singing of these hymns are given in the *Gānas*. These give the text of the *Sāmaveda* (which has been culled, with modification, from the *Ṛgveda* chiefly) with the syllables vocalized (i. e. with prolongation and modification of vowels) and farsed (i. e. with insertion of vocal syllables between those of the text). These insertions (*stobha*, praises) are the exact counterpart of the *jubila* interpolated in Plain-song in the ninth and tenth centuries, out of which 'tropes' were developed in the eleventh,[2] as the *bhakti* of the *Sāmaveda* are also of the 'strophes' of Plain-song, which, like them, were of indefinite number; the idea, too, of singing the hymn in *stotras* (stanzas) and *stomas* (groups) is reproduced in the sometimes single, sometimes repeated performance of the strophe.

Rhythm. The metres of the hymns are six (later eight) chief ones, in which the governing factor is the number of syllables, varying from twenty-four to forty-four for the stanza. Quantity of vowel is taken no account of except at the cadence. These need not detain us now, as the rhythm of the chants ignores the poetical metre entirely. In the true *Sāman* there are only three time-units: a short (*hrasva*) note for a quantitatively short syllable, a long (*dīrgha*) for a quantitatively long; syllables made long 'by position' count as short. An occasional important syllable still further lengthened or, especially at the end of a phrase (*parvan*), stressed, or both lengthened and stressed, is called augmented (*vṛddhi*) or prolate (*pluta*). This also finds its analogue in Plain-song.

[1] These are called *stotras*.

[2] See W. H. Frere, *Winchester Troper*, Introduction, p. xxxii seq.

The system of the *Mātrālakṣaṇa* (date?) is an advance upon this, and is placed here for comparison beside the modern South Indian scheme of time-values:

		MĀTRĀLAKṢAṆA.	MODERN SYSTEM (S. India).
1.	𝅘𝅥𝅮	Anumātrā, 'under'-mātrā	ANUDRUTA, 'under'-quick.
2.	♩	Ardhamātrā, half-mātrā	DRUTA, quick.
3.	♩.		Druta virāma.[1]
4.	𝅗𝅥	HRASVA short, or **MĀTRĀ**, unit	LAGHU, light.
5.	𝅗𝅥‿𝅘𝅥𝅮		Laghu virāma.
6.	𝅗𝅥.	Adhyardha, additional half[2] (sc. mātrā)	Laghu druta.
7.	𝅗𝅥..		Laghu druta virāma.
8.	𝅝	DĪRGHA, long	GURU, heavy.
9.	𝅝‿𝅘𝅥𝅮		Guru virāma.
10.	𝅝‿♩	Ardhatisraḥ, third halt	Guru druta.
11.	𝅝‿♩‿𝅘𝅥𝅮		Guru druta virāma.
12.	𝅝.	PLUTA, prolate, or VṚDDHA, augmented.	PLUTA, prolate.
13.	𝅝‿𝅗𝅥‿𝅘𝅥𝅮		Pluta virāma.
14.	𝅝..	Ardhacatasraḥ, fourth half	Pluta druta.
15.	𝅝...		Pluta druta virāma.
16.	+𝅝+		KĀKAPĀDA, crow's foot.[3]

These interminable theorizers also subdivided the *anudruta*. The *anudruta* is the equivalent of:

2 × 2 =	4 Kalā	syllabic instant.[4]
4 × 8 =	32 Nimesha	moment.
8 × 32 =	256 Kāṣṭhā	$\frac{1}{225}$ of an hour.
16 × 108 =	1728 Lava	$\frac{1}{2000}$ of an hour.
32 × 512 =	16384 Kaṇa	atom.

The use of astronomical subdivisions is interesting, though hardly illuminating (there are other explanations of the *kāṣṭhā* and *lava*). The only one of these terms in practical use is the *kalā*, which properly means $\frac{1}{16}$. The *kalā* is $\frac{1}{16}$ of the *Laghu* (their unit) as the semiquaver is $\frac{1}{16}$ of the semibreve (our unit). Cp. the German *Sechzehntel* and the American 'sixteenth note'.

[1] *Virāma* appears to be used indifferently for a rest or a dot with the time-value of an *anudruta*. The word means in general 'stop' (of punctuation); and is used in particular to show that a consonant is not followed by the *ă* which is inherent in it.

[2] Cp. German *anderthalb* = 1½, *dritthalb* = 2½, &c.

[3] The sign in one modern notation for the longest note is ×.

[4] The syllable *ka* has two 'instants'—*k* and *a*.

Scale. In the accompanying list of authorities for the *Sāman* scale the first six are ancient, the last four modern; the two sets are separated by something like twenty centuries. The list is probably not complete; there is no indication of place of origin. They are collated on two assumptions: (1) that the words *kruṣṭa*, *prathama*, &c., name the same note wherever they occur, that is, that *kruṣṭa*, for instance, was not at different periods applied to two different notes, and (2) that the two identifications of the *Sāman* names with the notes of the secular scale by authorities III, VII, VIII, and X are to be trusted. If either of these assumptions should be shown to be wrong the evidence would have to be reconsidered.

Names of the Sāman notes. As extensions of a nucleus—*prathama, dvitīya, tṛtīya, caturtha* (first, second, third, fourth)—occur three others—*kruṣṭa, mandra, atisvārya.*

Kruṣṭa. In more than one of these authorities the order in the original text is *prathama, dvitīya, tṛtīya, caturtha, mandra, kruṣṭa, atisvārya. Kruṣṭa* is used of the highest note; and as the sixth in a downward series this word has given trouble. Burnell proposed to read *kṛṣṭa*, 'that to which *karṣaṇa* has been applied.' He did not, however, explain why *karṣaṇa* should be applied in the sixth place especially, and it appears now that it is typically applied to the highest note. But there is nothing to show that the order of the names is the melodic order; and it is at least possible that in the order given above the first five name the ordinary notes of the scale (see p. 258, l. 12) and the last two the extraordinary ones (which happen to be at either end of the five). Meanwhile, if order does matter, that of No. III, in which *kṛṣṭa* actually occurs, is the order of the original. Moreover, No. V alludes to the seven *svaras* as *kruṣṭādi*, 'beginning on *kruṣṭa*'; so there is little doubt that the *kruṣṭa* is above the *prathama*, and that another statement of Burnell's that *kruṣṭa* and *prathama* are the same note is not universally true.

There is another interest attaching to the word *kruṣṭa*, 'highest.' It shows us, as do also the ordinals *prathama, caturtha*, that the Hindus regarded the treble as high and the bass as low; as we do, and as the Greeks, who named the lowest note *hypatē* (highest), did not. This reminds us that high and low in music are merely a metaphor, though a very natural one. In a somewhat similar way Europeans regard the harmony of a song as 'underneath' the

Authorities for the Sāman Scale.

I Ṛkprātiśākhya. At least fourth cent. B.C.		prathama	dvitīya		caturtha	mandra		1
		(also, aṣṭama, sama, and śukra)						2
II Bṛhaddevatā. At least fourth cent.	kruṣṭa head	prathama palate	dvitīya brow	tṛtīya ear	caturtha nose	mandra chest	atisvārya (formed by *karṣaṇa* from the *mandra*)	3 4
III Taittirīya-Prātiśākhya. At least fourth cent.	kṛṣṭa kṛṣṭa	prathama udātta Ga prathama	dvitīya svarita Ri dvitīya dvitīya	tṛtīya pracaya Sa . . . tṛtīya	caturtha anudātta Ni . . . caturtha	mandra . . . mandra	atisvārya (Āhvārakas) (Taittirīyas)	5 6 7 8 9
IV Sāmavidhāna-brāhmaṇa. Later than I, II, III.	kruṣṭa	prathama	dvitīya	tṛtīya	caturtha	mandra pañcama	atisvārya atisvāra anusvāra ṣaṣṭha antya	10
V Puṣpasūtra. Fifth to second cent.	Alludes to the whole series as 'kruṣṭādi', that is, beginning with kruṣṭa.							11
VI Sāmatantra. Prob. not modern.		gi	ji	ḍi	di	bi		12
VII Sāmaparibhāṣā. 'Quite modern.' (R. Simon.)	kruṣṭa Ni { C (G)	prathama Dha { B (F♯)	dvitīya Pa { A (E)	tṛtīya Ma { G (D)	caturtha Ga { F (C)	mandra Ri { E (B)	atisvārya Sa { D (A)	13 14

VIII Māṇḍūkiśikṣā. 'Quite modern.' (R. S.)		Ga first finger	Ri svarita first	Sa anudātta third	Ni udātta fourth (root)	Dha pracaya fourth (tip)		15 16 17
IX Dhāraṇalakṣaṇa. 'Quite modern.' (A. C. Burnell.)	kruṣṭa thumb (tip)	prathama thumb (root)	dvitīya second finger	tṛtīya third	caturtha fourth (root)	mandra fourth (tip)		18 19
X Nāradaśikṣā 'Quite modern.' (A. C. B.)	kruṣṭa first note of the scale = Ma	prathama second = Ga	dvitīya third = Ri	tṛtīya fourth = Sa	caturtha fifth = Ni	mandra sixth = Dha	atisvāra seventh = Pa	20 21
	crane	goat	bull	peacock	elephant	horse	koïl	22
	svarita	udātta	anudātta	svarita	udātta	anudātta	svarita	23
	kruṣṭa thumb (tip)	prathama thumb (root)						24
		Ga first finger	Ri second	Sa third	Ni fourth (root)	Dha fourth (tip)		25
	kruṣṭa	prathama		tṛtīya	. . .	. . .	(Āhvārakas)	26
		prathama	dvitīya	. . .	. . .	. . .	(Taṇḍibhallavins)	27
		prathama	dvitīya	tṛtīya	. . .	. . .	(The Ṛgveda)	28
			dvitīya	tṛtīya	caturtha	mandra	(Taittirīyas)	29

Relative pitch of the notes.

melody; whereas the Maoris think of the song as 'here, down below', and the harmony as going up to the roof under which they are singing and 'coming down' to them.

Mandra, low. This is the usual name for the sixth note; it is once (No. IV) called *pañcama*, in continuation of the ordinals. That it was a substantive note of the scale we see perhaps in No. I, where it appears even though the *tṛtīya* is omitted. But that it was on a different footing from the five notes above it is indicated in line 4, where they are all head-notes as opposed to the *mandra*, a chest-note. It gave its name also to the lower octave in the secular scale as opposed to the middle octave (*madhya*, or *madhyama*) and the upper (*tāra*, or *uttama*).

Atisvārya, extremity of the cadence. This is a curious name for the lowest note of the full scale, to which we should naturally have attached some idea of a tonic. But it is obvious that it is not a substantive note of the scale at all. In line 4 it only exists by permission of the *mandra*; in line 10 there is an uncertainty about the pronunciation of its name (*atisvārya*, *atisvāra*, *anusvāra*), and alternatives are suggested—*ṣaṣṭha* (sixth) and *antya* (last); in lines 17, 19, and 25 the 'musical hand' does not provide for it, and line 4 does not appropriate to it an organ of the body. It is clearly an 'extra' note; and it may be observed that the Greeks similarly regarded their scale as stopping normally at the B, while they called the note A below it 'extra' (*proslambanomenos*).

Tetrachords. There are indications that the nucleus of the scale was, successively perhaps, the tetrachords:

Ex. 349.  and 

The tetrachord E–B. In line 9 this is the *usus* of the *Taittirīyas*, confirmed by line 29. In line 16 these same notes are appropriated to the four *Ṛgveda* accents. Lines 1 and 2 are very difficult because we do not know how to place the three notes of line 2. *Aṣṭama* (eighth) in a scale of seven notes is surprising. But it will be seen at the foot of the diagram that the scale actually contains eight notes, and it is just conceivable that *aṣṭama*, which is obviously extra to the accepted seven, names the F♯, which is alternative to the F♮. This leaves *sama* (level) and *śukra* (bright) to fill three places; and all that can be said is that *atisvārya*, the 'additional' note, is the most likely of the three to have been left unfilled. In line 1, where we can place the notes, it is remarkable that *tṛtīya* should be omitted in the series of four; and this may be an indication that the D was not on the same footing with the others, and that in this treatise, at any rate, the real nucleus of the scale was held to be F E–C B, i. e. composed of the Fourths F–C and E–B.

The tetrachord F–C. On the other hand, the fact that the four ordinals (first to fourth) are assigned in every treatise to the notes F, E, D, C, and that in line 6 the *Ṛgveda* accents are appropriated to these notes, makes it clear that the tetrachord F–C has an equal claim with that of E–B to be considered the foundation of the scale.

The hesitation between these tetrachords is reflected in the 'musical hand' of line 17, where F and E are both assigned to the first finger, and C and B both to the fourth; and the hesitation remains, in respect of C and B, in lines 19 and 25.

It is clear also that the scale consisted normally of only five notes for a considerable time. In the *Puṣpasūtra* (9. 26) we find that 'the Kauthumas sing the majority of their chants to five tones, a few to six, and two of them to seven tones'. In line 12 we find Sol-fa names for five notes only. That no more than five were contemplated may be seen from the choice of consonants. They are the medials of the five classes of consonant (guttural, palatal, cerebral, dental, and labial) proceeding in regular order from throat to lips. Lines 17 and 25 are a further indication that the normal scale consisted of five notes. All this lends some support to the interpretation given above of line 1.

The scale was increased to six by the addition of *kruṣṭa*. That this was an afterthought is seen in the fact that it is independent of the nomenclature by ordinals, in the hesitation as to *kruṣṭa* or *kṛṣṭa*, and in the confusion introduced into the musical hand (lines 19 and 25). Finally, a seventh note was tentatively admitted in the *atisvārya*.

Consonance (*saṃvāditva*). The consonance which was suggested by two tetrachords, F–C and E–B, is carried out further in line 23, where the seven notes are divided into two similar tetrachords. This consonance holds whatever the intervals may be between the notes within the tetrachord. For the intonation of these we depend on the identifications in lines 14 and 21 of the *Sāman* notes with those of the secular scale, which, as we saw (p. 114), was at least as old as the oldest of these treatises.

In lines 6, 15, and 21 Sa is identified with *tṛtīya*, and this gives the *Sa-grāma* in a plagal form from N(i). In line 14 Sa is identified with *atisvārya*, and this gives the *Ma-grāma* in a plagal form from N(i), or the *Sa-grāma* in an authentic form from M(a). But S(a) and P(a) are *saṃvādī*; therefore the notes are D and $\overset{\sharp}{A}$ (not D and A). The two scales are therefore

Sa-grāma.

Ex. 350.

and

Ma-grāma.

Ex. 351.

We saw in Chapter IV that the *Gandhāra-grāma* was, according to one explanation,

Ex. 352.

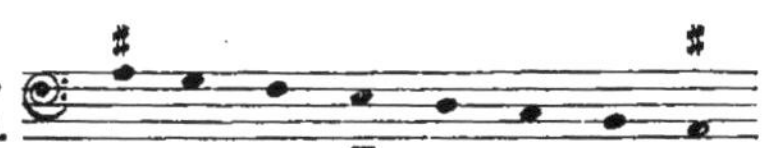

and it is possible that the *Sāman* scale may throw some light upon it. That scale is reckoned downwards, and therefore the note E is called R(i); but the *grāmas* are reckoned upwards, and therefore E is G(a). If the *Ga-grāma* begins on E, it has for its upward tetrachord E, F, G, $\overset{\sharp}{A}$, that is, a semitone and two major tones. These make more than a Fourth, therefore either the semitone is the Pythagorean comma ($\frac{256}{243}$, 90 cents), or one of the tones is a minor tone, as in the lower tetrachord, E, D, C, B. The upper tetrachord would in the first case be the same as the early Greek Doric, and would contain the ditone, instead of the major Third. It seems likely that in some way of which we cannot now trace the history, the *gāndhāra-grāma* is a relic of this old tuning. The Comma of Didymus ($\frac{81}{80}$) has to be negotiated somewhere in the scale. We, in Europe, put it between the A and the D (major tone, semitone, major tone), the Indians between the E and the A (semitone, major tone, major tone). In so placing it, it is possible that they reduced an original $\overset{\sharp}{E}$ $\frac{256}{243}$, F $\frac{9}{8}$, G $\frac{9}{8}$, $\overset{\sharp}{A}$ to a later E $\frac{16}{15}$, F $\frac{9}{8}$, G $\frac{9}{8}$, $\overset{\sharp}{A}$.

We have other hints which point to a correspondence between the Greek and Indian scale. The Aryans came into India from the North. *Gāndhāra* is the same word as Kandahar, which as late as Alexander's time (fourth century B. C.) included Afghanistan and the Panjab, with a capital near Peshawar. The *Gāndhāra-grāma* is the oldest of the three *grāmas*, and may preserve an early Aryan tradition. The Aryans spoke Sanskrit, which is closely allied to Greek. Evidence of the correspondence of the Greek and Indian systems has been accumulating in these pages; and that the fundamental scale of Greece, the Doric tetrachord, should be identical in form with the oldest form of Indian tetrachord would be more striking evidence than any. But it is unfortunately not more than circumstantial.

The *Gāndhāra* scale gave its name no doubt to the *Gāndhāra* note. The names *Madhyama* and *Pañcama* have been discussed in Chapter V. Of *Ṛṣabha, Dhaivata,* and *Niṣāda* nothing is known; they may be place-names, like *Gāndhāra,* or fancy names, like the majority of the *śrutis*. Of *Ṣaḍja* there is something more to be said. Referring once more to the list above we find in line 4 the seventh note left without an assigned organ of the body. In line 14 that same note is called Sa. We remember also that the *atisvārya* is not a regular note of the scale, but is introduced into it as an extension of the other six. Elsewhere, in the *Sangīta-sāra-sangraha,* for instance, *ṣaḍja,* which undoubtedly means 'born of six', is said to be produced from six organs of the body, viz. nose, throat, chest, palate, tongue, and teeth. Putting these together we see that the name *ṣaḍja* is merely the mythological expression of the musical fact that the *atisvārya* was an 'extra' note on a different footing from the others.

There is, however, another tradition as to the intonation of the *Sāman* scale. M. Śeṣagiri Śāstrī (*Descriptive Catalogue*, pp. 3, 4) gives the scale as Ma, Ga, Ri, Sa, Dha, and says that the sound is that of the Rāg *Abhogi*. That *Rāg* is:

Ex. 353.

Drone D[1] (which does not matter here, the drone being a later

[1] The European note (not the *svara*).

invention), *aṃśa* E, omitted notes C and A. This is an old tradition, as may be seen from three passages: (1) in an early book of the *Mahābhārata* the notes of the secular scale are given as Sa, Ri, Ga, Ma, Dha, Pa, Ni; (2) in the *Nāradaśikṣā* (I. 2. 16) the order is Ma, Ga, Ri, Sa, Dha, Ni, Pa; and (3) in I. 7. 4 it is Ma, Ga, Ri, Sa, Dha, Ni (Pa omitted). In all three passages the first five notes are the same, and the last two are out of order; this looks as if the first five were substantive and the last two optional, thus:

Ex. 354.

and this is the scale of Śeṣagiri Sāstrī and of the Rāg *Abhogi*; and since the *aṃśa* of *Abhogi* is at E, it divides thus:

Ex. 355.

and its lower tetrachord is similar to the *usus* of the *Āhvārakas* given in line 26 of the list. We must accept this transilient scale, therefore, as a collateral form of the *Sāman*.

The musical hand. The basis of numeration is in some countries five, in others a dozen (England) or a score (France); in India it is four. Rupees, for instance, are frequently counted by placing one finger on each and sweeping them into the hand. Bearing this in mind, it may be possible to introduce some method into these discrepant accounts of the musical hand. The root idea of this 'cheironomy' is that the thumb touches successively the tips of the four fingers. This is seen in the *svāra*, or cadence, where the hand is held 'in the shape of a cow's ear' (see the second of the two illustrations opposite), and the thumb passes over the four fingers in succession. Line 17 may accordingly represent two systems of counting:

	Ga	Ri	Sa	Ni	Dha
(*a*)		1st	[2nd]	[3rd]	4th
(*b*)	1st	[2nd]	3rd	4th	
(line 17)	1st	1st	3rd	4th	4th

Similarly line 19:

	Ma	Ga	Ri	Sa	Ni	
(*b*)		[1st]	2nd	3rd	4th	
(*c*)	thumb	[1st]	2nd	3rd	4th	(pentachord)
(line 19)	thumb	thumb	2nd	3rd	4th	

Sāmagaḥ, Madras

Sāmagaḥ, Bangalore

Lines 24 and 25 combine these. We have therefore:

	Ma	Ga	Ri	Sa	Ni	Dha	
(a)			E	D	C	B	(tetrachord)
(b)		F	E	D	C		(tetrachord)
(c)	G	F (F♯)	E	D	C		(pentachord)

as bases, perhaps successive bases, of the *Sāman* scale.

The accents.

	Ma	Ga	Ri	Sa	Ni	Dha	Pa
(i) line 6		U	S	P	A		
(ii) ,, 16			S	A	U	P	
(iii) ,, 23	S	U	A	S	U	A	S

There was a doubt, as we saw, about the relative position of *udātta* and *svarita*: in the *Ṛgveda* the *svarita* is above, but there is reason to think it may originally have been below the *udātta*. This doubt, reflected in (i) and (iii) above, is natural if we consider the nature of the *svarita*, which started on the *udātta*, rose a little above it, and fell much below it. It was natural that in recitation, where the question of exact pitch did not come up, the fall should be the conspicuous thing, and in its general effect the *svarita* come to be considered below the *udātta*; but that, when the pitch came to be defined in chanting, the rise should rather attract attention, since a fall or cadential phrase took place for other reasons than the fact that the syllable had a *svarita* accent, whereas the rise was peculiar to the *svarita* note, and therefore in its particular effect the *svarita* was above the *udātta*.

That in (i) the *pracaya* is above the *anudātta* and in (ii) below it need cause no trouble, since, as the *pracaya* is 'toneless', there is really no sense in assigning it to any particular tone.

The position of the *anudātta* above the *udātta* in (ii) is more difficult. Perhaps we are justified in calling Ga (in ii) *udātta* on the analogy of (i) and (iii). This would fulfil all that is required of the *pracaya* and *anudātta*, that they should be somewhere below the *svarita* (and the upper *udātta*). The lower *udātta* then appears as the other terminal of the tetrachord, with the *svarita* above it.

In (iii) the accents appear to lose their grammatical meaning entirely and to be given a musical meaning. The *udātta* is now the terminal of the tetrachord, at Ga and Ni, with the *svarita* above it and the *anudātta* below it. The *udātta* is 'raised' above the others not in pitch, but in musical eminence. The *svarita* loses its sense of 'graced' note, and becomes a note of certain relative pitch. The *anudātta* is no longer of indefinite 'low' pitch, forced under certain conditions 'lower' (*anudāttatara*), but becomes definite.

The theory of consonance thus determined has its counterpart in Greek music:

svarita	G	lichanos
┌ udātta	F	parhypate
│ anudātta	E	hypate ┐
│ svarita	D	lichanos │
└ udātta	C	parhypate │
anudātta	B	hypate ┘
[atisvārya	A	proslambanomenos]

These are quite different from Hucbald's *excellentes*, *superiores*, *finales*, *graves*, with which Burnell compares them, and which involved a series of disjunct, not conjunct, tetrachords.

An example of the chant as sung by a *Sāmagaḥ* in Madras shows the general musical effect. The breve at the beginning shows the actual pitch of the first note (a Fifth higher); the chant itself is given at the pitch which suits the scale just discussed. The fragmentary syllables are merely phonetic spellings of the apparent sounds of the phonograph, with gaps where the words are inaudible. It was extremely difficult to get even this short specimen.

Sāman chant. Madras. (Phonogram.)

Ex. 356.

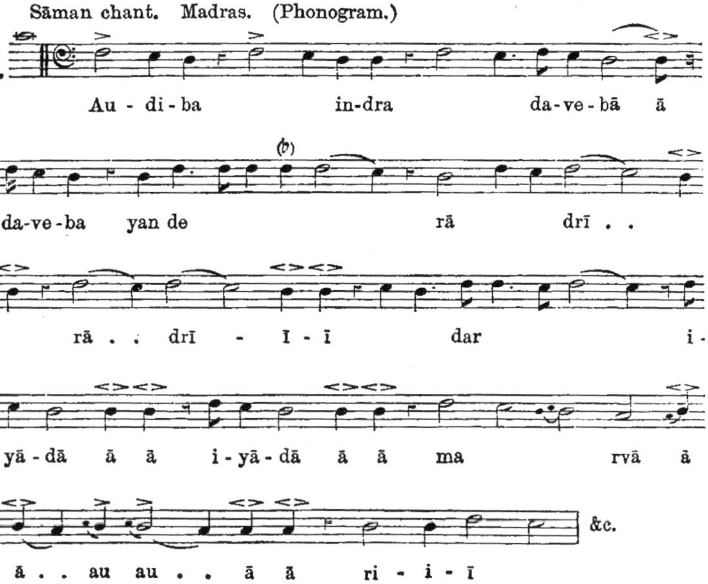

Herr Felix Exner was far more successful in 1904. His results have now been worked out by Dr. Erwin Felber, provided with text and translation by Herr Bernhard Geiger, and were published in 1913 under the title *Die indische Musik der vedischen und der klassischen Zeit* as a contribution to the history of recitation. Dr. Felber has very kindly given permission for their transcription here. The actual pitch is given, as before, by the breve at the beginning of each example. The *Sāmaveda* notation with which each of his examples is supplied is omitted here, because it is probably the notation of a different sect from that to which the singer belonged, who has, at any rate, taken no account of it except in a very general way. Felber's numbers are given for reference. He discusses the melodic structure of these chants in his third chapter (pp. 38–43).

No. 427. Sung by a Brahman priest in Calcutta, forty-two years old, born in Jodhpur. Original text:

Mahi trīṇām avar astu dyukṣaṃ mitrasyāryamṇaḥ |
duradharṣaṃ varu[ṇasya] |

Translation:

May the mighty aid of the three gods be ours—the help of Mitra and Aryaman and the invincible Varuṇa.

Felber. No. 427.
♩ = 79. *Sempre glissando, piano.*

Ex. 357.

This example (No. 427), and three others (Nos. 428–30) which it has seemed unnecessary to transcribe, shows, like the Madras example just given, little more than the scale of the *Ṛgveda* (see line 28 of the diagram on p. 259):

Ex. 358.

the F being, on the whole, the most prominent note.

Felber 443. Sung by two Brahmans of Tanjore aged forty and seventeen—a priest and a student in Madras.

Original text:

> punānah soma dhārayāpo vasāno arṣasi |
> ā ratnadhā yonim ṛtasya sīdasy utso devo hiraṇyayaḥ ||

Translation:

Purified, O Soma, by drops, thou movest concealed in the waters; rich in treasure thou residest in the womb of the sacrifice, a golden fount divine.

Felber. No. 443.

Ex. 359.

Felber, No. 444. Another version of 443, sung by the Madras priest alone.

Original text of the second verse:

duhāna ūdhar divyam madhu priyaṃ pratnaṁ sadhastham āsadat |
āpṛchyam dharuṇaṃ vājy arṣasi nṛbhir dhauto vicakṣaṇaḥ ||

Translation:

Milking the honey he loves from heavenly udders, Soma took his seat on his ancient throne. Mightily thy stream empties itself into a vessel of honour, and purified from the touch of men thine eyes behold what is far away.

Felber. No. 444.

Ex. 360.

The scale of these two (Nos. 443 and 444) is the same:

Ex. 361.

the melodies pivot on F and D. The chromatic beginning of No. 444 is quite common in secular singing, from which it seems to have been imported here, in order to establish a tonic.

The two which follow show a different scale:

No. 426.

Ex. 362.

No. 425.

Ex. 363.

The F♯ is essential in No. 425 and accidental in No. 426; in both it is used chromatically, which is on the whole unlike secular song. I heard something like it in Madras, but was unable to note it. Two chants were sung: one distinctly chromatic, described as *ucca* (high); the other as distinctly diatonic, described as *nīca* (low). I was more than once asked by the singer whether he should sing in the *ucca* or the *nīca* voice; and it seems possible that he may have been referring to a difference of scale rather than of pitch—*ucca* G F♯ F♮ E, &c., *nīca* (G) F E D, &c.

No. 426. Sung by a boy of fifteen in the Sanskrit College, Calcutta.

The text is not from the *Ṛgveda*, but a *stobha*, i.e. composed not of verses but of jubilations consisting of sentences and alleluias. (*ho-i*, &c.). In the Pada form:

ut nayāmi ādityam ādityam prāñcam yantam ut nayāmi ahorātrāṇi ahaḥ rātrāṇi aritrāṇi dyauḥ nauḥ tasyām asau ādityaḥ ādityaḥ īyate tasmin vayam īyamāne īyāmahe [. . .].

Translation:

I bear aloft the advancing sun, I bear it aloft; days and nights are the oars, the sky is the ship. On this fares forth the sun; and with it we are borne to that well-loved spot whose name consists of three letters.

Note. That which is named in the adoration of *om* (spelled a+u+m), which is an image of the world of Brahma.

Felber. No. 426.

♩=88. *Sempre accel.*

Ex. 364.

No. 425. Sung by a boy of twelve, a Brahman, in the Sanskrit College, Calcutta.

The original text is:

mūrdhānaṃ divo aratiṃ pṛthivyā vaiśvānaram ṛta ā jātam agnim |
kaviṁ samrājam atithim janānām āsan naḥ pātraṃ janayaṃta devāḥ ||

The translation:

The chief of heaven, the lord of the earth, Agni Vaiśvānara born of the sacred truth, wise, almighty, the guest of man—him it was whom the gods created as our chalice for their use.

Note. The sacrificial *ghee* is poured into the fire (*Agni*) which bears the gift up to the gods, that is, the fire is the vessel which conveys it to the mouth of the gods.

Felber. No. 425.

♩ = 73½.

Ex. 365.

NOTATION. The various systems are all modern—of the last few centuries, perhaps; and that followed in one MS. would not help to the elucidation of another. The signs employed are sometimes letters which appear to be abbreviations of technical terms, sometimes numerals which bear some as yet unexplained relation to the ordinals of the *Sāman* scale. They are written over the syllables of the text to indicate the substantive (*prakṛti*) notes, between them to indicate grace-notes (*vikṛti*), practically the 'ligatures' of Plainsong. Secular music has also till quite lately, the last century, dispensed with notation; and it must be remembered that a written notation would be a hindrance rather than a help when everything was learned by heart[1] or extemporized.

The form of the chant is recalled in its proper order by the aid of

[1] I saw in Mysore a *guru* who had received £10 for his life's work of committing to memory the text and the melodies of the whole *Sāmaveda*.

half a dozen sticks a span long, arranged much as we might arrange matches to mark whist-points.[1]

TECHNICAL TERMS (taken from R. Simon's *Puṣpasūtra*):

atikrama (transilience), disjunct motion, i.e. Thirds, Fourths, and Fifths in ascent and descent. The actual intervals prescribed by the *Sāma-paribhāṣā* (quoted by Simon, p. 516) are shown in white note-heads; those actually employed in Exner's examples in black.

Ex. 366.

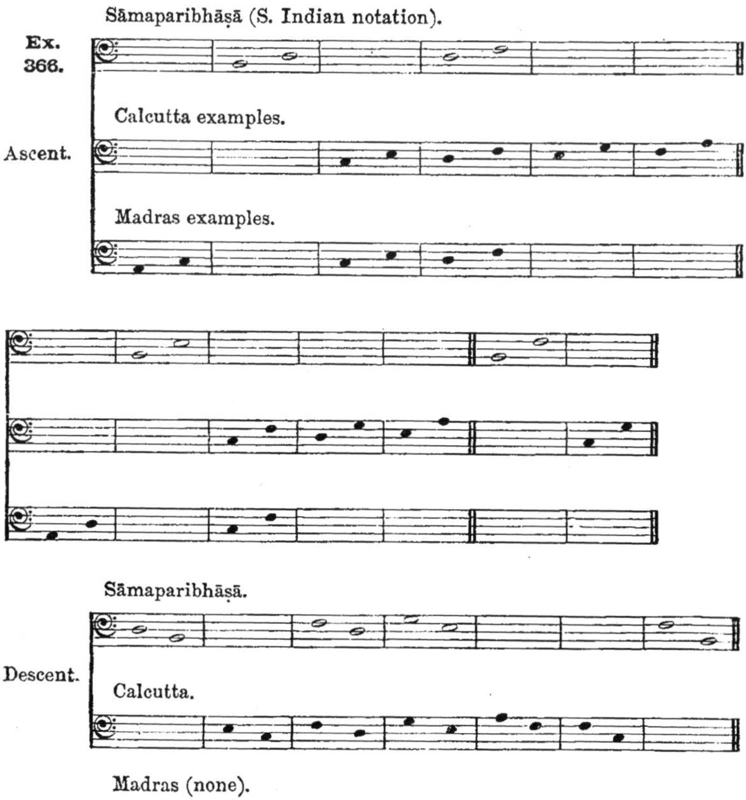

N.B.—It will be noticed that leaps are commoner in ascent than in descent and in the Calcutta chant than in the Madras.

udūha (upper completion) is the name for the upper consonant (*saṃvādī*).

[1] See Haug, *Ait. Br.*, vol. ii, p. 185, note, and p. 238, note; also Burnell, *Arṣ. Br.*, pp. xxviii and 105.

roha is a general name for ascent of one or more notes. The modern term for an ascending passage is *ārohaṇa,* for a descending, *avārohaṇa.*

svāra (lit. relating to sound), the cadence, used whenever the last syllable of the final section (*nidhana*) has the *svarita* accent. Examples:

Ex. 367.

karṣaṇa (lit. dragging, rubbing), the lengthening of a syllable by interpolated notes, is applied only to long or augmented (*vriddhied*) syllables. The most usual forms, though there are other varieties, are:

Ex. 368.

abhigīta (approaching note). Usual form:

Ex. 369.

udghāta (elevation). A downward *appoggiatura,* e.g.

Ex. 370.

vinata (crooked), a special case of *abhigīta*

Ex. 371.

or *karṣaṇa*
Ex. 372.

pratyutkrama (attack, initial step) is a progression to the next note above. Eight cases are given:

Ex. 373.

The definition does not appear to state, what seems evident, that in this progression one syllable is sung to two notes, that it is, in fact, the *podatus* of Plainsong.[2] No. 8 of these plays a great part in *Rāga* (see p. 158). These examples clearly presuppose the tetrachord E D C B, not F E D C.

gati (gait, passage). The lengthening of a syllable by the vowels i or u, e.g. ho—hoi—hoyi.

[1] We recognize in this semitonal elevation or depression the law of the mediaeval *Musica ficta,* which substituted a rising and falling semitone for a rising and falling tone.

[2] A good many of these figures find, of course, their analogues in the Neums, a list of which is given on p. 24 of H. B. Briggs's *Elements of Plainsong,* 1895.

atihāra (extremely long syllable, prosodial term). The carrying over of a syllable by means of a *jubilum* (*stobha*), e.g. ba—(auhova)—rhīṣī.

parvan (division). The smallest unity of a verse; practically, what can be sung in one breath, hence, musically, a phrase.

virāma. The *caesura* at the end of a phrase.

Melodic Figures. Mention should also be made of a method of handing down the traditional manner of singing. Melodic figures which constantly recur are directed to be sung after a certain well-known pattern. For instance, the cadence to the first line of the first hymn (given above) is:

Ex. 374.

Other syllables, then, which have this particular cadence are said to be 'done like *hīṣī*'. Thus:

Ex. 375.

Herr Simon gives about 100 examples; but until the *Sāmaveda* notation has been exactly interpreted it would be misleading to transcribe them.

If the cumulative effect of this evidence, chiefly circumstantial, may be said to have established any conclusion as to the original scale of India, we have found there, as in Greece, a starting point in a tetrachord of the form:

Ex. 376.

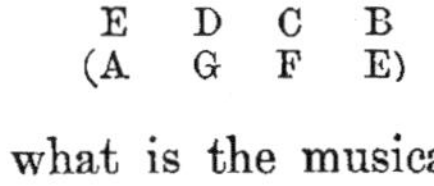

It is interesting to ask what is the musical justification of this particular series of notes, and of their development.

The music is purely vocal; no instrument is employed: and vocal scales are conceived downwards. They are so conceived because the telling notes of the voice are in its upper register, and this presents itself therefore as the starting point[1] for a vocal scale. In its search for consonance the ear hears in the first instance only quintal, not tertian, harmony, as was explained on pp. 123 foll. Quintal harmony provides only Fifths, Fourths, and major Tones. It has been shown on p. 150 that in looking for harmony to a given note the Fifth occurs first in an upward series, but the Fourth in a downward. A vocal scale, conceived downwards, establishes therefore the Fourth before the Fifth, the tetrachord before the pentachord. The intermediate notes can only be filled up by major Tones, for no other interval is as yet present to the ear. As soon as the major Third is heard it corrects no doubt one of these major Tones into a minor Tone.

In proceeding beyond this tetrachord there is nothing, apparently, in the nature of things to decide whether the F above should be first added, as consonant to C, or the A below as consonant to D. The F was, as a fact, added first. This is seen to be a result of the circumstance that the E was a graced note. It was, if we may judge from the modern secular usage (see Chapter VII), seldom sung pure; an upper note was, so to say, inherent in it; and this determined to an F rather than an F♯ owing to the C below. The A was added also; but, as the interest of the chant lay at the other end of the tetrachord, this A became more or less atrophied, and a G was never added below it. Meanwhile the F inherited the musical importance which had attached to the E, and the tetrachord F–C competed with the tetrachord E–B for supremacy.

It was here that the Greeks parted company; and the reason for their doing so is instructive. They continued their tetrachord A–E upwards through a B♭ and downwards through a D, but we do not make out that the tetrachord B♭–F ever attained any sort of eminence in their song. The B♭ did not come into their scale as a 'graced' A, as the Hindu F was a graced E. For they aimed at singing their notes pure, as Aristoxenus tells us.[2] They regarded

[1] The Hindus named the upper terminal of the tetrachord *graha* (beginning) and the lower *nyāsa* (end).

[2] He is contrasting (*Harm.*, ch. 10) the continuous (*synechē*) motion of the speaking voice and the motion-by-interval (*diastēmatikēn*) of the singing voice, and says, 'In speaking we avoid bringing the voice to a standstill (i.e. a pure note) unless we force it to that in moments of feeling. But in singing we do the opposite; we avoid continuous motion, and aim at making the voice, as far as possible, stationary'—i.e. we sing our notes not 'graced' but 'clean'.

their B♭ therefore merely as a consonant to the F below, not *also* as a kind of heightened A.

To return to the Hindus. The F, having inherited the prestige of the E, took on grace in its turn. But here a difficulty arose: should the grace-note have the same relation to the F as the F had to the E, and determine to a G♭ (F♯), or should it be consonant to the D below, and appear as a G? Both notes were taken in; and the scale had now two distinct sections: that from E downwards which was formed diatonically, and that from E upwards which was formed by grace, i.e. chromatically. These had distinct characters, and were distinguished as we saw by the names *nīca* and *ucca* (p. 271, and Exs. 362, 363). Moreover, the chromatic (*ucca*) style of singing is peculiar to the *Sāmaveda*, where it had, as we see, an efficient cause, and is not found in *Rāga*, where that cause is absent.

A purely vocal scale is so foreign to our music that, though we may understand it, we have difficulty in feeling its musical force. The following melody from the *Fitzwilliam Virginal Book* (i. 144) appears to be in such a scale; and its constituent notes happen, curiously, to be exactly those of the *Sāman* scale:

The woods so wilde.

Ex. 377.

Those writers on the modes who insist that the last note of a song must be the tonic would be delighted to find in this a rare—probably the only—instance of a Locrian (Mixolydic). But a tonic F gives a much better sense; and indeed Orlando Gibbons has harmonized it, if it was he, like a bagpipe tune on F and G pedals, though it must be confessed that harmony of any kind sadly impairs its delicious inconsequence and irresponsibility, and a calculated close on B does much to clip the wings of its fancy.

There is an abundance of tunes, too, which seem to have no definite tonality and to be divided in their allegiance to different tonics. Here is one from Böhme's *Altdeutsches Liederbuch*, p. 729:

St. Ursula, Königstochter von England.

Ex. 378.

The essence of the melody is that E is the predominant note; that it closes in A minor rather than C major is of the nature of an accident. In both these melodies we see the marks of a vocal scale not only in the high *tessitura* and the indefinite tonic, but in the way they tend to ascend by leap and descend by step.

CHAPTER XI

FORM

THAT principle of balance by which the several parts of a song, whether it lasts half a minute or half an hour, stand out from one another in strong contrast and yet help, each of them in its way, to build up the general sense of unity—that ordered disposition of its component parts by which music travels to an inevitable climax, neither postponing it nor anticipating it, and thence to a close—that variety which gives flesh and blood to the bare bones of structure—all this is 'Form'. Form is, however, rather an instinct than a principle, and it is dangerous to follow it too much into detail, because a composer may at any moment wrap his principle in new detail and justify it by success, and then analysis is apt to boggle.

Still, even instinct must work in elements of design which make on the whole either for variety or for unity, or which can be so used as to do the one or the other. The primal unity of our system is the tonic chord, and in a larger scheme the tonic key; and the sense of contrast reposes primarily in the dominant and subdominant chords and keys. These again can become unifying forces with related keys supplying contrast. It would be impossible for our music to get away from this as long as it continues to be harmonic, since all these chords are by implication in the triad itself (major or minor), and, by extension of its meaning, many others. The primal unity of the Hindu system is similarly the tonic note, or drone; and the sense of contrast is supplied primarily by the *aṃśa*, that note in which the lie of the song, its *tessitura*, centres, and the notes which are related to this (1) as consonants, *saṃvādī*, (2) as passage notes (*anuvādī*, *vivādī*) between the consonants. But whereas the dominant was implied in the tonic, and while contrasting with it still made for unity, the *aṃśa* stands out against the drone (*kharaj*[1]) as a matter of choice, and so makes for contrast; and yet since the varying relationship (in the different *Rāgs*) of the

[1] *Kharaj* is a vernacular form, through *śaḍ(a)j*, of *ṣaḍja* (Skr.).

aṃśa to the *kharaj*, its relative distance from it, is what gives its special character to the song, this very contrast may be said also to impart unity, the unity, namely, of that particular *Rāg*; and thus the general unity of the song proceeds not from intrinsic necessity, but from freedom of choice.

The first thing in a song is to put this relationship of the *aṃśa* and *kharaj* beyond doubt. This is done by the *Ālāp* (prelude). The notes of the *Rāg* are sung not in strict time, but in a loose kind of rhythm regulated by the convenience of the breath and by the amount of 'work' that is to be got on to the notes, and sung not to words, but to vocalizing syllables—Na, Ma, Ta, Ra, La, &c. The 'work' consists in elaborate graces, calculated to make the most of the important notes of the *Rāg*; and in order that these may be given with due impressiveness the *Ālāp* is taken at a slow or a moderate pace. Grace thus used to put the important notes in inverted commas is called *mūrchhana*. It is obvious that the *Ālāp* is a real necessity both for performer and listener; without it the listener would spend his time for some part of the song in ignorance of its tonal centres, and the melody would be for him an aimless running up and down hill, while the performer would, without a little preliminary practice, very likely play a note or two which was out of the *Rāg*, and that would upset the 'unity' altogether.

The scheme of the song proper, in its full shape, is as follows:

S. INDIA.	N. INDIA.
1. *Pallavi*, 'germ', 'sprout'. First subject, focussed on the *aṃśa*.	1. *Astai* or *Sthāyi*, 'at home'.
2. *Anupallavi*, 'after-germ'. Second subject, focussed on the 'consonant', generally the upper consonant.	2. *Antara*, 'interval', meaning perhaps change of voice-register.
3. *Caraṇam*, 'moving about'. Phrases taken from the *Pallavi* and *Anupallavi* to which the extra stanzas, if any, are sung.	3. *Sancāri*, 'alternation'; our 'development'.
4. Return to the *Pallavi* and close on the tonic (*śruti*) or Fifth above.	4. Return to the *Astai*, and close with the first note or phrase of the song, and for choice on the tonic (*kharaj*) or *aṃśa*. This return is sometimes called *Ābhōg*, 'coda'.

This is the form in South India for the full-fledged *Kīrtaṇam* (√*kṛ*, celebrate). The *Kṛiti* (perhaps from the same root) has no *caraṇam*, and this seems to be the more usual form in North India. The theme of the following is a repeated three-bar passage (*Cherarāvademirā*) with a link phrase (*Rāmayya*). In No. 3 variation the first bar of this is expanded to four, and in No. 4 to eight bars. The original theme is then dropped, and taken up again in No. 9. In Nos. 11, 12 comes a suggestion of the theme of the *anupallavi*, which follows at No. 13 at the upper consonant B♭, the *pallavi* having circled round the *aṃśa*, E♭.

Indian theory would not of course allow that the A♮ of the *anupallavi* involved a change of *Rāg*. That note is introduced only to form the 'strong' tetrachord (see Chapter XII), but the effect is indistinguishable from what we should call a key contrast. The *caraṇam* begins with phrases of the *pallavi* and ends with those of the *anupallavi*, and is preceded and followed by the cadenza.

Words. A girl is singing:—*Pallavi.* Why do you not come to me, O Rāma. *Anupallavi.* O infinite God, strong as Mount Meru, I can no longer bear (to be without you). *Caraṇam.* A fatherless and motherless child I pray to thee, I call on thee, I beseech thee, my own Lord. Again and again I cry in my sorrow to thee, my own dear Lord. Ah! with what yearning I gaze upon thy face, fair as the lotus. I send my petition to thee in strains that Tyāgarāja has made.

Cherarāvademirā, by Tyāgarāja (words and music).
Rāgam Rītigaula. (Aeolo-dorian.)
Tālam Deśādi ($\frac{2}{4}$, beginning on the up beat).

Devotamente. ♩ = 72.

Ex. 379.

4
5
6
7
8
9
10
11
12

Fine.
Anupallavi.
14
Me-ru-gā - du-rā i - ka ma-hā - -
15
16 Svarā.
ga-ma pa-da-ma pa-ga ma ga-ri-sa ni sa-ni
ga - ri-sa . . . ga-ga ma-ma ni-da-ma ga-ma ni-ni - sa ni-sa ga-ga-
- - ma ga-ri ga-ga-ri-sa ri - sa ni da-ma-ga-ri . ni sa-ga ga-ma Che -
- ra - rā - va - de - mi rā . . . Ra-ma-yya Che-ra-rā - va-
Caraṇa.
- de - mi - rā . . Ta - lli tan-dri le - ni - - bā -
17
- la . .
18
19

A few particulars of the different styles of song, collected chiefly from books [1] are here given. The distinction between them seems

[1] Pingle's *Indian Music*, Rajah S. M. Tagore's *Reprints from various Authors* and *Universal History of Music.*

to rest principally on the words, secondly on the time, hardly at all on the tune, but a good deal on the general form.

The oldest forms of Hindu song are the *Pada* and *Bhajana*. The *Pada* is generally some pithy saying taken from Sanskrit verse and enlarged upon. The *Bhajana*, 'adoration', is connected with *Bhakti*, 'faith in a personal God', 'love for him as for a human being, the dedication of everything to his service, and the attainment of *mokṣa* (emancipation) by this means rather than by knowledge, or sacrifice, or works'.[1] The *Bhajana* specialized in the Krishna literature; and as the Bengali *Kīrtaṇa* does the same they may be classed together. The former is a religious recital in which the congregation sing all the time under a leader, *Bovā* ('man of piety'), and takes place between sunset and sunrise. In the latter the leader has a long story to tell, of a dramatic nature, and the congregation act as chorus. Its invention is ascribed to Chaṇḍīdās, a native of Birbhaum, the birthplace of Jayadeva; it is mentioned in the *Ain-i-Akbari*. With it is associated the mystery play, *Jāttrā*, which circled round the love of Krishna and Rādhā.

The typical form of Hindu song, a development of the *Pada* and *Bhajana*, untouched by Mohammedan influence, is the *Dhrūpad* (*Dhruva-pāda*—*dhruva*, 'firm', 'enduring'; *pāda*, 'quarter-verse'; *Dhruva* is a name also for the 'constantly recurring verse' or 'burden' of a song). The *Dhrūpad* has a free masculine character; its words are religious, but not exclusively so. It is in slow time, and in selected *Tāls*—*Surphakta*, *Chautāl*, and *Dhamār*—the ionic and anapaestic metres in fact; and since to perform it requires a good command of the breath, there is a saying—'The man who has the strength of five buffaloes, let that man sing *Dhrūpad*'. When there is any doubt about the exact form of a particular *Rāg*, appeal is made not to the Sanskrit authorities, but to the traditional form of *Dhrūpad*. In that the *Rāg* is to be found in its purity with its *mūrchhanas* (the 'consonant' notes ornamented); a *Rāg* without these is called *Jhil* or *Dhun*. But the *Dhrūpad* is free from other grace-notes; and since these are considered essential to Hindu song, the *Dhrūpad* is somewhat at a discount; it is considered, for instance, unsuitable for public performance. Further, since most songs demand a compass of two and a half octaves, and since this can only be attained by *falsetto*, this kind of voice is prized

[1] L. J. Sedgwick, in the *Journal of the B. B. R. A. Society* for 1911.

for its 'liveliness', and the natural (*dhruva*) voice neglected; so that *Dhrūpad* singers are apt to form a special class. The great representative of the style was Rajah Mān of Gwalior (died 1518).

Another old form is the *Kathā*, or sermon in song. A text from the *Rāmayaṇa* or the *Mahābharata* is intoned (in about an octave of notes) and then expounded in the speaking voice and in the vernacular by a *Kāthaka*.

Another is the *Kabī*, a song of question and answer, such as the Garhwāli songs, pp. 50, 51. It is a popular form in the villages, and became in the eighteenth century a favourite in higher circles, when question and answer were elaborately prepared instead of being impromptu.

The commonest type is the *Khyāl*, a later form of *Dhrūpad*, supposed to emanate from Mahmud Sharqi of Jaunpur (1401–40). It is a song (*Chija*) or an instrumental piece (*Gati*) constructed of variations on, or rather episodes relieving, a short phrase; a Rondo in fact. The *Khyāl* ranges from a very simple little song to the following, which with its compass of three octaves probably represents the extreme of elaboration. Its highest development belongs to the Mohammedan period; this, *Kaba ho kapī*, is from the Panjab, where there are few but Mohammedan singers. The theme is variously treated on its three or four dozen appearances, and is not so monotonous to listen to as it is to write or to read, and the playful sweep of the episodes (*tāna*, 'divisions' in our eighteenth-century sense of the word) has nothing clumsy about it. The *Khyāl* is generally a love-tale and supposed to be sung by a woman; the procedure of love-making is in India, as so many other things are, the reverse of ours. It is the typically pathetic form of song.

Malkos. Velambit. Tīntāl.

Ex. 880.

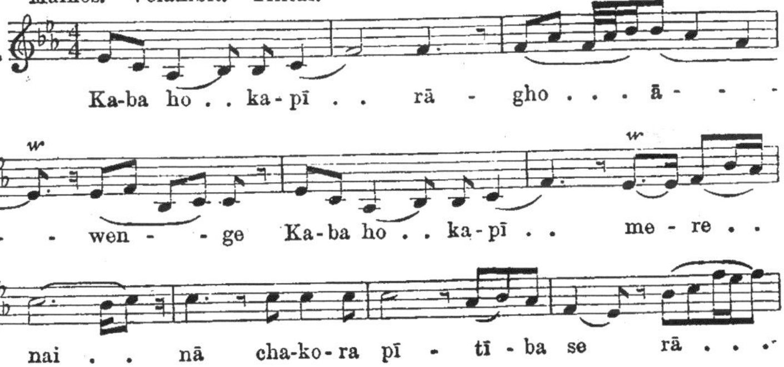

kā śa - śī mu - kha . . de - - - kha - na - - - a . .
. . . . ā - - - - - wen - - ge Ka-ba ho . . ka-pī .
. . A . . . . A . . . . Ka-ba ho . . ka-pī .
. . A . . . . . . A . . . .
Ka - ba ho . . ka - pī . . A . . . . . A . . . .
. . . . Ka-ba ho . . ka - pī . . A . . .
. . A . . . . A . . . A . . .
. . . . Ka-ba ho . . ka - pī . . A . .
. . . . A . . . . . . A . . . . . . A . . .
. . . . Ka-ba ho . . ka-pī .
. . . . A . . A . . . .

Ka-ba ho . . ka-pī . . A . . . .
. . . . Ka-ba ho . . ka-pī . . A . . . .
. . . . Ka-ba ho . . ka-pī .
. . . . . ī . . . . ī . .
Ka-ba ho . . ka-pī . . . .
. . . . . . ī . . . ī . . . .
. . . . ī . . . . ī . . .
ī . . . .
Ka-ba ho ka-pī . . . .
. . . . ī . . . .
. . . . Ka-ba ho . . ka-pī . . . . A

A
A
Ka-ba ho . . ka-pī . . . Ka-ba ho . . .
. . . . . . ka-pī . . . rā - gho . . . ā - wen -
- ge . . Ka-ba ho . . . . ka-pī ra-gho ā - wen - ge .
. . . Ka-ba ho . . ka-pī . . . . Ka-ba ho . . . . .
. . . ka-pī . . . . ī . . . .
. . . . ī . . . rā - gho ā - wen - ge . Ka-ba ho . ka-pī .
. . . . A . . . .

Ka-ba ho . . ka - pī . . . . . A . . . . A .
. . . . Ka-ba ho . . ka - pī . . A . . .
. . . . Ka-ba ho . . ka-pī .
. . ī . . . . . . Ka-ba ho . . ka-pī . . A . . . . . .
. . Ka-ba ho . . ka - pī A . . . .
. . Ka-ba ho . . ka - pī . . . .
. . . . Ka-ba ho . . A . . . .
. . Ka-ba ho . . ka - pī . . me - re nai . . nā . . A . .
. . . . me - re nai . . nā . . A . . . .
. . . . me - re nai . . nā .
. . . A A . . . .
. . . . me - re nai . . nā .

me-re nai nā cha-ko-ra pī-
tī-ba se rā
Ka-ba ho ka-pī
A
Ka-ba ho ka-pī
Ī
Ka-ba ho ka-pī
Ka-ba ho ka-pī rā-gho ā-wen-ge

Ka-ba ho ka-pī rā-gho ā - - wen-ge . . Ka-ba ho . . ka - pī .
. . Ka-ba ho ka - pī rā - gho ā - wen - ge
Ka-ba ho ka-pī rā-gho ā - wen-rā - ge . . . .
. . . . Ka-ba ho . . ka - pī .
. . Ka - ba ho ka - pī rā - gho ā - wen - ge
Ka-ba ho ka-pī rā-gho ā-wen-ge Ka-ba ho ka-pī rā-gho ā - wen - ge
Ka-ba ho . . ka - pī . . Ka-ba ho . . . ka - pī
. . rā - - gho . ā - - - wen - ge
. . Ka-ba ho ka-pī . . . Ka-ba ho ka-pī rā - gho ā - wen -
- - ge. Ka-ba ho ka - pī . . rā - gho ā - wen - ge . . . . .
. . . . Ka-ba ho . . ka - pī .

A
Ka-ba ho ka - pī
Ka-ba ho ka-pī
Ka-ba ho ka - pī
Ka-ba ho ka - pī
Ka-ba ho ka-pī

. . . . ī . . . . rā-gho ā - wen-
- ge Ka-ba ho . . ka-pī rā . . gho ā - - - - -
- - wen-ge . . . . Ka-ba ho . . ka-pī . . . .
Ka-ba ho ka-pī rā-gho ā-wen-ge . . Ka-ba ho ka-pī rā-gho ā-wen-ge.
. . Ka-ba ho . . ka-pī . . Ka-ba ho . . . . . .
. . ka-pī . . . . . rā - gho ā - wen-ge
Ka-ba ho ka-pī . . rā - gho ā - wen-ge . . Ka-ba ho . . ka-pī .
. . A . . . .
. . . . Ka-ba ho . . ka-pī .
. . . . . . A . . . .
. . . . Ka-ba ho . . ka-pī .

. . Ka-ba ho . . . . Ka-pī . .
. . . . . . rā - - gho ā - wen-ge Ka-ba ho ka-pī rā-
- gho ā - wen - ge Kaba ho kapī rāgho āwenge Kaba ho kapī rā - gho āwen-
- ge Ka-ba ho ka-pī ka-pī . rā - gho . . . .
. . ā - - wen - ge Ka-ba ho ka-pī rā-gho ā - wen-
- ge Ka-ba ho ka-pī rā-gho ā - wen-ge Ka-ba ho ka-pī rā-gho ā-wen-
- ge . . Kabaho kapī rā-gho ā - wen - ge A . . . .
. . Ka-ba ho . . ka-pī . . . A . . . .

Ka-ba ho . . ka-pī .
rā - gho ā - - - - - wen-ge
Ka-ba . . ho ka-pī . . rā-gho . .
ā - wen - - ge
Ka-ba ho . . ka- ī.
ī . . ī ī
ī . . ī

Ka-ba ho . . ka-pī . . . . A
Ka-ba ho . . ka-pī
Ka-ba ho . . ka-pī

Three other Hindu forms are the *Sargam* (for Sa, Ri, Ga, Ma), called also *svarāvarta*, or *surāvarta*, and in the South *Svarā*, a passage sung to the Sol-fa names instead of to words, taking the place of our cadenza; the *Tarāṇa* (*Tillāna*), the same thing with drum-words instead of Sol-fa syllables, and the *Trivaṭa*, the same thing to nonsense-words; and lastly the *Caturañga* ('in four sections') consisting of *Khyāl*, *Tarāṇa*, *Sargam*, and *Trivaṭa*.

The *Thumri*, love-song, is of Hindu origin. It is in the Vraj *bhāsa*. Vraj is the district round Agra and Mathurā, the scene of Krishna's juvenile adventures. The music is lively and adapted to pantomime or dancing. The subjects of *Thumri's* are: (1) beseeching the lover to be propitious, (2) lamentation over his absence, (3) imprecation of rivals, (4) laments over the watchfulness of the mother-in-law and sisters-in-law who prevent meetings with the lover, and over the tinkling bells of anklets imposed by jealous husbands to prevent clandestine visits, (5) appeals to female friends (*Sakhīs*) for help to secure an interview, (6) *Sakhīs* reminding their friend of the appointment and exhorting her to persevere.

The typical Mohammedan song is the *Tappa*, see pp. 188, 189. The trill (Hindost., *mūrki*; Urdu, *zamzama*), considered to be suitable to the female voice, of which the *Tappa* is full, and the marked rhythm are the Mohammedan contribution. The Mohammedan invasions did for India what the dissolution of the monasteries and the Civil War did for English music (see p. 84). The *Tappa* is exclusively in Hindi and Panjābi. It recites the loves of Hīr and Ranjha. It was brought to perfection by the songstress Shori (reign of Mahmud Shah, circ. 1700). It consists, like most Hindostani songs, of two movements (*tūk*), the *Astai* and *Antara*. The *Rekhtu*, another form of it, contains up to a dozen couplets. Other Mohammedan songs are the *Ghazal* (words Urdu and Persian) and the *Dādra* (confined to the lower classes). Both are in $\frac{6}{8}$ time, but commonly syncopated, ♩ ♪ ♪ ♩. In the *Ghazal* the lover makes a woful ballad to his mistress's eyebrow:

> Why not praise your moles more than the stars!
> Those are the ornaments of the cheeks of my beloved.
> The white of early dawn radiates from your cheek;
> The darkness of the night is a part of your waving hair.
> Since I was fated to moan in separation, O God,
> Why did I fall in love with one so beautiful?
> Your eyes with their long lashes were quite enough,
> Their side glances were not necessary for my annihilation.
> Do you not understand that you will be alone after killing me?
> Yet even the dust of my grave will cleave to you in my stead.
> The times are such that, in spite of all that I have said and sung there is no justice in this world.

There are also songs of local fame such as the *Abhāngas*, *Oṃvis*, and *Povāḍas* of the Maratha Tuka Rām, the first two religious, the last warlike; and the *Karkhās*, the war-songs of the Rājputs.

The *Kīrtaṇam* and the *Khyāl* that have been given above represent the highest flights of the professional musicians (*Ustāds*). Ordinary singers are content with humbler songs; and the following have been selected, out of twice their number in the books of the Poona Gayan Samāj (singing school), many of them for their beauty, others in order to give an idea of the principal *Rāgs* and *Tāls*.

Specimens of Rāgs.

Lydian. Hypolydic.

Hindol. Rūpak. 2 + 4.

Ex. 381.

Kalyāna. Tevra. 3 + 2 + 2.

Ex. 382.

Bhūp[kaliān]. Rūpak.

Ex. 383.

Hamirkaliān. Rūpak.

Ex. 384.

Ionian. Lydic.

Shankarābharaṇa. Tevra.

Ex. 385.

Nārāyaṇī. Tevra.

Ex. 386.

Bilāvala. Titai.

Ex. 387.

(The girl I left behind me.)

Kedāra. Eka Trisra. $\frac{6}{8}$. *Slow.*

Ex. 388.

Kedāra. Tīntāl.

Ex. 389.

Kedārā. Eka Trisra. *Slow.*

Ex. 390.

Kedāra. Dhamār. $\frac{7}{8}+\frac{7}{8}$.

Ex. 391.

Kedāra. Rūpak.

Ex. 392.

Mixolydian. Hypophrygic.

Jhinjoti. Eka Trisra.

Ex. 393.

Desh. Eka Trisra.

Ex. 394.

Desh. Eka Trisra. *Slow.*

Ex. 395.

Sorat. Tital.

Ex. 396.

Sārang. Rūpak.

Ex. 397.

Khamāj. Adi.

Ex. 398.

Dorian. Phrygic.

Kāfi. Dhamār.

Ex. 399.

Kāfi. Rūpak.

Ex. 400.

Bahār. Rūpak.

Ex. 401.

Bageshrī. Rūpak.

Ex. 402.

Myachā Malhār. Chautāl. 4 + 4 + 2 + 2.

Ex. 403.

Malhār. Tevra. *Slow.*

Ex. 404.

Bhimpalāsī. Chautāl.

Ex. 405.

Bhimpalāsi. Tintal.

Ex. 406.

Aeolian. Hypodoric.

Malkos. Eka Trisra. *Slow.*

Ex. 407.

Dhanāshri. Rūpak.

Ex. 408.

Dhanāshri. Tital.

Ex. 409.

Āsāvarī. Rūpak.

Ex. 410.

Āsāvarī. Eka Trisra. *Slow.*

Ex. 411.

Āsāvarī. Dhamār.

Ex. 412.

Darbārī Kānaḍā. Chautal.

Ex. 413.

Darbāri Kānaḍā. Rūpak.

Ex. 414.

Darbāri Kānaḍā. Eka Trisra. *Slow.*

Ex. 415.

Kānaḍā. Eka Trisra. *Slow.*

Ex. 416.

Pilū. Rūpak.

Ex. 417.

Pilū. Rūpak.

Ex. 418.

Phrygian-Doric.

Bhairavi. Eka Trisra. *Slow.*

Ex. 419.

Bhairavi. Rūpak.

Ex. 420.

Bhairavi. Rūpak.

Ex. 421.

Special Indian modes.

Rāmkalī. Tital.

Ex. 422.

Rāmkalī. Rūpak.

Ex. 423.

Kalangaḍa. Tital.

Ex. 424.

Jogi. Jhamra. 3 + 4 + 3 + 4

Ex. 425.

Bhairau. Chautal.

Ex. 426.

Toḍi. Rūpak.

Ex. 427.

Toḍi. Chautāl.

Ex. 428.

Multānī. Jhamra.

Ex. 429.

Shrīrāg. Rūpak.

Ex. 430.

Shrīrāg. Surphakta.

Ex. 431.

Pūrvi. Rūpak.

Ex. 432.

Gauri. Eka Trisra. *Slow.*

Ex. 433.

Sohani. Tital.

Ex. 434.

Paraja. Rūpak.

Ex. 435.

Lalat. Dhamār.

Ex. 436.

Lalat. Rūpak.

Ex. 437.

Māravā. Rūpak.

Ex. 438.

Māravā. Tintal.

Ex. 439.

Pūriakaliān. Triput. 3 + 2 + 2.

Ex. 440.

A European has great difficulty in giving himself account of these queer modes, because of the enormous difference between having the tonality condensed into a few contrasted chords and having it spread over a melody in successive notes which are epitomized as a scale. There is, however, a step between chord and scale in the arpeggio, as we may observe when immature pianoforte players sound the left hand before the right. It is useful sometimes to consider chords as scales, and scales as chords. Our harmony has gone through three chief moments in its history: the diminished seventh, the augmented triad, and now the whole tone scale, or chord,[1] have successively been regarded as the limit of permissible dissonance. Their double nature, scale and chord, becomes clear if we write them out as arpeggios:

Ex. 441.

From this point of view the modes too may be considered. The three chords just mentioned are practically statements that new notes are taken into the major scale (of C): the diminished seventh introduces A♭, the augmented triad D♯, and the whole tone chord E♭ and C♯. Other chords have, as they have appeared, introduced these or other notes.[2] The tonality of a scale may be quickly shown by taking all the constituent notes which are not part of the tonic chord, putting them upon the dominant note, and resolving them into the tonic. We will treat the principal modes thus in succession:

[1] The writer is indebted for this word to Dr. Walford Davies.

[2] The first eleven bars of Tristan introduce into C minor F♯, G♯, C♯; A♮, E♮; D♭, and C♭.

Ex. 442.

Kaliān.
Alahīya.
Lydian.
Ionian.
Jhinjotī.
Khamāj.
Ionian.
Mixolydian.
Kāfi.
Malhār.
Dorian.
Āsāvari.
Pilu.
Aeolian.
Bhairavi.
Ramkali.
Phrygian (Bhairavi).
Non-European (Rāmkali).
Toḍi.
Paraj.
Shrī.
Gaurī.
Pūrvi.
Lalat.
Then *Kaliān* again.

In this kinematograph of the modes they are seen to be each an isolated moment in the whole musical experience; or, to reverse the picture and the metaphor, the modes make a kind of stellar photograph of our harmony. The notes that give us difficulty are the F♯ and the D♭; the former yields freely, the latter persists surprisingly. In our scales we know two leading notes, upward to the tonic (B♮) and downward to the dominant (A♭). These modes show the other two, downward to the tonic (D♭) and upward to the dominant (F♯). But the whole of our harmony is based, of course, on the fact, which the ear, however, only gradually endorses, that any note may be treated as a leading note in either direction. It is in the same way that the ear endorses these extreme modes; to plunge suddenly into one of them is to be completely baffled. We have to take them as the native ear does, as extensions of some other more familiar mode, as accentuations of its poignancy, or as heightenings of its exhilaration.

CHAPTER XII

MELODY

> He will put a girdle round the earth in forty minutes and forget to mention the fact, but he may weep at the breaking of a pencil point. And as his poems come he knows not whence, so he is content to let them fly he knows not whither. You ask for yesterday's masterpiece, and it is not to be found. 'Did I write that,' he asks with Shakespearian negligence, 'and was it really good? Never mind, I'll do you another.'
>
> *The Perse Playbooks.*

AND now if some one should assert, and we were inclined to humour him, that the Hindus, having worked at the laws of melody for at least 3,000 years, must have something to teach us, what could we say in his support?

1. First that melody, both time and tune, is in a mode; that is, that it must be homogeneous, and that nothing can be allowed in it which would destroy that homogeneity. We also recognize this in our tunes, though it would not in every case be easy to say how or why. We realize that a melody is good in proportion as everything in it is in keeping; we at least feel that something is wrong if we patch two melodies together, thus:

Ex. 443.

Here the second half seems to defeat rather than to supplement the first, because the descending thirds, though they balance, do not develop the ascending, and the repeated quaver motion is monotonous. Or, if we reverse the process,

Ex. 444.

the one note we do not desire after the first section is the high E♭; but we get it three times, and the climax consequently drags. Also the sixth bar going over exactly the same ground as the third at half the pace forms an anticlimax.

The homogeneity of a melody is based differently with them and with us. The musical sentence is in both cases made up of salient and abeyant notes, just as the verbal sentence is made up of nouns and verbs in prominence, and the other parts of speech in subordination. But with them the salient notes are fixed by long association; with us they are made such by the momentary impulse of the harmony or counterpoint. The distinction is not unlike that between verse and prose as the chosen vehicle of a people's literature; poetry fills a form which is brought to it, and the words assert their value by fighting against it, though they yield to it; prose creates its own form in the process of uttering itself, and this form emerges from the conflict and balance of phrases rather than of words. In the same sort of way individual notes have in modal music their value as filling out with detail a form already supplied, while for harmonized music points of structure, such as melodic figures, have value as creating and articulating form as the music proceeds. In the first it is the note, in the second the cluster of notes that is to be true to 'mode'.

Still, phrases after all are made of notes; and just as the notes of Hindu melodies must be 'in' an assigned mode (of tune or time), so must the notes of ours, if they are to be strong, have a firm diatonic and rhythmic basis. Chromatic notes easily become sentimental—become 'weak forms of strong things'—when they are unduly dwelt upon and distract attention from the big words of the sentence (as in the march of the Persian soldiers in the *Fall of Babylon*), not when they are there only to make intelligible the big words which without them would be too startling (as in 'O du mein holder Abendstern').[1] Diatonic is, of course, an expansive word. The diatonic scale is not the same to one generation as to the next, any more than modes are stereotyped

[1] But we may fancy how, when later on these startling words had become commonplaces to him, Wagner may have smiled contemptuously at the greasy effect of the chromatics, as perhaps the mature Browning may have regretted the false note struck by the first word in the pretty jingle of 'Menace our heart ere we master his own'.

for every time and place. But inside the accepted diatonic the notes must move as a compact whole, or the melody become heterogeneous.

Again, they must have a firm tread along some high road of rhythm whatever flowers they may stay to gather by the wayside or whatever excursions they may make to points of interest. Rhythmic strength lies in subordinating the attractive figures to the steady march of the whole, not in pursuing them for their own sweet sake (as in some of the more dreamy episodes of Mendelssohn's Fugues), nor in hunting them to death (in the various forms of Rosalia).

These principles, which we recognize as the foundations of our melody, we find more naïvely formulated in the systems of *Rāg* and *Tāl*, much as we read in Plato simple statements of the eternal problems of ethics and politics. These systems lay it down that chromatic alterations can only take place on the weak (*alpa*) notes of the scale, that is, in unessential places; and that, though any amount of cross-rhythm is permissible, it must justify itself by resolution at a particular point (the *sam*).

2. Melody proceeds by step (conjunct) or by leap (disjunct). In Indian melodies the disjunct intervals amount to 10 per cent. and the conjunct to 90 per cent. We will deal first with the 10 per cent.

The surprising thing in Indian melodies is their frequent use of intervals which appear difficult to us. We consider, for instance, such intervals as:

Ex. 445.

to be unvocal, but they employ them quite commonly. What makes intervals vocal is the fact that the note to which the leap is made is familiar. For us, it is made familiar chiefly by its forming some intelligible harmony with the note which is quitted. We can realize this in the phrase at the end of Brahms's *Mainacht*:

Ex. 446.

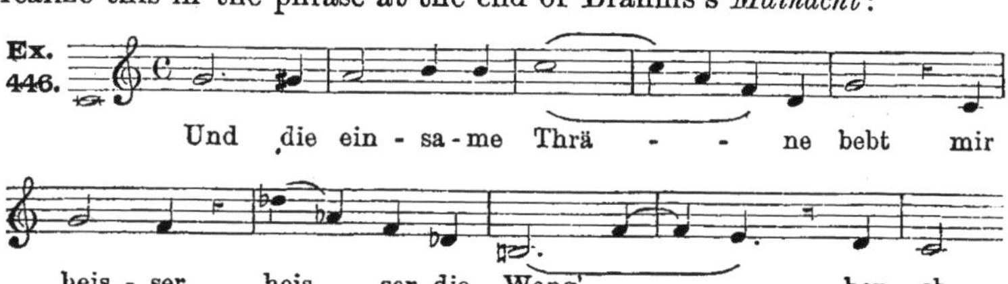

The leap 'die Wang'' is peculiarly dissonant; it consists of two diatonic semitones, which are greater than a whole tone by 20 cents; but it is made intelligible for us because it is a passage from the Neapolitan Sixth to the dominant chord, which is a perfectly familiar sequence. The other leaps are all justified to our ear as harmony notes.

But if we look at an Indian melody, one in *Bhairavi*, for instance:

Bhairavi.

Ex. 447.

of which the sixth of the scale (A♭) is *aṃśa,* with E♭ for its consonant, we see that the leaps are mainly to those notes, or round them, but not anywhere else. The tune swings between these two, generally in conjunct motion but with an occasional leap to one or other of them, and comes to rest between whiles on the tonic. Intervals as constituent parts of chords hardly ever occur, because chords form, for an Indian, no intelligible relationship.

The explanation of the augmented Second and diminished Third is that they are felt as conjunct intervals, not disjunct. The augmented Second is familiar to us in this sense in the 'harmonic' minor scale:

Ex. 448.

The B♮ has here a *melodic* appropriateness after the A♭ which the harmony immediately seizes upon and justifies; the harmony by itself (on double basses and drum) forms but a weak link. In Indian melodies the augmented second occurs also when the note between is transilient, that is to say, omitted not merely on that occasion but as a regular thing. The following instance in Sohani:

Sohani.

Ex. 449.

Scale.

consists almost entirely of conjunct motion. The G is transilient, and the F♯ optionally F♮. (This is the Poona form; elsewhere the A♭ is also A♮. Cp. Ex. 264.) It contains therefore, as conjunct intervals, one diminished Third (F♯–A♭) and two augmented Seconds (D♭–E and A♭–B); there is also a disjunct interval, the diminished Third, B–D♭. The *aṃśa* is E, the consonant B, and the melody swings between these two, making a pause on or otherwise emphasizing the tonic, C, on occasion. Hindus have said to me more than once that they like Wagner best of our music, and one sees perhaps in these two melodies a point of contact.

The augmented Fourth and diminished Fifth, which we avoid, are common with them. Although any sequence may be justified by its context, yet we consider on the whole the first interval slightly vulgar, and the second a little mawkish as melodic progressions, perhaps because they emphasize unduly the notes of a rather trite harmony. Where harmony is non-existent there can be no such feeling, and they are freely used in the following melody between the *aṃśa*, D♭, and the Fifth of the scale, G:

Gaula.

Ex. 450.

No less surprising than the presence of intervals which seem to us unvocal is the comparative absence of what we should call vocal intervals—the Thirds, Perfect Fourth and Fifth, and the Sixths. All these occur, but again are limited, as a rule, to leaps which approach a salient note. Such a passage as:

SCHUBERT.

Ex. 451. 

would be very unlikely to occur in their music. There would be no way of hitting the diminished Fifth ('ist des') unless the D were the *aṃśa*; and if it were, it would be impossible that so important a note should occur only once, and at such an insignificant point of the phrase. The intervals at 'Müllers Lust' would be practicable if C♯ were *aṃśa*, but they would not be at all typical, as the Third is which immediately follows ('Wandern'). A Third, in fact, is habitually taken as a changing note:

Ex. 452. 

or a grace-note:

Ex. 453. 

or, especially in ascent, in a sort of tentative way:

Ex. 454. 

indeed, in any way but as a harmonic interval:

Ex. 455. 

To continue Schubert's tune:

Ex. 456.

Here there is nothing unvocal from an Indian point of view, but the phrase repeated *totidem verbis* at different levels is not in their manner. A reason for this may be that their melodies swing from salient note to salient note, and that if the salient notes were in the important places in the first phrase they would not be so in the second, and vice versa, so that the point of the contrast would be lost; it would be like reading poetry thus:

> The *young men* march *before* him in all their *strength* and *pride*,
> *The* tender *little* infants *they* totter by *his* side.

It is conjunct motion that Hindu practice, rather than theory, accounts the stronger. It has been maintained[1] that melody tends to be developed along the line of the common chord. This appears to be the case in some parts of the world, among the Chippewas, for instance:

Ex. 457.

but it is emphatically not the case in India. The reason may be that there is more real contrast to be got out of step than leap; because the step must often be to a consonant interval, and in that case the second note repeats to some extent what has already been said by the first. It has often been noticed that Beethoven's melodies are full of conjunct motion—the great tune of the Choral Symphony, for instance, which matured during half a century with Goethe's *Faust*; and perhaps this motion was what he admired in our national anthem when he undertook to 'show the English'

[1] See Oskar Fleischer, *Ein Kapitel der vergleichenden Musikwissenschaft*, in the first quarterly volume of the International Music Society, p. 17.

what a fine tune they had—though they have hardly been as grateful as they should have been; perhaps, too, the injudicious use of disjunct motion accounts for some of the insipidity of the tunes of Shield, Henry Bishop, and T. H. Bayly, and the judicious admixture of both kinds of motion for the virility of Arne and Purcell.

Conjunct motion, too, is eminently suited to the speaking voice, which makes small changes in pitch; moreover small intervals seem to be more effective than large against a drone, as may be seen in Schubert's *Leiermann*. The song has contained plenty of disjunct motion, but in the last line:

Ex. 458.

where the maximum of effect is to be produced, it becomes suddenly conjunct.

Before we leave this point there is one thing that their songs have in common with our Folk-songs which seems worth mention. When a rising or falling Fourth is bridged by a passage note, this is usually nearer to the note which is being quitted than to that which is being approached. Thus:

Ex. 459.

are commoner than

Ex. 460.

The fact that the former kind is preferred suggests that such motion is really the stronger melodically of the two; and this seems to be borne out also in our music. We realize how much is lost by the not infrequent substitution of an A for the second note (G) in 'The bonny banks of Loch Lomond'.

Ex. 461.

We feel also that Beethoven's

Ex. 462. 

is better suited to a reflective *Andante con moto*, but Brahms's

Ex. 463. 

to an austere 'first movement', and Mozart's

Ex. 464. 

to a robust *Allegro molto*.

3. This leads to another point. The typical forms of ascent and of descent are apt to differ in one and the same *Rāg*, which is then called 'crooked' (*vakra*). The Hindus are most strict about the observance of the type. Its origin probably lies in this tendency which we have been discussing—the tendency to choose, between two consonant notes, the note of passage next to that which is being quitted, thus:

Ex. 465. 

Its effect certainly is the avoidance of tautology and anticlimax. There are plenty of instances in our melody where this principle of contrast is not employed, because the harmony can supply all the contrast which is required:

Ein' feste Burg.

Ex. 466. 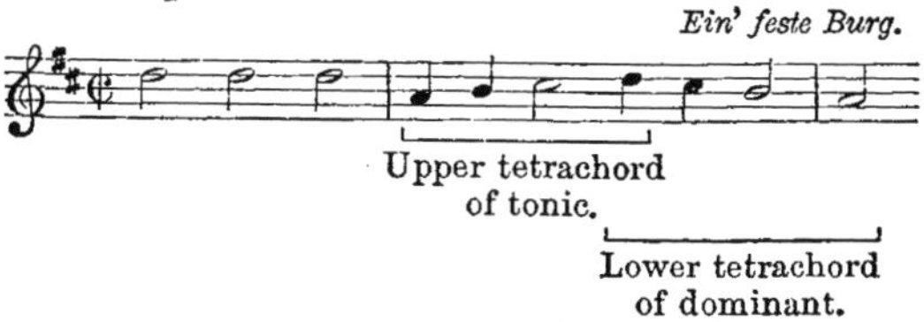

BEETHOVEN. Quartet, Op. 18, No. 5.

Ex. 467. 

But there are others in which a different form is adopted for ascent and descent, and consequently the contrast which harmony offers can be dispensed with:

SULLIVAN.

Ex. 468.

The whole of this departs but little from tonic harmony, and the main contrast lies in the scale:

Ex. 469.

But a large number of these 'crooked' forms of Hindu *Rāgs* consisted in creating gaps in ascent to be filled up in descent, or vice versa. This not only avoids anticlimax, but induces climax. To pass over a note immediately creates a desire for it, and it then becomes a fit note to bear the climax:

BACH.

Ex. 470.

BACH.

Ex. 471.

BACH.

Ex. 472.

BACH.

Ex. 473.

In the first three cases the notes marked (*) have only been heard as passing notes, and now they are made substantive; in the last case three of them have not yet been heard at all. There are special reasons, no doubt, for constructing the theme of a fugue in this way, but incidentally it has great melodic point. Two notes are similarly kept in reserve in the tune of Sullivan just given, and they (F and A♭) are the making of it. Similarly also in the 'Swanee River' the 7th and 4th of the scale are kept in reserve, in 'Come lasses and lads' the 4th, in 'Farewell Manchester' the 7th; whereas the 'Vicar of Bray' and the 'Bay of Biscay' put all their goods in the shop window. The last line of Schubert's 'Wandern', again,

Ex. 474.

where the D, hardly heard previously, now comes by its full rights, is a peculiarly grateful instance of this, and gains by the repetition of the phrase.

4. What gives its peculiar flavour to a melody, what defines more than anything else the character of a particular *Rāg*, is the position of the *aṃśa*. Round it, and round its consonant or correlative (*saṃvādi*)—a note at the distance of a Fourth or a Fifth from it—are grouped the phrases of the song. They derive their meaning, their point, from their relation to it. It is easy to see that the character of a phrase would completely alter according as the *aṃśa*, the salient note of the scale, were made the salient note of the phrase, or not. The *aṃśa* may be at any place in the scale, not excluding the keynote or drone note. The first section (*astai*) of the tune usually circles round the *aṃśa* and the second (*antara*) round its consonant. The aesthetic effect of a high and a low *aṃśa* is quite different, and in this respect the *aṃśa* and all that it implies may be compared with what we know as *tessitura*, though that is rather a 'range' of notes, whereas the *aṃśa* is a single note. Over against the *aṃśa* stands the drone note, or keynote (*kharaj*). These two notes divide between them the functions of our tonic. Hindostani music is apt to begin on the *aṃśa*, and to end, if not there too, on whatever was the first note, or the end of the first phrase, of the song. This leaves the melody, to our ears, in the air. In the Carnatic music it is the rule, rather than the exception, for the melody to end on the drone note, or its Fifth. Yet, even so, the drone note has not the finality of our tonic. When the *aṃśa* is at F, for instance, any meaning that we could attach to a tonic is utterly driven out of C. The purpose of the drone is rather to maintain a steady level by comparison with which the *aṃśa* appears as high (and the tune spirited) or low (and the tune reflective).

This is a conception which is and must remain foreign to our music as a whole; it is impossible for us to put any note besides the tonic in this position of 'central' except the Third or the Fifth; and to build tunes only on that principle would limit the possibilities enormously. Still we may realize the idea of this centre in those of our tunes in which the Third or the Fifth is so treated. Many of Mozart's circle round the Fifth and gain their sprightly character from that fact:

Andante. Sonata.

Ex. 475.

and

Andante. E♭ Symphony.

Ex. 476.

Allegro. Quartet.

Ex. 477.

All our composers have been fond of the Third as 'centre', in slow movements especially; it will be enough to look at the melody of the Finale of the Choral Symphony:

Allegro assai. Beethoven.

Ex. 478.

The 'central' note is F♯; and there is a skill in the way in which it is made central without being monotonous. It is central both because of the frequency of its use, and because, though the tune lies mainly above them, this is balanced by the dramatic drop to A at the climax. But it is not monotonous because (leaving aside repetitions of phrase, which are not strictly repetitions of note) it is never treated twice exactly in the same way although it occurs eight times; either the note is on a different beat of the bar, or of a different length, or it is an ascending instead of a descending phrase. And these are exactly the principles—position of central note, variety of metre, and contrast of ascent and descent—which India says are at the bottom of good melody.

The *aṃśa* need not, and frequently does not, occur in a melody any oftener than other notes; nor indeed need any of the other salient notes. But their presence is felt in the appoggiatura, which they render possible. It is difficult to imagine any system of music which did not give an important place to this the most emotional element of tune; the Chinese tunes seem, indeed, to show small trace of it; but we have not yet, perhaps, very trustworthy records of them. The Hindu tune to be quoted presently shows half a dozen instances of appoggiatura, and the poignancy of

Adagio molto. BEETHOVEN, *Rasoumoffsky Quartet.*

Ex. 479.

the tender grace of

BRAHMS, *Aeolsharfe.*

Ex. 480.

and the impetus of

BRAHMS, *Magelone Lied.*

Ex. 481.

are closely bound up with this device.

We may learn of this possibility in an Indian tune too, but we cannot instinctively feel it, because the *Rāg* is not ringing in our ears. We do not know, we have to be told, that in Behāg, for instance, B and E are strong and A and D weak notes, before we feel the force of the appoggiatura in:

Ex. 482.

But if we cannot select any other than these two notes (the Third and the Fifth) for 'central' note, because to do so would upset our tonality, and if to confine it to these two notes and insist upon it in every tune would cramp our harmony without securing for our melody any compensating variety, yet, on the other hand, harmony can establish a 'centre' anywhere and everywhere in a tune at will, and some of the most exciting tunes are built entirely on this change of centre (not of tonic); as, for instance, Brünnhilde's apostrophe to Grane at the end of the *Götterdämmerung*,

Ex. 483.

where, though the tonic, E, is clearly felt throughout, the 'centre' moves upwards to a climax,

Ex. 484.

and in so doing forms a broad 'inner' melody of its own, upon which an identical figure is carried up, and by its identity gives to the tune its unity.

This cannot be done in Indian melodies because each note has a fixed meaning, not, as with us, one assignable by the harmony at will. In them an identical figure, when it is transferred to another part of the scale, takes on a new meaning, because its relationship to the *aṃśa* has been altered. Consequently a principle of structure is then lost to Indian music. The Hindu melody has to get what symmetry of structure it can—and it will be seen presently that this may be a good deal—in spite of the fixity of the note values. As a result their melodies have, apart from the fact that they are of an extempore nature, less cohesion than ours.

5. With regard to rhythm Hindu melodies tell us two things. First, that variety of metre is more important than variety of accent, and secondly that cross-metre greatly enhances the interest.

With us, too, variety of metre is a sure mark of a strong tune. There is the often cited violoncello sonata of Beethoven:

Allegro ma non tanto. BEETHOVEN, Op. 69.

Ex. 485.

in which no two bars have the same metre. An even better instance perhaps is:

SCHUBERT, *Wanderers Nachtlied.*

Ex. 486.

Other themes attain the variety by syncopation:

BACH, *Wohltemperirtes Clavier*, No. 43.

Ex. 487.

But the truth is that we have not attached much importance to the breaking up of metre. One reason for this may be that, both for the sake of clinching the tonality and also because of the variety which is thereby obtained, we love to contrast different levels of pitch; and the best way of making this difference of level felt is to keep the melodic figure constant. This may easily degenerate into a mannerism.[1]

But the most infallible and effective way of lending interest to a theme is by cross-metre.

PURCELL, 'I attempt from love's sickness to fly.'

Ex. 488.

The pairs of phrases overlap. In each case the *ictus* of the phrase is shifted, thus:

Ex. 489.

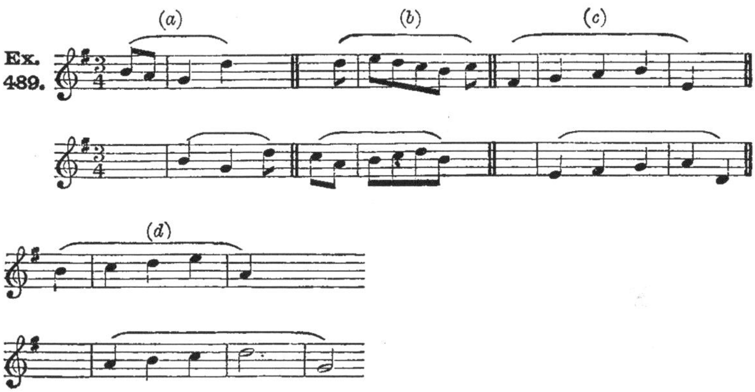

At (*a*) and (*c*) the reply arrives a beat late, at (*b*) half a beat early, and at (*d*) it is prolonged; and the result of it all is a flowing five-bar rhythm, a wonderful instance of art concealing art.

[1] The greatest sinner in this respect is Tschaikowsky who, in examples too numerous to need quotation, works some poor little rhythmical figure literally to death; and the same is also true of a large number of Franz's songs, of *Für Musik*, for instance:

FRANZ, Op. 10, No. 1.

In the Andante of Brahms's 3rd Symphony the whole theme is built on a subtle cross-rhythm:

Ex. 490.

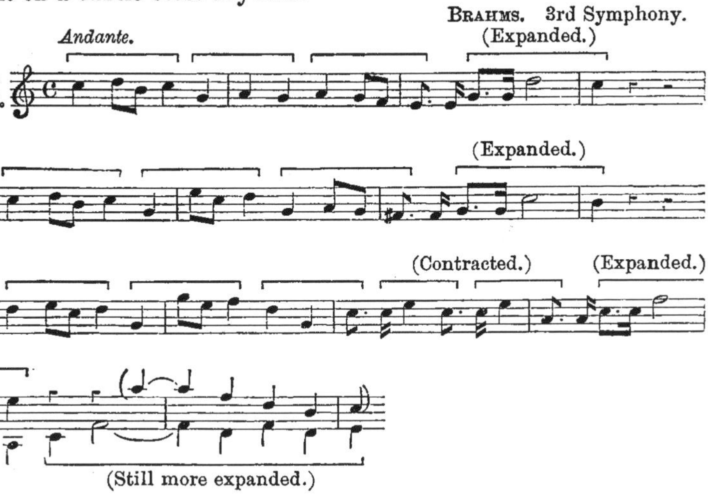

The slow movement of Beethoven's seventh violin sonata may be simplified thus:

Ex. 491.

The four phrases marked *a*, *b*, *c*, *d* have this in common, that they all make the high or the low F the climax of the rhythmical figure (it might almost be called the *aṃśa*). They also increase in sweep and complexity. But the point here is that they are 'strettoed'—that the F in *c* and *d* increasingly antedates its arrival, and that the cross-metre which this involves does much to heighten the interest.

We will now put side by side a good specimen of each system, for comparison of method, not of merit. For it must be remembered that the Indians do not make 'tunes' in our sense; all they do is to display *Rāg* and *Tāl*. Still, most of those given in the last chapter are tunes with a beginning, middle, and end, though it may be doubted whether a Hindu would consider them to be typical of his music at its best. Florestan's air from *Fidelio* compresses the maximum of point and balance into four bars, and a singularly beautiful tune in *Rāg Kānaḍā* attains with curious felicity a more ornate symmetry in sixteen:

BEETHOVEN.

Ex. 492.

Following the skeleton given below the tune, the four sections are of equal length (practically three crotchets) but iii begins one quaver late, and iii and iv overlap. The A in iv is an appoggiatura for G, and is to be considered as a long G. The semiquaver in III corresponds to the acciaccatura in II. Then, ii repeats i in double time, at a higher level, preceded by a link note; iii reverses ii; iv repeats ii at the level of i, doubling the time of ii (quadrupling the time of i) and lengthening out the link note. Again, I is unadorned, II adds a semiquaver (acciaccatura), in III this becomes two semiquavers, and in IV three semiquavers. There is not a single note which is not doing duty. What makes this closeness of structure possible is that harmony allows of any note being taken at any interval; in an Indian tune, for instance, if the leap in II were possible that in IV would be less possible, and vice versa, and that in III would be impossible in any case; or again, if the downward progression in II were possible the upward in III would very likely not be so in that particular *Rāg*.

Now we will take this tune in *Rāg Kānaḍā*, which is obviously well balanced; but before it is dissected and its beauty explained away the reader is recommended to turn back to p. 310, Ex. 416, and enjoy it. It is set to a delicately constructed *Oṃvī* (a Maratha form of verse), of which the English is unfortunately not forthcoming. The words are:

Māgō sān|gītălēṇ | lākṣănēṇ
Mūrkhā āṇ|gīṇ cātŭ|ryă bānē
Ātēṇ ē|kā săhā|nē ăsō-
nă mūrkhă

and the scansion:

Ma Ra Ra
Ma Ta Ya
Ma Ra Ra
[Ma Ta] Ya (see p. 196.)

The bars in the music follow this scansion roughly, the first and second lines being farsed with a 'jubilation' (see p. 255); but beyond this the music pays, as far as its structure is concerned, no attention, as indeed our best melodies do not, to the poetical form; it only sees that a long syllable is provided with a long note as ours see that a stressed syllable comes on the musical accent.

The tune has 16 bars; 5 + 5 in the *astai*, and 6 in the *antara*. There is thus a suggestion of cross-metre (4 time and 5 time) in the general plan. The *astai* ascends to a climax for three bars and descends for two (twice over); the *antara* does the same for three and three bars, enlarging the intervals for its downward sweep from the second (the higher) climax. The *aṃśa* of *Kānaḍā* is E♭, with consonant note B♭ above and below; and at these places the most conspicuous figure (marked ⌴‿⌴) is introduced. The *astai* is concerned only with the lower tetrachord, the *antara* (until the final cadence) only with the upper, according to rule. *Kānaḍā* is one of the *Rāgs* with a queer intonation (see App. II); but though that makes it more difficult (and more beautiful) it does not affect the question of structure:

Ex. 493.

The main interest here centres in the metrical plan. This is based on a contrast of what we may irreverently call pot-hooks and hangers. They are marked *a* throughout, placed for the former below the stave and for the latter above. A succession of these makes up a section which is understood to be *A* in contrast to *B*. *B* is itself an expansion of *a*; it is a trisyllable as against a disyllable, an opposition which we saw to be important in verse. But for fear the *a*'s and *B*'s should become monotonous they vary in length; the *a*'s are of 2, 3, or 4 quavers, the *B*'s of 6, 7, or 8. The 'pot-hooks' have on the whole the best of it in the *astai*, but the 'hangers' drive them off the field in the *antara*; *B* acts as an impartial umpire, giving decisions in favour now of one side now of the other. The ingenious way in which in the first five bars the last note of the ascending metre is made the first note of the descending melody is worth notice. It will be seen here too that, though on quite different principles, not a note is idle.

It is true no doubt that these tunes could be analysed in quite other ways, and equally true that their respective composers never thought for a moment of this or any other analysis. But it is only by analysis that those of us who are not composers can realize such a complex thing as the act of composition. The point is that a tune is not a tune at all until it has something that we must call closeness of structure. It might seem as if nothing could be less fettered or more impulsive than melody; beauty is there—wherever it is that tunes come from—and the composer has only to stretch out his hand and seize it. Man's will is free, no doubt; but he is bound by his own past—in a tune, as in anything else; his tune must be a related whole, just as his life must be a consistent one. That is what is meant by structure. The closer the structure, the more lasting the pleasure which the tune gives; and to make such tunes is art, through whatever conventions.

These two tunes epitomize for us the music of West and East. On the one side a repression of what is petty, a rejection of what is transient, a soberness in gaiety, an endurance in grief. On the other a vivid insight, the eager quest after wayside beauty, the dexterous touch that turns it to account. The one seems to say—Life is puzzling, its claims are many, its enthusiasms hardly come by; but we will hammer out a solution not by turning away from ugliness but by compelling it to serve the ends of beauty. The other—Life is simple, and beauty close at hand at every moment whenever we look or listen or wherever we go; the mistake is in ourselves if we do not train our eyes and ears and hearts to find it.

Who would wish to decide which way was the best? Both are human. There is no need to decry one in favour of, or to exalt one at the expense of the other. Are those Europeans who smile at 'tomtoms' sure that they understand the grounds of their faith in their own music? And are those Indians who scoff at Equal Temperament, at the dullness of European song and the screaming tones of the European voice, able to reach the governing principles of their own art through the mass of tradition and imagery in which it has become involved?

Art expresses. It finds words or tones for what was hitherto unnamed; it actually calls into being an experience which has not previously existed; it does not communicate to us, or acquaint us with, an antecedent experience. And what it expresses is the fact of emotion, not particular feelings. It is not that words or tones cannot indicate these, but that directly they do so the result ceases in so far to be a work of art. That music can, as most would agree, express emotion more immediately than other arts, depends on the fact that 'in its ideal, consummate moments, the end is not distinct from the means, the form from the matter, the subject from the expression; they inhere in and completely saturate each other; and to it, therefore, to the condition of its perfect moments, all the arts may be supposed constantly to tend and aspire'.[1]

But if music at its best obliterates those distinctions, it will be at something less than its best when it maintains them. Thus both the 'popular' music which exalts matter at the expense of form, and extreme 'absolutism' in which the form dwarfs the matter, depart, to some extent, from the ideal. Indian music knows perhaps less than ours of this falsehood of extremes. It seldom descends to the merely popular because it refuses to compress itself into a square tune, something that you can carry away with you like an

[1] Pater, *The Renaissance*, 1904, p. 139.

umbrella, and, as Corney Grain used to add, 'it doesn't much matter if you never bring it back'. Nor has it the deadly insistence of the cook's song in the *We're Here,* which was 'like something ever so bad but sure to happen whatever you did', because it is never sung twice in the same way. Nor is the tune a mere adjunct to the words, as rhyme or alliteration are to an advertisement, for the words are set to the tune, not the tune to the words.

On the other hand, it seldom runs riot in absolutism. Since it is vocal rather than instrumental, melodic and not harmonic, it seldom travels far from those broad human requirements which gave, in song, the first impulse to musical expression, and which, through whatever subsequent developments, still form its ultimate justification.[1] Since concerted song is rare the personal element is not put in commission, and the appeal of the music is therefore more immediate. At the same time it never ceases to be a purely musical appeal. For whereas in our songs development has proceeded increasingly on other lines than those of pure melody,[2] in India the singer's tones can still carry all the artistry which his mind can conceive. And while in England, especially, concerted music has always been highly prized, and rightly so, for its social element,[3] it is apt to fall short of the highest ideals, since it is never so easy to find an artistic crowd as an artistic individual.

Again, the fact that in India the composer and executant are one and the same person, brings it about that he sets, as composer, no problems which he cannot, as executant, himself solve, and that mere academicism is non-existent and that his songs 'come off'.

[1] A string quartet, for instance, which may be taken as our highest achievement in absolute music, still finds its final justification in the fact that the instruments individually or collectively 'sing', that is, are employed upon phrases which are thoroughly 'vocal' in all but the grace of words. Modern composers seem increasingly to ignore this fundamental of their art and to forget to 'sing'. If they will not take warning by the fate of Spohr's saccharine harmonies and of Berlioz's evasion of the main issue, they can expect no immortality.

[2] Since Schubert the centre of interest has been more and more transferred from the voice part to the accompaniment. To hear the accompaniment alone would give a better idea of the composer's thought than to hear the voice part alone. The latter would, in fact, be wholly unintelligible in a large number of modern songs, especially in those which aim at creating atmosphere or at elaborating niceties of declamation.

[3] And there is something, therefore, to be said even for the Crystal Palace and other monster concerts.

When all composition is improvisational, and when notation is rarely employed for recording music and never for performing it, there can be no such thing as 'visual' music—music which makes a pretty pattern to the eye but disappoints the ear; and of this we have a surprising number of examples in the madrigal period, and it is by no means unknown in later times.[1] The Indian practice, described on page 85, of setting the syllables of the words to notes which bear the same Sol-fa syllable, is quite as childish; but it appeals, at any rate, to the ear, not the eye.

Are there not singers amongst us who have felt a desire to break loose, if it were possible, from the trammels of our tonality—from its 'closes' and 'half closes', its 'conceded modulations', its 'unity of design', its rhythmical rigidities and its fussy logic—and to let the melody bear them along on light wings of fancy; to find, in fact, a music which is free like that of the woods in spring-time, where, without rule, the uncouthest tones like the crudest colours all harmonize, where, unguided and unthwarted, sound and silence answer one another, where the inchoate and incomplete are made good by the motherly bounties of Nature, and 'unbroken perfection is over all'? Something of this is in the careless profusion and the unstudied rapture of Indian song:

Singing hymns unbidden,
Till the world is wrought
To sympathy with hopes and fears it heeded not.

[1] See an article by Alfred Einstein, *Monthly Journal of the International Musical Society* for October, 1912.

APPENDIX I

The scale of twelve notes, as given on p. 86 of the *Introduction to the Study of Indian Music*, is here written out, distinguishing the notes derived from quintal harmony by capital letters and those from tertian harmony by small letters, and placing above them the available common chords:

G	a♭	C	d♭	D	e♭			Major.
e	F	a	B♭	b	C			
G		b	C			e		Minor.
e♭		G	a♭			C		

C d♭ D e♭ e F g♭ G a♭ a B♭ b C

This scale is the plagal form of the *Sa-grāma* beginning on *F*; hence the notes are *g*♭, *a*, and *B*♭, instead of (as from *C*) *f*♯, *A*, and *b*♭. *F* was chosen as a more convenient starting point than *C* because then all the 'black' notes can be called flat, instead of one of them being an *f*♯. Taking the scale as it appears above, it will be observed that no chord but a first or second inversion can stand on *D*, *e*♭, *B*♭, or *b*; so that none of these notes could, if harmonized, be used in a prominent or a final sense. The writer suggests, however, that these 'natural' harmonies would be sufficient for the harmonization of Indian melodies.

With regard to this suggestion, attractive as it sounds, there are several difficulties.

In the first place, there is no such thing as natural harmony. Nature 'gives' a note, with its Fifth a good deal fainter, and its Third much fainter still. We make the three notes of equal loudness, and call them a chord. But Guido d'Arezzo did not get so far as that. Adam de la Hale did not hear the Third as a satisfactory note. Josquin des Prés could not endure the minor chord as final. Palestrina inserted the minor chord at that place, but surreptitiously altered it to major. Bach, in the first part of the forty-eight Fugues, prefers on the whole the *Tierce de Picardie.* Beethoven's favourite ending is in the unison—like Guido's—which, indeed, is all that can truly be called 'natural'; and that is not a 'chord'. Without wishing to press the word 'natural' too far, the argument goes to show that the employment of the very first chord is the knell of modal melody.

Secondly, the modes (*Rāgs*) all have an *aṃśa*, and this *aṃśa* is seldom the drone note. In the many *Rāgs* in which the *aṃśa* is at *e*, or *a*, the melody would have to close on a minor chord; when it is at *e*♭ the final note, which the *aṃśa* as a rule is, could only bear a second inversion; when at *b* (as in Behăg) it could have no chord at all. It would not be possible to end the melody (in this last case) on *b* with an *e* minor chord below it, for that would make the *e* really final instead of the *b*, and so falsify the *Rāg*.

Again, is there not at the bottom of this suggestion a misunderstanding of the nature of harmony? That was not a fortuitous thing, but directly necessitated by what went before it. There had been melody, with some notes salient and others in abeyance, upon a drone (explicit or implicit). To support the salient notes better the drone took other positions, and so, breaking up, became an independent part, long before any 'chord' was invented. To these two parts another drone was added, to form what was called the *Triplum*, which similarly broke up; and another, to form the *Quadruplum*. There is no thought of chords in all this; only of concurrent melodies, of whose successive moments chords were later generalizations. A chord cannot be used in music for its own sake, any more than can a word in language; it has a before and after, and that is its only reason for existing.

It would be a rash thing to say that the European method of harmony is the only possible one. All that can be said is that it is perfectly logical. This breaking up of the drone is, at bottom, the moment when the desire arises to contrast not one note with another, but one whole passage of the song with another passage, and that is the way in which music has always advanced. We saw something that looked very like this in Exs. 93 and 99. All that really happens in the second of these examples is that the mother and son sing the same tune at different pitches. But it reminds us of a stage in our own art when, as in the times before Tye and Tallis, in whose music there are still traces of it, the soprano and tenor parts had a flat less in the signature than the other two parts.

And, lastly, would not this suggestion defeat its own end—the preservation of just tuning—and lead after all straight to the accursed thing, Equal Temperament? For as soon as harmony came to be valued for its own sake it would be impossible not to feel an enormous difference between, say, a major and a minor chord. If then, closing on *a* (in Imankaliān), the composer had nothing but an *a* minor triad and a second inversion at his disposal, could he resist the forbidden *a d♭ e*, which is so near and yet so far? And if the *d♭* would not do, would it be long before he altered it—and then chaos?

Still, it is conceivable that a step in the argument could be jumped, and that a nation should go straight to harmony without first having felt the impulse which led to it, just as it is possible that Esperanto will become a living language although it is based on a different motive from that of all other languages on earth. The possibility depends on the actual achievements of composers in one case and of authors in the other, and it is vain to attempt to prophesy.

But this question of harmony is only a side issue in a book whose main purpose is to establish the true principles of Indian intonation—a purpose which it excellently fulfils. And every one who is interested in the music of India will look forward eagerly to another by the same hand, which is perhaps hinted at on p. 4, containing a 'census of Indian *Rāgas*' grouped 'according to the principles of correct intonation'. If such a book appeared, written with authority, it would supersede all the books on the subject.

APPENDIX II

It was not noticed until after the plate containing the Table of *Rāgs* had been set up that of the eight scales, which according to Ashreka (see p. 151) exhibit quarter-tones, the intonation had been correctly given only for the first two. The intonation for all the eight is as follows:

2. Bibhās	C	$\overset{\flat}{D}$	E		G	$\overset{\flat}{A}$		C
26. Mālkos	C		$\overset{\flat}{E}$	$\overset{\flat}{F}$		$\overset{\flat}{A\flat}$	$\overset{\flat}{B\flat}$	C
33. Kānaḍā	C	$\overset{\flat}{D}$	$\overset{\flat}{E}$	F	G	$\overset{\flat}{A}$	$B\flat$	C
35. Jogi	C	$\overset{\flat}{D}$	$E\flat$	F	G	$\overset{\flat}{A}$	B	C
36. Rāmkalī	C	$\overset{\flat}{D}$	E	F	G	$\overset{\flat}{A}$	B	C
40. Toḍi 41. Multānī	C	$\overset{\flat}{D\flat}$	$\overset{\flat}{E\flat}$	$\overset{\sharp}{F\sharp}$	G	$\overset{\flat}{A\flat}$	$\overset{\sharp}{B}$	C
49. Māravā	C	$\overset{\flat}{D}$	E	$F\sharp$		$\overset{\flat}{A}$	B	C

BIBLIOGRAPHY

OF WORKS IN EUROPEAN LANGUAGES

General.

1. C. R. Day, *The music and musical instruments of Southern India and the Deccan,* London, 1891, pp. xvi, 173; 17 coloured plates,

   gives a good general introduction to the subject as regards S. India.

2. A. M. Chinnaswami Mudaliyar, *Oriental Music in European Notation,* Madras, 1892, 36 pages of Introduction, 106 pages of musical examples.

   The Introduction contains much useful information. The examples are carefully done, provided with marks of tempo and expression, and with words (Tamil, Telugu, and Sanskrit, which are often transliterated). Relates to S. India.

3. Bhavānrāv A. Pingle (of Wādhwān, Kāthiāwār), *Indian Music,* Byculla, 1898, pp. xviii, 341, Index xxii; 2nd edition,

   is a mine of information on many details of performance; it suffers from obscurities of style, and the few musical examples are not altogether intelligible; it is the only good account in English of the music of N. India.

   Nos. 1 and 3 have long been out of print: a few copies of No. are possibly procurable.

See also Nos. 5, 9, 13, 14, 15, 50, 52.

Descriptive.

4. A. K. Coomaraswamy, *Essays in National Idealism,* Colombo, 1909,

   has twenty pages on music.

5. Mrs. Maud Mann, *Some Indian Conceptions of Music, Proceedings of the Musical Association,* 1911–12, p. 41,

   gives an account of the S. Indian system.

6. Pierre Loti, *L'Inde (sans les Anglais).* Paris, n. d. 38th edition.

   Chapter v describes a concert. (See p. 11 of this book.)

7. Anne C. Wilson, *A Short Account of the Hindu System of Music.* London, 1904. pp. 48.

See also Nos. 1, 3, 16, 44, 53, 54.

SANSKRIT THEORY.

8. J. Grosset (Lyon), *Contribution à l'étude de la musique hindoue*, place and date not given,

gives the Sanskrit text of the twenty-eighth *adhyāya* of Bharata's *Nāṭyaśāstra*, with translation and notes. The date of Bharata is probably the fifth century A.D.

9. *The Indian Music Journal* (monthly), editor, H. P. Krishna Rao, Mysore,

of which ten numbers have appeared, is translating *Somanātha's Rāgavibodha* (A.D. 1609).

See also Nos. 20, 22, 23, 27, 41, 42–46.

MUSICAL EXAMPLES.

10. Max Wertheimer, *Musik der Vedda, Journal of the International Music Society*, Year XI, pt. 2, p. 300. 1910.

Phonograms of songs of the Ceylon Veddas, closely analysed.

11. Charles S. Myers, *Vedda Music*, chap. xiii (pp. 341–65) of *The Veddas* by C. G. and B. Z. Seligmann. pp. xx, 463. Cambridge, 1911.

Phonograms, closely analysed.

12. O. Abraham und Erich M. von Hornbostel, *Phonographirte indische Melodien, Journal of the International Music Society*, 1903–4, pp. 348–401,

ignoring Indian theory, treats twenty-eight tunes simply as musical phenomena.

13. Ratan Devi, *Thirty Indian songs, with texts and translations by A. K. Coomaraswamy*. London, 1913. 7 illustrations.

From the Panjab and Kashmir. This with its excellent translations gives a better idea of the song as a whole than any other collection.

14. Rajah Sourindro Mohun Tagore:

(*a*) *The seven principal musical notes of the Hindus, with their presiding deities*. Calcutta, 1892. pp. 51.

15. (*b*) *Six principal Rāgas with a brief view of Hindu music*. pp. 88, App. xvi. 6 plates. Calcutta, 1877.

16. (*c*) *The eight principal Rasas of the Hindus, with tableaux and dramatic pieces illustrating their character*. pp. 161. 8 plates. Calcutta, 1880.

17. (*d*) *The musical scales of the Hindus*. Calcutta, 1884. pp. 118.

N.B.—There are thousands of specimens (words and music) to be found in books in the vernacular; and, no doubt, hundreds could be transcribed by any musician who possessed a working knowledge of Urdu, Panjābi, Hindi, Gujarāti, Tamil, Canarese, or Malayālam, but more especially of Marathi, Bengāli, or Telugu. Those which have been drawn upon for the present work are Vishnu Degambar's books

(Panjābi), the books of the Poona Gayan Samāj (Marāthi), and the hymns of the Brahma Samāj (Bengāli), although it has not been thought worth while to print more than a few dozens of them. Even a smattering of Indian languages helps; it is useful to be able to recognize under the forms Dhol, Dholka, Dholaka, and Dolu the same instrument, and under Saurashtra, Surati, and Sorat the same *Rāg*, and to be able to check to some extent the vagaries of proof readers. A great number of songs are contained in *Sangīta Prakāśika*, vols. i–viii, *in progress.* Calcutta (in Bengāli notation).

See also Nos. 1, 2, 9, 22, 40.

Scale.

18. Alexander J. Ellis, *On the musical scales of various nations, Journal of the Society of Arts,* March 27, 1885, pp. 485–527.

The results for India are based on insufficient data, but the article is valuable as a *conspectus* of scale in general.

19. Ludwig Riemann, *Über eigentümliche bei Natur- und orientalischen Kulturvölkern vorkommende Tonreihen und ihre Beziehungen zu den Gesetzen der Harmonie.* Essen, 1899. pp. 133.

Gives full particulars as to the apparent scales of various instruments found in European museums. pp. 27–41 relate to India.

20. Krishnaji Ballal Deval, *The Hindu musical scale and the twenty-two shrutees.* Poona, 1910. pp. viii, 49.

A careful study of intonation, based on the Sanskrit prescription and the practice of living musicians.

21. E. Clements, *Introduction to the Study of Indian Music.* London, 1913. pp. ix, 104.

See also Nos. 1, 8, 11, 34, 42, 50, 52.

Grace.

22. Richard Simon, *The Musical Compositions of Somanātha critically edited with a table of notations* [Lithographed MS. in Nāgari]. Leipzig, 1904. pp. ii, 33.

23. Richard Simon, *Die Notationen des Somanātha.* A reprint from the *Sitzungsberichte d. Königl. Bayer. Akad. der Wissenschaften,* 1903. Heft III. 2 plates [facsimile]. Munich.

These give the system of grace-notes adopted in the *Rāgavibodha*, with full explanations. The great authority on this subject (and on much else) is said to be a book in Telugu by *Subrama Dikshitar of Ettyapuram, Tinnevelly*; and there is a work in Bengāli by S. M. Tagore, *Yantraksetradipika*, Calcutta, 1872, on grace as performed on the *Satār*, 317 pages with many musical examples. See also H. P. Krishna Rao, *First steps in Hindu music.* 1906. Weekes & Co. pp. 52.

NOTATION.

24. O. Abraham und Erich M. v. Hornbostel, *Vorschläge für die Transkription exotischer Melodien*, *Journal of the International Musical Society*, Year XI, pt. 1, p. 1. Leipzig, 1909. 24 pages.

25. Charles S. Myers, *The Ethnological Study of Music*, in *Anthropological Essays presented to E. B. Tylor*, pp. 235–54. Oxford, 1907.

These two contain useful suggestions for investigators and collectors of songs in extra-European systems.

26. S. M. Tagore, *Victoria-Sāmrājyan*. Sanskrit stanzas on various dependencies of Her Most Gracious Majesty the Empress of India. Calcutta, 1887 [30 plates of unnamed instruments].

The melodies purport to belong to the various countries, and they are noted according to the *Bengāli* system, in *Nāgari* characters and also in staff notation.

See also Nos. 23, 42, 43, 46.

POETICAL METRE.

27. Albrecht Weber, *Indische Studien*, the eighth volume of the *Beiträge für die Kunde des indischen Altertums*. Berlin, 1863. pp. xii, 468, and index.

A critical study of the earliest authorities, contains quotations from Sanskrit works relating to the earliest forms of the scale.

28. Rudolf Westphal, *Allgemeine Metrik der indogermanischen und semitischen Völker*. Berlin, 1893. pp. x, 502, and index.

29. Monier Williams, *A practical grammar of the Sanskrit language*, pp. 392–7. 4th edition. Oxford, 1877.

30. H. T. Colebrooke, *Miscellaneous Essays*. 1st edition. London, 1837. 2nd edition. Madras, 1872. 2 vols. I, pp. x, 419, 23. II, pp. 531, 31.

31. S. H. Kellogg, *A grammar of the Hindi language*. 2nd edition. pp. xxxi, 584. London, 1893.

An account of Hindi metre at the end of the book gives examples (in *Nāgari*) of the *Dhrūpad*, *Ṭhumri*, and others.

32. Hermann Oldenberg, *Zur Geschichte der vedischen Anuṣṭubh*. *Zeitschrift d. d. morg. Gesellschaft*. Vol. 54. pp. 181–94.

33. Josef Zubaty, *Der Bau der Triṣṭubh- und Jagati-Zeile im Mahābhārata*. *Zeitschrift d. d. morg. Gesellschaft*. Vol. 43. pp. 619–52.

34. Hermann Jacobi, *Über die Entwickelung der indischen Metrik in nachvedischer Zeit. Zeitschrift d. d. morg. Gesellschaft.* Vol. 38. pp. 590–619. Leipzig, 1884.

35. Hermann Jacobi, *Zur Kenntniss der Āryā. Zeitschrift d. d. morg. Gesellschaft.* Vol. 40. pp. 336–42.

36. Charles S. Myers, *A study of rhythm in primitive music.* Reprint from the *Journal of Psychology,* vol. i, pt. 4. pp. 10. Cambridge, 1905.

37. Hermann Oldenberg, *Die Hymnen des Rigveda.* Berlin, 1888. Bd. I. pp. vii, 545.
Chap. i (pp. 1–190) deals with Vedic metres.

Harmonization.

38. A. J. Polak, *Die Harmonisierung indischer . . . Melodien.* Leipzig, 1905. pp. 107.
The first forty pages deal with India.

39. Abraham and Hornbostel, *Über die Harmonisierbarkeit exotischer Melodien. Journal of the International Musical Society,* vol. iii, p. 138. Leipzig, 1905–6. 3 pages.
An answer to No. 38.

40. A. C. Macleod (Lady Wilson), *Five Indian songs.* Edinburgh [1912].
The accompaniments have atmosphere.

See also No. 17.

Sāmaveda.

41. Martin Haug, *Ueber das Wesen und den Werth des wedischen Accents.* Munich, 1874. pp. 107.
Gives particulars about accents, notation, and the musical hand.

42. A. C. Burnell:
(*a*) *The Ārsheyabrāhmaṇa (being the fourth Brāhmaṇa) of the Sāmaveda.* Mangalore, 1876. pp. li.
The introduction of fifty-one pages is in English.

43. (*b*) *The Saṃhitopanishadbrāhmaṇa (being the seventh Brāhmaṇa) of the Sāmaveda.* Mangalore, 1877. pp. xx.
Introduction in English.

44. Friedrich Chrysander, *Über die altindische Opfermusik, Vierteljahrsschrift für Wissenschaft.* Leipzig, 1885 [14 pages].
Describes ritual and form.

45. Oskar Fleischer, *Neumen-Studien, Abhandlungen über mittelalterliche Gesangstonschriften.* 2 vols. Leipzig, 1895. pp. 128 + 136. Index to each volume.

Details of musical hand.

See also No. 3.

46. Richard Simon, *Das Puṣpasūtra. Abhandlungen d. K. Bayer. Akad. der Wiss.*, 1. *Kl.*, XXIII. Bd., III. Abt., pp. 484–779. Munich, 1909.

Pages 510–526 give lists of the various forms of ligature (*Tontypen*) and of technical terms. This is the latest and most authoritative work.

47. A. A. Macdonell, *Vedic Grammar*, being vol. i, pt. 4, of the *Grundriss d. indo-arischen Philologie.* Strassburg, 1910.

Pages 76–9 give a succinct account of the musical character of accent, and its marking in the *Sāmaveda.*

48. Martin Haug, *Aitareyabrāhmaṇa of the Ṛgveda.*

A full account of the Soma ritual.

49. M. Śeṣagiri Śāstrī, *Descriptive Catalogue of the Government Oriental MSS. in the Madras Library*, vol. i, pt. i, pp. 3, 4.

The only account by an Indian in English.

50. Erwin Felber, *Die indische Musik der vedischen und der classischen Zeit. Sitzungsberichte der Kais. Akademie der Wissenschaften in Wien, philosophisch-historische Klasse*, 170. Band, 7. Abhandlung. 1912. pp. 189.

Indian recitation and chant. Contains forty-six Phonograms taken by Felix Exner in 1904, of which eight are *Sāman* chants, provided with *Ṛgveda* text and *Sāmaveda* text and notation critically edited.

See also No. 27.

51. R. Simon, *Das Pañcavidhasūtra.* Breslau, 1913. pp. 82.

Instruments.

52. Victor-Charles Mahillon, *Catalogue descriptif et analytique du Musée instrumental du Conservatoire de musique de Bruxelles.* Gand, 1893. pp. 535. Indices. 2nd edition.

Pages 99–158 (about one illustration to a page), together with the description and illustrations in Day's book (No. 1), give a fairly complete idea of the principal instruments.

See also No. 54.

Musicians and Styles.

53. S. M. Tagore, *Universal History of Music.* Calcutta, 1896. pp. 345, xxxiv.

    Has a good deal of information about Bengali musicians and styles.

54. S. M. Tagore, *Hindu music from various authors.* Calcutta, 1882. pp. 423.

    Reprints of articles by Sir W. Jones, Captain Willard, and others.

See also No. 9.

Musical Analogies.

(*a*) Religion. See No. 5.

(*b*) Colours and Castes. See No. 53 App. and No. 17.

(*c*) Pictures. See Nos. 15, 16.

(*d*) Medicine, Astrology, &c. See No. 53 App.

(*e*) Drama. See No. 16.

GLOSSARY AND INDEX

NOTE.—Individual *Rāgs* and *Tāls*, Tribes, Localities, and Indian and European Musicians are indexed under those heads. The spelling of the Index is to be preferred whenever it differs from that in the body of the book.

abhañga, Maratha song, 300.
abhigata, upward appoggiatura, 275.
ābhog, section of song, 281.
'Abroad as I was walking', 128.
absolute music, 341 and note.
absolute pitch, 148, 149, 249 note.
accelerando, Ex. 330.
accent and quantity, 191, 192.
accidentals, loosely used, 17, 27.
āḍa = crooked, 216.
ādi or *tīntāl*, common time, 15, 204–17, 231.
āditālaḥ, 202, 203.
aeolian, 136, 178.
aeolo-dorian (change of mode), Ex. 379.
Āhvārakas, 258, 259, 264.
Ain-i-Akbari, 84, 286.
āk, eye, see *sīyahī*.
Akbar, 83.
akṣara, syllable, 156, 200–4.
ālāp(a), prelude, 186, 235, 281.
alcaic, 195, 196.
alpa, weak (note), see *balin*.
aṃśa, predominant note, 150, 177, App. I.
  central note of *tessitura*, 330 seq.
  in Bharata, 141.
  graced, 152.
  aesthetic effect, 156.
  contrast to drone, 280.
  = *mesē*, 142.
  see *graha*.
Andaman islands, 208.
añga, tetrachord, 141.
  = *aṃśa*, 142 note.
animals, sense of pitch, 149.
aniṣṭa, disagreeable; identified with *vivādī*, 114.
antara, interval, 119.
  section of song, 281.
anticlimax avoided, 328.
anudātta, 'not-raised' sound, 246, 258, 259, 264.
anudāttatara, comparative of *anudātta*, 247, 266.
anudruta (quaver), and its subdivisions, 256.
anupallavi, section of song, 281.
anuṣṭubh, 194. See *śloka*.
anuvādī, imperfect consonance, in particular the major third, 108, 114.
appoggiatura, 146–8, 248, 275, 332; Ex. 274.
  double, 182.
Appunn's Tonmesser, 101.
Apsaras, nymph, 76 and note.
Arab music, 19, 37, 185.
arcika, of the *Ṛgveda*, 122.
Aristoxenus, 103, 114, 121 note, 125, 200 note, 277 note.
ārohaṇa, ascending passage, 159, 275.
arpeggios as chords, 317.
āryā, a metre, 200.
'ascending' minor, 138.
āsh, the 'slide', 183.
association, its part in music, 1–3.
astai, section of song, 281.
aṣṭama (eighth), a note of the *Sāman* scale, 260.
āṭa, or *dhamār*, a rhythm (5 + 5 + 2 + 2), see *Tāl*.
āṭa, flour, used for tuning drum, 29, 227.
Atharvaveda, 249.
atihāra, farsed syllable, 276.
atikomal, very flat, 107, 142.
atikrama, transilience, 274.
atisvārya, seventh note of *Sāman* scale, 260.
atitīvra, very sharp, 107.

augmentation and diminution, 241.
Aurangzeb, 83.
āvard (*āvarta*), section, aggregate of bars, 205 note, 218.
avarohaṇa, descending passage, 159.

bagpipe, *see* Scotch.
bahusāmi, having many melodies, 250.
balin, strong (note), 154, 159, 177, 178.
Bande Mātaram, Ex. 250.
bansri, bamboo flute, 30, 102.
bārobāri, normal time, 241.
barypyknon, lower note of a cluster, 121.
bayan, left hand (drum), 226.
beating time, 209.
'bee-string', or drone, 79.
beggars, &c., 22–4.
Behār, its folk-song, 22.
Bengal, language, 84, 92.
  musical system, 122.
  tune, Ex. 1.
  see Tagore.
bhajan(*a*), kind of song, 286.
bhakti, faith, 286.
bhakti, section of *Sāman*, 255.
bhāṣā, dialect, 82, 299.
bhatial, boatmen's song, 7.
bīn, North Indian *vīṇā*, 89.
boatmen, 33, 37–41.
boat-songs, Ex. 1, 51–77.
Böhme, *Altdeutsches Liederbuch*, Ex. 378.
bol, drum-stroke, 227, 229, 233.
braces of drum, 226, 227.
brāhmaṇa, 246, 249.
Brāhma samāj, 162.
Breton song, Ex. 73.
bṛhaddevatā, treatise, 258.
budubudike, hand drum, 228.
Burnell, A. C., 250, 251, 254, 257, 266.
Burns, Robert, 250.
Butler, Samuel, 162.

C major mode, 178.
cadence, *see* close.
cadenza (*svarā*), 282.
caraṇam, section of song, 281.
Carnatic system, the, 15, 47 note, 139, 149 and note, 150, 209.
catuḥśruti, of four *śrutis*, 118, 119.
caturañga, form of song, 299.
caturguṇi, double diminution, 241.
caturtha, note of *Sāman* scale, 257 seq.
  of time, 203.
cents, 115, 116 note, 185.
chakravādya, tambourine, 34; cp. 228.
Chaṇḍīdās, Bengali poet, 286.
chanterelle, 88.
chanties, 19, 39–41.
chapu, syncopated, 210.
character of sound, 124.
chartāla, 'four-beat' (six unit) time, 216.
chattu, wall of drum, 226.
chaugan, see *caturguṇi*.
chautāla, see *chartāla*.
chāyālaga, 'altered', 138, 139, 153, 155.
cheironomy, *see* musical hand.
children's songs, 68, 69.
Chippewas, 163, 174 note; Ex. 457.
chords, 100 and note, 317, 318.
chorus, *see* solo and chorus.
chromatic scale, 119, 120.
  notes, 271, 278, 321.
Clements, Mr. E., 105, 111, 116, 119 note, 125, 171, App. I.
climate, its effect on music, 9, 10, 14.
climax, 329.
  and anticlimax, 320.
close, 36, 57, 342.
cluster, *see* Greek.
Cock o' the North, The, Ex. 296.
comma of Didymus, 127, 132, 263.
compass of songs, 123, 286.
  of *Ṛgveda*, 249.
  of *Sāmaveda*, 257 seq.
  of *Yajurveda*, 249.
concerted music, 14, 341.
conjunct motion, 48, 160–2, 322–7; Ex. 72.
consonance, 108, 141, 261.
consonants, 280.
convention, its part in music, 1–3, 5.
'convergence', 241.
counterpoint, 101, 238.
cradle songs, 62–7, 90.
crescendo, 183.
cross-rhythm, 72, 99, 169, 236, 240, 334 seq.; Ex. 41, 42, 48, 86, 129, 139, 333, 334, 336.
'cumulation' (of time), 242.
Cuttack dance, 59.
'cyclical' dactyl, *see* Greek.
cymbals, *āghāṭa* (Vedic), 78.
  see also *tālam*.

dādra, form of song, 300; Ex. 177.
daina, right hand (drum), 226.
dancing, 17, 29–32, 36, 52, 57, 59, 61, 80.
dardara, drumming, 245.
Day, Captain, v, vi, 18, 200 note, 201, 202 note, 228, 346, 351.

day, periods of, 153.
'deflect', 88, 183, 190. See *dolana*.
descant, **Ex.** 273.
Deval, Mr., 116, 348.
devanāgari, accents in, 247 note.
dhā, drum-beat, see *bol*.
dhā (of time), see *bārobāri*.
dhaivata, note of the scale, 142, 263.
dhara, the 'slide', 183.
dhāraṇalakṣana, musical treatise, 259.
dhol, drum, 29, 59, 226–8; Ex. 141, 142, 333, 334.
dhrūpad, old Hindu form of song, 160, 286.
diatonic intervals, 103, 321.
 scale, *see* Greek, *nīca*.
Didymus, *see* comma.
digan, see *duni*.
diminution, *see* augmentation.
diṅmātrā, general, i.e. indefinite time, 186.
dīrgha, long (prosody), 200, 251 note, 255, 256.
disjunct motion, 35, 36, 158, 322.
 tetrachords, 266.
dissimilar tetrachords, 138.
dīwal, braces (drum), 226.
dolana, the 'deflect', 182, 183.
dolu, see *dhol*.
dominant, 178, 317.
'dor-aeolian', pentatonic, 135.
dorian, 136, 178; Ex. 333.
doric, 47 note. *See* Greek tetrachord.
Dravidian, *see* Carnatic.
drone, 31, 79, 137, 141 note 2, 171–4, 208, 263, 330, 344.
drum and drumming, 10, 15, 24, 53, 76–9, 83, 89, 228, 230; Ex. 330–5.
druta, quick note, 200.
 quick tempo, 241.
duni, diminution, 241.
duration, *see* stress.
dviguṇi, see *duni*.
dvitīya, note of *Sāman* scale, 257 seq.
 of time, 203.

ecclesiastical music, 3, 4, 6, 70, 147, 169, 179, 255, 266, 275 note.
ekasāmi, having one melody, 250.
Ellis, A. J., 115 note, 184 note.
emotional content of music, 5, 6, 155, 340. See *ēthos*.
English verse, reading of, 202.
epithalamium, Ex. 163.
equal temperament, 118, 344.
equivalence, 199, 200.
Erewhon, 162.
ēthos, 20, 153–6.
European drumming, 225.
European folk-song, 128, 134, 135, 154 and Table opposite; Ex. 193, 208, 209, 461.
European mediaeval songs, 84.
European modes, 47 note, 137, 138, 169 and note, 177, 178.
European music, 2, 18, 339, 340.
European musicians:
 Adam de la Hale, 343.
 Bach, 173 note; Ex. 290, 328, 335, 470–3, 487.
 Bantock, Ex. 271.
 Beethoven, 343; Ex. 239, 240, 262, 290, 318, 337, 338, 443, 444, 462, 467, 478, 479, 485, 491, 492.
 Berlioz, 341 note.
 Brahms, 136, 224; Ex. 182, 290, 339, 446, 463, 480, 481, 490.
 Chopin, Ex. 321.
 Ducoudray, 164.
 Dufay, 84.
 Franz, 335 note.
 Gevaert, 103 note, 173 note.
 Guido d'Arezzo, 343.
 Handel, 220; Ex. 262, 323, 329.
 Haydn, Ex. 319, 320.
 Henschel, 91.
 Hucbald, 266.
 Josquin des Prés, 343.
 Luther, 177; Ex. 466.
 Mendelssohn, 322; Ex. 290, 293.
 Mozart, Ex. 443, 444, 464, 475–7.
 Orlando Gibbons, 278.
 Palestrina, 84; Ex. 169.
 Purcell, Ex. 488.
 Schubert, 133, 341 note; Ex. 290, 451, 456, 458, 474, 486.
 Scott, Cyril, 224.
 Smetana, 133.
 Spohr, 182, 321, 341 note.
 Stanford, 164.
 Strauss, Ex. 262.
 Stravinsky, 224.
 Sullivan, Ex. 468.
 Tallis, 343.
 Thomé, Ex. 290.
 Tschaikowsky, 208 note, 220, 223, 335 note; Ex. 324, 325.
 Tye, 343.
 Vaughan Williams, Ex. 207.
 Wagner, 12, 133, 182, 208, 224, 321 and note; Ex. 236–8, 262, 448, 483.
 Weelkes, 206.
 Wesley, Ex. 290.

European rhythm, 218 seq.
European songs and singers, 340.
evening, *see* day.
Exner, Herr F., 267.

fakīr, a begging ascetic, 22, 23.
false relation, 132.
falsetto, 286.
feet in Indian versification, 196.
Felber, Dr. E., 248, 267.
Fifth, *see* Fourth.
Finland, 204.
Fitzwilliam Virginal Book, Ex. 377.
five-rhythm, 203, 204, 222 seq.; Ex. 339.
flute, bamboo, 9, 78. See *bansrī*.
  scales, 101–4.
folk-song, *see* European.
form (in melody), 337, 338, 339.
four-bar section, 218–20; Ex. 339.
Fourth (the interval), 25, 31, 48, 69, 70, 103, 124, 150, 173, 277.

ga-grāma, 106, 110, 111; Ex. 352.
gamak, *see* grace.
  two kinds, 182, 183.
gāna, text of *Sāmaveda* as sung, 251, 255.
gāndhāra, note, scale, locality, 142, 262, 263.
Gāndharvas, 76 and note.
gāthika, non-Vedic, 122.
gati, farsed syllable, 275.
gaṭṭa, tuning blocks (drum), 226.
gāyatrī, a metre, 194.
gesture, *see* singing.
gharṣaṇa, the 'slide', 182.
ghasīṭ, the 'slide', 183.
ghazal, form of song, 300; Ex. 333.
ghe, one of the drum-strokes, 227.
Gilchrist, Miss, *see* Scotch music.
gipsies, 13, 46, 62 note. *See* Magyars.
Gīta-Govinda, by Jayadeva, 157, 187.
Gītānjali, by Tagore, Ex. 267.
Goorkha regiment, first, 56 note.
  second, 57–9.
Gopīs, Krishna's houris, 78.
grace, 17, 19, 22, 27, 32, 56, 59, 90, 181–90, 227, 281.
graduated scale of trochees, 211.
graha, initial (note), 141, 153 and note, 277 and note.
grāma, 82, 106, 109, 148. See *sa-grāma*, *ma-grāma*, *ga-grāma*.
grāmarāga (see *melakarta*), 119, 120.
gramophone, 16.
Greece, 8, 122.
Greek absolute pitch, 148, 260.
  chromatic scale, 120 note.
  chronos prōtos, 199, 251 note.
  consonance, 266.
  cyclical dactyl, 211.
  diatonic scale, 120.
  diesis, 103 note.
  drone, 140, 141.
  enharmonic scale, 121.
  harmoniā, 140, 141.
  hypatē, 257.
  mesē, 142.
  modes, 47 note, 179.
  musicians, *see* Aristoxenus, Didymus, Olympos, Plutarch, Ptolemy, Pythagoras, Thamyris.
  pyknon, 121, 247 note.
  rhythm, 204.
  singing, 277 and note.
  tetrachord, 140, 262, 263, 266, 276.
  tonoi miktoi, 139.
  tonos, 140 seq.
Gurkhas, tribe in the Himālaya, Ex. 94–124, 127, 128.
guru, long note, 196, 200, 256.
  priest, 251.

haṇ, yes, 235; cp. 57.
hand clapping, 33, 48.
harmoniā, *see* Greeks.
harmonic minor, 138.
harmonium, 16, 18, 63 note, 163 and note.
harmonization, 3, 4, 31, 164, App. I.
harmony, 4, 19, 101, 163, 180, App. I.
Haug, 246 note, 247, 250.
Hindostani music, 47 note, 139, 149 and note, 150, 216.
history, Indian, *see* India.
hrasva, short (prosody), 200, 251 note, 255, 256.
Hungarians, 5. *See* Magyars.

iambs and trochees, 211.
imitation, 48, 72, 179.
India, climate, effect of, 9.
Indian history, 73, 74.
Indian instruments, 9–13, 77–80, 88, 89, 101, 228.
Indian music, 11–13, 75–86, 340–3.
Indian musicians:
  Ashreka Ganga Ram, 151, 345.
  Balwant Rao, 151.
  Banerji, Sourendro, 88.
  Bhāgavatār of Trivandrum, 89.
  Bharata, 105, 112–17, 139, 347.
  Deval, Krishnaji Ballal, 116, 348.

Indian musicians (*continued*):
Jayadeva, 83, 157, 286.
Mān, Rajah, 287.
Mārār, 85, 86.
Miranbaksh, 228, 237.
Mudaliar, Chinnaswami, 156, 346.
Nanne Khan, 230.
Nārada, 75.
Panna, 236.
Pingle, 151, 230, 285 note, 346.
Prabhu, Chandra, 90.
Rāmachandra of Trivandrum, 89.
Ray, Upendrakisor, 152, 161, 162, 166.
Sahasrabuddhe, Trimbak Balwant, 151.
Śār(a)ṅgadeva, 105, 154.
Seshanna of Mysore, 86, 87.
Sharqi of Jaunpur, Mahmud, 287.
Shori (songstress), 300.
Somanāth, 105, 347.
Subbanna of Mysore, 86, 87.
Tagore, Rabindranath, *vide sub voce*.
Tagore, Rajah S. M., 285, 347 seq.
Tānsen, Miyan, 83, 84.
Tiagarāja, 84–6; Ex. 379.
Tuka Rām, 300.
Tumburu, 75, 76.
Indian mythology, 76.
rhythms in European music, 223, 224.
singing, 13.
infinite series, 125.
instrumental, *see* vocal.
instruments, *see* Indian.
intensity of sound, 123.
intervals, the Fourth, 31, 44, 327.
mediately and immediately perceived by the ear, 125.
quarter-tone, 108, 113, 117 seq.
septimal, 125.
sharpened, 104.
the Third, 36, 325.
three-quarter tone, 21, 38, 39, 184.
tone and semitone, 101 and note, 109, 110 note.
vocal and unvocal, 322 seq.
intonation, 17, 18, 27, 100–33.
Irish pentatonic, 126 note.
iṣṭa, agreeable, identified with *anuvādī*, 114.

jagatī, a metre, 194.
jātaka stories, 74 and note, 78, 80, 81.
jāti, species, Bharata's name for *Rāg*, 112, 113, 140, 155.
jāttrā, mystery play, 286.
Jayadeva, author of *Gita-Govinda*, 83, 157, 286.
jayaghaṇṭa, gong, 79.
jhil or *dhun*, 'ungraced' melody, 160, 286.
jubilum, 'jubilation' of Plainsong, 250, 255, 276.

kabī, song of question and answer, 287.
kaiśiki, hair's-breadth, 119.
kākali, flat, 119.
kalā, $\frac{1}{4}$ of *anudruta*, 256.
kāla, speed-unit, 241.
kanār, rim of drum-wall, 227.
kanjari, tambourine, 228.
karadivādya, arm-drum, 228.
karane, see *āṭa* (of drum).
karkhā, Rajput song, 300.
karṣaṇa, ligature, 257, 275.
kathā, form of song, 287.
Kauthumas, a sect, 261.
Keats, 192.
khālī, the blank beat, 29, 30, 57, 61, 208, 209, 230.
kharaj, drone, 280.
khyāl, a kind of song, 165, 287.
kinnara, stringed instrument, 76 and note, 81.
kīrtaṇa, song (Bengali), 286.
kīrtaṇam, song (South India), 282.
kokkara, instrument of percussion, 44, 45, 228.
komal, flat, 107, 108, 142.
Krishna, 26, 76, 83, 286.
kṛṣṭa, 'graced', supplied with ligature (*karṣaṇa*), 257.
kṛti, song (South India), 84, 282.
kruṣṭa, first note of *Sāman* scale, 257, 261.
kruṣṭādi, 'kruṣṭa, &c.', 257.
kuzhal (*kuṛal*), South Indian pipe, 32 and note.

laghu, short (note), 196, 200, 256.
laraz, fifth string of *satār*, 78.
lascar, sailor, 19.
laya, tempo, 82, 241.
legend, *see* India.
limma of Pythagoras, 127, 132.
Localities:
Achilgarh, 60.
Allahabad, 231; Ex. 9–13.
Alleppey, Ex. 51–4.
Amritsar, 231.
Bangalore, 251, 252; Ex. 17–26.
Bhavnagar, 60, 90, 209, 229.

Localities (*continued*):
Bombay, 231; Ex. 3, 7.
Calcutta, 24, 88, 91–9, 231, 267, 271, 272; Ex. 16.
Dehra Dun, 53–9.
Dharmsāla, 56.
Gāndhāra, 262.
Gwālior, 8, 151, 287.
Jaunpur, 287.
Jhelum, 59, 60, 68, 69, 231.
Lahore, 230, 231.
Madras, 86, 87, 248, 251, 266, 269; Ex. 6, 27.
Maratha songs, Ex. 92, 93, 161–3.
Mussouri, Ex. 14, 15.
Mysore, 9, 86, 230, 251, 252, 273 note.
Nagpur, Ex. 28.
Negapatam, Ex. 72, 74–7.
Peshawar, 262.
Pind Dādan Khān, 231.
Poona, 247, 324, 340; Ex. 4, 5.
Raipur (C. P.), Ex. 29, 30.
Tanjore, 8, 9, 46, 84, 85, 253, 268; Ex. 90, 91.
Trichur, and neighbourhood, Ex. 31–50.
Trivandrum, 88, 89; Ex. 78–89.
Vraj, 299.
locrian (mixolydic) mode, 278.
long by position (syllables), 255.
Loti, *see* Pierre.
lotus, its connotation, 161 and note.
lullabies, *see* cradle-songs.
derivation, 62 note.

maddale, cylindrical drum, 228; Ex. 37, 48.
madhya, middle (octave), 107, 114.
middle (*śruti*), 108 and note.
of *tempo*, *moderato*, 241.
madhyādi, a form of common time, 207.
madhyama, 142 seq.
ma-grāma, 106, 110, 136, 140; Ex. 351.
Magyars, 186.
Mahābhārata, 114, 264, 287.
mahāvyutpatti, dictionary, 155.
Mahommedan music, 16, 62, 89, 90, 125, 203, 287, 300.
Maitra, Mr. S. M., 6, 7.
major Third, *see* interval.
major Tone, *see* interval.
mālavikāgnimitra, play, fifth cent., 82.
Malay Archipelago, 204.
mandra, low, 114.
lower octave, 107.
note of *Sāman* scale, 260.
mandragati, lower tetrachord, 140.
māṇḍūkiśikṣā, treatise, 259.
mantras (spells), recitation of, 201.
Maoris, 260.
Maratha songs, *see* localities.
mātrā, time-unit, 82, 156, 211, 256.
mātrālakṣaṇa, treatise, 256.
mātrāvṛtta, 'time-unit-fixed', 193.
mediaeval Europe, 203.
melakarta, group of *Rāgams*, 47 note, 106, 120 note, 139.
melodic figure, 70, 158, 159, 276.
melody, 4, 48, 49, 69–72, 100, 174, Chap. XII.
memoria technica, 120 note, 139, 209.
'merging', 118, 119, 127.
mesē, *see* Greek.
mesopyknon, 121.
middle note of three, 121, 208.
Milton, 202, 203.
mīnd, the 'deflect', 183.
mīrh = *mīnd*.
miśra, 'mixed', 138, 155.
misrāb, plectrum, 88.
mixolydian (hypophrygic) mode, 135, 136.
mixolydic, *see* locrian.
mode, *see* scale and mode, European modes, and 217 (of time).
modulation, 136, 137.
Mohammedan, *see* Mahommedan.
mood, 5, 8, 107, 174.
mordent, *see* grace and 152.
morning, *see* day.
morris dancers, 16, 31.
mṛcchakaṭikā, play, sixth cent., 76, 81.
mṛdanga, drum, 10, 89, 226, 227.
mūrchana, mode, 82, 107, 113, 141.
mūrchhana, grace note, 106, 152, 281, 286.
mūrki, trill, 300.
musica ficta, 42, 134, 152, 175, 178, 275 note.
musical Ass, the, 82.
musical hand, the, 260, 261, 264.
Myers, Dr. C. S., 48 note.

nāgari, kettle-drum, 228.
nāgasaram (South India) or *shahnai* or *surnai* (North India), oboe of strident tone, 46, 59, 78, 236, 237.
naqqārah, *see* drum.
Nārada, patron saint of music, 74, 75, 76.
nāradaśikṣā, treatise on music, 74, 75, 259, 264.
nasal tone, *see* singing.

nāṭyaśāstra of Bharata, 74, 75, 105, 193.
nīca, low, diatonic, 271, 278.
nidhana, coda of *Sāman*, 254, 275.
niṣāda, note of scale, 142, 263.
North American Indians, *see* Chippewas.
notation, vi, 83, 157, 267, 273.
notes kept in reserve, 329.
nyāsa, final (note), 141, 153, 277 note.

'occupation' songs, 19–26.
Olympos, 76.
oṃvi, Maratha song, 300, 337.
organ, 162.
Organum, 163; Ex. 272.
oxypyknon, 121.

Pachtikos, 141, 156.
pada, song, 286.
pāda, quarter-verse, 193, 286.
pallavi, section of song, 86, 281.
pañcama, fifth note of secular scale, 142.
  fifth note of *Sāman* scale, 260.
  of time, 203.
Pañcatantra, fables about the fifth cent., 82.
parand, drum-variant, 230, 231.
partials, *see* upper partials.
participant, 178.
parvan, what can be sung in one breath, 200, 251, 255, 276.
passing notes, *see* substantive.
Pater, *Renaissance*, 340.
pentatonic scales, 122, 123, 126 and note, 135; Ex. 353.
perfect consonance, see *saṃvāditva*.
Petrie, 126 note.
phonograph, 17, 50, 90.
phonographed tunes, Ex. 42, 43, 103, 154–7, 330, 333, 334, 356, 357, 359, 360, 364, 365. *See* pp. 48 note and 348.
phrygian (doric) mode, 178, 276–8.
pianoforte, 16, 18.
picotta, water-raising apparatus, 21, 22.
Pierre Loti's *L'Inde*, 10–14.
plagal tunes, rare, 48.
Plain-song and *Sāman*, 250, 255, 275 note.
pluta, prolate (prosody), 200, 255, 256.
Plutarch, 130, 173 note.
Polak, Herr, 164.
'popular' music, 152, 340, 341.
povāḍa, chivalric song, Maratha country, 46, 300.
pracaya, 'drone' note of *Sāman*, 247, 258, 265.
prakṛti, substantive (notes), 273.
pramāṇa, indicative, determining (*śruti*), viz. the comma of Didymus, 112 seq.
prastāra, changes (as in bell-ringing), 155.
prastāva, introduction, 253.
prathama, note of *Sāman* scale, 257 seq.
pratihāra, section of *Sāman*, 254.
prati-madhyama, 'false' *madhyama*, 119, 133, 139.
pratyutkrama, acciaccatura, 275.
prosody, 196, 203.
Ptolemy, 140.
pūrvārcika of the *Sāmaveda*, 250.
puṣpasūtra, treatise, 258, 261, 274.
pyknon, *see* Greek.
Pythagoras, *see* limma.

quantitative language, 191.
quarter-tones, 129, 130, 151, 345.
quintal harmony, 124, 173, 277.
quintuple, *see* five-rhythm.

Rāg	*Instances* Examples	*Discussion* Pages
Alahiya		318.
Āsāvari	410-12	170, 171, 318.
Bāgeshrī (Bageshvarī)	402	90.
Bahār	401	
Behāg (Bihāg)	220, 482	50, 152, 158, 171, App. I.
Bhairau (Bhairo, Bhairav)	216, 294, 426	122, 156, 171, 173.
Bhairavī	175, 176, 419-21, 447	83, 90, 156, 170, 318.
Bhimpalās(ī)	405, 406	
Bhūp(kaliān) (= Mohanna Rāgam)	306, 383	170, 174, 210.
Bibhās(a)		83, 90, 173, App. II.

Rāg	*Instances* Examples	*Discussion* Pages
Bilāskhānī Todī	218	
Bilāvala	387	
Darbārī Kānadā	413–15	
Desh	221, 394, 395	171.
Dhanāshrī	408, 409	
Dīnkapūria		155.
Dīpak (=Māravā)		155.
Gaula	450	
Gaurī	433	318.
Hamīr(kaliān)	384	159, 171.
Hindol(a)	381	154.
Jhinjoti (Jhijhit)	179, 219, 308, 393	170, 171, 318.
Jogi	425	154, App. II.
Kāfī	180, 301, 399, 400	89, 170, 318.
Kālangadā	424	
Kaliān(ī)	268, 382	89, 156, 159, 170, 318.
Kamod(kaliān)		159.
Kānadā	416, 493	154, 171, App. II.
Kedārā	278–81, 388–92	175.
Khamāj (Khambāz)	178, 300, 398	89, 171, 318.
Lalat(a)	436, 437	318.
Lalit(a)		152.
Mālkos (Mālavakauṇs)	380, 407	150, 173, App. II.
Mallār(a) (Malhār(a))	404	318.
Mand	226, 307	
Māravā	438, 439	App. II.
Multān(ī)	429	121, 152, App. II.
Myāchā Mallār	403	
Paraj(a)	435	318.
Pilu	417, 418	128, 318.
Pūria(kaliān)	440	170.
Pūrvī	432	318.
Rāmkalī	422, 423	318, App. II.
Sārang	330, 397	126, 154, 174, 175.
Shām(kaliān)		155, 159.
Sindora	334	
Sohanī	264, 434, 449	
Sorat	396	
Śrī-(rāg(a))	430, 431	318.
Tilang(a) (Tilak)		171.
Todī	217, 427, 428	121, 173, 318, App. II.
Vasant(a) (Basant)	298, 299	83, 90, 155, 170, 186.
Yaman(kaliān) (Iman-kaliān)	265–7	90, 159, 171, App. I.

Rāgam (see p. 107)	*Instances*	*Discussion*
Abhogī	353	
Ārabhī		174.
Gaurī-manoharī		155.
Mayamālavagaula		120.
Mohanna	173	86, 210.
Mūkhārī		119, 120.
Nārāyaṇī	386	
Ritigaula	379	
Śankarābharaṇa	308, 385	
Śrī(rāgam)		86.

rāga, particularization of mode, 8, 14, 15, 44, 56, 82–4, 89, 90, 107 and note, 112, 282, and Chap. VI.
rāgavibodha, treatise by Somanātha, 74, 105, 106, 155, 182 note, 186.
rāgmāla, 'picture' of a *Rāg*, 163 note.
Rāmāyaṇa, the, 287.
ratnākara, treatise by Śārṅgadeva, 74, 105, 110, 111, 119, 201 and note, 202 note.
Ray, Indu Bhūṣan, poet, 6.
recitation, 201, 267.
reckoning by *akṣara*, 200, 201.
by *mātrā*, 204 seq.
rekhtu, form of song, 300.
religious basis of music, 5, 6.
resonance of drum, 29, 227.
rests, 192, 193, 200.
Ṛgveda accent, 246 seq., 260, 265.
recitation, Ex. 340.
rhythm, 27, 29, 49, 72, 98; Ex. 34, 42, 72, 129, 141; *see* Chap. VIII.
ṛkprātiśākhya, treatise, 114, 258.
roha (= *ārohaṇa*), 275.
route through India, 17.
ṛṣabha, 142, 263.

ṣaḍja, 'born of six' (note of the scale), 142, 263.
sa-grāma, the, 106, 109, 136, 140, 343; Ex. 350.
'sailor's life, A', 135.
sālanka, 'altered', 138, 139, 155.
Salvation Army, 6, 43.
sam, the first of the bar, 208 and note, 226, 230, 231, 322.
sama, applied to a note of the *Sāman* scale, 260.
sāman, hymn melody, Chap. X.
scale, 258, 259, 263.
chants, *see* Ex. 344–8, 356, 357, 359, 360, 364, 365.
sāma-paribhāṣā, 258, 274.
Sāmaveda, 80, 142, 190, and Chap. X.
saṃhata, struck together = *saṃvādī*, 114.
saṃhitā, text of Veda, 249.
sāmika, of the *Sāmaveda*, 122.
saṃpūrṇa, heptatonic, 122.
saṃvādī, perfect consonance, 108, 114, 138, 145, 266.
saṃvāditva, theory of consonance, 111, 261 seq.
sañcāri, section of song, 281.
śaṅkha, conch, 79.
saṅkīrṇa, 'mixed', 138, 153, 155.
sannatara, lower than *anudātta*, 247.
Sanskrit language, 10, 190–3.
poems recited, Ex. 8, 346.
authorities, 74, 80, 105.
sapphic, 195.
saptaka, octave, 107.
saraband rhythm, 213, 223.
Saraswatī, goddess of music, 16.
śārdūla vikrīḍita, a metre, Ex. 307.
sargam, see *svarā*.
satār, musical instrument, 78, 106, 172.
scale, Chap. IV. *See* Greek and *Sāman*.
scansion, 193–200, 338.
schools of music, 9.
Scotch music, 71, 126 note, 174 note, 184, 185.
Scott's ballad metre, 193.
'Seeds of Love', the, 154.
Seligmann, Dr., 48 note.
semitone, *see* interval.
septimal interval, *see* interval.
Śeṣagiri Śāstrī, 248 note, 250, 263.
shāḍava, hexatonic, 122.
shahnai or *surnai*, see *nāgasaram*.
Shakespeare, 169.
sharp and flat, 107, 108.
sharp Sixth, 122, 125, 127.
shaṭkāla, six-fold speed (treble diminution), 85, 86, 241.
shatśruti, of six *śrutis*, 118, 119.
śikhariṇī, a metre, 197.
similar tetrachords, 138.
singāra, stringed instrument, 31.
singing, 89–91.
Sir William Jones, 187.
siyahī, black plaster on drum, 227.
'slide', 66, 88, 190. See *gharṣaṇa*.
śloka, 'flowing' metre, 193, 194.
snake-charmer, 208; Ex. 274.
solmization, 84, 149; cp. the musical hand.
solo and chorus, Ex. 3, 9, 17, 18, 42, 54, 58, 72, 73, 74, 76, 77, 115, 122, 129.
soma, plant, 249, 250.
song, 78, 80–4, 341.
sopānam, temple songs, South India, 43.
South Indian scale, *see* Carnatic.
'Sovay, Sovay', 134.
śriṅga, horn, 79.
śruti, enharmonic interval or note, 112, 113, 117, 127 and note, 132, 133.
sthāna, voice-register, 82, 114.
sthayi, see *astai*.

stobha, jubilation, 250, 255, 276, 338.
stoma, group, 255.
stotra, stanza, 255.
stress and duration, 192, 223.
'strong', see *balin*.
structure, 337–9.
'substantive' and 'passing' notes, 4, 100; *see* 141.
śuddha, pure, natural diatonic, 107, 118, 119, 138, 153, 155.
śukra, applied to a note of the *Sāman* scale, 260.
'super-particular' fractions, 124.
superscript accidentals, 17, 108, 109.
surāvarta, see *svarā*.
surbahār, instrument, 88, 172.
surnai, see *nāgasaram*.
surphakt(a) (*sulafakata*), 'zigzag' time, 216, 241; Ex. 111. See *Tāl*.
svara, diatonic or chromatic interval or note, 82, 107, 109 note, 142.
svarā (*sargam*, *svarāvarta*, *surāvarta*), sol-fa syllables to form cadenza, 84 and note, 85, 299, 314, 315, 342.
svāra, cadence, 264, 275.
svaramela-kalānidhī, treatise, 105, 119.
svarāntara, of four notes, 123.
svarita, *Ṛgveda* accent, 190, 246.
'sounded' or graced note of *Sāman*, 258, 259, 265, 275.
symbols of notation, 18, 200, 201.

tabla, pair of drums, 226, 227.
Tagore, Rabindranāth, of Calcutta, 91–9.
his melodies, 92, 99.
his songs, Ex. 176–80, 263, 264, 266.
his portrait (frontispiece), 92.
his method, 96 note, 250.
Tagore, Rajah S. M., 285 note, 347, 348, 351.

Tāl	*Instances* Examples	*Discussion* Pages
Āḍa-chautāl(a) (=Dhruva)	330	216, 217.
Ādi (=Tīntāl)	173, 308, 398	209.
Āṭa (=Dhamār)	315, 316	209.
Brahma		242.
Chautāl(a), or Chartāl(a)	334, 403, 405, 413, 426, 428	216, 217.
Dādra (=Eka Trisra)	177	
Deśādi	309, 379	
Dhamār	333, 391, 399, 412, 436	216.
Dhruva		209.
Eka (Ekka, Ektāl(a), Ekatālī)	178-80, 267	209, 216.
Eka Trisra	388, 390, 393-5, 407, 411, 415, 416, 419, 433	
Jhampa (Jhap, Jap)	266, 314	201, 209, 216, 217, 218.
Jhamra	425, 429	
Khaṇḍajātī Laghu	311	
Khaṭṭ		216.
Madhyādi	310	
Madhyamāvatī		216.
Māṇṭ (=Māṭya, and Surphakta)	280	201.
Matta		216.
Māṭya	172	209.
Rūdra		242.
Rūpak	312, 381, 383, 384, 392, 397, 400, 401, 402, 408, 410, 414, 417, 418, 420, 421, 423, 427, 430, 432, 435, 437, 438	209, 216, 218.

Tāl	*Instances* Examples	*Discussion* Pages
Savārī		242.
Surphak(a)t(a) (Sulafakata)	263, 264, 431	216, 217.
Tevra (Teora) (=Tripuṭa)	176, 294, 306, 382, 385, 386, 404	216–18.
Tīntāl (Tītāl(a), Tritāla, Trivaṭa)	300, 301, 387, 389, 396, 406, 409, 422, 424, 434, 439	208, 216.
Tripuṭa	313, 440	209.

tāl, beat, 208, 217 note.
tāla, time, 14, 83, 89, 90.
tāla(m), cymbal, Ex. 42, 86.
tambūra, stringed instrument to accompany voice, 78, 85, 171, 173, 227.
Tamil, 120 note.
tāna, *fioriture*, melodic figuration, 82, 287.
tappa, form of song, 188, 300.
tāra, high (octave), 106, 114.
tāragati, upper tetrachord, 140.
tarāna (*tillāna*), form of song, 299.
Telugu, 84.
tempering, 118.
tempo, see *druta*, *madhya*, *vilambita*, *kāla*.
tertian harmony, 125, 277.
tessitura, 4, 107, 143, 279, 280.
tetrachord, 70, 71, 121 note, 128 and note, 141, 260. *See* Greek.
teyāttam, exorcism, 34.
thā, augmentation, 241.
Thamyris, 76.
thāṭ, setting, 106.
ṭheka, drum-phrase, 230, 231; Ex. 330, 336.
Third, *see* interval.
thumri, form of song, 165, 299; Ex. 268.
Thurston, Mr. E., 48 note.
'tierce de Picardie', 132, App. I.
tillāna, see *tarāna*.
time, see *Tāl*, *Tāla*, *tāl*.
time of day, *see* day.
tīvra, sharp, 107, 108.
tīvratar, *tīvratam*, sharper and sharpest, 107.
tonality, 19.
tonic, 18, 19, 36, 48, 144, 145.
tonos, *see* Greek.
transilient scales, 48, 122–7, 128, 152, 158, 263.
tribal song, 154.
Tribes:
  Arabs, 37.
  Chitrālī, Ex. 138.
  Garhwālī, 50–7.
  Gond, 28–31.
  Gurkha, 56–9.
  Kadar, 31.
  Kāfīr, Ex. 139.
  Kānika, 44, 45.
  Kanwar, 31.
  Malayan, 36.
  Malya, 31, 32.
  Pāṇan, 34.
  Pāndaran, 41.
  Pulaiyar, 42.
  Velan, 33.
triṣṭubh, a class of metre, 194.
tritone, 103, 104.
trivaṭa, form of song, 299.
Troubadours, 8.
tṛtīya(ḥ) = third, of time, 203, 207.
  note of *Sāman* scale, 257 seq.
tūk, movement (of song), 300.
tuning of drum, 227.
twelve sorrows, the, 61, 62.

ucca, high, chromatic, 271, 278.
udātta, 'raised' sound, 246, 258, 259, 265, 266.
udghāta, downward appoggiatura, 275.
udgītha, section of *Sāman*, 253.
udukku or *udukkai* drum, shaped like hour-glass, 43, 228.
udupe, goblet-shaped drum, 228.
upadrava, section of *Sāman*, 254.
upendravajra, metre, 194–6.
upper partials, 123, 124.
uśniḥ, a metre, 194.
ustād, professional musician, 89, 301.
ut queant laxis, 84, 85.
uttama, see *tāra*.
uttarārcika of the *Sāmaveda*, 250.

vādī, unison, i.e. starting point of consonance, 108.
vakra, crooked, 153, 328.
valam, covered boat, Travancore, 38, 39.
varek, the 'deflect', 183.
variation form, Ex. 12, 27, 38, 42, 43.
varja, transilient (q.v.).
varṇavṛtta, 'syllable-fixed', 193.
vasanta-tilaka, a metre, 197; Ex. 280.
vibhāg, see *āvard*.
vikṛta, chromatic, 107.
  passing-note, 273.
vilambita, *adagio*, 241.
vīṇā, stringed instrument, 9, 78, 79, 88, 112, 148, 171, 172, 183, 227.
vinata, lengthened appoggiatura, 275.
violin, 8, 162.
virāma, rest (in music), 200 and note, 256, 276.
'visual' music, 342.
vivādī, dissonance, in particular the semitone, 108.
vocal and instrumental, 150.
vocalizing syllables, 23, 280.
vocal scale, 276–9.
vṛddha, increased (prosody), 251, 255, 256.

warka, drumhead, 227.
watch, *see* day.
'weak', see *alpa*.
whole tone consonance, 173.
Wilson, Lady, 164, 226.
'woods so wilde, the', Ex. 377.
words of songs, 14, 50, 53.

Yajurveda, 248.
yama, twins, 114.
Yāma, death, 78.
yoni, a borrowing fro the *Ṛgveda*, 250.

Zakmi Dil, Ex. 123.
Zalzal, Arabian musician, 185.
zamzama, see *mūrki*.
Zoroastrians, 250.